# REBELLIOUS PROPHET

A Life of Nicolai Berdyaev

# REBELLIOUS PROPHET

## A LIFE OF
# NICOLAI BERDYAEV

### BY DONALD A. LOWRIE

### HARPER & BROTHERS, NEW YORK

# CONTENTS

PREFACE                                                    ix

*Picture Section*                              following 150


1. TURNING POINT                                            1

    *Riga, 1926.*


2. "CERCLE DE FAMILLE"                                      7

    *Berdyaev's French ancestors, the Choiseuls; the Berdyaevs; Major-General Michail Nicolaievitch.*


3. A DOLL NAMED PRINCE ANDRÉ                               14

    *Berdyaev's father and mother; his brother Serge; the family's high social connections; Berdyaev's nurse; illness; the tic; lack of discipline; early reading; the Cadet Corpus; loneliness; preparation for the university.*


4. THE BAROMETER OF SOCIETY                                31

    *The University of Kiev; revolutionary activities; the near-marxist.*


5. THE ATHENS OF THE NORTH                                 47

    *Prison in Kiev; Vologda; how exiles lived; the Union of Exiles; "obituary."*


6. THE UNSPEAKABLE MYSTERY                                 67

    *Release from Vologda; a semester in Heidelberg; the Union of*

v

Liberation and political activity; acquaintance with Bulgakov; courtship and marriage; Rozanoff; Berdyaev's convictions about sex, marriage, and the family.

7. THE IVORY TOWER                                              81

St. Petersburg in *1905*; the cultural renaissance; V. I. Ivanoff; Ivanoff's "tower"; Bulgakov; Merezhkovsky; Hippius.

8. "SUB SPECIE ÆTERNITATIS"                                     99

Further spiritual evolution; the St. Petersburg Religious-Philosophical Society; contemporary periodicals; the New Way; Life's Questions; Sub Specie Æternitatis; social life; Berdyaev leaves St. Petersburg.

9. "THE PILLAR AND BULWARK OF THE TRUTH"     111

Paris; Moscow in *1909*; the Novoselov Circle; Put; Bulgakov; Florensky; the Religious-Philosophical Society; life in Moscow; in the country; his love for animals; Berdyaev as seen by his friends at this period.

10. A DECLARATION OF INDEPENDENCE                              126

The Pit; Steiner and Anthroposophy; Mintzlova; The New Religious Consciousness; Milestones; The Philosophy of Freedom; open letter to Archbishop Antony; Florence; The Meaning of the Creative Act; friends and enemies; "Quenchers of the Spirit."

11. WAR, REVOLUTION, BANISHMENT                               140

Russia's unpreparedness; The Destiny of Russia; Berdyaev's activity after the Revolution; forced labor; writing; the Free Academy of Spiritual Culture; first arrest; conversation with Dzerzhinsky; the Authors' Bookshop; banishment.

12. BERLIN                                                     160

Cordial attitude of the German government; hostility of the emigration; the Russian Scientific Institute; the Religious-

*Philosophical Academy; youth in study groups; The New Middle Ages.*

13. PARIS IN THE FALL                    170

*Home life; table talk; daily schedule; finances; Sunday evening groups; religious life; how he wrote; opinions of his own books.*

14. IN AND OUT OF ORGANIZATIONS          192

*The Russian Student Christian Movement Outside Russia; Berdyaev's appreciation of art; St. Sergius Theological Institute; the Fraternity of St. Sophia; the Religious-Philosophical Academy; Put; ecumenical contacts; the YMCA Press.*

15. BROKEN FRIENDSHIPS                    203

*Prewar friendships; wartime discords; the Berdyaev temper; the value of suffering; Berdyaev as aesthete; friends, old and new; Berdyaev's correspondence; personal characteristics.*

16. "THE LIGHT OF RUSSIA"                 215

*Berdyaev's changing attitude toward the church—in early years, during spiritual crisis, and at the time of the revolution; his final attitude toward the authority of the church, and of the Bible; the sacraments; dogmas; Berdyaev as a theologian; other confessions; the ecumenical movement; the church's attitude toward Berdyaev; his hope for the Russian Church; Berdyaev as a mystic.*

17. RELUCTANT PRECEPTOR                   230

*Berdyaev as teacher; as leader; books written in Paris; extension of Berdyaev's world-wide influence among Russians; his influence—constructive, personal, Christian.*

18. THE THINKER                          241

*How Berdyaev thought; intuition vs. logic; radical; Christian; Berdyaev's basic concepts; the God-man, man as co-creator* with God; three epochs of history; thinkers who influenced Berdyaev: Kant and Hegel, Nietzsche and Marx, J. Boehme, Khomiakoff and Solovieff, Dostoievsky.

19. THE PROPHET                                    259

Berdyaev as a speaker for his time; as a seer; Berdyaev's eschatology; a prophet's reward; Berdyaev's faith in Russia; the Russian soul; the mission of Russia; optimism for Russia's future.

20. WAITING FOR THE LIGHT                          267

The war years; the exodus; life under German occupation; Lydia's death; surgery; postwar problems; attitude toward Soviet Russia; books produced in the period; a Cambridge degree; visits to Switzerland; death and burial; the autobiography.

21. THE SUMMING UP                                 282

A summary of Berdyaev's life and character; of his thought— its originality, its emphasis on freedom; Berdyaev's philosophy of history; his Christian conviction; Berdyaev's significance for our time.

NOTES                                              289

BIBLIOGRAPHY                                       303

INDEX                                              305

# PREFACE

Nicolai Berdyaev's *Self-Knowledge, An Essay in Philosophical Autobiography* is as different from most autobiographies as Berdyaev was from most men. It is the story of the development of his thought, with only enough personal detail to serve his philosophic purpose. It seemed desirable to me, as one of his long-time colleagues, to assemble the more usual biographical data while numerous living witnesses were available. Of course, such a monograph cannot be the final, definitive biography of a great man. It appears only twelve years after his death, and hence perspective is lacking—yet "one may speak of whether a man [has] justified what he taught by the way he lived and died."[1] To this end, "not alone events are dear," as he said in one of two biographies he wrote, "dear also is that general-psychological music which accompanies them, the breath of the epoch."[2] With this in mind, an attempt is made here to present the man as "concrete, unrepeatable, . . . as a center of life."[3] These quotations state my purpose and my method in preparing this book. It contains only factual material, most of it concerning Berdyaev directly and the rest selected to fill in the background. Berdyaev wrote about his thought; I am writing about him.

The work has been made possible by the generous assistance of friends, many of them members of the Berdyaev Society but some who have no connection with it and share no special interest in "extending his teachings." Yet all of those approached, have, without exception, given all possible aid. They are too numerous to receive separate mention here, but individual gratitude is due certain of them. Research on Berdyaev's ancestry and the early part of his life was greatly facilitated by Mme Helena Nicolaevna Fedotoff, long a friend of Berdyaev and his family. To the unstinted collaboration of another close friend, Mme Tamara Feodorovna Klepinin, the author is indebted for many reminiscences and historical details. Generous contributions from old friends of Berdyaev like Kartasheff, Remizoff, and Zaitseff are evident in the text. My thanks also go to Miss Claudia Michailovna Pereshneff for both counsel and technical assistance. I am especially obliged to the librarians of the Lenin Library in Moscow, the Public Library in Lenin-

grad, and the University Library in Kiev, for providing facilities for
my recently completed research in the U.S.S.R.

Philip Guedalla once remarked: "I am not sure you can write a
truthful and effective biography of anyone who leaves behind him a
devoted relict."[4] In one sense this is true of the present work, but in
another, it must be said that only the constant and sympathetic aid
of Mme Eugenie Yudifovna Rapp has made possible some sections of
the text. Sister-in-law and member of Berdyaev's household during his
last forty years, her keen intuition and sympathetic comprehension
were important factors in his life. He said she was "one of the few people who have understood me . . . [and] of very great significance in my
life; . . . I am greatly indebted to spiritual dialogue with her."[5] Much
of the material presented here was assembled from her answers to questions arising from a study of the autobiography. Some of these replies
were oral, but in many cases Eugenie Yudifovna preferred to give them
in writing, and her manuscript is quoted time and again.

Eugenie's is not the "Euclid" type of mind. She does not remember
dates—"even that of her own marriage." Time is irrelevant to one
who, like Berdyaev himself, is so conscious of living in eternity. A lack
of scientific approach qualifies most of the material she supplies. For
several years after Berdyaev's death she studied the archives he left,
copying what selections she thought suitable for publication, then de-
posited the original documents in the Bibliothèque Nationale, Paris,
under seal "until they can be returned to a free Russia." Even Berdyaev's letters to Lydia and to Mme K are available only in the excerpts
Eugenie has selected. Most of the quotations and other material she
has so generously provided are from memory. But while scientific ac-
curacy thus is not assured, her general presentation is unimpeachable.

And of Helen Ogden Lowrie it must be said that without her constant aid and support the book might never have been written. She
has typed the manuscript and helped prepare it for the publisher, in
addition to serving as critic and counselor throughout the process of
composition. Gratitude, here, is a feeble word. In acknowledging my
obligation to the many others who have helped make this book possible, let me express the hope that upon reading it they will be as
happy as I have been about their participation.

*New York City*
**August 15, 1959**

                                                        D. A. L.

# 1

## TURNING POINT

The ancient shrine of St. Nicolas in the quayside market of Riga shelters the saint's gold-haloed icon under a canopy upheld by bulbous, Russian-style pillars. A man had stopped before the shrine to add his candle to the large cluster of tapers already burning there. Moved by some deep emotion he struggled to control, the man stood a long time, head bowed in prayer. Patches of snow still showed on the shrine's green tin roof, the gold cross at its peak agleam in the watery sunlight. Spring was late—it was March, 1927—and the ice had not yet gone out of the Dvina River bordering the market. The man was Nicolai Alexandrovitch[1] Berdyaev, recent exile from the U.S.S.R.: a prophet who wanted to be a philosopher, an aristocrat who had always tried to be a democrat, once a marxist but now a confessing Christian, a former professor at Moscow University now living in poverty in a Paris suburb.

He made a handsome figure as he stood there, hat in hand, his fine head with its well-kept shock of scarcely-graying hair and small pointed beard, his firm, straight shoulders, his eyes dark with the world's tragedy. Three days ago he had arrived in this old Hanseatic city, now the capital of the new Republic of Latvia, for a series of lectures. The three days had marked a new stage in his development, in his thought of himself and of his calling in the world.

This was Berdyaev's first visit to the ancient city on the Dvina, with its chivalric traditions, its somewhat confusing modernity. Founded in 1202 by the Brothers of the Sword to protect the port and market from surrounding barbarian tribes, it soon became headquarters for the Teutonic Knights, a German city in a non-Germanic land. Riga surrendered to the Russians under Peter the Great in 1710, but despite two hundred years of Russian control the city always retained German elements which, mixed with the native Latvian, gave it an atmosphere all its own. German, Russian, and now Latvian in architecture and

*1*

style of life, Riga was pre-eminently a Baltic city, its three principal
national cultures striving each to maintain itself. The existing confusion of thought in a country like Latvia, not yet a decade after the
collapse of two ancient empires, was typical of most of Europe. New
and old were still commingled in people's thinking.

Here was a medieval city, suddenly become the capital of a new
republic, struggling valiantly to be Latvian instead of German or, even
worse, Russian. In government offices one saw men toiling over great
dictionaries, "modernizing" the Latvian language; the university, the
opera, the whole of civil life had had to become Latvian. The old Russian population and still more the new groups of Russian émigrés were
anything but popular. The whole emphasis was on Latvian culture.
Was there any place left for the Russian culture which so long had set
the tone of the city? How permanent would this new Republic be?
What were its basic ideas, valid under any regime, as distinguished
from what was merely transitory? To a visitor from Riga attending a
student conference near Paris in the summer of 1926, one of the
speakers brought the clearest answer yet to all these questions. As a
result, the lecturer had been invited to speak in Riga. After months of
negotiation to secure passport and visas—here was a man without a
country, another Russian émigré, seeking to visit the new Republic—
the necessary papers were in order and Berdyaev made the journey. To
Berdyaev, arriving from the gray Paris suburb, Riga was like a home-
coming. He was "surprised and moved at Latvia's resemblance to
Russia: the broad plains, the snow, the poor little villages."[2] Here,
despite the prevailing new nationalism, Nicolai Alexandrovitch found
himself in a Russian atmosphere. He lived with the family of the
editor of the Russian magazine *Perezvony*. He lectured in Russian in
one of the oldest secular buildings in the city, the great Hall of the
Black Heads, seat of a quasi-chivalric order that had survived six centuries of war and revolution.[3] The walls of the hall were hung with
portraits of Russian tsars who had been patrons of the Black Heads.
For a moment one could believe the revolution had been only a passing nightmare—this elegant hall, this cultured Russian audience.
Berdyaev often recalled later the "at home" feeling the place had
given him.

The lectures had been organized and well advertised by the community educational society Prosvetitelnoe Obschestvo, one of the principal Russian cultural organizations in Latvia, and nearly a thousand
persons, young and old, attended. Berdyaev's first lecture, on a theme

which he had developed into one of his most widely known books *The New Middle Ages*, was almost over his audience's head, but he corrected this, and the following talks were very popular. The whole city talked of Berdyaev. His days were crowded with personal interviews and consultations. At a dinner given in his honor, it seemed as though the congratulatory speeches and toasts would never end. Berdyaev was greatly embarrassed: "Can't you stop all this speech-making?" he asked the hostess. When the flood of admiration continued, Berdyaev lost his appetite and wanted to leave, and only the insistence of friends persuaded him to remain to the end. His first experience of praise and commendation had been a shock which affected the remainder of his stay in the Baltics.

When he returned to Paris he told the family about it: "On the entire journey there was really only one unpleasant impression. I was met as though I were an important person, as though I were some famous man. Coming out of the station, I was astonished to see the presidents of various social organizations, who had come to do me honor; I was surrounded by photographers and reporters." It was somehow like the deaf Beethoven after the first performance of his *Ninth Symphony*, unaware of the frenetic applause until the soprano soloist turned him around to face his public. So Berdyaev, concerned primarily with the presentation of his message, now suddenly realized how favorably it had been received.

Yielding to pressure from his friends on his last day in Riga, Berdyaev was put into a carriage and taken to a tour of the town. He had seen the famous Dvina River view as he entered the city: the old castle and the tall, Baltic-style steeples of the cathedral and St. Peter's. Now he visited the old town, its twisting, narrow streets lined with old-world houses with painted gables, and gray stone storehouses dating from Hanseatic times. Street signs were in three languages; in every block of the old streets some remarkable bit of the past looked at him. He visited the cathedral, almost as old as Chartres, with its typical Baltic square tower topped by a high lantern. He smiled comprehendingly at the epitaph on a tomb near the high altar:

> O beautiful man,
> Consider me.
> What you are, I was.

The note seemed particularly fitting; Berdyaev was a "beautiful man." (The day after the tour a friend asked his hostess: "Who was that very

handsome man driving with you yesterday?") At fifty-two, with his
leonine head, his kindly but piercing eyes and his erect carriage, Berdyaev was a man to be looked at.

Then they came to the market, noted by guide books as "the most
interesting part of Riga." Not unlike the *gostinny dvor* in a typical
Russian town, it stretched half a mile along the Dvina quay fronting
the "old town," row on row of open-faced shops where one could buy
anything from a packet of needles to a *pood* of meal, from secondhand clothing to seeds and flowers. It was characteristic of the mixture
of nationalities in Riga that different sections of the market were occupied by different national groups: the fish stalls by Latvians and,
from time immemorial, the gardening section by Russians—bearded
peasants with white aprons over their blouses. The only language of this
area was Russian, of course. Berdyaev descended from his carriage and
walked slowly along the gardeners' row, speaking briefly with one after
another of the traders. They called him *barin* ("sir"). He had known
these Baltic-Russian accents since his early days in St. Petersburg. For
a few moments the exile was once more at home.

Here was the shrine of St. Nicolas, Berdyaev's patron saint, the
favorite saint of the whole Orthodox world—dozens of tapers flickering
before the icon. Placing his own candle among the others, Berdyaev
stood with bowed head. It is not difficult to imagine some of the
thoughts flowing through his mind. One of a small group of intellectuals too prominent to kill and too dangerous to be left in Soviet
Russia, he had been banished by the communist government four years
before. And life in those four years had not been easy for Nicolai
Alexandrovitch. In Berlin, center of the Russian emigration, he had
not only been unwelcome but openly attacked as a bolshevik agent. He
was ostracized by practically all leaders of the emigration, many of
them his old friends and co-workers. Life in Paris, where he had moved
two years later, proved not much better. No one understood better than
he the ephemeral character of the emigration: scarcely a man among
the "homesick million" was not sure that within a few months, or a
few years at the most, they would all return to a liberated Russia.
Berdyaev was not so certain—but he comprehended fully the instability
of the émigré groups, with their shifting political views, their economic
incapacity. There were many experienced leaders: Struve, Miliukoff,
Wrangel—each with his own loyal party and his own political program
for the Russia of the future. Even had he wished it, Berdyaev would
not have been accepted by any of these influential groups; his views

were too different from theirs. Hating communism as ardently as any of them, he was concerned, not with the political readaptation of Russia but with its spiritual problems, its spiritual regeneration. Standing almost alone among his fellow countrymen in Berlin and Paris, had he wondered sometimes whether he truly had a message for his fatherland? Scorned, isolated, constantly attacked by other Russians, he was able to publish his views only with the sponsorship of a non-Russian organization.

Knowing this background, it is easy to appreciate the impact of the Riga experience on Berdyaev's sensitive spirit. The enthusiastic acceptance of his lectures by cultured Russian people had given him a new sense of assurance sadly lacking through the past four years of exile. And now, if he still doubted his mission to the Russian people, this visit to the market place made things clear. Yesterday it was acceptance by the elite; today, his free, easy contact with the people, the Russian workingman and the peasantry, had completed the picture. He still belonged to them, to all of them. He had a message and it would be accepted. New courage flowed through him for the task ahead.[4]

Did he foresee that Russia's travail would continue through more than a generation and that one after another of the political efforts to "save" his country would collapse into apathy? Had this enthusiastic reception by the Russians in Riga given him some faint hint of the world-wide fame that would one day be his? Head bowed in meditation before the shrine of St. Nicolas, Berdyaev stood a long, long time.

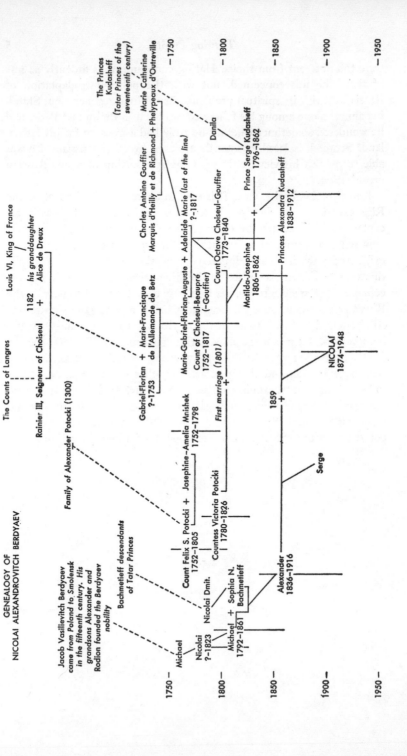

GENEALOGY OF
NICOLAI ALEXANDROVITCH BERDYAEV

The Counts of Langres

Louis VI, King of France

Rainier III, Seigneur of Choiseul

1182    his granddaughter
  +     Alice de Dreux

Family of Alexander Potocki

Gabriel-Florian  +  Marie-Francisque
?–1753              de l'Allemande de Betz

Marie-Gabriel-Florian-Auguste  +  Adelaide Marie (last of the line)
Count of Choiseul-Beaupré          ?–1817
1752–1817
(–Gouffier)

First marriage (1801)

Josephine–Amelia Mnishek
1752–1798

Count Felix S. Potocki  +
1752–1805

Countess Victoria Potocki
1780–1826

The Princes
Kudasheff
(Tatar Princes of the
seventeenth century)

Marie Catherine

Charles Antoine Gouffier
Marquis d'Heilly et de Richmond + Phelypeaux d'Outreville

Danila

Count Octave Choiseul-Gouffier
1773–1840

Matilda-Josephine
1806–1862

Prince Serge Kudasheff
1796–1862

Princess Alexandra Kudasheff
1838–1912

NICOLAI
1874–1948

1859
+

Serge

Alexander
1836–1916

Jacob Vasilievitch Berdyaev
came from Poland to Smolensk
in the fifteenth century. His
grandsons Alexander and
Radion founded the Berdyaev
nobility

Bachmetieff descendants
of Tatar Princes

Michael

Nicolai
?–1823

Michael  +  Sophia N.
1792–1861    Bachmetieff

Nicolai Dmit.

1750 —

1800 —

1850 —

1900 —

1950 —

— 1750

— 1800

— 1850

— 1900

— 1950

# 2

## "CERCLE DE FAMILLE"

When, in 1924, Nicolai Alexandrovitch Berdyaev went to France, where he was to spend the last third of his life, he was returning to the birthplace of his maternal great-grandfather, Antoine-Louis-Octave, Comte de Choiseul-Gouffier. As Berdyaev wrote in his biography of Leontieff:

> National, class and family instincts and traditions are transmitted into an unique individuality, and so a man is formed. A man's organic inheritance, his origin, the traditions which surround his childhood—all this is not the man's accidental shell . . . from which he may and should completely free himself. . . . All these are profound connections which determine his destiny.

Berdyaev's own life and character proved the truth of these words. Like his French grandfather, he was both child and victim of revolution. The French revolution forced the grandfather to emigrate to Russia; the Russian revolution brought Berdyaev back to France an exile, thus in a sense returning to France the intellectual values of one family which had left it in 1793. As in Schlumberger's novel *Cercle de Famille*, the family circle had come full-round.

The story of the Choiseuls in Russia, though not unlike that of many others of the French nobility given asylum by Catherine the Great, is worth recording briefly here. The father, Marie-Gabriel-Florent-Auguste, Comte de Choiseul-Gouffier, was an outstanding personality in both countries. He came of a long line of French nobility which had played important roles in French history. Born (1753) Count of Choiseul-Beaupré, he married (1771) the only child of the Marquis de Gouffier, last male member of the De Gouffier line, and, along with the bride's dowry, received the right to add this title to his family name. A precocious young man, his personal interests turned to science

7

and travel, although like most French aristocrats he served in the army, where at twenty-four he was already commanding a regiment. With his military service finished at the end of the 1770's, when most of his comrades were off to America to fight in the colonial army, this young aristocrat elected to join one of the earliest French scientific expeditions, and headed for Greece on the frigate *Atalante*. The book he published upon his return, *Voyage Pittoresque de la Grèce*, was generally considered one of the literary events of the time. The young Choiseul at twenty-nine was made a member of the *Académie des Inscriptions et Belles Lettres* and a year later was elected to the *Académie Française*. The *Voyage Pittoresque* helped establish Choiseul's reputation as a specialist on the Near East, and at thirty-two he was appointed to one of the most responsible of French diplomatic posts, the ambassadorship at Constantinople.

Constantinople was not only a "responsible post," it was a difficult position for any Frenchman, and particularly so for Choiseul. Although officially friendly to the Turkish government and supervising the armament of Turkey by French engineers, the young ambassador became more and more interested in Turkey's enemy, Russia. Himself an ardent monarchist, he, like many others of his generation, was attracted to Catherine II, then the leading supporter of Europe's old regime. Moved by a natural sympathy and also, possibly, by foresighted thought for a place of refuge later, the French ambassador followed a line of conduct calculated to win the confidence of the Russian court. He rendered service to Russian war prisoners in Turkish hands, even aiding some to escape. Such evident partisanship did not ingratiate Choiseul with the Turks, and his resultant unpopularity is doubtless responsible for the fact that the Parthenon marbles now repose in the British Museum instead of the Louvre. An ardent collector, Choiseul dreamed of securing for France the sculptured treasures of the Acropolis and raised the question with the Turkish government. Despite his urgent request, however, all he was able to obtain were the two pieces now exhibited in the Louvre. That this was largely a matter of personality is evident from the fact that only a few years later (1780) Lord Elgin secured the rest and took them home to the British Museum.

Choiseul was profoundly shocked by the revolution at home. His sympathies were with the losing side, and he began to say so in correspondence with fellow aristocrats who had escaped from France. By mischance, sections of this correspondence fell into the hands of the revolutionary government, and he was at once recalled. He was too well informed, however, to accept the order to return, and a warrant for his arrest was issued in Paris. He left Constantinople hurriedly and, traveling via Transylvania, arrived safely in St. Petersburg. His literary reputation, together with reports of his Russophile attitude in Turkey, had preceded him, and records of the time say that Catherine "awaited his coming with great interest." He was at once awarded an allowance, and, bringing his family from France, he established himself in the Russian capital.

Count de Choiseul was not the only French émigré in St. Petersburg. As an expression of her dislike for the new regime in France, Empress Catherine not only permitted but, for a time at least, encouraged the exiled French aristocracy to emigrate to Russia. As in our day, when intellectuals driven from home by a Hitler or a Stalin have been highly esteemed and profitably employed in their land of refuge, Catherine appreciated the qualities of her French guests and assigned them suitable places in the service of the state. One Frenchman accepted by the Empress, Count Esterházy, wrote (1792): "She takes a truly sincere interest in the misfortunes of France. . . . Our princes and nobility have no other refuge than the kind service and influence of the Empress." For some reason, Choiseul did not make a favorable impression on her at first. But he overcame this and was soon receiving one important evidence of the Empress' favor after another. She made him a gift of two thousand *chervontsi*, enough to provide a comfortable pension for life. He was given the rank of Privy Counsellor. She promoted his elder son Octave (Berdyaev's great-grandfather) to the guards and placed the younger in the Cadet Corps with sons of the Russian aristocracy.

In the meantime, French émigrés continued to arrive in Russia. Count Esterházy wrote: "From now on I am not going to forward the requests of others . . . since their number is increasing beyond measure." As a sort of unofficial ministry for French émigré affairs, the Empress formed a triumvirate to advise her. This group, Count Esterházy, the Marquis de Lambert and Count de Choiseul, took over the management of virtually all émigré business. When, in 1795, Catherine confiscated the properties of Polish nobles held responsible for a rebellious uprising, the three Frenchmen were among the beneficiaries in the redistribution. Choiseul received a large estate near the Galician border, one which had not been confiscated from a private party and thus would not be in danger of litigation in event of the former owner's rehabilitation at court.

In 1795, Louis XVIII offered Choiseul the position of Ambassador at Vienna, and Choiseul was prepared to accept. But Vienna for reasons of its own refused to receive him. As a result of this awkward situation, Choiseul retired to his estate until Catherine's death in 1796. Her successor, Paul I, not only renewed but considerably augmented the favor and authority accorded Choiseul by Catherine. Choiseul was again named Privy Counsellor[1] and made president of the Academy of Arts. He was also appointed director of "all the Imperial libraries." But, as Michaud says: "at a court everything is transient, especially under a prince like Paul I, naturally generous, but . . . capricious."[2] Romantic interest in the French émigrés had begun to fade after a few years of living with them, and not a few Russians envied the high positions held by the Frenchmen, among them Choiseul. Add to this jealousy the Count's incompetence, and the result was disastrous. Choiseul had large ideas—too large to be realized. Authority at the Academy of Arts was soon placed in the hands of a vice-president. Choiseul's experience with the libraries was even less successful. In 1800 he was removed from office, and retired to his estate. After the assassination of Paul I (1801), Choiseul sought no further positions in Russia and in 1802 returned to France where he devoted the rest of his life to scientific studies, dying in 1817.

But Choiseul's eldest son Count Octave remained behind, founding the Russian branch of the family. When at the age of twenty he had gone to Russia with his father, he was already an officer in the French royal bodyguard and was taken at once into Russian military service. He rose rapidly and was awarded the St. George Cross for "bravery against the Polish rebels" by Suvorov, under whom he served in Poland. Military records show that Choiseul was assigned as captain to the Riga cuirassiers regiment but removed within two months "for nonarrival" in Riga. Subsequently appointed by the Empress to her Cavalier Guard regiment, he left the army in 1795. Later (1812) he became a royal chamberlain busied with civil affairs.

Despite his record in the war against the Poles, Count Octave married a Polish countess, Victoria Potocki, in 1805. One of the oldest of aristocratic families, the "little kings of Polonia and the Ukraine" whose records go back to the 1300's, the Potockis had been pro-Russian. The second partition of Poland was partially brought about by the appeal of a group of aristocrats headed by Count Felix-Stanislas

Potocki to Catherine to save Poland from the dangerous ideas of the
French Revolution. After the third partition of Poland, Catherine accepted Count Felix into her army with the rank of general. His daughter married Count Octave Choiseul and became Berdyaev's great-
grandmother. When Octave, already a subject of the Tsar, inherited
the title "Peer of France" at his father's death, he attempted to arrange
double nationality for himself (one of the earliest known such instances in Russian history). He seemed to be on the way to success,
but in 1827 Tsar Nicolai I "with his own hand" crossed Count Octave's name off the list of royal chamberlains. He died (1840) in
Florence.

Octave's sons, like their father, all chose Polish Catholic wives, but
his only daughter Josephine-Mathilda married a Russian Orthodox
prince. According to family tradition, she met Prince Kudasheff in
Paris at one of the court balls of Napoleon III. Their daughter became
Berdyaev's mother.

Berdyaev's father also came of a long line of patrician ancestors. The
Berdyaev family first immigrated to Smolensk from Poland toward the
end of the fifteenth century. Somewhere there was also a Lithuanian
ancestor, for the family coat of arms contains elements neither Polish
nor Russian. At the end of the sixteenth century, Boris Godunoff
granted the Berdyaev family large estates and the name was first listed
among the nobility. By 1863 eighteen Berdyaevs were registered as
landed gentry. These early grants of land and title required the re-
cipient and his descendants to appear with "their people" (peasants on
their estates) at the call of the Tsar in the event of war.[3] A young
aristocrat did his military service, obtained officer's rank, and could
then choose to continue in the army or retire to a quiet life on his
estate.

Berdyaev frequently spoke of his military forebears as having influenced his own character. His great-grandfather, General Nicolai
Michailovitch, was a lieutenant-general under Catherine II and Paul I
and was named by the latter to be governor of the newly annexed "New
Russia" district at the eastern end of the Black Sea. His correspondence
with the Emperor from this post was later published in *Russian An-
tiquities*. But his son Michail, Berdyaev's grandfather, was the outstanding military figure in the Berdyaev line. Like all the Berdyaevs before
him, Michail Nicolaievitch was an officer in the elite Cavalier Guard
regiment. During the Battle of Kulm (August 30, 1813) when it
appeared certain that Napoleon was defeating the Russian and Ger-

man armies, and all the senior officers of young Lieutenant Berdyaev's division had been killed, he took command and rallied his troops to a strong counterattack. The French retreated and lost the battle. Lieutenant Berdyaev was awarded the St. George Cross, traditional decoration for military valor, and the Prussian Iron Cross for good measure.

Later, as a major-general, Michail Nicolaievitch was made *Ataman* —commander of one "region" of the Cossack troops. Tsar Nicolai I had, as part of his reactionary program of unification, decreed the elimination of the "Cossack freedoms," certain rights that the stubborn, independent Cossacks had obtained in recompense for their loyalty to the Tsar during half a century of military "pacification" in the Caucasus. The Tsar came to review General Berdyaev's troops in Novocherkassk and ordered him to carry out the imperial rescript. General Berdyaev, to the astonishment of everyone present, told the Tsar that he considered such a measure detrimental to the country, and on the spot presented his resignation. The Tsar, at first offended by anyone who dared decline obedience, suddenly changed countenance, embraced the General, and countermanded his order.

Despite his generally reactionary views, Nicolai I was much concerned with improving the condition of the serfs. Berdyaev's father used to tell the boy how grandfather Michail had considered the whole institution of serfdom shameful. The General, putting into practice his feelings about the lower classes, was so exceptionally kind to the soldiers in his regiment that they presented him with a medal inscribed "God guard you for your kindness to us." Bedyaev recalled the medal hanging in his father's study and a reproduction of it carved on the grandfather's tombstone. Berdyaev's own liberal tendencies seem to have been a direct inheritance from his father and grandfather.

Berdyaev's paternal grandmother was Sophie Nicolaevna Bachmetieff, who traced her descendence from Tatar nobility of the fifteenth century. (The last imperial ambassador in Washington, Boris Bachmetieff, came of this line.) Until the revolution there were some Bachmetieffs in Russia who, true to their ancestral traditions, were still Moslems. One of the most significant items of information about the grandmother is that, living close to the famous Petchersk monastery in Kiev, and under the spiritual direction of the "Elder" Parfenii, she secretly took the veil—a form of religious devotion not rare in Russia. The family first learned of this when she died, and Berdyaev recalled vividly his astonishment at seeing his grandmother in her coffin in the robes of a nun. On the other side of the family, Berdyaev's maternal great-grandmother also took the veil, after the death of her husband Prince Kudasheff. Her portrait as a nun, with its "very severe face," was left hanging on the wall of the Berdyaev home in Moscow when he was banished by the Soviet government. The Kudasheffs were also of Tatar descent; applied to Berdyaev, the old adage "scratch a Russian and you'll find a Tatar" was doubly true.

What a rich and varied heritage was Berdyaev's: a mixture of nationalities—French, Polish, Lithuanian and Russian, a mingling of races—white and yellow; on his mother's side there was scarcely an ancestor without a title, count or prince or even king (the Choiseuls were descended from Louis VI of France), and the entire Berdyaev line was of the untitled nobility. Inbred aristocracy, inherited mysticism, the best traditions of military valor and ancient chivalry, independence of thought almost to the point of agnosticism, all these characteristics were mingled when in 1859 Alexander Michailovitch Berdyaev married the beautiful Princess Alexandra Kudasheff. Berdyaev felt he could trace most of these ancestral elements in his own personality.

# 3

## A DOLL NAMED PRINCE ANDRÉ

Berdyaev's father, Alexander Michailovitch,[1] lived in a period that may be described as the twilight of the landed gentry. The eighty years of his life (1836-1916) spanned a period of social change almost unparalleled in Russia's history—the reigns of four tsars, with policies fluctuating from black reaction under Nicolai I through the reforms of the "Tsar Liberator," Alexander II, back again to the reactionary regime of Alexander III and the feeble do-nothingness of Nicolai II. The elder Berdyaev had lived through two "eastern wars" and the disastrous conflict with Japan, the abortive revolution of 1905, the liberation of the serfs, and the institution of the Duma. These movements affected most of all the class of people living luxuriously on the backs of their serfs, as their families had for hundreds of years before them. To one born in the twentieth century, such living is almost unimaginable. The landowner lived with a minimum of care—there was usually a more-or-less honest manager to oversee the operation of the estates. If the master did not serve in the army or the civil service, he had few responsibilities, and life was indolent and easy. Balls, clubs, hunting, travel abroad, in some cases individual study, filled his timeless days.

Alexander Michailovitch Berdyaev was typical of this class. After serving in the elite Cavalier Guard the one year necessary to assure officer's rank, he gave up the army and retired to what were at first considerable properties. He lived the life of a country gentleman at Obuchovo, the family estate on the banks of the Dnieper. But, as Berdyaev says in his autobiography, his father "always had a tendency toward ruination," and Obuchovo was sold when Berdyaev was a very small child. His earliest memory was of walking with his nurse in the grande allée at Obuchovo, but all other childhood recollections are of the house and garden in Kiev, purchased at the time Obuchovo was sold. All his days Alexander Michailovitch grieved over the loss of the estate and longed for life in the country. The boy Berdyaev felt this and "always dreamed of the village and hoped that father would buy a new estate, even more modest"; he pictured in his imagination that it would be "of course near the forests"—which he loved so much.

In fairness to Berdyaev's father, it must be said that the loss of his estate was not altogether due to a lack of business capacity. The abolition of serfdom meant radical change in the economic life of the country. Miliukoff calls this the "period of impoverishment of the gentry." Ruined by the liberation of their serfs, they had to seek some other means of livelihood—often business ventures which ended in disaster. Alexander Michailovitch apparently undertook no commercial ventures on his own but accepted election as "marshal of the gentry," serving also for a score of years as president of the Agrarian Bank of the Southwest Region. He was an honorary justice of the peace for more than twenty-five years. One brief military interlude, when Alexander Michailovitch re-entered the army at the time of the Turkish War (1877), brought no special distinction. Berdyaev writes that his father had no inclination toward making a career for himself. Fortunately there was another estate in western Poland, granted to Berdyaev's grandfather in recognition of his services to the state, and it could not be sold because it was entailed. "This," Berdyaev says, "saved us from complete ruin." The Berdyaevs never lived there, but income from the estate served to support Berdyaev and his family until the outbreak of the first World War. Alexander Michailovitch frequently visited it, but Berdyaev saw it only once as a young man, en route home from Germany.[2]

Berdyaev's father loved travel and frequently visited western Europe. In sharp distinction to many of the "retired gentry,"* Alexander Michailovitch was a man of considerable culture and learning. His library contained books in half a dozen languages and he had read them all. French was the language of the family, and he used German and Italian easily in his travels. So young Berdyaev grew up surrounded by the books—chiefly philosophy and history—of his father's extensive library. Alexander Michailovitch was greatly influenced by Voltaire and like many other Russian intellectuals moved gradually toward a new world view, breaking with old traditions even to the extent of criticizing the monarchy, and hence coming into conflict with the society around him. He belonged to the small minority of landed gentry who advocated reform laws for the peasants, and had great

* Retired from military service.

sympathy and respect for N. A. Milutin, who helped prepare the decrees that liberated the serfs in 1861. He used to point to a framed
picture of Lincoln that stood on his desk, calling Lincoln "one of the
greatest of men: he liberated a whole people from slavery." His religious thinking was largely influenced by Tolstoi, and while he believed
in God "in the deistic sense" and reverenced Christ, his Christianity
was summed up in the second of Christ's commandments—love for
one's neighbor. He had no use for church dogmas because he felt they
distorted the original Christian teaching. He was proud of his ancestry and never tired of recounting to his son tales of the military
prowess of his father and grandfather. Alexander Michailovitch was
equally proud of his own "high connections," chiefly through his Cavalier Guard regiment. Prince Lopuchin-Demidoff of one of the oldest
families of Kiev, Alexander Michailovitch's comrade in the regiment,
was Nicolai's godfather. Berdyaev writes that the Lopuchin-Demidoffs
also "had a tendency toward ruination" and were periodically rescued
from bankruptcy by grants from the imperial family. Alexander Michailovitch was a close friend of the Governor-General of Kiev and had
such intimates at the St. Petersburg court as Prince Kotchubey, *Ober-
hofmeister* to the Tsar, and the Commandant of the imperial court,
General Cherepin. Despite his intellectual liberalism, he never envisioned life in any other framework than that of the traditional patriarchal, aristocratic system where rank and family play a decisive role.
That his father occupied an influential position in Kiev is evidenced
by Berdyaev's description of the moment in his student years when
the police came to search his room and arrest him: they "moved on
tiptoe and spoke in whispers so as not to disturb Father."

Alexander Michailovitch was strong-willed but very temperamental.
Berdyaev says this was characteristic of the Russian gentry. His sudden bursts of violent anger caused much unpleasantness within the
family. The fact that Alexander Michailovitch was at odds within himself, particularly during the transition from patriarchal, Orthodox traditions to Voltairianism, partly accounted for the stormy temperament
that brought him into frequent conflict with those about him and
isolated the Berdyaevs from most of their neighbors. Because his
father had quarreled with Princess Lopuchin-Demidoff, Berdyaev never
visited that family. Berdyaev's mother often said the Berdyaevs were
all abnormal and that sanity in the family came from the Kudasheff
side.

As a "freethinker," Alexander Michailovitch took pleasure in criticizing religion and the church. At the table he would often read aloud portions of the Bible, adding his own sarcastic comments regardless of the effect they might have on an impressionable son. This would go on until the mother threatened to leave the table unless he stopped. He never punished his son and on at least one occasion held a "very important conversation" with the boy, in the course of which the father wept. This changed many things in the son's life. Berdyaev says his father's love for him increased with the years, but asserts that while he was grateful to his father and fulfilled all the usual filial duties, he never really felt he belonged to either of his parents. When the German invasion of Poland in 1914 stopped his father's only source of income, Berdyaev brought him—already an invalid—into his home in Moscow, where he died in 1916. Berdyaev, in the only considerable series of his letters that has been preserved, wrote: "I always had good relations with my parents, but I always had the feeling that I was not born of them, but came from some other world." Berdyaev's attitude toward the other boys in school, as he describes it, is a perfect description of a "mama's boy," but he seems not to have been unusually close to his mother. He "liked her, but was not in love with her." He "loved both parents, considered them fine people" but felt more toward them as a father toward his children than vice-versa. He took good care of them, always fearful lest they become ill and tortured by the thought that they might die. He never was interested in family life as it is known in the west, Berdyaev explains. Like Dostoievsky, he loved humanity in general but not in particular. He disliked intensely the family resemblance of brothers and sisters; such resemblance seemed to him a contradiction of the dignity of the individual. Was this in compensation for the fact that the boy had no sisters and grew up almost completely alone? In his earliest years he began to feel a conviction of his own peculiarity, a lack of resemblance to others.

Berdyaev seems to have resembled his father in character more than his mother. Perhaps his good looks came from her, the delicately arched brows and the graceful hands. In her youth she was a noted beauty, and Berdyaev says that at fifty she was still very beautiful. Her photograph, made in Kiev sometime in the mid-eighties, reveals a delicately molded face with dark hair curling away from a high forehead, a rather coquettish turn of the head, smallish eyes with a hint of a twinkle beneath arched brows, and a mouth that seems capable of smiling although her general countenance is one of sadness. Nicolai loved his mother in the sense that he loved beauty. Unlike her husband, who was pure Russian in character and temperament, she evidenced her French upbringing and descent. Her school years had been spent in Paris. She always spoke French, never learned to write good Russian, and in many other ways was strikingly different from him. Perhaps one reason she went abroad every year to Vichy or Karlsbad to take a "liver-cure" was the opportunity it gave her to stop in Paris for a visit with her sister. She loved the city and he preferred life in the country. This was the cause of frequent family quarrels.[3] Even in her religious life she was more French than Russian; although born and baptised in the Orthodox Church, she felt more at home in Catholicism and always used her mother's Catholic prayerbook for her private devotions. Nicolai felt she never took them very seriously and jokingly said she was never on first-name terms with God. She loved the life of the aristocratic society to which both families belonged, but she felt that her family connections were higher than the Berdyaevs. Her father was at one time governor-general of Kiev. Her cousin, the Polish Countess Branicky, was one of the wealthiest women in the empire; she owned the entire city of Belaya Tserkov and 160,000 acres in the Kiev province—breadbasket of Russia—and "palaces in Warsaw, Paris, Nice and Rome." Nothing could better illustrate Russia's feudal aristocracy at the turn of the century than the Branicky family. Their great summer palace "Alexandria," on the outskirts of Belaya Tserkov, was a regular feudal institution with its court, its multitude of retainers, its stables of blooded horses, and its renowned hunts that brought together all the landed gentry of southwestern Russia. Fifteen course dinners were the usual thing at "Alexandria." Like many other great houses in Russia, "Alexandria" was sacked and burned during the revolution.

Although he insists that he did not like this aristocratic world "and even in childhood was in opposition to it," Berdyaev remembered with pleasure the autumn months he and his mother used to spend at "Alexandria": the solitude of the great park, "one of the finest, not alone in Russia, but in Europe," where he could walk and "dream of another world." A special pavilion was reserved for the Berdyaevs to live in whenever they were with the Branickys. Berdyaev had a small buggy with a pair of ponies, and he was permitted to drive them himself, with a liveried footman sitting up behind. There was also a donkey that he could ride in the long avenues of the park. In such company Alexandra Sergeevna Berdyaev felt more at home than in her own household. With her French background, her grace and beauty, she fitted admirably into the gay, carefree life of high society. She dressed herself in elegant taste—and her little boy as well; all his life he was to be noted for his concern about clothing, and in his younger days, when money was plentiful, he was one of the most stylishly dressed young men in St. Petersburg.

It was a strange home into which Nicolai Berdyaev was born in 1874. His parents had been married sixteen years but there was only one other child, his brother Serge, fifteen years his senior. Serge, like the rest of the Berdyaevs, was of a highly explosive temperament and broke off relations with his parents shortly after his marriage outside the patrician circle, with the result that Nicolai grew up in a family consisting solely of his father, his mother and himself. Berdyaev's description of his brother seems to witness to the truth of his mother's assertion that all the Berdyaevs were abnormal—a gravely sick man (many considered him psychopathic). As a youth he suffered from occasional "nervous seizures" resulting in convulsions and loss of consciousness, and occasional outbursts of almost insensate rage. Very gifted, kind, but lacking in character, he never was able to realize his gifts in actual life. Generous to the point of giving his last ruble to a needy friend, he was always in financial difficulties. The magazine he tried to launch in Kiev was short-lived, although Serge himself had some success as a poet and placed his verses in other journals. Handsome in a classic way, he vacillated between an appearance of elegance and that of a tramp—there were periods when he went unshaven, even unwashed, and dressed in rags.

Berdyaev admired in him certain capacities lacking in himself: language ability—he even wrote verses in German—and a gift for mathematics. Unlike his brother, Serge had no philosophic turn of mind. He greatly disturbed Nicolai and his parents by his interest in the occult. Sometimes he would go into a trance, speaking rhythmically but in an unknown tongue, and considered himself a medium transmitting messages from long-dead Hindu teachers. During the time he lived at home, Serge was in frequent quarrels with his parents. Serge scandalized his relatives by refusing to follow a military career. While preparing for the university he was involved in some student "revolutionary" activities, arrested, and exiled for a year, and for a long time thereafter he was under special police surveillance. Was this bizarre nature, like the unusual character of his young brother, partly a result of inbreeding through long generations of aristocracy? At all events the Berdyaev line ceased with these two brothers. Nicolai had

no children. Serge himself died young; his son Alexander, now living in
the U.S.S.R., recently wrote a friend in Paris: "We are the last of the
Berdyaevs—with us the family dies out."

The arrival of a child in a family where there have been no births for
fifteen years creates a difficult situation. Perhaps this helps to explain
the strange lack of spiritual contact with his parents that Berdyaev
describes. Older parents forget the adjustments and adaptations necessary when there are babies in a home. Their lives have become
settled in routine, and the presence of a small child is disturbing, often
subconsciously resented. This seems to have been true with Berdyaev.
He was left largely to his own devices. Neither father nor mother offered spiritual companionship or much in the way of what used to be
called "bringing-up."

Fortunately there was his *nyanya*, that peculiarly Russian institution in wealthy families. A nurse who was more than a servant, a
member of the family in all but social activities, she was almost solely
responsible for the health and nurture of the children, often actually—
if unintentionally—preventing them from having enough companionship with their parents. Like the "mammy" in many old southern
families, she helped form the child's thought world—her folk tales
trained his imagination, her religious feeling laid the foundations for
such religious life as the child might have. Anna Ivanovna Katamenkova
had been a serf belonging to Berdyaev's grandfather. She had been
the *nyanya* of Berdyaev's father and of his brother Serge. Berdyaev
reports that his father, not normally a respecter of persons, greatly
loved and respected the nurse—even though she was "an ardent
Orthodox." Her care and kindness surrounded the young Berdyaev
until he was fourteen, when she died "at a great old age." Berdyaev
says little more about her, but she must have been for him a great
stabilizer, sure refuge from his doubts and sufferings.

Despite her own deep faith, Anna Ivanovna evidently did not take
the boy Nicolai to church very often; he says definitely that memories
of services in the village church, usually a rich portion of normal Russian childhood, are not a part of his recollections. On the contrary, he
was unfavorably impressed as a child by the occasional services to which
he was taken at the Governor-General's church in Kiev. The atmosphere there was one of official rather than spiritual orthodoxy, and
even as a child Berdyaev was aware that the generals and other be-
medaled officers were in attendance only because it was a part of their
official duties. He was further repelled by Petchersk, the monastery

quarter of Kiev adjoining Lipki where the Berdyaev home was located. Lipki was the official and aristocratic "upper" part of Kiev, its fine houses set in extensive gardens. These gardens were Berdyaev's delight, but the proximity of the great monastic establishments added an element of the unpleasant. Both his grandfather and his father felt a strong aversion for the many monks they passed on the street—long-haired, long-bearded, wearing rusty black robes—and made no effort to hide their displeasure. Some of this must have been communicated to the child. His father's mother, the one who secretly took the veil, had forced her son into such strict religious observances—he said it seemed to him that life was just one long Lent—that it turned Alexander Michailovitch against all formal religion for the remainder of his life.

With the death of Berdyaev's grandmother, when he was six, the family's only connection with Petchersk was broken, and even his nurse did not communicate her beliefs to him. Berdyaev could truly say he never had a traditional Orthodox childhood.

Nyanya must have been a great comfort to the oversensitive child in the tense family atmosphere: mother quarreled with father over where the family should live; Serge was in constant argumentation with his parents, who rarely found anything in his tastes or actions that they could approve. Later the boy would try to play the role of mediator in these recurrent quarrels, but as a child his parents' bitter criticism of his brother, for whom he always had a strong affection, must have been a painful experience. Both father and mother were frequently ill. The boy would be wakened at night by his mother's shrieks of pain during an attack of gallstones, and he would tremble with terror lest she should die. In such emotional crises the boy could turn to Nyanya for comfort and reassurance.

Yet from early childhood the young Berdyaev felt himself "alone, and rootless in this world." Unlike most other Russian homes, theirs was cold and formal. Guests at the table were rare occasions. The proper calls were exchanged with the proper persons, and that was all. Most other families kept permanent open house, with friends dropping in at all hours of the day and young folks continually organizing excursions or amateur theatricals. Even the children led gay, exciting lives.

In our time it is difficult to imagine the social life the gentry of those days pursued. With practically no economic limitations—unrecognized limitations produced families "with a tendency to ruination"—life went along on a grand scale: travel, palatial homes, hospitality of the broadest sort. Eugenie says there were usually twenty or more guests at her mother's table, some of whom—friends of friends— were total strangers to the hostess. The wife of a tsarist official, traveling with her two daughters to their estate on the Volga, met another lady on the steamer with two daughters about the ages of hers. Within a day's travel the two groups became such friends that it was decided they would all spend the summer at the first lady's home. And that was what they did. Princess Jashwill tells of being seated at luncheon one hot summer day and noticing a cloud of dust approaching up the driveway that developed into a small caravan: two carriages, a cart stacked high with luggage and a cow tied on behind. Neighbors from an adjoining valley had heard the heat was less oppressive on the Jashwill estate and just moved over, unannounced, to spend a month or two. They took along the cow because they did not want to change the baby's milk.

In the Berdyaev home there was none of this. Probably the father realized his difficult financial position, and this precluded much social life. At all events the father was an unsocial individual, living much in his own thoughts and studies, and he ruled the household. Perhaps his frequent journeys to the estate in western Poland were an escape from family bickerings and tensions. The mother, yielding to her husband's social mood, could go to her cousins in Belaya Tserkov or, profiting by a trip to Vichy, enjoy the social life of Paris for a month or two. There was a dour and formal atmosphere about the Berdyaev home.

Then there was illness. In the family, someone was always under a doctor's care. Serge was unbalanced physically as well as emotionally. His father was always taking medicine. Nicolai, in early childhood, spent a whole year in bed with rheumatic fever. No wonder he reports that one of his earliest philosophical thoughts was "life is illness." He never recovered from his childhood trauma; all his life he was terribly afraid for himself and for members of the family. Courageous, almost fearless, in great crises, Berdyaev says the idea of illness filled him with "an almost mystic terror." He drank only boiled water. His fear of drafts was almost comical. A friend recalls the reprimand he once gave a maid who went out after making up his study in the morning, leaving the window open. Berdyaev came in without the woolen scarf he usually wore to protect his neck from a *courant d'air* and called the maid back to express his horror. She must remember how dangerous it was for him to step into fresh air unprepared for it. He admonished her never to let this happen again. Another friend who spent a season with the family at Vichy tells how Berdyaev, returning from the cinema evenings, would hastily wrap his scarf over mouth and nose at a certain corner, urging the rest of the party to do the same. "You know here is where the wind comes up off the river, and how dangerous that is!" Illness or the fear of it "played a great role" in his life.

Further, there was the tic. From earliest childhood to the day of his death he was plagued with this nervous affliction. Those who knew him well became so accustomed to it that they, like Berdyaev himself, almost failed to notice it, but for strangers it was a painful, almost frightening experience. Almost without warning the head would be thrown back, the fine face distorted with a tortured grimace, and from the twisted, wide-open mouth the tongue would be thrust out. In a few seconds the spasm would pass and the face return to its normal state. Berdyaev was more subject to the tic in moments of high nervous tension, but sometimes in the midst of an ordinary conversation one would tactfully stop and glance in some other direction until the facial convulsion had passed. In his mature years Berdyaev learned a gesture that sometimes prevented these seizures. When he felt one coming on, he would raise his right hand to the back of his head, a movement like that of a woman fixing her hair but without touching hand to head. Sometimes this was effective, but again it would fail and the lecture or conversation would stop for a few painful seconds. For both boy and man, this infirmity was doubtless a significant element in Berdyaev's psychology. It certainly increased the child's feeling of peculiarity, a part of his earliest consciousness. Berdyaev says that in the family atmosphere he "always felt a certain infelicity, inadaptability to life, depression, super-sensitivity." Left largely to his own devices in a gloomy, inhospitable house, the little boy took refuge in stories and dreams. He created an inner world of his own, different from the "real" world around him. From earliest childhood, Berdyaev says, he was convinced that our "real" world is illusory and that he—apparently he alone—belonged to quite another. We do not know who taught him to read, but at a very early age—certainly several years before he was sent to school at eleven—he had read all sorts of books from his father's library. He was still playing with dolls when he read *War and Peace*; his favorite toy was a doll named André, an officer gradually endowed by the boy with all the high qualities of Tolstoi's Prince André. This doll was his constant companion, and its personality and personal history became

more real to Berdyaev than his comrades at school. The boy read scores
of novels and dramas, in three languages: French, German, and Russian. Their heroes meant more to him than the people actually living
around him. As a matter of fact, he says, he merely pretended to participate in the life of the "real" world but with all his powers defended
himself against its influence like a feudal baron besieged in his castle.

He had ample occasion to become acquainted with the real world,
however. At seven he made his first trip abroad when his mother took
him with her to Karlsbad, visiting Vienna en route. The boy usually
accompanied her on her annual trips abroad, and there were the long
visits to "Alexandria" to remove him from the inner world of his
imagining. He resisted these influences stubbornly, clinging to his own
thoughts and convictions, far more concerned with himself and his
feelings than with society.

Consequently, the child grew up almost uninfluenced by the outside
world. From his first childhood steps he never knew any authority and
never recognized any—never experienced such a thing as external control. He was neither scolded at home nor punished, he says, because he
was too proud to do anything for which he might be reproached—also
probably because of his delicate health. Apparently his outbursts of
anger, when he would beat his head with his small chair, were not considered anything for which he should be corrected. Perhaps, too, the
old patriarchal traditions were no longer valid in the family. Unconsciously, the search for a substitute made the family too little sure of itself to enforce direction on the child. He seems to have had no companions of his own age; early childhood set a pattern in this as in many
other aspects of his life. He disliked competitive games, probably because he came upon them suddenly in school with no previous experience, and the only sports in which he took an interest were riding
and shooting. From a Cossack riding master he learned both Cossack
and cavalry riding styles at the age of nine. Here, he thought, the blood
of a long line of military ancestors made itself felt. These were sports
he could pursue alone, without much competition from other boys. He
was also an enthusiastic mountain climber in Switzerland. Again, however, there is little of the competitive about alpinism.

The child lived and did exactly as he wished. He collected his own
library. He made order in his own room and went wild with rage if
anyone interfered with it. All through his autobiography, even in the
account of his childhood, we find "I decided," "I made the plan for my
study," "I refused to accept. . . ." As a child, he decided he would

never work for anyone else because he could never accept orders from a superior. Berdyaev says this was all due to his "innate sense of individual freedom." One wonders if he was thinking of his own experience when years later he wrote: "How many lives have been deformed and ruined by the wrong ideas of authority, of parents or of leaders!" Apparently even the shock of his brother's arrest, trial, and sentence to exile when Berdyaev was only ten did not inspire him with any respect for authority. It may even have served as a precedent for his own stormy student years, resulting in his own exile. For the first ten years of his life, he followed only his own very strong likes and dislikes—a truly self-made child.

But although he would not submit to the influence of living persons, the boy was profoundly and permanently affected by the authors of the books he read. The James Fenimore Cooper and Jules Verne of his first reading soon gave place to more serious writers. Toward the poet Zhukovsky, Berdyaev must have felt considerable personal sympathy, for Zhukovsky had grown up in a family atmosphere so sheltered that he faced his early school years as sort of a freak, quite unappreciated and uncomprehended by his teachers. Karamzin, the Russian historian, may have first attracted the boy with his sentimental descriptions of the toil and suffering of "the people," giving him an early sense of social injustice and of evil in the world. But Karamzin also gave the boy his first strong sense of belonging to a great land and a great people. These ideas were vastly strengthened by young Berdyaev's reading of Tolstoi, and even more by Dostoievsky. The two authors were reread until their characters became a part of the boy's being. He always felt himself closely bound up with Ivan Karamazoff and Stavrogin and with Prince André. No other writer left such deep traces in Berdyaev's thought as Dostoievsky. The boy lived into the lives of Dostoievsky's characters; they "shook his soul." But if these books and writers gave the boy ideas, they did not greatly influence his character and temperament. He remained his own peculiar self, living within the closed circle of his stubbornly defended personal world.

One of the differences between a man and a tree lies in the fact that a tree, growing up alone, assumes a form of beautiful symmetry, while a man, left completely to himself, is almost certain to be one-sided. So it was with young Berdyaev. Along with his consciousness of being different from others, he had a keen sense of his incapacities. He was unable to adapt himself to the ideas or wishes of others; he detested the thought of conformity. In later life, he considered this in-

adaptability one of his basic characteristics. In school he felt a strong
aversion for formally directed study. As a child he played at different
forms of handicraft: woodwork, painting, and even gardening, but in
later life he was incapable of replacing a burnt-out fuse or building a
new fire in a stove.

More significant in the boy's development was his consciousness of
spiritual apartness. The more the world pressed in upon him, the more
he strove against it. In defense of his inner world, he was forced to
appear unsocial, almost sullen, although he always tried to hide his
peculiarity and pretended he was just like other people. He was continually astonished how those about him could be a part of the world
and play a natural role in society. In later years he was surprised that
he himself came to have a place of importance in the world's thinking,
which he had neither desired nor intended. This attitude was later to
find expression in his book *Of Man's Slavery and Freedom.* In many of
his books Berdyaev speaks of "this world" between quotation marks.
After all, his own world was distinct and different.

The boy was different from most others in the matter of class. Although he struggled throughout his life to overcome it, he never could
rid himself completely from what the Russians call his *barstvo,* his
consciousness of coming from and belonging to a privileged class. In
later life it was more an unconscious than an active knowing, but as a
child he could stamp his feet and scream at the servants—only recently freed from serfdom. Driving his pony through the park at "Alexandria" with a footman up behind was most natural for a lad of noble
breeding. His parents were very conscious of their high social standing
and relationships and never hesitated to use them for their own benefit. Owing to their high connections, the boy was granted special conditions upon entering school. Friendly relations with the Governor-
General of Kiev and other important officials greatly softened the rigors
of "exile" during his student years. His lifelong conviction of the necessity for an elite in society was probably rooted in his privileged childhood. He grew up knowing the angels were on his side.

And others knew it also. At the age of ten, this strange, dreamy,
pampered, self-willed boy was plunged into the life of a military school.
His lineage gave him the inherited right to study in the Pages' Corpus
at St. Petersburg, but he was enrolled instead in the Cadet Corpus in
his home city, Kiev. Perhaps his parents were reluctant to have him so
far from home, particularly in view of his delicate health, and hence
decided against the pages' school. Upon his placement in the Kiev

school, his parents obtained two special concessions at the outset. He was permitted to skip the first class, starting at once in the second, and, privilege still more unusual, was permitted to live at home whereas the cadets were almost without exception boarders. More than this, they were all of the bourgeois class, and young Nicolai seems to have been the only patrician among them—a future Royal Guard officer—all of which prepared for him anything but a friendly reception. Coming of a pampered noble family, he was so little interested in the usual things that occupy schoolboy minds that he scarcely spoke the same language. His tic made more trouble. The older folk with whom he had been almost exclusively associated up to now could understand and overlook it, but his classmates made full use of the chance it gave them to ridicule the new pupil. Like Kierkegaard, "his physical idiosyncrasies fostered a precocious brilliance at the cost of social misery."[4]

The boy's reactions may be easily imagined. He had never liked the company of boys his own age. He felt the cadets were especially rude and coarse and, even worse, "immature." To the end of his days Berdyaev thought there was "nothing more repulsive than boys' talk among themselves . . . a source of corruption." The classroom was bad enough, but the intermissions were pure torture. He could not—even would not—take part in the games. From his earliest years he had a strong aversion to any conversation about sex or physical functions in general; the small talk around him was as disagreeable as everything else about the school. Later, Berdyaev said he felt his incapacity for close comradeship or intimate friendship was based on his complete lack of spiritual contact with other boys in these early years.

He disliked the school program and discipline. To a boy who "had never felt authority over him," the stiff order and discipline of a military school was almost unbearable. An individualist like Berdyaev could never be at home in the collectivism of the Corpus. Here, at school age, his "incapacity to conform" was strongly evident. He refused to cut his long hair as military regulations prescribed. Even before entering school he had disliked the military, partly because he sensed the empty formalism behind uniforms and decorations and parades, partly because his father and his brother had both broken away from the martial tradition. Furthermore, the military system "made a person a subordinate part of a collective," and subordination was something Berdyaev, boy or man, never could endure. This school experience intensified his aversion to things military. He would go out of his way to avoid meeting a general—one had to stop and stiffen to a salute:

three drill steps, a half-turn on the heels, "one, two, three, four." If
one went into a teashop—restaurants, where ordering wine lent a
"manly" air, were off-limits for cadets—and discovered an officer sitting
there, it was even more humiliating: "Mr. Lieutenant, permit me to
take a seat." Any general one met on the street could ask: "Cadet, why
aren't you in school at this time of day? Let's see your card." A generation later, when he was introduced to General Alexeev during the
revolution, Berdyaev said it was the first time since his cadet days that
he had used the official military greeting.

If not on the street, where officers might be encountered, the young
man was in his room at home during a considerable part of the time
he should have been in the classroom. He hated directed study as much
as he hated the rest of the school discipline. Consequently he was a
poor pupil. His having learned German and French at home gave him
an advantage over his classmates in these two subjects, but he lagged
behind in all the rest. Nicolai's next best subjects were history and
natural science. His compositions were "not bad," although his spelling
was. He was incapable of memorizing a four-line verse; he seemed to
understand mathematical theory but could not solve a problem. The
boy once set a scandalous record within the Corpus by getting the
lowest possible grade ("one" in a twelve point scale) in "The Law of
God," as the Russians call the catechism. Examinations were "unbearable things." Berdyaev could not limit himself to a mere answer;
he wanted at once to add his own thought on the subject. Looking
back on it later, Berdyaev noted that he had no ability to absorb knowledge passively—that it was only when he was developing his thought
on his own that he progressed in knowledge. At this early period as
through all his life, Berdyaev was an avid student, but not by swallowing the books and thoughts of others. Rather, he says, his study has
been a system of "communion with the world's thought, toward which
I determine my own attitude."

Instead of following the courses set by the school, young Berdyaev
was making his own plans for his reading and thinking. As a boy, he
had known that he would devote his life to philosophy. Unlike most
boys in their early teens, his thinking involved nothing specifically religious; he had no childhood religious memories. The meaning for him
of the Christ of the "Grand Inquisitor" was still in the future. His
thinking was "a search for meaning and a search for eternity." Here is
how he describes what was, in a sense, his conversion:

One day, on the borderline between puberty and youth, I was shaken by the thought, "I may not know the meaning of life, but the search for meaning gives meaning to life, and I will consecrate my life to this search for meaning." This was a true inner transformation, which changed my whole life. I experienced it with enthusiasm. This was my true conversion, the most powerful in my life, the turning to a search for Truth, which by this very fact was a belief in the existence of Truth, spelled with a capital letter. After this inner revolution, I began to read philosophical books with great enthusiasm, almost exaltation.

At exactly what age this conviction came to him Berdyaev does not say, but by fourteen he had read Hegel and "deeply breathed in" Schopenhauer and, before taking the final cadet school examinations at about seventeen, had mastered John Stuart Mill's *Logic*, and Kant's *Critique of Pure Reason*. He must have astounded the officer who gave him the examination in logic.

Despite his poor scholastic record, young Berdyaev passed the sixth form examinations in the Corpus. It had been his parents' plan that he should go from there to the upper classes of the Pages' Corpus in the capital and thus be launched on a career in the Cavalier Guards. Instead, to realize his own dream, he left military school and began preparing for the "certificate of maturity" needed to enter the university. By what means he persuaded his family to permit this pivotal decision he does not say. It probably involved some strong arguments, but the young rebel won out. His brother had also rebelled against family ties and had already left home and set up his own household. A little later Nicolai did the same thing, but not at this moment. Was there also a hint already of revolt against the monarchy, for which, as a student, he was exiled a few years later? We have no record, but this was in the air breathed by the youth of that day. From his school, Berdyaev would not have received any revolutionary notions. But against his entire milieu and the traditions back of it the seventeen-year-old was in complete and stubborn opposition.

Now ensued a strange situation: to pass the maturity examination meant three years of intensive study, including some difficult subjects like Greek and Latin to which great importance was attached in the Gymnasium but which did not occur at all in the military school curriculum. This young man, with his acute distaste for any kind of external discipline, had to discipline himself most sternly in order to obtain the diploma that would open to him the doors of the university. Berdyaev tells us nothing of these three years, but it is easy to imagine the intense struggle required to master a score of subjects that did not interest him and kept him from his single passion, philosophy. For three years the youth sat alone at his studies, forcing upon himself a discipline he could not accept from others.

Alone—six years at school had given him no comrades. He had nothing in common with boys his own age. The only exception Berdyaev indicates was "the sailor Mukalov," but this friendship had evidently begun earlier. It was one of the few friendships in his entire life, that Berdyaev never broke off. Mukalov was a youth in whom Nicolai's father had become interested to the point of paying for his education. He seems to have been older than Nicolai, and one has the impression that he was physically more robust. Did the boy's father wish to provide a protector for his delicate son amid the rude contacts of the Corpus? Berdyaev only says that he was very close to Mukalov, who was his companion not only in school but later during the Vologda exile. Eugenie says he was a social-revolutionary, hated the monarchy, and participated in the revolutionary struggle. In the calm years before World War I, Mukalov often visited the Berdyaev family in Babaki. By that time he had attained a good position in the Russian commercial fleet. He later fled from Soviet Russia and served as a captain in the British Navy. Berdyaev corresponded with him and once[5] visited him in London, not long before Mukalov's death. One would like to know more of this sailor, although Mukalov probably could not have been of much assistance to Nicolai during the three years after he left the cadet school. Nicolai had to depend upon himself alone. All we know is that the lonely battle with ancient languages, mathematics, and other unpleasant, nonphilosophical, subjects was won at last and the maturity diploma attained. At twenty, Nicolai Alexandrovitch Berdyaev, forsaking the traditions of his forebears, could enter the university.

# 4

## THE BAROMETER OF SOCIETY

The university life into which young Berdyaev now entered (1894) was something quite new, not only to him but to Russia as well. A statute granted by Alexander II in 1863 had radically changed the position of all institutions of higher learning in the empire. For the first time universities had a considerable measure of academic liberty—faculties could elect their own officers and replacements, and could teach their own courses without censorship. A decade before Berdyaev entered, the doors of the universities had been opened to students of any social class, and new life flooded into higher education.

But the grant of new liberties to the universities was accompanied by almost equal restriction of student rights. Attendance at all lectures was limited to regularly registered students, cutting off a widely practiced custom of open doors to anyone who wished to attend a university course without seeking academic credit. Further, it was specified that registered students be considered "separate visitors" and hence have no right to their own organizations or existence as a corporate body. The response to these restrictive measures was instantaneous, as it would have been among students in any age or country. The press of the times reports frequent "student disorders" and "street demonstrations," often accompanied by clashes with the police, expulsion of students from their schools, and on occasion, the temporary closing of the universities. In an effort to produce a more tractable generation of university students, the curriculum of the Gymnasia (the only high schools giving access to higher education) was revised to eliminate most science courses, which the minister of education felt encouraged materialism, and these were replaced by enlarged doses of Greek and Latin.

At practically the same time these new restrictions on student privileges went into effect, there arose a series of student "circles"—study groups or informal clubs. Some circles were directed toward self-education and confined their activities to that purpose. Others, however, engaged in the propagation of revolutionary ideas. These were the reflection in the universities of powerful undercurrents abroad among Russia's intelligentsia. Many were not satisfied by the extensive reforms already granted by the "Tsar Liberator," Alexander II. Widespread unrest was fueled by the writing of Chernishevsky, with its social-revolutionary theories and its efforts to draw the intelligentsia into closer contact with "the people," and of Pisarev, outright nihilist and anarchist demanding the complete abolition of existing governmental forms for the sake of a "bright future." (This is more or less the same "bright future," still just around the corner, that the Soviet government has been promising for a whole generation.) These movements found partial expression in a series of clandestine publications, some printed in Russia, some abroad, that had become an accepted part of Russian intellectual and political life by the time Berdyaev entered the university.

Revolutionary organizations were responsible for the assassination of Alexander II (1881) and hence, indirectly, for more than a decade of reaction in government that followed. Despite all sorts of obstacles placed by the government, university teachers conducted for the general public an ever-widening circle of lectures on general cultural themes, not without an occasional admixture of political topics. Cat-and-mouse play with the police was almost comical. Lecturers were officially permitted to speak, then jailed for what they had said. An increasing volume of liberal literature was published despite an increasingly rigorous censorship. This struggle against reaction could not fail to affect university life, that "barometer of society." For the first time, close contact was established between students and professors. Some of the more liberal faculty members initiated discussion groups with their students. Many meetings were held in secret; most of them discussed forbidden political questions. As Miliukoff says, "the signs of coming change were creeping out through all the cracks."

The years before Berdyaev entered the university were crucial in Russian history. A turning point was 1891, when the great famine in the Volga regions finally forced the government into co-operation with nongovernmental social workers and agencies. Hitherto the government had opposed any contact between the intelligentsia and "the people"— by which was usually meant the peasantry. Now voluntary committees were formed, funds were collected, Tolstoi made his famous appeal to the outside world, and the majority of Russian intellectuals gained almost their first acquaintance with the actual living conditions of not "the other half" but more nearly the other four-fifths of Russia's population.

The shock of this contact with real life was felt most strongly in the universities. The revolutionary movement that had been suppressed during the reign of Alexander III now began to stir into new life, with new leaders replacing the old. An even greater role in directing public thought was now taken by the universities. Despite government disapproval, professors formed groups concerned with social—meaning *political*—problems. Their meetings frequently took the very Russian form of long evenings in the "salon" of some professor and his wife, with unlimited quantities of food and tea, and discussion as limitless as the food. In one such salon in Moscow there was a table with all the latest British and American magazines concerned with social and political questions laid out. How these passed unobserved each week through the censorship, no one was so impolite as to inquire.

Into this university world, seething with the ferment of changing social thought, shadowed by a sense of tragedy ahead, stepped young Berdyaev. He had observed university life from outside and possessed a fairly complete knowledge of its exterior manifestations, for he had always lived in Kiev, but his attention must have been particularly centered on it in the difficult years of his struggle for the "matura." As a cadet he had looked with envy on the university students, "for they were occupied with intellectual problems, and not with marching back and forth." He knew university people, saw street demonstrations, and had contact with one young man exiled for "revolutionary activities," his brother Serge.

Partly out of reaction to its suppression in the Gymnasia, young people felt a burning interest in science. (Those were the years when Lenin and Lunacharsky and other Bolsheviks were also in their university stage, and one wonders if out of this atmosphere developed the passionate faith in omnipotent science so characteristic today of the doctrinaires of Russian communism.) It was quite natural, therefore, for Berdyaev to enroll in the department of natural science. He evidently found it offered little philosophy, for within a year he had transferred to the department of law. From his first student years stemmed the negative reaction toward science and "scienticism" one often finds in Berdyaev's writing. Science, he felt, was discovering truths, while he sought Truth—spelled with a capital. Even the lectures on philosophy did not greatly impress this student; he was in-

capable of swallowing whole any subject presented by someone else.
Regarding subjects and particularly textbooks, the university offered
anything but academic liberty. In a course on the French revolution, for
instance, Michelet was forbidden and Taine utilized chiefly to empha-
size the dark and negative aspects of that epoch-making time. Even
in the Gymnasium, literature courses were never allowed to consider
"modern" writers, although students were permitted some acquaintance with Pushkin, dead these sixty years. All Russian students read
forbidden books, and we may be sure Berdyaev was no exception.
Not all his professors were first rate. In view of the flood of youth
crowding into the universities, teachers were scarce and even had to
be imported from other Slavic countries, particularly Bohemia. One
such man was obliging enough at the end of the year to ask each
student on what portion of the course he wished to be examined.
The examinations were the important thing and attendance at lectures was not obligatory; this gave Berdyaev the chance to continue for
himself the philosophical reading in which he had delighted, the past
few years.

About the time he left the Corpus, there occurred the great
spiritual crisis in Berdyaev's life previously noted. His "whole life
was changed." He experienced a new sense of "spiritual firmness,"
a great spiritual uplift, and read "almost rapturously" all the philosophical books that came into his hands. He felt deeply with
Schopenhauer. It was characteristic of Berdyaev at the time of his
spiritual awakening that the philosophy of the German thinker, not
the Bible, should kindle his inner fire. And although he later moved
away from Schopenhauer philosophically, certain elements of his
early affinity never left him. He read books on metaphysics—on eastern religions, especially Buddhism—that made a deep impression. He
never forgot his shock of pleasure on discovering Carlyle's *Heroes*. It
gave him a love for biography that lasted throughout his life. He said
such reading increased his faith in the possibility of human greatness,
although by this he meant not the military heroes or the statesmen
but the great reformers and the "wrestlers of the spirit."

Within the crowded life of the university, Berdyaev "moved out of
solitude" and began certain friendships which, for him, were remarkably
lasting. Among these was almost the only one of Berdyaev's youthful
friendships that remained unbroken to the end. He called his Jewish
friend, Shestov, "one of the most remarkable and one of the best men it
was my fortune to meet in my whole life." Their respective world out-

looks differed, but in their approach to problems they were much alike, and they were one in their intense searchings for the meaning of life. They quarreled with good humor in St. Petersburg and Paris over the most varied topics, trivial and profound, but never broke off the basic friendship that united them. Another friendship helped bring the young man out of his isolation. Although he was registered in the science department, Berdyaev began cultivating the acquaintance of professors from the department of philosophy. Among the most popular was Professor G. I. Chelpanoff; from attending his lectures on a critical approach to materialism Berdyaev developed a personal friendship. Chelpanoff was one of the "new type" of professor, and he knew how to stimulate the interest of others. Berdyaev used to visit him for long conversations on philosophical themes, apparently the first time the young man—who from childhood had known he would be a philosopher—had talked with a specialist in the field. The process was rewarding; it brought the budding philosopher out of his self-contained, intuitive thinking, and made him compare it with more systematic and more generally accepted theories. This contact with Chelpanoff apparently continued throughout Berdyaev's university study and the two years before he left Kiev.

As might be imagined in a youth of Berdyaev's concentrated nervous energy, the student years were not untouched by what he calls the spirit of Dionysus. During his loneliest period in Kiev, he says he had no men friends who could share his views and was much in the company of women, who were less negative and "gave the illusion of understanding me." Throughout his life he was popular with the ladies, and this tendency, he says, was often in conflict with his spiritual interests. It is characteristic of Berdyaev's self-analysis that he attributes the loose living of his student days and the years in Kiev immediately after, not to his reading of Nietzsche, but to "Dionysian elements present although not preponderant in my nature." All his life, he says, he loved "the momentary ecstasies," despite a tendency to rationalize inherited from his French ancestors. Unlike German students, Russians were not given to frequent drinking bouts; tea was the usual stimulant to the nightlong discussions. But Berdyaev was less inclined than most to drinking. Wine was not frequently used in his family, either in Kiev or later when he had his own home, and he records the fact that wine never made him drunk. Even when others at a student party were under the table, he remained sober. He thinks this is due to a "trace of the Socratic" in him, another indication of the individualism that made him different from others.

His "radical and innate revulsion from the prose of life, from the empiric actuality" under whose compulsion he lived, plagued him to the end of his days. "Rupture with my surrounding milieu," he writes, "moving out of the aristocratic world into the world of revolution—this is the basic fact of my biography, not only external, but internal as well." This was a part of his struggle for free and creative thought. From early youth he avoided contact with the military; if a fellow officer was calling on his father, he would not go near the study. He says he broke away completely from his aristocratic family connections, but Eugenie insists that instead of a complete severance of relations with the Gudim-Levkovitches, the Mozhaiskys, the Lopuchin-Demidoffs and others of the aristocratic circle frequented by his mother, he merely reduced his calls to the socially permissible minimum. "Everything of the family is the opposite of freedom," he said. "Race is of the order of necessity and not of liberty, and hence the struggle for freedom is the struggle against the power of the racial over man."

This aversion to the tribal, racial element did not mean that he disliked his own immediate family—parents or brother. His brother was very close to him. He was always especially interested in his brother's elder son, whose photograph occupied a place over the divan in his study. As a man he was particularly attentive to his father and mother in any misfortune or illness. It appears that both parents sometimes exaggerated the importance of a passing illness and used it to call him to their side. Wherever he was, he never failed to respond. Once in the midst of an exciting, creative year in Italy, he dropped everything and hastened back to Russia on receipt of a telegram saying his mother was ill. He says his revulsion for the family idea and for aristocracy in general led him to select most of his student friends among the Jews. At any rate he could be sure they were neither kin nor of the nobility. His mother, greatly disturbed by the despised residents of the Podol—the ghetto of Kiev—who came to see her son, would ask: "*Nicolai, est-ce un monsieur, ou ce n'est pas un monsieur?*" Berdyaev protested so vehemently against her use of the common term *zhid* that she was afraid even to use the word "Hebrew" and spoke of them only as "Israelites," a term far less current in the nineties than in our own day. One wonders, parenthetically, whether this penchant for Jewish comrades was motivated exclusively by the young Berdyaev's turning away from family ties. It could have been partly because the rare individualist was so difficult to get along with that members of his own group avoided him, whereas the Jews, crowded into the ghetto but tolerated in the university, would welcome this unusual contact with gentile society. Be that as it may, these friendships, unpleasing to his mother, and perhaps other relationships, social or political, impelled him to leave home toward the end of his student days and take his own apartment in a poorer section of the city. It is interesting to note that he did just as he desired in this move. Not every student could suddenly undertake the financial obligations involved. Berdyaev evidently expected his father to provide the necessary funds, as had always been the case. Now he was free from parental tutelege; here he could live his life as he chose.

We can see this move as another attempt to dissociate himself from his patrician background. Time and again he insists every hierarchic feeling, every differentiation of people according to social position, is alien to his thought. Berdyaev says he belonged to the "repentant nobility"—a term current in his father's generation to indicate that group of liberal-minded noblesse troubled in their consciences by the injustice of serfdom. Just how he qualified for this classification Berdyaev does not say; he never owned any property in Russia and hence did not have the problem that faced Tolstoi as a land owner; yet for the first forty years of his life he lived on the income from property still held by his father. "I never liked the elite," he says, "who pretend to be aristocrats." One phrase indicates his feeling of revulsion toward all "parvenus and arrivists, elbowing their way up from lower to higher layers of society." Conversation with the *tovarischi* (comrades) was, he maintained, more fruitful than with the "decadents," but he admitted an exception here. "For personal contact I prefer people who use a handkerchief to blow their noses, rather than their fingers." When he was a child, he said, he had certain prejudices natural to one of the seigniorial class, but he overcame them. He certainly believed his sympathies extended to men of any group, most of all to the oppressed. Yet he would never accept the idea of a classless society, so essential in the marxism to which he was soon to be attracted. And throughout his writings we find the implicit approval of the idea that society is necessarily divided into classes. He even wrote in defense of social aristocracy. It is not always evil, he said; "it has much of positive value, also: its sense of

magnanimity, its capacity for self-sacrifice, its understanding of the
viewpoints of others, the absence of struggle to get above the others."
This last, the striving for success, is definitely not aristocractic he
insists; indeed, it is not necessary for the aristocrat who believes he
is already at the top. But natural selection is one of nature's privileges,
it is a part of biology, and so there are naturally different classes of
society. Like Tolstoi, Berdyaev resented this fact, but like Tolstoi he
accepted it in principle. In his *Slavery and Freedom,*[1] Berdyaev
attempts to clarify his ideas on this topic.

> A class society is founded on injustice. . . . Society must in-
> evitably be differentiated, but differentiated not in the sense of
> social classes. The differentiation . . . should be human, personal,
> rather than social, class, impersonal . . . Class differences of bour-
> geois and laborers are false, and should disappear. A classless so-
> ciety is not a utopia . . . it signifies the humanization of society.

In these student years, and even as a professed marxist, he had
no hestitation in accepting the hospitality of Countess Branicky,
staying in the summer at "Alexandria" for a month's study alone or at
the winter palace in Belaya Tserkov. One can imagine the conversations when he would take refuge at "Alexandria" "after arguments on
marxism with Lunacharsky"; one of the noble qualities of the Countess must have been "understanding of the viewpoints of others," albeit while Berdyaev was sitting in her salon defending the teachings
of Marx, neither of them—as she later said—foresaw its results for
that fine family and the social forms it represented.

In his own private apartment the young rebel was not troubled by
such contradictions. Here he could choose companions against whose
opinions and arguments he did not rebel. Long before his entrance
into the university, Berdyaev had been affected by revolutionary
theory. He says his revolutionary point of view took form in the second
half of the eighties, when work was being conducted underground.
He does not say how closely concerned he was with political unrest
during his pre-university years, but owing to omnivorous reading, and
in spite of his lack of social contact, he must already have been well
informed about it in his teens. After the world-renowned "movement
to the people" of the intelligentsia in the seventies had failed, a new
sharpening of political opinions had taken place. Then Alexander III
died and new hopes were raised that his successor, the unhappy
Nicholas II, would inaugurate a new and enlightened policy in place

of the black suppression of his father's regime. But when, during Berdyaev's first year at the university, the new Tsar made the famous announcement: "Let everyone know . . . that I shall defend the monarchy as unfalteringly as did my father," revolutionary spirit rose to new furor. There was scarcely a student who did not share the conviction that the monarchy must be overthrown. Most students were engaged in some form of conspiratorial activity. That this was carried out at grave personal risk is indicated by Miliukoff's account of how in his first year in the university he was asked to receive in secret a person in whom he could have complete confidence and who later was discovered to be the infamous *provocateur* Azeff.

Revolutionary sentiment found its expression in two groups that were eventually organized into two clandestine political parties. Legal political parties were, of course, unknown in tsarist Russia before 1905. It is a simplification to distinguish the two parties by their attitudes toward the West, but it will help to understand them to say that one, the Social Revolutionary, was more or less the successor of the "movement to the people," with a fairly new doctrine of Slavophilism— according to which the Slavic world and especially Russia should follow its own destiny, basing social and political development on "the people." To these enthusiasts, anything coming from the West was suspect, even marxism, which about that time began to make its way among Russian intellectuals. The opposing group, the Social Democrats, held that a push from the West was needed to move Russia out of her century-long stagnation. To this group "scientific" marxism was a doctrine wholly acceptable, and its emphasis on the proletariat—in a country with only an infinitestimal proletariat—became the basis for all subsequent thought and action. Out of it came Lenin and the 1917 revolution.

The university world was agitated by discussions of the two opposing doctrines, not pro and contra revolution—everyone was for revolution —but for one or the other of the political theories. Jewish students were among the prominent political thinkers, and Berdyaev's association with them may have been partially responsible for his involvement in clandestine organizations. Later in describing another Russian rebel, Constantine Leontieff, Berdyaev quoted Leontieff's words about his youth: "At that time it was very hard for me to live in the world. I suffered from everything: . . . from life in the family, where a great deal displeased me, . . . from physical infirmities, from lack of faith." Leonteff might have been describing the youthful Berdyaev instead of

himself. In the university Berdyaev could not help contrasting his own
easy situation with the traditionally poverty-stricken students of Russian universities. One has the impression clandestine literature was
read more widely than student textbooks. In one of his earlier books,
*Sub Specie Aeternitatis* published in 1907, Berdyaev described his student generation as lifted by "the mighty new wave" of social thought,
of their passionate discussions of the works of Michailovsky, leader of
the nonmarxist faction, and how eventually they outgrew him, adhering
to marxist philosophy. He was safely past marxism when he wrote this,
but he said that at the time the marxists were certain the future belonged to them. The students, Berdyaev among them, extended their
revolutionary enthusiasm beyond the university walls and became the
champions of the oppressed workers. In the midst of his university
career—June, 1896—after other less notable incidents of the same sort,
the empire was startled by what almost amounted to a general strike
of thirty thousand workers in the textile mills of St. Petersburg. Nothing
on this scale had ever happened before. Here was the factory proletariat
taking things into its own hands. Now the marxist theories seemed to
assert their validity. Marxism would save Russia and the world.

Berdyaev was carried along by the general attraction to marxism,
although—as might be expected—he refused to conform strictly to its
tenets. But in general he gave himself to the cause, fully conscious of
the possible personal consequences for himself. He had seen too many
other students, on becoming acquainted with "modern" thought,
graduate from their sophomore year into prison or exile. He realized
this could be his own fate. But even as a youth he had often pictured
himself suffering for a great cause, and emotionally he was ready for
it. He already had other reservations about marxism, among them an
aversion to violence, and to the idea that even such concepts as truth
and justice derived solely from the economic process. Berdyaev threw
himself wholeheartedly into clandestine activity. Today, after a generation of the Soviet secret police, it is sometimes forgotten that Russia
had excellent masters before the revolution, that the G.P.U. and its
successors merely added refinements to the processes of the tsarist
police. At the time Berdyaev was a student, all movement of persons
from one city to another was subject to police control. No meeting,
even a private gathering in a private house, could be held legally
without police permission. Thus the conduct of underground political
effort involved not only grave personal risks but demanded techniques
that only a revolutionary student generation could contrive. Berdyaev

had well-prepared associates. His Jewish friends put him into contact with the "Bund," a secret and powerful workers' organization active largely in Poland. Although Berdyaev had "never prepared himself to be a professional revolutionary," we find him an active member of one of the several student "circles" in Kiev that, strangely enough for those times, had close contact with clandestine organizations of workers in some of the factories of Kiev. This was one of the first Social Democratic groups in the city. As early as 1894, Berdyaev's first student year, it had adopted a definitely marxist position.

In his autobiography Berdyaev devotes several pages to a denunciation of politics in general and his own reasons for disliking it. Politics, he writes, is always based on falsehood; it is largely a fiction, a parasitic growth on human society. Political revolutions contain no new spirituality; either they deny the spiritual in principle or they act on the old spiritual bases. But also, and this is characteristic, all the political systems of the world are calculated on the basis of "the ordinary mass-man, in whom there is nothing creative." But by 1897 we find him a member of the Union for the Liberation of the Working Class—not to be confused with the more important Liberation Union, organized 1903-4. Despite their traditional distrust of the intelligentsia, and even more of the nobility, the labor leaders in Kiev seem to have had confidence in Berdyaev. He was considered the principal ideologist of the "SD" (Social Democrat) party group in Kiev. He attended many secret meetings; his speeches carried considerable weight because of their brilliant handling of social questions and even more because of the evident sincerity of the speaker. In a treatise on the origin of the Social Democrat party published (under the communist regime) in Moscow in 1921, Berdyaev is mentioned with gratitude as having been useful in finding lodging for out-of-town members assembled to elect a delegate to the 1895 conference in Minsk, where Russia's Social Democratic labor party was born. In the summer of 1897, between his junior and senior years, Berdyaev attended a meeting of European trade unions in Zurich. There he met with Plechanov, one of the great marxist theorists, living in exile in that city. This was probably the time he also met Axelrod, another revolutionary leader living abroad, who later wrote to friends in Russia recommending Berdyaev as "a young writer, useful for preparing pamphlets." On this or another trip abroad he collected all the marxist literature available and brought it triumphantly back to Kiev in a false-bottom trunk. It provided excellent material for the printing plant in a Kiev suburb without which effective party propaganda would have been impossible.

Both Berdyaev himself and his friends have given considerable thought to the reasons why a man of his clear intelligence could have been converted, even temporarily, to marxism. The process seems to have begun with Berdyaev's acquaintance in his freshman year with another student in the natural science department, David Longvinsky. Berdyaev says he was his only friend among the students then. Living alone for the first time in his life, he felt he "had nothing in common with anyone." Longvinsky had a brilliant mind, "heads above other students," and Berdyaev found it easy to have contact with him "on a high level." To a young man who had digested Schopenhauer and Kant, most university freshmen must have appeared immature, but he learned a great deal about sociological questions from his tall, stoop-shouldered friend. They apparently went through the four years together, and then Longvinsky was arrested for his connection with the same secret print shop that was the cause of Berdyaev's eventual trouble, imprisoned for months, and finally exiled to Siberia. Under the terrible conditions there he developed tuberculosis. Berdyaev appealed to his father to use his high connections to lighten the conditions under which Longvinsky was living. This was arranged, but to no avail. Longvinsky died in exile.

A permanent member of the Social Democrat group was A. Lunacharsky, communist and future People's Commissar of Education. Like Berdyaev, Lunacharsky was a native of Kiev, and apparently the two had known each other in boyhood. This friendship, too, seemed based on Berdyaev's passion for argumentation. The debate began in the student years in Kiev, continued through their youthful exile, and closed only with Berdyaev's banishment from Soviet Russia, an event in which it appears the Commissar of Education had a hand. Although he leaned strongly toward marxism, Lunacharsky accepted both Avenarius and Nietzsche into his thought patterns and, while not an authority, played all his life with an interest in art and sometimes even religion—to the extent that on one occasion after the revolution Lenin told him: "Whatever your good intentions may be, Comrade, your flirtations with religion do not make us smile—they are disgusting." Writing of him later, Berdyaev said he was a widely read man of great gifts, but light-minded.

Berdyaev recalls his first contact with Russian marxism. It was at a secret meeting in a private home in Kiev, and his first impression was negative. Marxism seemed to him something airless, choking freedom.

But further contact reversed this opinion, and Berdyaev admits he had a soft spot in his heart for marxism throughout his life—theoretical marxism, he was clear to point out, rather than marxism as practiced. "At that time," he wrote in 1940, "I considered Marx a man of genius, and I still do." Eugenie says it was not only his attraction to the high intellectual quality of Russian marxist leaders that drew him to Marx in those university years but a conviction that marxism was the only form of struggle that could overturn "capitalism, which he considered the ultimate evil." But this seems a bit like putting the cart before the horse; he could have held that belief only if he had already accepted at least a part of the gospel according to Marx. More likely it was Berdyaev's passion for justice—including social justice—rather than economic theory that led him to what proved to be a passing belief in marxism. In those years when the traditional Russian revolutionary movements were evidently losing their vitality, marxism seemed to open a new way to success.

With its teaching that socialism, sacred goal of all revolutionists of the day, would result inevitably from the development of economics, marxism seemed so convincing, so "scientific." The socialists had been conscious all along that their aspirations were far more emotional than rational; this had weakened their self-confidence. Now there was new light and hope from the West, and the socialists could hold up their heads. Russian socialists became less emotional and sentimental—more firmly reliant on intellect. Berdyaev was at once impressed with the historic claims of marxian socialism—the breadth of its world perspective. By comparison the old Russian socialism seemed to him narrow and provincial. As he later said, the rise of Russian marxism caused a crisis among the intelligentsia, shaking the very basis of their world outlook. To most of them it was true revelation.

One of the amazing things about marxists in general is their completely academic approach—the blind acceptance of a theory without too much appreciation of what it might mean in practice. Tyrkova-Williams says of the Russian pioneers of marxism, "they swam in that doctrine, accepted it as something real." The marxists were least of all concerned with the people for whose supreme benefit the marxist theories had been concocted. Leaders of Russian marxism like Struve and Tugan-Baranovsky were simply not interested in people. Gathered in their salons for interminable discussions, these enthusiasts accepted the word of Karl Marx as Moslems accept the Koran—any argument could be confirmed by the proper quotation. Like many boudoir bol-

sheviks of our day, they believed the gospel of Marx would bring a
golden age of happiness for all mankind. As Tyrkova says, "They did
not know life, and considered it unnecessary to know it."

It was this theoretical side that appealed to the young intellectuals
of the day. Marxism was "scientific." Plechanov, the patriarch of Russian marxism, expounded this at length. Just as Darwin had scientifi-
cally explained the rise of man, so Marx explains man's social history
with theories just as scientific. That early fervent acceptance of Darwin
has faded with the years. It is strange there should still be adepts who
think marxism scientific after all that has happened in Europe in the
past four decades. This was the basis for many of Berdyaev's disputes
with Lunacharsky and other still more "integral" marxists. Lunacharsky would argue that Berdyaev's insistence upon the independence
of the intellect and man's right to personal judgment was contrary to
marxism, which subordinated such concepts as truth and justice to the
furtherance of the class struggle. For Berdyaev, truth, goodness, and
beauty were positive rather than variable categories; it was merely the
degree of man's comprehension that was relative.

Even in those early days of Russian marxism, its two essential phases
were evident: on the one hand, insistence that man's fate is determined
wholly by economic materialism, and on the other, the passionate
messianic faith that a time would come when, in a perfect society,
man would no longer be dependent upon economics. True to the
historic traditions of his race, Marx believed in a coming Messiah, but
with a new "chosen people," the proletariat. The saving agent, the lever
that could overthrow the world and liberate man from slavery, was the
factory working class. This is where, in one of its sharpest inner contradictions, marxism switches from materialism to idealism. Marx
confused the economic and the ethical categories. Berdyaev remarks
that only the second of these could ever inspire revolutionary will and
self-sacrifice. There is nothing scientific about this "myth of the proletariat"; it is a matter of faith, a creation of marxian imagination. As
Berdyaev says, marxism is not only science and politics, it is also a
faith, a religion. At the close of the century, he says, marxism undoubtedly aided the process of Europeanizing Russia's intelligentsia,
affording, as it did, contact with the west. It had little resemblance to
the marxism out of which bolshevism later developed. Less dogmatic
and less totalitarian than in later years, it had not yet set up its pre-
tention to control the whole of man's life and still permitted a "differentiation of spheres of thought"; thus Berdyaev was free to do his own

thinking in matters of spiritual culture and could become a "critical marxist," which permitted his remaining an idealist in his philosophy. This critical attitude excluded any acceptance of "integral marxism," and within a short time Berdyaev had left marxism completely, moving to other philosophical positions on his way to a full Christian faith.

Although he was still in the university, Berdyaev devoted most of his time to revolutionary activity among the workers. There was even a special movement among the laborers calling for organized activity of their own, free from the tutelage of the intelligentsia. One of its leaders was a Jewish printer, a giant of a man with rusty red hair and beard. He became interested in Berdyaev, liked to come to his flat for nightlong discussions—one can imagine how this showed up in the police files!—and actually hoped that Berdyaev, despite his "idealist" heresies, would undertake leadership of a workers' group. Propaganda activity among the laboring class was officially considered the proper pursuit of a Social Democrat. The party considered the equally strong and well organized revolutionary movement among the students not properly zealous, and not only had a tendency to look down on them, but by the tragic exclusiveness that has plagued Russian organizations ever since, had practically no contact with it. But when news reached Kiev that a woman student Vetrova, a prisoner in the Petropavlovsk fortress in St. Petersburg, had committed suicide in protest against the regime, and the students summoned everyone into the springtime streets for a demonstration (18th and 19th of March, 1897), Berdyaev felt it his duty to participate. Student demonstrations were not new events in Kiev, and when they went out into the street, Berdyaev knew —as all the others did—that they could be fired upon by the police or trampled under the hoofs of Cossack horses. Now might be the time he would have to suffer for his ideas.

The demonstration took its usual course. Someone produced a red flag, the crowd sang the "Marseillaise," there were occasional shouted slogans of the Social Democratic party, but that was all. There was some scuffling with the mounted police, but no shooting, no use of Cossack whips, and the whole group was surrounded and marched off to prison. Of course the police searched Berdyaev's quarters, but found only personal papers, and after a few days he was released like most of the others with a severe warning to avoid trouble in the future.

Berdyaev continued steadfastly in his underground activities. The next year was a notable one for the Social Democrats. A series of secret lectures was organized with one party member V. O. Vodovozov speak-

ing on the political and social systems of western Europe. As usual
these lectures were followed by endless, often violent argumentation,
with Berdyaev, Longvinsky, Lunacharsky and other future communist
leaders like Ratner participating. One of the members of this group,
the woman in whose apartment the printing press was concealed, recalls
in her memoirs the lively participation of Berdyaev with his philosophical approach. Later they all came to realize what important political
training these meetings had given them. All this time Kiev continued
to be one of the chief centers of the underground party movement.
Kiev supplied much propaganda either by lecturers or by the printed
word. The clandestine press was of crucial importance in the whole
Social Democratic party effort. And then one day it was discovered by
the police, a list of names and addresses was found, and there was a
mass roundup of those suspected of complicity (March 11 and 12,
1898). Among them Berdyaev was again arrested. He never returned to
the university lecture halls.

# 5

## THE ATHENS OF THE NORTH

Together with Berdyaev, about one hundred and fifty others were arrested. Police records show that almost half of them were intellectuals, the remainder workmen. Under arrest came all the members of the Social Democrat central committee. The entire company was imprisoned in the great Lukianovsk prison on the edge of the city. With a twinkle in his eye, Berdyaev compares life in a tsarist prison with that in a Soviet jail. Of course there were the frightful prison fortresses of Petropavlovsk and Schlusselburg in tsarist days, but otherwise, at least in Kiev, the prison regime was not too severe. Berdyaev explains there was a difference then in what guards felt. Under the tsar prisons were guarded by soldiers, usually kindhearted peasants to whom the prisoners were not "enemies of the people" but of the government toward which they themselves felt no affectionate attachment. Even the prison director maintained a patriarchal regime, with considerable latitude for his charges. Under the Soviets, on the contrary, guards are told their prisoners are "enemies of the revolution," and the regime in prison is of the same fabric of terror as the rest of the government.

Perhaps it was because single cells were not available for all the one hundred and fifty new additions to the prison population, but for the first two or three weeks they lived in large dormitories, were fairly free to exchange visits, and even held meetings in the prison courtyard. Here Vodovozov could continue his hitherto secret lectures under the very eyes of the police. Berdyaev usually chaired these meetings and others where he himself was the chief speaker.

The day after the arrest, they were assembled to receive an imposing visitor. Accompanied by the state prosecutor and the general of the gendarmerie—the latter a friend of Berdyaev's father—in came Governor-General Dragomirov himself. He gave a long talk, seemingly revealing himself as partly sympathetic with the prisoners. Out of it Berdyaev recalls one phrase: "Your mistake is that you do not see the

47

social process as something organic, rather than logical, and a child cannot be born before the ninth month." The gendarme general, on the contrary, was manifestly not in sympathy with the governor or with the students. This half-implied sympathy of the governor helped raise the morale of the prisoners even higher than it had been already. Berdyaev describes the atmosphere as one almost of exaltation. He himself felt it as never before in his life. Save for the few days in jail a year earlier, this was his first experience living in a community—the first time he felt himself truly part of a group. Instead of being downcast, these young intellectuals felt a spiritual uplift. They were sure their arrest marked the beginning of a new era in the liberation struggle and that news of the event would spread across Europe, moving all true liberals to increased revolutionary effort.

The stir in Kiev created by this massive police haul may well be imagined. As was usual in such cases, families having influential friends at once busied themselves with appeals for the release of "poor innocent students present at the meeting on the street purely by accident and not because of revolutionary sympathies." This procedure was effective for some imprisoned with Berdyaev in Lukianovsk. For Berdyaev unhappily it failed. One of his aunts was on friendly terms with the state prosecutor, and she pleaded with him to speak with the young hothead to convince him of the error of his ways. Under her pleading, he yielded and agreed to have the young man in for a talk. When the aunt inquired a few days later about the result of the interview, the "procurator" replied: "What could you do with a fellow who, invited to sit down and talk, just sticks out his tongue at you?"

After two or three weeks, prison authorities shut down on the general meetings and Berdyaev was put into a cell by himself, but even here he was privileged. His cell door was left open; he could move about inside that wing of the prison and even make his way up to the women's floor above, where among the prisoners were several good friends of his. And at the exercise hour, when all the prisoners were in the courtyard, Berdyaev continued giving lectures. Thereupon he was moved once more, into a cell with the door locked. But even here he felt happy, for although, as he says, social contact had ceased, "I was able to read."

What did he read at this time? Many of the books he wished to have, Plechanov, Bakunin, Marx, possibly also Nietzsche, he could not legally receive, although he probably had them anyway. He had Shestov's new book on Nietzsche and Dostoievsky. He reread Tolstoi, and this reading in these special surroundings intensified his earlier "contempt for all false gods, all the false greatness in history . . ." and his profound conviction that "this civilized and socialized life, with all its laws and all its comforts, is not the real, true life." During this period he reread all of Schopenhauer and for the first time discovered Maeterlinck and Ibsen. Like Andre Byeli, he felt "Ibsen was the explosion of a bomb" in him. He felt himself identified with all the great rebels of history: ". . . with Luther, rebelling against authority, with Marx rising against capitalism, with the anarchistic Bakunin, with Leo Tolstoi against history and civilization, with Nietzsche against reason and morality, with Ibsen revolting against society." From then on Ibsen was, next to Dostoievsky, his favorite author. The first stirrings of what he later referred to as his "inner conversion" began in this prison solitude.

Meanwhile friends of the prisoners, at work to secure their release, began to achieve results. In Berdyaev's case his family's connection with the Governor-General proved helpful. Instead of being transported at once to some far corner of the empire—by "administrative" rather than legal proceedings, as was often the case—he was released after six weeks on heavy bail under the recognizance of professors of the university, was required to report personally to the police at stated intervals, and was forbidden to leave Kiev until his case should be decided by the courts. Court proceedings were no more expeditious in Kiev than they often seem to be in our day, and the case of these young revolutionaries dragged on for two years. It was finally closed by administrative order rather than a formal sentence. Years later, Berdyaev learned from records in police files that he had been charged with the desire to overthrow the government and the church and with plotting the abolition of private property and the family. For crimes such as these the normal punishment would have been exile to Siberia. In the present case, however, only a few of the accused received that severest sentence. The remainder, almost all the Social Democrats, were given exile to the northern province of Vologda. Berdyaev was sentenced to live there for three years under police surveillance. The text of this document is interesting:

### Sentence in the case of the
### Society of Struggle for the Liberation of the Working Class

By order of His Imperial Majesty to the prosecuting attorney of the Kiev Tribunal of Justice, May 23rd 1900. His Majesty the Emperor, upon my most humble and loyal report on the circumstances in the case of the commoner Boris Eidelman and others accused of crimes against the state, was pleased on March 2nd 1900, to decide the matter by administrative order as follows—

I. To exile under police surveillance:
a. to Eastern Siberia, Boris Eidelman . . . .
b. to the Vologda province, Nicolai Berdyaev and . . . for three years."

Among the others exiled to Vologda was Nicolai Mukalov, Berdyaev's schooldays friend.

Berdyaev says he recalls the two years of waiting for trial and sentence with a feeling of pleasure. It was one of the happiest times of his life, "a period of uplift and flowering" he called it. He suddenly found himself a very popular lecturer. His first appearance, even with a subject so abstruse as one chapter from what later became his first book, *Subjectivism and Individualism in Social Philosophy*, was greeted by a standing ovation. This was partly due, as Berdyaev himself noted, to the fact that all of Kiev knew of his recent imprisonment and impending trial. Except for the tic, he had everything necessary for popularity on the lecture platform and elsewhere: enthusiasm, a brilliant wit, passionate faith in the cause he advocated, patrician background and breeding. He was a handsome figure, as a photograph of that period proves: clearcut profile, a mass of curly brown hair that hung over his collar, neatly trimmed beard and mustache, chin lifted slightly in a pose some people thought arrogant—and then his eyes, large, dark, ablaze with enthusiasm when he was in argument or exposition. He dressed in the latest style, was always fastidiously groomed—externally the true aristocrat. That he advocated nonaristocratic ideas must have been a hard blow for his parents, but even they must have appreciated his popularity.

It was at this time that Berdyaev began to write. His first published article appeared in 1899 in Kautsky's *Neue Zeit*, a marxist journal published in Germany. Berdyaev's title was characteristic of the time: "F. A. Lange and Critical Philosophy, in Its Relation to Socialism." This article began a correspondence between the German Social Democrat[1] and the young Russian. Kautsky wrote that he had great hopes for the theoretical development of marxism that the Russians would provide; they were more academic than the German communists, who were so busy with practical politics that they had no time for theory. The theory developing in the young Russian's mind, however, was not what

Kautsky hoped for. Berdyaev was already questioning the very basis of marxism. Like the first faint notes of the Russian hymn in Tchaikovsky's *1812 Overture*, something finer than communism was making itself felt in him. There was a springlike atmosphere in his mind, he says, with a new sense of poetry.

This feeling was strengthened by Berdyaev's visit to St. Petersburg. With special permission from the police he made a brief trip to the capital, where he had many more contacts of the widest variety. One day he lunched at the house of his cousin, Prince K, with an important official in the Ministry of the Interior, the government department that controlled the police who were watching Berdyaev. That evening he had a meeting with Struve and Tugan-Baranovsky where he first met Skvortsov-Stepanoff, the future bolshevik editor of *Izvestia* and author of much communist anti-religious literature. Although Berdyaev's position then was further to the left than that of Struve and Skvortsov, these St. Petersburg contacts hastened his evolution away from marxism. He met other thinkers who leaned toward "idealism"; he discovered that, like them, he too looked forward to a better world resulting not from the necessary evolution of economics, but rather from man's creative activity. His revolutionary feeling, he began to see, was more ethical than social.

Those were difficult years for Berdyaev's family. In addition to concern for Nicolai Alexandrovitch's future, there was great anxiety about his brother Serge. He lived in St. Petersburg, moving from one job to another, and then undertook to publish a magazine, *By Sea and Land*. Like all his other ventures, it was a financial failure. About this time, possibly under the influence of his economic situation, Serge suffered a mental depression that brought him to the verge of insanity. Berdyaev was deeply concerned, since it was largely through his personal intervention that relations between his father and Serge had been maintained in recent years. Now there was even talk of placing Serge in an institution for the mentally ill. Berdyaev says the "confused, dramatic situation" of his brother shadowed his life at this time as it had all through his youth, but nothing could suppress the new upspring of energy of these two pre-exile years.

Part of this uplift came from his reading. The necessity of making a personal appearance at police headquarters once a week did not, of course, hinder his having at home any books he wanted. Nietzsche and Marx were striving for the young man's allegiance. There was a wave of Nietzschean pessimism among students. Against this background he read and reread all of Ibsen's plays. *The Master Builder* struck him with particular force. It made him wonder if all idealists carried within themselves the seed of their own destruction. But Ibsen, and above all Dostoievsky, made him conscious of the philosophical weakness of the marxist position. He was more and more dissatisfied with a philosophy that was content with "the closed circle of this earthly world." This was part and parcel of the stirrings of the new spirit that within the next decade was to sweep into one of the most fruitful spiritual revivals in any nation's history. His first book was written in these years, but the development of his thought left it far behind before it could be printed. Although he still held to the "scientific" economic theories of Marx, he was firmly convinced that man does not live by bread alone.

Once the Tsar's administrative order was issued, there were no delays in its execution. A considerable group of those sentenced to exile in Vologda was rounded up and started on its way. The party as a whole was cheerful. Vologda was well known as a fairly "easy" center of exile, but as they neared their destination a wave of melancholy came over Berdyaev, partly a reaction from the exciting months of his popularity in Kiev, partly in reaction to the dreariness of the northeastern Russian landscape, particularly the section between Jaroslavl and Vologda. Another reason was his loneliness. These exiles were all fellows in the same misfortune, but Berdyaev already felt himself in disagreement with most of them on many questions that both he and they considered important. The majority were "common people," workmen and others who had been involved in the revolutionary activities, men of little education or culture. Although Berdyaev maintains he had no sense of social difference, it was enough for these men to know he was a *barin*, a "gentleman"—they could tell it by his stylish clothing, by the mountain of luggage traveling with him, if not by his bearing and his accent—to make him feel the difference and the distance between them. But worse in his fellow travelers' eyes than the difference in caste was Berdyaev's complete incapacity to accept discipline. Already those who knew him considered him a "hopeless individualist." He felt a powerful reaction against the "revolutionary ascetic regulations" of party organizations; they oppressed the personality and denied creative liberty to their members, demanding the subservience of the individual to the collective conscience. As though it had been planned to set Berdyaev apart from the rest at the very outset, an incident occurred upon their arrival at Vologda. They knew they would be met by police officials. In a meeting in the train it was agreed that none of the exiles would shake hands with these agents of the Tsar. Berdyaev made them a short speech in which he declared that this question, like all others of a similar nature, would be decided by himself alone. It was all right to talk of revolutionary "military discipline," but in moral questions Nicolai Alexandrovitch wished to fight his own battles, and he refused to accept in advance any group judgment. Of course he did not shake the hand of the police inspector who received the group at the station, but the decision was his own.

The wave of depression passed and his spirits lightened soon after arrival. Vologda turned out to be not such an unpleasant place. Unlike most northern Russian cities, this one had a long history and certain cultural traditions. It had been a member of the medieval Hanseatic League and consequently had engaged in commerce with much of northern Europe. Its cathedral was one of the architectural monuments of Ivan the Terrible. Although of course none of the exiles ever entered it, it embellished the landscape. Essentially a commercial town of some thirty thousand inhabitants on the latitudinal level of Stockholm, it had its hotels, cafes, and theater. It had no institutions of higher learning. Berdyaev took the best room in Vologda's best hotel, the Golden Anchor. Life here might not be so disagreeable after all.

Although most of these exiles were assigned to residence in one or another of the smaller towns scattered over the Vologda "government" or province—about two-thirds the size of Texas—Berdyaev had been given freedom to choose his own place, and of course he chose the city. Within six weeks another choice was offered him; he was handed a document from St. Petersburg granting him the privilege of residence in any city of southern Russia provided it had no university—he would be dangerous company for students, with his revolutionary ideas. Again his aristocratic background had caught up with him. As he discovered later, his godfather Prince Lopuchin-Demidoff had taken occasion to speak to his friend the Grand Duke Vladimir Alexandrovitch about this brilliant godson, scion of a noble family, forced to endure the rigors of a northern winter. The Grand Duke at once intervened with the Ministry of the Interior, and Berdyaev was faced with what must have been somewhat of a temptation. As a southern-born Russian he dreaded the legendary northern winters with the thermometer often touching −40 degrees Fahrenheit. But he felt that as long as the others must remain in Vologda he had no moral right to an easier berth. We do not know what his godfather told the Grand Duke when asked what southern city the rebel godson had selected.

This incident quickly became known among the other exiles and must have gone far to overcome their dislike of Berdyaev's "individualism." They all knew that he lived a protected life. The Governor-General of Vologda, Kniazeff, was his distant relative and a close friend of Berdyaev's uncle. Kniazeff exercised a certain leniency toward his exile guests, and he certainly was not unaware of the one who had taken up residence in the city's first-class hotel where only "the quality" stayed. The gentleman in Room No. 1 was the special care of all the hotel staff. Most exiles lived in the most modest of rented rooms, and anyone could drop in on them at any time of day or night. Not so Nicolai Alexandrovitch. To call on him one had first to get the desk man to ask the *corridorni*—valet in charge of the second floor. If he felt like it, the valet would inquire if the gentleman in No. 1 would receive the caller. And more often than not the reply was negative. An interesting commentary on the rigors of Berdyaev's exile is the fact that both in 1901 and 1902, his second and third years in Vologda, he returned to Kiev for a long summer vacation. The second time, his fellow exiles noted he was very "late in returning." And on at least one occasion in between, his father came to Vologda for a surprise visit. Other social contacts helped make life interesting. Although his fellow exiles must have looked askance at it, Berdyaev was a frequent visitor in some of the city's "best" homes. The president of the local *zemstvo*, a sort of general nongovernmental welfare council, often invited Nicolai Alexandrovitch in for a long evening of conversation.

Then there were the pleasures of the northern countryside, particularly in spring and summer. Nicolai Alexandrovitch loved to make long trips away from town on foot or on his bicycle. He discovered the ruins of an old monastery, where he could sit against a wall in the vernal sunshine and rethink the "idealistic" problems from which he could never escape. The northern rivers—great and small—abounded in fish, and fishing usually offered opportunity for meditation.

Perhaps it was his new-found sense of beauty, but in this, his first acquaintance with the Russian north, the newcomer found special pleasure in nature. His fellow exile Alexis Remizoff, that painter with words, describes it:

> Nowhere else in the whole world is there such a sky, as in Vologda, and where will you find such colors as those which shine on the

Vologda River? The midnight sun and the white nights—look how blue and green the Vologda flows. . . . And in winter the northern lights across half the heavens and over the river shackled in its seven feet of ice pour a purple like a June midnight, and a green more vivid than the Suzdal luster, and a red like the berries of the north . . . or in the autumn, when the clumps of damp moss blossom with all the colors of a Persian carpet. For the unique and unmatchable colors of the season—for its sonorous springtime, and the forty-degree cruelty of its winter—it's no use—you have to see it with your eyes and feel it with your senses.

Remizoff first met Berdyaev in Vologda at one of Berdyaev's lectures, and the friendship then begun lasted throughout their lives. Watching the man, so carried away by his subject, his flow of speech occasionally interrupted by the spasmodic tic, Remizoff thought the speaker must be completely unconscious of what was happening to him; how otherwise could he have such an air of self-confidence and go right on talking after the enforced momentary break without losing poise. But Remizoff was charmed by the speaker's face, with its wonderful eyes—deep and brilliant—and by the kindly smile. Further acquaintance justified his first favorable impression.

Remizoff's story is much more typical of a northern exile than that of Berdyaev, with which it became so closely associated. Throughout his life this eccentric Russian genius had no interest whatever in politics. Perhaps the Vologda exile cured any early enthusiasms he may have had, yet as a student he had been caught by the police in a street demonstration. Having no influential family to be taken into consideration by the authorities, he was sentenced to exile in a small county seat, Ust-Sisolsk, three hundred miles northeast of Vologda. In youth Remizoff suffered from a disease of the eyes that now has made him nearly blind. With this as a pretext he secured permission to go to Vologda for a month of medical treatment. These trips were repeated several times in the course of a year, and then Remizoff simply remained in Vologda and the authorities did nothing about it. For the writer, life in Vologda after vegetating in Ust-Sisolsk was like the explosion of the Siberian spring after the somber last months of winter. Socially, life could not be very expansive on the exile's standard allowance of six rubles and forty kopecks per month (about three dollars), but books were available, the various meetings and lectures of the exile group were of course open to him free, and even for the theater and an

occasional concert one might contrive to crash the gate. Despite the
surprisingly low cost of living, this stipend barely sufficed for food and
lodging, and most exiles had to have additional income—either sent
from home or earned on the spot. This latter was Remizoff's only recourse. An occasional piece appeared in *The Northern Region*, local
Vologda paper with a comparatively large circulation and considerable
influence even in St. Petersburg. In addition to such sporadic income
Remizoff earned some money doing translations. He had undertaken
to translate a German book on "monistic gnosseology" and, being a
budding poet rather than a budding philosopher, found some of the
terminology almost unintelligible. Shortly after his first contact Remizoff decided to ask Berdyaev to help him. He was emboldened to approach the aristocrat in the Golden Anchor by what other exiles told
him: that Berdyaev was always available to people needing his help.
"There's your real nobleman," they said.

Berdyaev lived up to his reputation as far as Remizoff was concerned.
He had done translations himself, although not because he needed extra
income. He not only helped with "the many clever words without which
philosophers cannot do anything, like subsummation or predicate," but
entered into "literary conversation." Remizoff was charmed by his new
friend: his courtly manner, his impeccable dress—Remizoff used to
marvel at how such good taste could be possible in the far distant Vologda—his beautiful long-fingered hands, perhaps even a little by the
elegance of his room. Remizoff lived in the watchman's hut in a courtyard. It was pleasant to have a room alone, but it was terribly cold. The
little stove could be red hot, but the wind in the cracks and under the
door made one shiver. Even at this early date Remizoff's passion was
for what he calls "the art of words"—actually symbolist poetry in prose.
He was surprised to discover that Berdyaev with all his fine intelligence
had no interest, not even any feeling, for the art of writing. He never
thought about his own vocabulary; he used the words that came as he
wrote. In later years Remizoff said it had always troubled him that his
friend was so little interested in style—to the extent that once when
Berdyaev in a book review said Rozanoff wrote well, Remizoff felt it
was an irresponsible statement because Berdyaev had no basic knowledge of the subject. Perhaps what charmed Remizoff most was the manner in which Berdyaev received him on a basis of absolute equality, with
no sign of condescension or annoyance at being asked to help. During
their subsequent lifelong acquaintance he never saw Berdyaev refuse, or
pass judgment on, a petitioner. Berdyaev evidently found his new ac-

quaintance interesting, and thereafter the *corridorni* in the Golden Anchor never said no when Remizoff asked for an appointment.

These "literary conversations" continued throughout Berdyaev's lifetime, and always without an altercation. Remizoff was the one friend with whom Berdyaev never quarreled. Shestov, one of the few others with whom Berdyaev never broke relations, told Remizoff how in the heat of argument Berdyaev would shriek at him in defense of his own ideas. In a sort of frenzy of polemics, he would refuse to listen to his opponent, pounding his fist on the table and occasionally being seized with a spasm. Berdyaev would be angered by Shestov because the latter insisted upon starting from some definitely accepted viewpoint, while Berdyaev wanted to wipe out all previous positions and start afresh. One reason why Berdyaev never railed at Remizoff was that the younger man "never discussed any difficult questions with him." Another reason was Berdyaev's having assumed a sort of protective role for his friend that continued through many years and many circumstances.

Acquaintance with Berdyaev was advantageous for Remizoff in several ways other than the assistance in translating German philosophy. He came to know many sides of his friend. He would notice how he stopped to stroke a cat on a bench at the street corner—although Berdyaev was unusually fond of animals, he had no pets in his Vologda room—and how he liked good fare and fine perfumes. Remizoff enjoyed Berdyaev's quiet smile and his mild sense of humor. He was even one of a select group that would be invited to Berdyaev's room on some special occasion, a birthday or the departure on "vacation," to share a bottle of champagne. In general, there was little drinking among the Vologda exiles. Most of them, as part of their idealism, were opposed to the use of alcohol. Besides, there were no bars in Vologda. Berdyaev was not a teetotaler, but if he had wine it must be of the best. "He would not drink trash," said Remizoff. Although Remizoff was one of the humblest of the exile company, at least from an economic viewpoint, he "hopped right into the very eyrie of Parnassus where sat Berdyaev, Lunacharsky and the rest"—thanks to Berdyaev. For, regardless of the fact that all these exiles believed ardently in equality, there soon developed in Vologda a fairly clear division into classes. It is true that this separation was based on intellectual interests and capacities, but the "Olympians," as they were locally known, lived rather exclusively within their own group.

Vologda was full of exiles, of all ages from seventeen upward, of all

social groupings from simple workmen through "half-intellectuals" like
Berdyaev's friend Mukalov[2] to the very elite who had never done a
stroke of manual labor in their lives. One of the latter told how, arriving one winter night in a cheap hotel in Prague, he suffered from the
cold: "There was a stove, and wood in the room, but of course I don't
know how to build a fire, and I nearly froze." Among the "Olympians"
were a number of men who later made their mark in Russian history,
men of the widest variety of character and interest. Some went the way
of Lenin, who had not yet chosen his staff of bolshevik leaders.
Berdyaev mentions a fellow exile who became one of the most cruel
and bloodthirsty commissars in northern Russia, and another, Otto Aussem, who turned up as Soviet consul in Paris long after Berdyaev was
established there. Another kindly bolshevik, who remained true to him
throughout the revolution and after, was the philosopher A. Bogdanov, who held his marxist faith with such simple-mindedness that
he could not understand why anyone else should stray from it. He
was a psychiatrist, and when he learned that Berdyaev was leaning
away from orthodox communism toward "idealism," he began frequent calls and what Berdyaev soon discovered to be a series of
psychiatric interviews, inquiring about his dreams and reactions to
various stimuli. To Bogdanov, a tendency toward idealism and the
metaphysical was evidence of a deranged psyche, and he wanted to
discover how far the process had gone in Nicolai Alexandrovitch.

Then there was the already familiar Anatole Lunacharsky—thin
pince-nez, that badge of the Russian intellectual, astride a prominent
Roman nose; neatly trimmed goatee—who achieved communist fame
in many ways, not the least in being one of Lenin's few original comrades to survive a decade of Stalin's regime and die a natural death.
Lunacharsky's was a typical Russian revolutionist's career. After the
failure of the 1905 revolution he fled abroad where he had a check-
ered history of activity, part of the time opposing Lenin, part of the
time with him. Returning to Russia after the 1917 revolution was well
under way, he became People's Commissar of Education, a post he
held for more than a decade and almost to his death (1933). During
the worst days of the earlier red terror he used his great influence to
protect many fellow exiles from Vologda, among them Berdyaev.
Arriving in Vologda during the second half of Berdyaev's sojourn, he
was at once adopted into the circle of the elite, and the long disputations he used to have with Berdyaev in Kiev were resumed. Berdyaev
could not accept the overall dialectic in marxism, which, he saw,

inevitably denies the absoluteness of truth, subjecting it to the struggle for power. From his early years Berdyaev had had the conviction that the Truth he sought was an absolute. The leading lecturer in the town, Berdyaev attracted to his "subversive" views many of his listeners, especially the younger ones. Lunacharsky writes in his memoirs that Berdyaev at that time was just beginning his evolution from "an idealistically-tinted marxism into the dusk of mysticism, whence he plunged straight into the night of a philosophical Christianity." Shocked by this situation, Lunacharsky began at once a series of lectures in opposition.

Oddly enough this public polemic did not result in estrangement between the two old Kiev friends; under normal circumstances it would have meant breaking off personal relations. But various exiles of the period agree with a sort of wonder that despite all their differences of opinion, especially political opinion, there reigned an atmosphere of peace and concord on Parnassus. It would be an interesting psychological study to inquire why it was in this Vologda exile that men of such violently contrasting opinions could still remain on friendly terms personally. Was it their sense of a common fate, or the fact that here a collective striving for revolution outweighed any differences in method proposed for making it? Perhaps the spirit of concord was partly because so many of the Vologda exiles came from Kiev and were, as Remizoff says, all devoted to Berdyaev. At any rate, Remizoff remarked how "tolerant" Berdyaev was in contrast to his explosions of wrath during public arguments in later life. Although Lunacharsky invited Berdyaev to come to his lectures and make public rebuttal, Berdyaev never accepted. Perhaps he could not trust himself to that much "tolerance." Aside from one outburst of anger in defense of injured womanhood, Remizoff never saw Berdyaev quarrel with anyone during his entire stay in Vologda.

It is strange that one of the most despotic governments in Europe, with its studied repression of liberty in the press and the schools, with its secret police, its withering censorship, its Siberian exiles, should have produced the amazing variety of individual types, many verging on genius, that characterized Russia at the turn of the century—so very different from the more regimented man of central Europe. In this respect the Vologda population was typical of Russian youth, in or out of prison. The tremendous spiritual renaissance of the 1900's was unfolding.

Like the intelligentsia, the other exiles were a variegated lot. They represented all the possible and impossible revolutionary groupings of the empire, as well as the young fellows who had not developed their political ideas far enough to belong to a party. In his autobiography Berdyaev recognizes that although he was not a rich man, the externals of his life gave that impression. This must have been especially true in Vologda, but it did not hinder his contact with all classes of society. He says he was always surprised at his capacity, quite unusual in a "gentleman," for contact with the common people. In Vologda, he says, he was the only man among the intellectuals who had social contact with the nonpolitical exiles, those sentenced for crimes or misdemeanors—"the very dregs of society," Berdyaev called them. All the others were afraid of them. Berdyaev says one among these "cagey ones," a veritable tramp whose name he apparently did not know, was his friend. This was the case later, in Moscow during the revolution, when many workmen and sailors attended his lectures at the Institute of the Word. A typical incident from the Moscow period, after Vologda but before the revolution, may help explain Berdyaev's relationships with "the people." "Look at that cobbler across the way," he told his wife. "He works all day long, bent over those dirty boots— and this for his whole life through! How can he endure it? Why doesn't he break down and destroy this social order?" One day they learned that the cobbler across the street had killed himself. Berdyaev's great sense of pity was a fundamental characteristic. In one of his letters to Lydia (Vichy, 1930) he wrote: "In recent years the feeling of pity has terribly increased in me—pity for everything and everyone, and if I did not restrain it by coldness, and limit it by my dryness, I would often weep." In the autobiography there are some paragraphs on this topic well worth quoting. Berdyaev is speaking of the conflict between pity and freedom:

> Pity may lead to a renunciation of freedom, while freedom may lead to loss of pity. On man's road there are always two ways, movement upward and movement downward. Man rises to the heights, toward God. . . . But he remembers those left below, deprived of the enjoyment of higher values, and here begins a movement downward in order to help his brothers . . . to rise, as well. In his uprising a man must not fly away out of the world, slip away from his responsibility for others. . . . Only collectively can we be saved for eternal life. Freedom must not be

release from responsibility for one's neighbor. . . . Here we
come upon an incomprehensible paradox in Christianity: "The
first," that is those who have attained spiritual height, shall be
"last." This is a serious warning for those on the heights. In order
not to be "last" they must descend, must show active love for
their neighbors, for those who by their position are "last." Hence
Christianity is based upon freedom and compassion, upon love for
the divine heights and upon love for those who suffer, below.

Aside from this adventitious contact with "the people," however,
Berdyaev's life was centered largely on the intelligentsia among the
exiles. They organized the Union of Exiles, with a prominent lawyer,
Zhdanov, as its president. Even here exile society was divided into two
groups, "the aristocrats" made up of Berdyaev, Remizoff, and a budding Danish author Madelung and others, and "the democrats" headed
by Lunacharsky and Bogdanov. The "aristocrats" were more independent in their thinking, more individualistic in their action than "the
democrats." This division did not prevent them all from belonging
to the Union of Exiles or attending the frequent meetings with lectures by various of its members. Prominent among them was Berdyaev.
Unless he was the speaker, he usually sat quietly, avoiding public controversy. Lectures were given on a variety of topics, from Lunacharsky's
series on "empiriocriticism" to Berdyaev's on Ibsen. This was the
period in Berdyaev's evolution away from marxism when he was fascinated by the Norwegian dramatist. His article on Hedda Gabler,
published at this time in the St. Petersburg *God's World*, caused a
stir in Russian intellectual circles. This was another point on which
Berdyaev stood out from all his fellow exiles. They were all writing
books, Lunacharsky, Savinkoff, and Remizoff—who reworked the
manuscript of his first book twenty times. But Berdyaev was already
an author. Not only had several articles been published, but a book as
well. His *Subjectivism and Individualism in Social Philosophy* was published during the first year of his exile, followed shortly (June, 1901)
by a striking article in *God's World* entitled "The Struggle for Idealism." Both book and article attracted attention to their author throughout the Russian reading public. Berdyaev's opinions were too "spiritual" for the orthodox marxists, who condemned him vigorously for
what in our day would be called "deviationism." And for the majority
of the intelligentsia, traditional free thinkers, it was also unpalatable;

both in Vologda and the rest of Russia comment was predominantly censorious.

The fact that everyone in Vologda could read the polemics on Berdyaev's writing is a commentary on its lack of real isolation from the rest of the world. Every new book published in Russia came straight to Vologda, first arriving not by way of the principal city bookstore but direct to Schegoleff, the literary historian, one of the exile leaders. Furthermore, the exiles were in general correspondence with all the leading writers of the country: Filosofov, Struve, Zhukovsky, Valery Brussov, and Leonid Andreev among others. The exiles must have had all the St. Petersburg magazines including the sensational New Way with its emphasis on spiritual problems and the intelligentsia. Whether published material arrived uncensored is not certain, but the vivid correspondence with political exiles abroad certainly came in surreptitiously. Remizoff says they had a regular "direct wire" to Paris, Zurich, and Geneva, where Lenin was already planning the revolution. Berdyaev seems to have taken this freedom of contact for granted; he does not mention it among the privileges of exile life. Latitude of movement applied not only to life within the exile group; it enabled social contacts outside, at least for the "aristocrats." Within the exile circle was "a very nice and highly educated woman," Valentina Dreling, with whom Berdyaev had especially friendly relations. He calls her "a true philsopher." Among his other women friends were the actresses of the local theater. Although theatrical people were esteemed at about the same level as they were in the Britain of Queen Victoria—who died the previous year, 1901—Berdyaev's relations here seem to have been purely on the basis of camaraderie. One fellow exile reported Berdyaev was always having a "romance, in plain view" of course, and enjoyed saying: "Mlle X is deeply in love with me, but at the moment I am only interested in Mlle Y." Berdyaev never had a real "affair" in Vologda. "He was in love with love," according to this source. Others of the "aristocrats" also enjoyed the normal society life of Vologda, and there were parties, concerts, and occasional evenings at the theater. Once, for a long-heralded gala performance, Berdyaev and some of his friends bought the box next to that of the Governor-General and, dressed in evening clothes of the latest St. Petersburg cut, attended in a body. Although the members of the group were too young to have earned any decorations, save for Mukalov who had a silver medal for lifesaving, they must have attracted no small amount of attention.

Berdyaev himself attracted public attention on another occasion of which he used to tell in the family circle. He was sitting one day in the cafe of the Golden Anchor with some of his friends when a young woman of their acquaintance burst into the room, tears in her eyes. She said she had been followed on the street by a man who was at that moment standing outside waiting for her to come out. Seizing his cane Berdyaev rushed out, and finding the offensive young fellow, began beating him regardless of the fact that his uniform indicated he was a government employee. "Tomorrow you'll be discharged, you rascal," Berdyaev shouted. How a political exile could make such a threat was difficult to explain. In telling the story, Berdyaev used to smile and say it was probably the heritage of a long line of men accustomed to command. For weeks the incident was a chief topic of conversation in Vologda—what punishment would descend upon one who so flagrantly affronted authority? To anyone who did not enjoy the protection of the Governor-General, some sort of punishment would surely have come swiftly. In Berdyaev's case, nothing happened, at least to him. Whether Berdyaev's friend was again molested we do not know.

Berdyaev felt himself mentally superior to most of the exiles he met in Vologda. Those not sentenced to live in the city passed through it on their way to Archangel in the north or the wastes of Siberia, farther east. They sometimes came to Vologda on visits. Twice during Berdyaev's stay "the little grandmother of the revolution," Catherine Breshkovskaya, came from her Siberian place of exile to visit friends in Vologda. But with almost all of the exiles Berdyaev felt ill at ease. He recognized their high devotion to the revolutionary cause and the sacrifices they had accepted, but he was pained by the terrible narrowness of their minds, even among those with a good education. He says they considered him a romantic individualist. His conduct seemed to justify their opinion. In a phrase from Berdyaev's biography of Leontieff, he might be describing himself (he is discussing Leontieff's religious type): "only a *barin*, an aristocrat, can talk like this. The democratic type of religiosity does not permit this play of the mind, this love of contradiction, this freedom, this mingling of the Psalms of David with Voltaire."

There was something of this mixture of King David and Voltaire in Berdyaev's first book. *Subjectivism and Individualism in Social Philosophy*, "that book so youthful and so incomplete" as Berdyaev later called it, was a critical commentary on a volume with a similar title by Nicolai Michailovsky, *The Subjective Method in Sociology*. Michailovsky was the great leader of the "movement toward the people" that a generation previously had so captured the minds of Russia's educated youth. For most young people of Berdyaev's age he was the leader and inspirer. Berdyaev approved of Michailovsky's ideas in general but felt they rested on a feeble philosophical basis. Believing the problem of the conflict between personality and society was basic, he ventured farther along individualist and idealist lines than Michailovsky. In view of Michailovsky's great prestige among the liberals of the day, this was a daring thing to do. Berdyaev's book had a preface by P. B. Struve, already somewhat of an authority himself, but carried considerable weight on its own. Although only twenty-seven when he wrote it, the author astounded his readers by his vast erudition. Besides pure philosophy, the book revealed such a knowledge of European literature, particularly in the fields of psychology and sociology, that it might have come from the pen of a man twice Berdyaev's age. Berdyaev's article "The Ethical Problem in the Light of Philosophical Idealism," published later in a symposium entitled *Problems of Idealism*, revealed a strong personalism based upon such widely differing authorities as Kant and Nietzsche. Berdyaev headed this article with the lines from Pushkin:

A king thou art—live on alone!
Go thy free way, thy proud mind leading on.

This is the way Nicolai Alexandrovitch quoted the poet, from memory as usual. There is probably some psychological significance in his quoting "thy proud mind" where Pushkin had written "thy free mind." In later years, he might better have anticipated the impression this epigraph would make on his readers, particularly on those who disagreed with him. Prince Trubetskoy, also a contributor to the symposium, said he never would have written for it had he known it would contain "such a Nietzschean article." This article further estranged Berdyaev from his Vologda colleagues, for most of whom he was a traitor to marxism. Long and fiery debates ensued, in which Berdyaev wasted much time, he says, in conflict with the orthodox marxists and in criticism of the traditional mentality of the Russian intelligentsia. The marxists were openly hostile to this presumptuous young apostate. The liberals, on the other hand, considered his type of idealism harmless and treated him with amused contempt.

It was all a part of Berdyaev's rapid evolution away from marxism toward a new spiritual religion. It was evolution, not conversion. As Berdyaev points out, a sudden and complete change from lack of faith to its full possession is little known in the Orthodox world; and in his own life, although the movement from materialism to Christianity was completed within a few years, there was "no sudden rending of the veil." As he saw later, the search for life's meaning was the search for God. Beginning with Berdyaev's exile, and at the same time with Struve, Frank, Bulgakov, and others in St. Petersburg, there was a swift spiritual movement that took them all through a similar evolution. As Eugenie once said: "Most of us grow slowly into a full Christian faith, especially if we start from agnosticism, Berdyaev made it in one leap. We go afoot; he went by plane." As Berdyaev wrote describing those years between 1900 and 1903:

> Marxism first postulated that only a material social organization can be the basis for the ideal development of human life. . . . And under the conditions of the historical moment, all theoretical and practical effort went into the development of material means. . . . The means were taken for the ends—the purpose of life was understood in too material a fashion.

When a materialist is converted, says Berdyaev, he accepts the spirit as authority, and often in some definite confessional form, whereas a "spiritualist," one conscious of the primacy of the non-material, accepts it as freedom. He stood at a point free from the restraints of marxism but not yet arrived at a conscious Christian position when exile ended late in 1902.

Just before his departure, as was the custom in Vologda, there was a party at which an "obituary" of the one about to depart was read aloud. This time it was Remizoff who composed the notice and Schegoleff who gravely intoned it. The document, in the form of a scroll, ornamented with Remizoff's inimitable "hentracks," was then solemnly presented to Berdyaev. Remizoff describes the pleasant character of "the departed" and what a vacancy will be left by his going: "Who can replace him? Even Lunacharsky, with all his rich oratory, cannot fill that abysmal hole." And then he comes to his main point:

> There are people one meets in life who are "as-it-should-be." They take all the joy out of life. I have met such well-trained

persons, without any bursts of impulse or hints of madness. They pass through life smoothly (probably calmly)—rise on time, eat at the proper hour, everything "as-it-should-be"—but by their very looks, "sobriety, caution, calculation," they induce a deadly boredom. In the departed there was no trace of this. His whole life he has lived without any "as-it-should-be" and hence life has always been easy and has smiled upon him and he on us.

Then, presuming that "the departed" is now somewhere in heaven, Remizoff talks about the stars as seeds of life in the sky.

And you certainly cannot say there is no sort of spirit there— No, this is evident, you can almost feel it with your eyes—these spermatozoids are the bearers of life—Nicolai Alexandrovitch, do you hear? I feel very strongly, but cannot quite imagine angels or bodiless powers. —Well, go where you will, only not into any most normal "as-it-should-be" heaven!

# 6

## THE UNSPEAKABLE MYSTERY

For a while after his return from Vologda, Berdyaev's life might have appeared to follow the "as-it-should-be" pattern. Late in 1902 he was permitted to leave Vologda and live out the remainder of his three-year sentence in the south, with the explicit condition that he should not live in Kiev. He chose Zhitomir. Of his months in this provincial town in Volhynia we have only fragmentary information. He seems to have spent most of his time in gay "normal" social life. Surrounded by a circle of young people, especially young women who were attracted by the romantic, handsome figure just returned from "terrible" exile, he participated in picnics and games, boating parties on the sunlit river, fell in love once or twice—all "as-it-should-be." But beneath the surface there was deep unrest and even dismay. Berdyaev spoke of this as a period of "downward, rather than upward movement." He was drawn toward the poetry and beauty in life, and would have liked to enjoy it to the full, but could not blind himself to the gray prose and the ugliness that underlay its surface gayety. This critical sense seemed to push all creative impulse out of his life. He almost stopped writing; he even felt he was making no intellectual progress. The "breath of Dionysus" had brought him to the "worst, the most decadent period" of his life.

This mood persisted when after a few months he could finally regain Kiev. It was accentuated by the isolated position in which he found himself. His former marxist friends had been estranged by his heresy, his persistent and increasing idealism. Berdyaev described his position at this time in a letter to the publishers of a biographical dictionary. On May 9, 1903, he wrote them at length, calling himself a "publicist":

> . . . Beginning with my article "The Struggle for Idealism," I finally move from positivism to metaphysical idealism, and in

conformity with this I change my attitude toward marxism, from which I still retain a series of realistic social ideas but which I deny as a whole world-view. At the present time I belong to the idealistic tendency which is becoming ever more definite, and which is expressed in the symposium "Problems of Idealism." I consider P. B. Struve as the man whose thinking most nearly corresponds with my own.

Although he maintained some individual friendships in the marxist group, it was officially hostile to him. The other liberal, premarxist group, with its standardized skepticism, refused to take Berdyaev seriously or have any intercourse with him. He felt the increasing width of the chasm that separated him from his former associates and at the same time had found no other friends to take their place. But here began a new friendship that was to continue throughout his lifetime. On his second "vacation" from Vologda he had made the acquaintance of Serge Bulgakov, young professor of economics in the Kiev Polytechnical Institute. At that period no one could have discerned in the marxist teacher the future Orthodox priest, ardent theologian, and "father in God" to the famous Academy of St. Sergius in Paris. To his delight Berdyaev discovered that Bulgakov, like himself, had matured past the marxism expressed in his book on *Capitalism in Agriculture*, published two years earlier, and had already proceeded further along the "idealistic" road than he himself. Three years older than Berdyaev, Bulgakov was at this period growing rapidly away from the materialism with which he had become infected in his own student years. With Bulgakov, Nicolai Alexandrovitch found himself for the first time in his life discussing purely religious problems. He never ceased discussing them to the end of his days.

Perhaps it was this new religious interest, perhaps the desire to escape the stifling atmosphere of tsarist Russia, or some more personal motive, that prompted Berdyaev's next move. In the spring of 1903 he went to Germany and enrolled for a semester in the old University of Heidelberg. The famous professor Windelband was attracting much attention in the philosophic world of that day with his revival of interest in Kant. Berdyaev was no longer a Kantian, although he had not forgotten his earlier readings of the sage of Königsberg. Now he sat under Windelband. No further data are available about Berdyaev's relationship with his professor or his other activities in the special atmosphere of a German university town. But we do know he did not remain continuously in Heidelberg. In Stuttgart, a few miles away, his St. Petersburg acquaintance Struve was living, together with a large number of other Russian exiles, and directing the "Liberation Movement."

The actual Russian liberation center was not in the city of Stuttgart itself but in a workmen's suburb Gaisburg. Most of the suburb's population belonged to the German Social Democrat party; Struve felt at home in the spacious rambling farmhouse where he lodged his large family and many guests, together with some of his assistants, and the editorial office of *Liberation*. This revolutionary paper, published in Germany, was the organ of an underground group in Russia. Its backers managed to slip large quantities past the tsarist censors, and it had a fairly wide circulation in the empire, with every governor-general on its mailing list. The Struves lived comfortably, generously supported by funds received from sympathizers in Russia. Imagine the Soviet government today permitting the passage of mail, books, and money orders to some center of Russian anticommunist organizations abroad such as the "Solidarist" group in western Germany! Protective techniques have improved since 1903. A very social atmosphere prevailed, and the family at once took to the lively, talkative visitor. On one of their picnics they spread their tablecloth on a stone bench in a ruined old Benedictine monastery. The calm and seclusion of the place appealed to Berdyaev. "I would like to spend my whole life here, in meditation," he said with a sigh. This may have been a passing impression. But later in life, Eugenie reports, "he often would say: 'Sometimes I wish I could enter a monastery. I am fascinated by the rigorous living, the solitude, the austere battle of the spirit, the separation from a world to which I can never accommodate myself.'" It is difficult to imagine one of Berdyaev's temperament in a monastery. Despite his proud bearing and authoritative combativeness, which often gave an impression of pride, he was essentially a very modest man. This might have made him an obedient novice. But if ever a question of moral principle should arise—. At least life would not be dull with such a member in the community.

On another occasion the same group was traveling on a train. It was a hot summer day, and as the train stopped at a small station along came a waiter, his fists full of mugs of foaming, amber beer. Berdyaev leaped gaily from the train, handed the waiter the necessary pfennigs, took one of the mugs, and downed its contents almost at one gulp.

Then he stood, empty mug in hand, until the bell rang for the train
to start. "Get aboard," his friends called, "the train is starting." "But
I have to give this mug back to the waiter." "Put it down on the platform!" they urged. "Never in my life have I set a glass down on a dirty
floor," he protested.

Another trip was made from Heidelberg to attend the meeting near
Chaux-de-Fonds, in Switzerland, of a committee from which eventually
developed the famous Union of Liberation. This was in late summer,
1903. Berdyaev reports having attended another meeting of the same
group in 1904, at Schaffhausen, Swiss enclave on the German frontier,
making a special trip abroad after he had finished the semester in
Heidelberg. At this second meeting, with revolutionary figures like
Petrunkevitch, Zhukovsky, and Shachovskoy participating—in all,
twenty delegates came from Russia as "tourists,"—the Union of
Liberation was formally organized.[1]

This Union attempted and achieved something that in our day
various forces have sought vainly to recreate: a workable coalition of
all or most of the diverse groups in the Russian emigration. In effect it
brought together most reform-minded Russians save the various shades
of marxists. At the outset the Liberation organization did not consider itself a party, although it was embarked upon a program of political change.

It soon developed that various groups held widely divergent opinions
about procedure, but they all rallied around one magic and romantic
word "constitution." This was their slogan and their goal. The first
formulations of their demands were comparatively mild. "The elementary and necessary preliminary conditions for life in a free society"
are freedom of the person guaranteed by an independent judiciary,
equality before the law, and the right to control legislation and approve
the budget. When it became evident the Tsar would never of his own
free will grant a constitution, they recognized the validity of "all forms
of action," and demands became more radical. For a year or more the
organization remained clandestine, but with the institution of the
Duma by Tsar Nicolai II (August, 1905), it became the central
political force in Russian life. Kerensky's provisional government in
1917 was made up largely of its members.

Although he had no special taste for politics, Berdyaev felt in this
period of "spiritual ferment" and revolutionary fervor that he could
not remain aloof from the movement to free Russia from the mon-

archy. He joined the Union of Liberation, remaining in sympathetic contact with it until it later became the Constitutional Democratic ("Cadet") party. (At that time Berdyaev, who continued to think of himself as a socialist, decided the Cadet party was "bourgeois" and refused to go along with it.) On some occasions he represented the party in negotiations with other groups. Among these was the Jewish "Bund," where he had long had good personal contacts. As a matter of fact he would have been more at his ease with the Social Democrats than with the Cadets, but the marxist group "could not forgive him for his 'reactionary' bent toward the spiritual and the transcendental." Yet here, also, Berdyaev was occasionally engaged in negotiations for his group with the Social Democrats.

At home again in Kiev, Berdyaev was restless. His political activity did not satisfy him; he needed further outlet for his energy. He gave a few lectures. He renewed his contact with Bulgakov, and their long discussions provided the impetus for his next move. Bulgakov was just at the point of leaving all free thought behind and turning to Christianity. Berdyaev was not yet ready for that final step but felt great sympathy with his friend. They both were much interested in the new literary and philosophical tendencies beginning to attract attention in St. Petersburg, and they talked of moving to the capital, but Bulgakov was tied to Kiev by his position in the Polytechnical Institute; and for one widely considered a marxist, government jobs were not easily to be had. This was a new idea to Nicolai Alexandrovitch; he had always been able to move as his fancy indicated. He knew that workmen were captives of their jobs, but intellectuals as well—that seemed strange. At all events, they could plan together in Kiev. They talked of a new magazine to bring into the current literary and artistic movement a more serious note of philosophy and sociology, even perhaps, of religion. It would have a sufficiently broad title to include almost any topic or tendency along these lines—something like the New Way then appearing, only more philosophical.

Planning for the proposed magazine went farther than Berdyaev's discussions with Bulgakov. Two letters to Zinaida A. Wengerova, then well known both as a writer and as a translator of foreign-language literature, indicate the extent of the project as well as the difficulties in the way of a new journal. In one letter (May 30, 1904) Berdyaev announces that the financial and editorial support of "V. M. Sablin, publisher and translator of Maeterlinck, Schnitzler, Hauptmann and

others" has been promised. "Thanks to Sablin a whole series of perspectives is open to us and I begin to hope that the literary section
of the magazine will not be dry and talentless." They are almost certain to have Leonid Andreev, perhaps Chekhov, and "are even planning an approach to L. Tolstoi." Berdyaev writes that they have
decided to invite Minsky, Merezhkovsky, and Hippius and asks Wengerova to make preliminary contact with them and "let me know if we
may send them official invitations from the editors." Then Nicolai
Alexandrovitch outlines the policies of the proposed magazine: "You
explain to them that the journal will be definitely idealistic, but with
broad tolerance: every new seeking will find sympathy in it (especially
in me, personally) but in political relations it will be radical."

A second letter, undated, reports "complications." The chief financial
supporter, Sablin, "has left us." Consequently plans have had to be
changed, but the editors still hope to issue the first number in January.
And in January, 1905, after many further "complications," Bulgakov
and Berdyaev could realize their long-discussed project in *Life's Questions*, of which more later.

One day Bulgakov mentioned another matter. He had recently received the visit of two young Kiev ladies, just released from the prison
where they had been sent for revolutionary activities. They wished to
consult Bulgakov about their desire to continue "serving the people,"
but he had found their esthetic and modern artistic ideas somewhat out
of his line and thought Berdyaev could be of more use to them. They
had seen Berdyaev at one of the many "liberation" meetings and hoped
to meet him. Would Berdyaev see them? Of course he would, and
thus he made the acquaintance of two women who became the most
intimate companions of his life. They were Lydia and Eugenie Trusheff, daughters of a prominent Kiev attorney. They represented, here
in Kiev, some sparks of the cultural renaissance that had begun to fire
the capital. In many ways they were typical of the intelligentsia of the
period: widely read, widely traveled, liberal to the point of religious
agnosticism (religion was "reactionary"), yet aflame with a desire for
social justice and political liberty. Although they still retained their interest in efforts for social improvement, they were now especially
concerned with the possible role of art in the promotion of political
reform. Eugenie was a sculptress; her sister already showed signs of
talent in poetry. The two sisters were almost inseparable. They had sat
together in jail for revolutionary activity. Together they had carried on

such projects as teaching peasants to read, but much worse in the eyes of the government, had aided in the distribution of subversive literature. One night their home was suddenly surrounded by the police. Lydia jumped from a side window right into the arms of a policeman. Eugenie was taken with her to jail. Now they were free. They were used to doing things together, and together they fell in love with the attractive young philosopher. Now although formal marriage with its wealth of church ceremonial was treated rather lightly in the circle of the Russian intelligentsia, and partnership without external sanction was not exceptional, more than one partner was decidedly not in good taste. Nicolai Alexandrovitch chose Lydia Yudifovna. Even her women friends agree that Lydia was very beautiful; dark, well built for her height, she was most pleasing in her attitudes toward other people but always with a hint of sadness behind her graciousness. Nowhere in books or articles, or even in personal conversation, has anything very definite been said about Berdyaev's swift courtship and marriage. Eugenie said "he loved her with a beautiful and ethical love." In reply to a series of direct questions about it, however, Eugenie wrote:

> Nicolai Alexandrovitch based his attitude to marriage, as to all problems of man and his destiny, on revelation and on his own spiritual experience. Hence he understood marriage as the accomplishment, the realization, of the image and likeness of God in man, which image was divided in the Fall into man and woman, and which ought to unite for the attainment of one Divine image in man. This sacrament is accomplished before God, in man's soul, and has no need of church sanction, which in Nicolai Alexandrovitch's view is a juridical act, and carried out for earthly, rather than heavenly purposes. Nicolai Alexandrovitch's marriage with my sister was a spiritual marriage. They lived as brother and sister, like the first apostles.

All this is in line with Berdyaev's description of his attitude toward "general, universally valid morality." He felt that all kinds of vows, marriage or monastic, even taking an oath in court, were actions against man's freedom. All his life, he said, his attitude toward legalism had been one not merely of hostility but of moral indignation. He considered getting out from under the power of the formal law his moral duty. In matters of sexual morality and marriage his ideas were almost as radical.

Berdyaev's approach to the problem was, naturally, first theoretical

and philosophical, even mystical. He does not say so, but by the time
(1913-14) he was writing the book that contained his major pronouncements about sex he must have seen some of Freud's earlier works.
Berdyaev's book was *The Meaning of the Creative Act*, and although
the problem of sex and related questions appears in many of his later
books, this one treats the topic more fully. Berdyaev was among the first
Russian writers to call attention to the (then) new theories of sex and
its basic function:

> . . . men begin to realize, scientifically, philosophically and
> religiously, that sexuality is not a special, different function of the
> human . . . , but is diffused throughout his whole being . . .
> determines the whole of his life. . . . Sex is the meeting-point of
> two worlds in the human organism . . . the metaphysical roots
> of man's being.[2]

In the St. Petersburg days later on, Berdyaev entered into controversy about the subject of sex with Rozanoff, "one of the most unusual,
most original" men he ever met. Rozanoff was unusual even in appearance, with frowsy red hair and beard, and a pronounced lisp; he con-
versed with Berdyaev in whispers accompanied by a light shower bath
because of the sputtering way he spoke. The friendship lasted for years.
Rozanoff called Berdyaev "Adonis," and Berdyaev says no one else
showed him such attention. Despite his wonderful literary gift, his
"regular magic of words," and the special attention he showed Bedyaev—very flattering from a prominent figure like Rozanoff toward a
young newcomer—Nicolai Alexandrovitch could not agree with Rozanoff's cult of the flesh. For him the basic problems were of the spirit
which is free, rather than of the flesh, captive to necessity. Berdyaev
disputed Rozanoff's assertion that Christianity was thoroughly hypo-
critical in its attitudes toward sex, and defended the Christian viewpoint which he felt stood for personality as against race. He did admit
"the so-called Christian family is . . . a pagan compromise, like the
'Christian' state." And he deplored the pretense that in the "Christian"
family the problem had been solved: "The chaos of sex surges beneath
the family, just as it surged in the blood of mediaeval hermits."[3]
Berdyaev quotes Rozanoff's statement about himself: "I am a man
devoid of talent, but my theme is talented,"[4] and feels Rozanoff applied
great erudition to the great subject of sex as a religious problem.

In several statements Berdyaev commented that in the entire course
of human history thinkers seem nearly always to have ignored the

problem of sex. He felt only two philosophers had given adequate "doctrines of sex and love," Plato and Vladimir Solovieff. "Plato's *Feast* and *The Meaning of Love* by Solovieff, are the most profound, the most penetrating things which men have written on this theme."[5] Although he could not accept Solovieff wholeheartedly, he seems to have felt that much of *The Meaning of Love* was pertinent and acceptable. In his own thoughts about sex, Berdyaev passed beyond the purely philosophical into the theological—although he would not admit it was theology—and the mystical.

The mystical origins of sex Berdyaev finds in various aspects but especially in the bisexual nature of man that was marred by Adam's fall, resulting in the division of humanity into male and female. But the Fall can never "wipe out the basic, true bisexuality, the androgynous quality in man—the image and likeness of God in him. In truth neither man nor woman is the image and likeness of God, but only the androgyne—the youth-maiden, the integral bisexual man."[6] Berdyaev combined this idea, which dates back at least to Plato, with his own theory of the three epochs of creation, the epochs of the Law, of the Redemption, and of Creativity. In this third epoch man will realize his divine calling to be a co-creator with God, and at the same time by some mystical process will regain his shattered virginity, and humanity will be restored to its original sinless androgyneity. Because the first man was sinless, androgyne, the new Adam, Christ, was "perfect man and never knew a woman."[7] On the cross, He "restored the androgynous image of man." And in the third epoch the eternal mystery of man will be disclosed with "the revelation of the absolute Man in creative power and glory." Berdyaev felt this experience was already under way.

Continuing his theological concept of sex mysticism, Berdyaev feels male and female are cosmic rather than mere anthropological categories. "The Christian symbolism of the logos and the soul of the world, of Christ and His Church, speaks of the cosmic mysticism of male and female, and of the cosmic conjugal mystery."[8] He wrote frequently about relationships and differences between the sexes. "Woman," he says, "is the bearer of the sex-element. . . . In man sex is more differentiated and specialized, while in woman it is diffused through the whole . . . organism."[9] In his letters to Mme K, Berdyaev asserts:

> The typical male nature is many-planed; it can contain at one
> moment both joy and suffering, a sense of oppression along with

a feeling of uplift. This is why man has been able to accomplish so much in so many spheres, in history. This is why woman is more integral in love, while man with rare exceptions is only partial. . . . You place love at the center of life, and you write it with a capital "L." Let me express a few bitter thoughts about love. Love (I am speaking of erotic love between man and woman) has become so vulgarized and defiled that it is scarcely possible to use the word. True love has a deep significance, but it is rare, and other words and gestures are needed to express it.

Men speak much of sex but forget about love. Love is not the sexual act; in a very profound sense love is just the opposite. The sexual act is essentially a drive for the preservation of race; in love there is something individual, unracial, surpassing the average racial consciousness. In its essentially animal element the sexual thirst for union leads, tragically, not to mystical union but to childbirth, which Berdyaev equates with a disintegration of personality. "It shackles man to that decadent order of nature, where reigns the endless relay of birth and death."[10] In the deepest sense, however, love is not necessary to the continuation of the race. "We cannot theorize about love, nor moralize, nor socialize, nor even biologize—it is a foreign flower" in the midst of our world. This "other-worldly" love Berdyaev speaks about, "the love which creates eternity," overcomes sex for the sake of a higher, absolute union. The sexual act is divisive, but real love can create new integral life, overcoming the race and natural necessity. The individual personality is confirmed in the "unique and unspeakable mystery of love." True love is "a tormenting search for the androgynous image, for cosmic harmony"—the fusion of male and female natures into the image and likeness of God, into the androgyne. And this reveals the ultimate meaning of love: the restoration in man of the image of God.

From this position, Berdyaev views the Christian approach to sex. The most persistent Christian attitude toward sex had been refusal or denial—the way of the great wrestlers of the spirit. This being manifestly too much to demand of the average man, the Church justified sex in the "bourgeois and utilitarian" institution of the family. In truth, says Berdyaev, Christianity as a religion of redemption refuses to accept the elemental necessity of race. The old Adam is racial; the new Adam is divested of this old nature. In asceticism Christianity has denied sex in denying the old Adam, but the Christian family, a compromise, has not yet provided a revelation of the mystery of sex outside the racial element. Only now we begin to see the change implicit in Christianity: ". . . never before has there been . . . a recognition of man's bisexuality."[11] Berdyaev says the "natural" boundaries between male and female are becoming confused: "It becomes possible to ask whether, in a higher sense of the word, birth-giving, racial sex is . . . normal."[12] Real Christianity recognizes as normal and proper only birth by the spirit and in union with the spirit. "The family was born of necessity, not of freedom. Even the Christian-moral ideology of the family is deeply tinctured with economic utilitarianism."[13] In "blessing family life the Church renders harmless the sin of sexual life,"[14] while true marriage is a sacrament of union in love. Love is a sacrament above and outside the law—outside racial necessity.

What is the answer to such an impossible challenge? How can man "escape the body of this death?" Berdyaev avoids being very specific on the level of present-day living, but in general he argues for a sublimation of sex. It ties in with his theory of the third epoch, when pro-creation must give way to creation. "Sexual activity will be directed toward the production of a new world, the continuation of original creation."[15] In the present world order sex energy is used in the begetting of children, mortal creativeness in place of immortal. "In the depths of sex, creativeness must conquer begetting, personality must overcome race, union in the spirit must conquer natural union by flesh and blood . . . this can only be the revelation of the androgynous, God-like nature of man."

For everyday people Berdyaev does not offer much guidance. Neither, he says, do the teachings of the Church; all that has been said by the fathers and the theologians is on a rather low level, and much of it seems to consider marriage chiefly from the contractual standpoint. But the revelation of Christian love demands a creative act. "It calls us to another union, not of this world, . . . the union of all in the free Spirit."[16] Berdyaev declares "only a few achieve the true mystery of marriage . . . it is something aristocratic and predicates election."[17] And there is another cryptic thought: "Any union of man and woman in which the sin of the sexual act is overcome and in which integrity is re-established is not a family union." It is evidently something higher, since "the family appears as a lower form."[18]

How did Berdyaev apply these theories in his own living? Conjecture in the matter would be perilous, and the facts are not too plentiful. What is known, however, helps to form a picture, even if it leaves some questions unanswered. In many places Berdyaev emphasizes his aversion to "this world" of necessity and to the material. This applies to all physical functions, he says, even to that of eating. He really preferred the simplest food, a vegetarian diet where one was possible. He speaks of his "squeamish attitude" toward life and his "small capacity for the erotic idealization of actuality."[19] He thinks his aversion to "life" has spiritual rather than physiological causes since, although his was a normally strong physical organism, he had a feeling of scorn for everything of the flesh. "I love only the forms of the flesh,"[20] he says. Not that he stood above life's temptations, but he did not like them. From childhood, he disliked talk about sex or the "dirty grimaces when sex is mentioned." In theory the sexual act was degrading, he insisted, since "personality becomes the toy of the genius of race."[21] And in practice it is a delusion—it sets up expectations that are unrealizable; it is made up of inward contradictions and "goes against the meaning of the world."[22] The life of genius is not a "natural life, it is incompatible with a bourgeois-ordered sex life."[23] Berdyaev always knew he was different from the normal. Of course he never said he thought himself a genius, but others must have told him he was. His sense of his creative calling undoubtedly played a part in his idealization of marriage.

Nicolai Alexandrovitch lived with his parents until he was past twenty. He held apart from other boys. He did not feel at ease with men; they accepted him but paid him no special attention, which may explain why he felt more at home with women. All his life he had closer relationships with women than with men, although it sometimes seemed to him that he did not love the feminine element. If any conversation turned to affairs of love he would break it off at once. In one letter to Mme K, he wrote: "It is torture for me to read in a novel a description of love—it is torture to listen when . . . people talk of love affairs."

Berdyaev attributed Leontieff's success with women to the fact that he was a very handsome man. Berdyaev's good looks were a factor in his attractiveness to women, and in this sense he "had great success with women" also. But one of his old friends said his success was as an artist, a Beau Brummell, and that even in the St. Petersburg days there was never any gossip about wrong relations with women. His intense "affair" with Hippius was purely platonic. He never knew a cult of *la belle dame*, and his was always a knightly attitude says another— perhaps prejudiced—witness. He frequently received love letters from women, some of whom he did not know. With one such lady, who had seen and heard Berdyaev at only one of his lectures, he carried on a long correspondence because he felt she was on the verge of madness —he also corresponded with her husband. Whether the lady's eventual suicide was the result of unrequited love is unknown. A close friend said he preferred to captivate rather than be conquered by women. Once a lady told him, "You are better fitted to be a monk," and he replied, "I have often thought so, myself." There was the case of the "unusually beautiful" woman from southern Russia who left her husband and followed him to Vologda during his exile. Berdyaev said he had "cruelly refused her." Some of Berdyaev's friends consider the "brother and sister" relationship with his wife to have obtained throughout their married life; others feel this was true only later, as in the case of his friend Bulgakov. With Hippius, Berdyaev must have discussed his love for his wife, because one of the letters to Hippius in 1907 closes with the strange phrase: "I never doubt that Lydia Yudifovna is with Christ. I have a real sense of this. And I will love her as long as I love purity." In his later years Berdyaev had at least two "affairs"—sudden deep interest in certain women that caused considerable talk—but as with Hippius, these were evidently quite platonic relationships. They left their mark on him though. Friends felt he never fully recovered from the break with Hippius. Some of the letters to Mme K reveal Berdyaev's ideas about the love of women. "Venera was born of the sea foam. In Greece she was a goddess: in our world she has become a café singer or a cocotte." And later: "I fully believe in woman's love: I consider woman capable of love in the highest degree, but the character of that love inspires revulsion in me. . . . I am not in the least inclined to be ruined by any sort of relation with women. This contradicts my consciousness of my calling in the world."

His concept of his calling influenced all of Berdyaev's ideas about marriage and family life. He said Russians were "less family-minded than western people, but infinitely more communal."[24] He felt his love of freedom and his concentration on the value of the personality explained his "revulsion to social life, to everything which is connected with birth-giving."[25] Like Kierkegaard, Berdyaev was conscious of the difficult dilemma the Christian faces in marital life. One wonders whether he might have been thinking of himself when he wrote of Leontieff: ". . . all these characteristics presuppose the presence, along with a series of strong masculine traits, of feminine traits as well. Not a uni-sexual, but a duo-sexual structure of spirit . . . the thirst for love . . . and the impossibility of finding one satisfying, truly conjugal love."[26] "He felt the impassable chasm between the poetry of romantic[27] love, and marriage, the family." The Greeks knew, Berdyaev said, that Hades and Dionysus were the same god, and "in the birth-giving life of sex there is a foreboding of death."[28] "The racial element is the chief obstacle to the revelation of . . . man's creative nature."[29] In *The Meaning of the Creative Act,* Berdyaev airs the Christian attitude: "The New Testament reveals . . . a way out of . . . racial necessity, but this way predicates a heroic struggle to overcome . . . sexual inclination. . . . In Christianity only the ascetic denial of sex . . . is religious. . . . The new sex, in a positive form, was not revealed in the religion of redemption."[30] In his ardent youth Berdyaev felt mankind was just entering the third—the creative—epoch in history when this revelation would finally come.

Berdyaev's marriage took place in the summer. Then almost at once, leaving Lydia to come later, he set out for St. Petersburg and the ferment of the new intellectual life there.

# 7

## THE IVORY TOWER

Berdyaev arrived in St. Petersburg in the autumn of 1904, leaving his young bride behind. The handsome young dandy—"no one else but an actor in a theater could have worn such extremely cut clothes"— entered headfirst into the maelstrom of new and daring Russian thought that later came to be recognized as a real renaissance. It was a time of crisis—political, cultural, religious. Everything was in a flux; as Kartasheff says, "People were not making history; history made people." Following an amnesty under Svatopolk-Mirsky, the majority of political exiles, their ideas sharpened by long years in Siberia, flooded into the capital. Scores of new "thought-systems" arose; more quasi-religious cults appeared. The hitherto clandestine political parties began to emerge from hiding and were later joined by half a dozen new ones. Although most of the intellectuals seem to have been little concerned with it, 1905 was the year of the disastrous Russo-Japanese War and the "disgraceful" treaty of Portsmouth. The year had begun with "Bloody Sunday," when government troops fired upon an unarmed mass of workmen led by a priest, cross in hand, in the square in front of the Tsar's winter palace. In June the crew of the cruiser *Potemkin* mutinied. On August 6, the Tsar's manifesto first proposed an advisory parliament. In October the first Soviet of Workers' Deputies, with their paper *Izvestia*, appeared as the directing organ of a general strike that included even the railroads. The outburst of hope for better times accompanying the famous imperial manifesto of October 17—which this time proposed a legislative Duma—was soon drowned in disappointment. Again reaction set in. Again there were revolutionary demonstrations, with peasants burning and pillaging great country houses and "counter revolutionary" mobs beating up the intelligentsia and the Jews. An armed uprising in Moscow, in December, ended the calamitous year.[1]

Against this bloodstained backdrop of social and political ebullition the Russian cultural renaissance began its flowering. In Moscow the

81

Religious-Philosophical Society was founded, with sometimes two hundred persons attending its meetings: students and artists, priests and marxists, terrorists and religious fanatics. In St. Petersburg there were a score of "circles," closed groups gathering more or less regularly for endless discussions on the most abstruse and varied problems. Some of these groups were political. But one sign of the times was the fact that, in an atmosphere saturated with political revolution, large numbers of intellectuals were far more interested in philosophies and cults and the metaphysical than in civic and political questions.

Berdyaev devotes an entire chapter in his autobiography to the Russian cultural renaissance at the beginning of this century. In an earlier book he described its atmosphere of intense creativity—a flowering of poetry and philosophy, a profound spiritual disquiet and religious searching. It derived from a juncture of social factors. The tsarist bureaucracy was a brilliantly educated corps, its members probably as deeply moved by the spiritual forces abroad in Russia as others were but mostly silent for fear of losing their jobs. They provided a vast readership for the quantities of writing produced by younger men— most of them economically independent—suddenly returned from exile, voluntary or otherwise, and now at liberty to express themselves. Berdyaev was among the young writers who began to vociferate in the explosive atmosphere of these early 1900's. It must be said that he made no special impression for either originality or power at that moment. The period of exclusive domination in Russian thought by positivism and materialism was ended. The new tendency sought to build an ethical foundation within socialism, and the search for an absolute was directed toward religion instead of revolution. From Plechanov and other materialists the young intellectuals turned to Tolstoi and Dostoievsky. Germany, hitherto setting the tone for most of European thought, was still in its neo-Kantian stage, thinkers in Russia had moved on their own into the fresh field of metaphysics. They were captivated by themes of "the divine cosmos and of cosmic transfiguration, of the Creator's energies in creation, of the divine in man, of man's creative calling, and the meaning of culture[2]—albeit this fresh thinking occupied only one small portion of the intelligentsia; a majority continued to live with the old materialist and positivist ideas. A cultural elite was formed that gradually lost much of its contact with the general population and any action for social betterment. Berdyaev said there was a complete schism. It was as though the intelligentsia lived on another planet with its exquisitely refined culture bordering on decadence. Nowhere else in modern times has there been anything like it. The breadth of reading in a dozen languages typical of the thin social layer known as the intelligentsia, its theoretical and philosophical approach to every question, astonished any ordinary westerner having contact with them then or since.

To all appearances, Berdyaev entered completely into the glare and excitement of the intellectual society in the capital. Life seemed to be an endless succession of visits, parties, and discussions. It was like children enjoying the pleasures of a wealthy father's home. Berdyaev enjoyed these pleasures with the best of the circle. Always gay, always alert, his hearty laughter punctuated every social gathering. He was still the Beau Brummell; with his mass of brown hair worn long, he was a handsome figure. He enjoyed it when friends would ask "where ever did you find the material for that beautiful new coat?" He used the most expensive perfumes. Although his tic was somewhat of a shock to people meeting him for the first time, they soon got used to it and after a few months never noticed it at all. With the others—Remizoff tells how Rozanoff taught them always to go in a flock—he went from one to another of the salons or the intellectual "circles" gathered about one person or one main interest. More and more his interest moved away from materialism, and he battled openly for something finer— for which he was denounced as a heretic to marxism and called by the horrible name "bourgeois." Berdyaev gave as good measure as he received, particularly in his articles collected in Sub Specie Aeternitatis. For like almost everyone else in this supercharged crowd of intellectuals Berdyaev continued his writing, although one wonders how he accomplished it in the whirl of social events.

His life in St. Petersburg differed from that later in Berlin and Paris; he seems to have been more an observer than a participant. There was no effort to organize his own "circle"; he moved from group to group, absorbing what pleased him. It was a pattern he followed almost up to the revolution. "I wanted to penetrate into the spiritual tendencies of the time" he said, "to find their meaning, but I did not surrender to them. And therefore I remained outside and alone, in marxism as in orthodoxy." After he had learned what he wished from one group he left it, usually with something like a slammed door, and passed on to another. From the (at first) indefinite "Social Democrat" group in Kiev he had moved toward marxism; from here, under the influence of Bulgakov and Merezhkovsky, he entered the "idealist" camp in St. Petersburg. But although he continued his contacts with the intellectual circles of the capital, he was deeply dissatisfied inwardly. In a letter from a country place he wrote:

> In all the St. Petersburg literary society I have scarcely met any purity or nobility. I am so painfully surprised at the impurity and shallowness of this milieu, that I am resting my spirit in the country, and dream of living at least one winter away from St. Petersburg. . . . In this musty mess of "circles," there is no interest in God's world and in world-problems . . . and they esteem themselves to be the salt of the earth!

Berdyaev could already see that the new intellectual ferment lacked moral foundation as well as contact with the people. "An aesthetic softening had taken place. There was no willed choice." Again he was finding it impossible to go along with the crowd.

"Crowd" is the right word—with a bizarre medley of personalities and interests. After the Tsar's October manifesto one could talk about anything almost, without fear of police espionage. And talk they did, occasionally listening to each other as well—they were all slightly intoxicated with their freedom. Berdyaev once said that an intellectual, a thinker, is in a certain sense a freak. The whirling "circles" in Petersburg held many such. They lived abnormally, and mostly at night. The Merezhkovskys had supper at one in the morning, then went on talking until three or four, rising the next day after noon. Sometimes, if very heated, the discussion would go on without a pause the whole night through and the opponents would separate, tired but unreconciled, with the rising of the sun. Occultism flourished. There was tremendous, very nearly hysterical, interest in all sorts of cultural problems, almost all of it pure theory. If the thought of doing something about the burning social questions of the time ever occurred to them, they dodged. They were interested in ideals, not people. As Byeli said, they "had no will for noble deeds." They all were critics; all wrote and spoke "dark words" about the suffering of the masses. But the members of the intelligentsia did not suffer; they were inwardly filled with a satisfied confidence in themselves and a happy future. No one seemed to have any material needs. Many of the intelligentsia, like Berdyaev, lived comfortably on some sort of family allowance. If that failed, as in the case of Leontieff a generation earlier, government service was always a last resort. Berdyaev says Leontieff, "in despair, finally decided to take a job, and selected the diplomatic service. Through an acquaintance of his brother . . . he was placed in the Asiatic department."[3]

Almost everyone was writing. Because it took too long to compose a book, they found a few fellow writers of more or less similar interests and produced a symposium. Such collections of articles, often on the most abstract of themes, became very popular. The books were widely read and then, of course, discussed. These discussions sometimes finished with a cruel separation of people who yesterday were friends. This was especially true of political discussions. Tyrkova, writing of the period, says: "Party differences had not yet drawn an impassable line between me and Nadya"—her girlhood friend Nadezhda Krupskaya, later the wife of Lenin. Berdyaev wrote for such symposia, among them *Problems of Idealism* (1903), *From Marxism to Idealism*, and the provocative *Milestones* (1909). The first sentences of the preface to *Milestones* give the tone: "It is not in order to judge the Russian intelligentsia from the heights of truth we have perceived, and not with any supercilious disdain of its past, that these articles are written, but with pain because of this past, and burning anxiety for the future of our fatherland." Of the seven authors, four were to play important roles in the emigration: Berdyaev, Bulgakov, Struve, and Frank. Berdyaev's article "Philosophic Truth and the Justice of the Intelligentsia" made a deep impression. It was almost the first of his writing that attracted special attention amid the chorus of new writers of the time. His *New Religious Consciousness and Sociality* was viewed as merely part of the stream of new books that year, 1907.

In those early revolutionary years all the intelligentsia were interested in politics—at least in theory. None seems to have dreamed that a given revolutionary program, if realized, could concern one personally. They all believed, with Plato, that politics should be managed by philosophers. All were agreed that revolution must come, and for most, any thought of revolution seems to have begun and finished with the overthrow of the monarchy. Berdyaev also was concerned with revolution. His participation in the Union of Liberation was "as-it-should-be" but none too enthusiastic. He rebelled against political revolution, which from his spiritual viewpoint seemed reactionary. But these political contacts brought about a better acquaintance between some of the more idealistic political revolutionaries and the "idealist" group they had been calling reactionary. Mutual understanding helped the idealists to establish themselves in the intellectual world. Berdyaev says it was a bit awkward to denounce as reactionary the very people with whom you were working on revolutionary planning. Thus Berdyaev's conditioned political interest helped prepare the way for his spiritual message.

If politics interested large numbers of the intelligentsia, the position of religion was exactly the reverse. The old idea that religion was equivalent to reaction still persisted in many minds. The intelligentsia, says Tyrkova-Williams, did not understand the difference between the divine truth of the eternal Church and the mistakes of the church on earth. Many considered the Gospels a collection of myths. It was even difficult for one of Christian faith to be considered a member of the intelligentsia.

Aesthetic as well as religious and political themes occupied the minds of the intelligentsia during these first years of the twentieth century. They never could tell what subject would come up next. One evening, the *jour fixe* of the editors of *Life's Questions*, a lecture had been announced on "The Beauteous Helen." Chulkoff, who was an editor at the time, tells the story: about forty people were listening to a brilliant speaker. Coming into the room in the middle of the lecture, Chulkoff found the chairman struggling to restrain his own excitement while asking the audience to remain calm and the lecturer to continue. At the rear of the hall was a group of policemen whose appearance had thrown the audience into near panic. In front of them stood Berdyaev blazing with anger, stamping his feet, and shouting at the scared-looking police sergeant already backed up against a wall. In the midst of his tirade, Berdyaev was seized with the tic and stuck his tongue out at the officer. He, taking this for personal insult, ordered his men to arrest the entire crowd. When they hesitated, Chulkoff suggested they go into an adjoining room and establish a police report. The sergeant started writing. Name of the speaker? Subject? "The Beauteous Helen." "What? Don't try to joke with me." It was some time before the brave policeman could be convinced such a recondite subject did not conceal some sort of revolutionary motif. This particular meeting had been duly reported to the police in advance; hence the sergeant's descent upon it was unjustified. It illustrates the general confusion of authorities, confronted as they were with the fervid activity in the capital of hundreds of young people just released from prison or exile for "revolutionary" activity. The government itself was uncertain, and as a result people did very much as they pleased.

Symbolism was a popular movement. Andre Byeli describes the basic symbolist idea:

The curve of European thought passes from Kant through Schopenhauer to Nietzsche. Now we can hear the music of the symbols, which speak to us of another world. But our art is not the final goal—art must give place to theurgy. We strive for the incarnation of eternity by means of the transfiguration of resurrected personality, the perception of spiritual reality behind the visible.

The movement was notable for its uncanny awareness of catastrophe ahead, its experimentation with the occult, and its toying with the apocalyptic. That many highly cultured intellectuals should be passionately concerned with such mystic-philosophic abracadabra when revolution was marching in the streets seems almost incredible now. Berdyaev must have been in St. Petersburg on the "Bloody Sunday." but it is not mentioned in his autobiography. Berdyaev said in defense of the intellectuals that they were mostly literati and had neither theoretical nor practical preparation for solving questions of social order. He considered it a weakness in himself that his normal social interests slackened in this period of his close contact with the movement of minds and spirits. He explained it as typical of the self-centeredness of the elite.

With such a purely academic approach, was it any wonder their meeting place came to be called the "Ivory Tower?" It was in V. Ivanoff's top-floor apartment opposite the Tauride Palace. The large corner room was round with a domed ceiling, up a few steps from the rest of the apartment, the small cupola over it visible from the street. For a year and a half the whole of St. Petersburg's intelligentsia—professors, literati, journalists—attended the "Wednesdays" held here. Meetings began late at night and often continued until sunrise the next morning. The subjects discussed were varied in the extreme: "not only literary, but philosophical, religious, mystical, occult."[4] Ivanoff was preaching a new theater of mysteries with Dionysiac sacraments. The atmosphere was almost hypnotic. "You forget in what country you are, and at what time. Everything is turned around and day becomes night, night day. Even Ivanoff's 'Wednesdays' were Thursdays, for they began after midnight."[5] A. Byeli presented a paper on the two forces struggling in the world—the sphinx and the phoenix. Once or twice Lunacharsky, editor of Lenin's organ, attempted to introduce a political note, but with small success. Others including Berdyaev were advocating a "mystical anarchy." This romantic period, Berdyaev said, was characterized "by the predominance of the erotic and aesthetic over the ethical." Looking back at it after half a century, Kartasheff said "it was a poetic time. We lived like children."

V. Ivanoff was the instigator of one experiment that caused much gossip both in and outside the press. The prevailing mood was one demanding a return to the ancient sources of culture—to the mystic of the Earth and to a cosmic religion. Berdyaev said Ivanoff very nearly identified Dionysianism with Christianity. Ivanoff was always insisting that for Dionysianism the important thing was not "what," but "how—the significant thing was experiencing ecstasy, regardless of the subject concerned. "Orgiasm became stylish," said Berdyaev, and "Eros got the upper hand over Logos." Even people not the least ecstatic-minded joined in the search for ecstasy. "They were more interested in ecstasy than in truth." So one night (in 1906), in Minsky's apartment, they undertook to create something like an imitation of the Dionysiac mysteries. In the group were Rozanoff and V. Ivanoff, which was not surprising, but Sologub the serious-minded poet and Berdyaev himself must have been somewhat astonished to find themselves there, although young Russians more than most Europeans have a tendency to go out after strong sensations—anything, of whatever quality, if it takes them out of the ordinary. Berdyaev said they hoped to attain a Dionysiac uplift and escape out of the usual. Just what took place was never made public, and at this distance details are insignificant. St. Petersburg gossip accused the group of having celebrated a "Black Mass." Remizoff, who was one of the group, says it was "frivolity to the point of oblivion. In Rozanoff there was some sort of evil spirit: there was nothing of this in Berdyaev." Remizoff never afterward mentioned this evening at Minsky's to Berdyaev.[6] "I always felt that there had been something in it which should not be, and it would have been unpleasant for both of us." The incident, however, reveals what Berdyaev called the "hot-house atmosphere" of this ultrarefined cultural group.

Berdyaev was usually the chairman and occasionally the chief speaker at Ivanoff's "Wednesdays." His topics we do not know, but about that time he gave a public lecture on "The Grand Inquisitor," and we may be sure he brought Dostoievsky and Ibsen into the discussions. Despite the bizarre and ephemeral nature of much that went on in the "Tower" with this collection of "lilies of the valley abloom in January," it represented the flower of the current renaissance, and much of value has come from its participants.

During his first year in the capital Berdyaev confirmed friendships that remained significant for the rest of his life and thought. There was Bulgakov. A passionate Social Democrat with a most utilitarian approach, he had small respect for such people as artists. But throughout the next sixteen years Berdyaev and Bulgakov collaborated in various literary-philosophical enterprises. Together they were banished by the Soviet government, and they remained friends through the score of years they lived in Paris.

Then there was the strange "mystic three" of the Merezhkovskys: Dmitri Merezhkovsky, his wife Zinaida Hippius, and D. V. Filosofov, poet-philosopher and critic. Filosofov lived with the Merezhkovskys throughout a large part of their married life, moving when they moved, within Russia or abroad. He was so wrapped up in the Merezhkovskys that he evidently had little time for other interests, and there was not much active contact between him and Berdyaev.

With the two Merezhkovskys, however, Berdyaev's life was to be closely bound up for some time. Dmitri Sergeevitch Merezhkovsky was at this moment a sort of leader among intellectuals and "the most widely read man in Russia." On his book-piled desk one might find any strange combination of authors: Eckharthausen, Dionysius the Areopagite, Bakunin, St. Isaac the Syrian, Shelling, on top of a collection of Arabian folk legends. He was a thin little man with a rusty goatee, a waxlike color to his sagging jowls, a large nose, and slightly bulging eyes with only a dull grayish color in them. But these cold eyes could, on occasion, suddenly light up "with the hidden flame of frenzied enthusiasm"—to quote Andre Byeli. A man so strangely self-contained that not even his wife was admitted to his deepest interests, he gave the impression of coldness or even unkindness to his associates. His wife says he never had a friend. He never sought popular acclaim, and friends wonder if he would ever have attracted much attention without the services of his wife as press agent. Very active, very vocal, she "sold" him to all sorts of people. A brilliant essayist, mostly on historical themes, he was deeply concerned about religious problems, "played a major role in arousing religious interest in literature and culture,"[7] and had a lively interest—theological, not ritualistic—in all religions, Christian and non-Christian. His effort to find some combination of religious beliefs that could satisfy his peculiar mind resulted in what many felt was a new mystical sect of which the principal members were himself, his wife, and Filosofov. In this thinking, the powerful moral sense so strong in Russian writers of the nineteenth century was lacking. Berdyaev said Merezhkovsky was "trying to find a synthesis of Christianity and paganism, and mistakenly identifies this with a synthesis of spirit and flesh. And the impression sometimes remains that he wants to synthesize Christ into anti-Christ."[8] Not that he was constant to one idea or theorem; his lecture at the Palazzo Vecchio in Florence, in 1933, was a tirade against the thoughts expressed in his own most widely read book *Leonardo da Vinci*.

Thanks to Mme Kuskova we have one incident sufficiently revealing of those times to be included here. It was after 1905, and the Stolypin reaction had already set in. One night there was a secret meeting for members of the Union of Liberation in the Merezhovsky apartment. All the servants had been sent away, when towards midnight the doorbell rang, Hippius sent Berdyaev to answer it. There stood a police sergeant with a group of his men. At that moment Berdyaev was seized with his tic. In astonishment the sergeant at first fell back but then brushed past Berdyaev and began bitterly to protest to Merezhkovsky at the insult he had received. The group surrounded him, explaining it had been an accident. After a long time the sergeant calmed down enough to announce that he had orders to arrest everyone in the house. There were about thirty, and the sergeant marched them two by two through the midnight streets to the precinct station. He led the way, and behind him marched Zinaida in her long, white, sheathlike robe, lorgnette to her eyes, with Berdyaev trotting along beside her, his hand under the elbow that held the lorgnette. On the way Zinaida asked the sergeant: "What are you going to do with us?" "I don't know," he replied. "I was told to arrest all present and bring them to the station."

Arrived at the police station, all members of the group were registered and then told to go, each to his own home. As they gathered in the street outside, Hippius suggested they sing a revolutionary song. Others in the group felt this might be unwise, and someone proposed they return to Merezhkovsky's and continue their meeting, which they did, breaking up at five in the morning.

Berdyaev was attracted to the Merezhkovsky orbit by the "atmosphere so opposite to the ordinary," a kind of "magic atmosphere." This contact, he said, was the most significant of his three years in the capital. The Merezhkovsky thesis was characteristic of the romantic attractions that fascinated the young intellectuals of the day, and this for a time included Berdyaev himself. He described it in his autobiography. The talk was of the relationship between Christianity and culture, but the center of attention was the flesh—the sexual. Berdyaev considered this important, but his philosophically trained mind pointed out the confusion in the ideas of romantic minds like Merezhkovsky's. He asserted, in opposition as usual, that the history of Christianity held not too little but too much of the flesh. Even the contrast between spirit and flesh seemed false. Berdyaev felt Merezhkovsky was preaching a "Nietzscheanized Christianity." In his "mystic materialism of sex," Berdyaev said, Merezhkovsky had launched into an aesthetic amoralism, against which he revolted "as complete indifference to human dignity." To Merezhkovsky, Berdyaev gave the impression of a man uncomfortably close to an orthodox religious position. Berdyaev said that perhaps in arguing with Merezhkovsky he appeared to be more orthodox than he really was, but the long-drawn-out argumentation actually helped bring him nearer to the Orthodox Church. A mysterious process was at work in him, he felt, that had not yet found expression in words. Within a year he was writing that the (then) religious crisis of the cultured elite indicated the necessity of a new approach to Christianity; neither the "old," ascetic, nonsocial religiosity with its lack of cultural appreciation nor the current nonreligious culture can satisfy. There must be a new and fuller realization that the religion of Christ is for this world as well as the next. A new mysticism and a new love that will give a higher unity to all mankind must overflow the earth.

If Berdyaev discussed all this with Merezhkovsky, it was at meetings in the presence of others. With Mme Merezhkovsky there were almost scandalously long tête-à-têtes devoted to the same themes. Nicolai Alexandrovitch met Hippius soon after his arrival in the capital in 1904, before his wife joined him, and for the next year the two were very close; they discussed everything, and spent so much time together, especially in the late hours of the night, that even St. Petersburg society talked of it. Hippius tells of one such conversation that ended in the wee, small hours with Berdyaev rushing out of the apartment and she calling down the stairs after him: "Do you want God to exist, or don't you?" For a time, beginning with the New Way, Berdyaev thought they could collaborate in the literary-cultural field. But after a period of intense communion and genuine friendship with her the greater part of their lives was spent in an atmosphere of hostility, until at last it was impossible even to meet. When he wrote this toward the close of his life, Berdyaev could see that part of the difficulty arose from their too-aggressive temperaments.

In temperament and otherwise Hippius was a most unusual woman. Even other women admitted that while not beautiful she was fatally attractive. Berdyaev said she was remarkable but tormenting, with a serpentlike coldness. Stepun also commented on her lack of spiritual warmth but "her indescribable charm" as well. Together with this charm she possessed a brilliant mind. When once in Heidelberg she was presented to the philosopher Rickert, the good German professor could not believe he would be able to discuss philosophy and mysticism with this "aggressively dressed" and highly perfumed person who looked as though she had stepped out of some French novel. There was a mixture of the sexes in her, and their constant conflict made her and those about her suffer. Byeli noted in her the disharmony between the thinker and the artist: "In her creative work there is mind, taste, culture, but the wisdom in her overpowers the artist, and the artist weakens the earnestness of religious appeal."[9] Small, slender, so well proportioned that she seemed taller than she was, she dominated a salon where most of the literati of the day were frequent guests. And she was a poetess of sorts, one of the first to use free verse. Together with her husband she was much interested in mystical, almost occult, religious ideas and was trying to bring other men into the small circle of those who shared them with her. This effort somehow never succeeded, and the "mystic three"—the two Merezhkovskys and Filosofov—carried on by themselves in what Berdyaev calls "a church of the Spirit in which would be revealed the mystery of the flesh." They were always talking in terms of "we" and tried in vain to get Berdyaev to join. But his character was incapable of accepting anything like the inner discipline that "we" implied. Byeli, too, was at one time almost persuaded to join. Byeli has given a vivid description of Hippius in her salon:

> A human-sized wasp, with a mass of reddish hair (they say it lets down to her heels) that half concealed a very small, somehow crooked, face, greenish eyes behind her lorgnette fixed on me, a shining gem hanging on her brow on a black cord, on her breastless breast a black cross dangling. She lay on the divan before the fireplace, legs crossed, the train of her white dress pulled tightly across her. She went to bed at dawn and rose only in the middle of the afternoon to spend her day on the sofa, chain-smoking with her long slender cigarette holder.[10]

The air was heavy with her favorite tuberose perfume. She was a greenhouse combination of the "advanced" poetess and a shy high school girl.

Byeli spoke of the "most significant, most refined discussions" as leaving their mark on his whole life. "Here at Merezhkovsky's," he said, "they truly created culture." In effect, the cream of St. Petersburg cultural leadership gathered here in Hippius' brick-red salon: Bulgakov, Sologub, Chulkoff, Ternavtseff, Minsky, Pertsoff, and of course Berdyaev. We are indebted to Byeli for a symbolist poet's description of Berdyeav at one of these meetings:

> Tall, swarthy, a curly mane almost to his shoulders, high forehead, rosy cheeks contrasting neatly with his black beard and trusting blue eyes—he might be demolishing the thrones of the Nebuchadnezzars with some daring word, or an ancient Chernigoff prince caracoling, not on a tabouret, but in the saddle, to do battle with the Tatars.
>
> A dark blue suit, setting off his face, a varicolored silk handkerchief like a bouquet in his breast pocket, white vest as always. He came in with a light resolute step, head thrown slightly back, broad shoulders up. With an almost imperceptible movement he shook back his hair, kissed her hand with a slightly mournful smile, and sat down on the pouf almost beneath the feet of Hippius. Eyes shining, he would try to keep silence, like a well-trained epicurean rather than a philosopher. In his effort to sit upright he squeezed the pouf, twitched his neck, straightened his tie—a St. Bernard in a dovecote.
>
> And all of a sudden a jerk to hold himself back—he has been touched (someone has questioned his viewpoint). With a squeak of the pouf, nervously crossing and uncrossing his legs as though to avoid falling into some yawning abyss, with his trembling hand he grasps the arm of Hippius' chair, and he's off: "In general— no—I affirm"—with piercing force, as though he were on his charger and the pencil in his hand were his lance—in an instant Hippius is not there—she has collapsed under the heels of this knight's attack—on a Tatar, not on a lady. . . .
>
> But there sits the lady, and the knight goes over his horse's head into the abyss. This is not what happens. Rather, a nervous reaction to that "I affirm": the head drops into his hands, which claw his lips before the bared teeth; rounded shoulders shaking, the enormous red tongue hangs out. With one hand he struggles to put it back in place and with the other he paws the air as though he were batting at a fly. And after that brief unpleasant moment, hand, mouth, tongue and head are all back in their proper places.
>
> And then "I affirm," and a Niagara of short, sharp, pointed

sentences, each one like an ultimatum: subject, predicate, period, his pencil-lance jabs the space between the pouf and that white deviltry. Neither age, nor sex, nor class could stop him. If God the Father was sitting there, if it were a paralytic or a puppy, he would stab forth his own viewpoint with the same conviction.

Now that he has had his say, he sits meditative, sad, all quiet attention, and his dark eyes shine, there is just the trace of a smile and he straightens his tie. There is something almost unbearable and at the same time childish about this pathos. He is still immovable in his own viewpoint.[11]

Berdyaev was not an easy opponent in an argument, at least for Byeli.

Berdyaev would splutter forth intolerable, meticulous truths, . . . but personally he was not narrow—he was even broad, up to the moment when he would break off: "Enough, that's clear." And that is the finish for his opponent, thinker or politician. Berdyaev the Crusader builds a wall of dogma, sets himself to guard the wall which separates him from the further course of the half-understood thought. He would narrow himself terribly; his uninhibited imagination would put forth the latest chimera, fetter it with dogma, and having done so he paid no attention to what was hidden beneath the hard shell of the dogma. . . . And he would declare a crusade against the chimera of his own creation, flashing out with a machine-gun fire of sentences, prancing on his chair, leading a flock of worshipful ladies in an attack sometimes only on the fourth dimension. . . . He always seemed to me a subjectivist from the effect of dogmatic Orthodoxy or on the contrary, an orthodox dogmatician of the world of illusion.

In contrast with this, Byedi painted another picture of Berdyaev at home. They lived in the building where the office of *Life's Questions* was lodged, and here, as anywhere they happened to live, there were many guests.

At home he would be so quiet and distrait, hospitably but somewhat sadly welcoming his guests. He would appear from his study to enthrone himself in his mahogany armchair. He has just finished scratching out a clever article which will be published tomorrow demolishing Merezhkovsky's position. Then after this literary battle, he has his supper, silent, weary, leaving to his wife and her sister the monopoly of ideas, which he, cigar in mouth, quietly takes in.[12]

As with other of Hippius' intimate friendships—Byeli for example —this with Berdyaev was soon clouded by disagreements and an eventual break that never healed. Extracts from Berdyaev's letters of this period trace both the widening rift between him and the Merezhkovskys and the swift development of his own spiritual life. The Merezhkovskys moved to Paris toward the end of 1905 and lived there for nearly three years. Early in 1906, we find Berdyaev writing Merezhkovsky:

> I desire union with you and value you highly, but I do not see
> that you know much more than I, how to react to the world
> around us. . . . I can say that I have never felt the tragic horror
> of empiric existence as now, and in many ways I can no longer
> have such a light-minded attitude, as before. Everything in life
> seems much more serious and significant. The life of every being
> is not a trifle—it is full of religious importance. The blood of
> all of us is poisoned with nihilism. We take a nihilist attitude
> toward too much in life, and toward too many living beings. I
> can no longer bear nihilistic feelings and am conscious of all the
> difficulty of transition from nihilist emptiness to some new, posi-
> tive content. A mystical consciousness of personality has always
> been the basic motive of my life and perhaps it is here that we
> disagree. I . . . hope that in winter I can come abroad. Then
> we shall talk heart to heart about everything.

In the summer of 1907, Berdyaev left St. Petersburg to live in the country. From Lubotin, the village where his mother-in-law had her estate, he writes Hippius that he cannot go along with the new religious society, and his attitude toward things of the spirit is no longer that of the mode prevailing among the intelligentsia of the capital:

> I have recently re-thought and re-felt many things, I have been
> living a very serious inner life free from the pressure of Petersburg
> styles, and I do not know yet, in what degree this harmonizes
> with what you have been experiencing and gaining. I now look
> at religion much more seriously and severely, and it seems to me
> that none of us has the power, and none of us is ready for the
> role either of religious preacher or creator of a religious move-

ment in the world: none of us yet has sufficient gifts of the Holy
Spirit . . . we do not give the impression of messengers from
heaven. . . . I fear that you are threatened with . . . temptation to play politics in religion, and politics leads to love of power,
and finally to falsehood. You think too much of religious organization, of an artificial religious society (although it be very intimate at the beginning) and perhaps you do not think enough
about a religious change in men's hearts. . . .

Consideration of the sect of the "mystic three" continued in another letter shortly after. All at once Berdyaev talked of faith in God:

Reading your letter, it seems that in St. Petersburg there is not
a single person with whom it is worthwhile having contact or conversation. . . . On what do you base your belief in the future:
where will you find your chosen ones? If I believed only in myself and two or three of my own circle, I would cease to believe
altogether. I would lose faith in God and in the meaning of the
world's life. The greatest and most terrible temptation is the assertion and deification of some kind of "we," some sort of human center through which everything should pass, and from
which everything should receive sanction. . . . The beginning
of religion is when one ceases to consider oneself as especially
important—the refusal of self-assertion is denial of self. . . .
Hatred of religious groupings and sectarianism is very strong in
me now. I would wish for something greater in every scale: man
and God, man and the church, man and the universe, man and
Russia. Universality should be our instinct and this I do not find.
I see my own chief task in this: to lead the new religious consciousness out of sectarianism—that we should permeate the
world and the world should permeate us. In the past I experienced a very great disillusionment in the decadent-literary
sphere. . . . Development is organic process, and chipping off
(into groups) is opposed to genuine development and revelation.
Without connection with millennial roots we cannot expect new
revelations.

This thought of the need for contact with the past, for some sort of
apostolic succession of ideas, is more clearly expressed in a letter to
Filosofov at about the same time:

I am greatly concerned about the organic connection with the
holiness of the old church. . . . It is becoming clearer to me that

there cannot be some kind of special and new religion of the Holy Spirit. The religion of the Holy Trinity will be only the final fulfillment of the commandment of Christ, i.e. the appearance of the Holy Spirit.

Perhaps the influence of Bulgakov now began making itself felt. At all events here was Berdyaev already longing for life in the church as represented in the sacraments. Again the man's essential modesty found expression:

I still fear that with your intimate pseudo-monasticism you are breaking the chain of history, its mystic organic quality. The new church will not appear without some action on the part of the old church. The third commandment cannot be without a successive relation to the second. "*Sobornost*"[13] is not merely a conscious effort, say of you three, to live together, think together, take communion together (not in the church)—there is contact with the world-spirit and the world-reason. . . . One question troubles me and makes me unhappy: the question of sacraments in the church, without which there is no true religious life. . . . The sacraments are the very essence of life; the joy of religious being. . . . Without the sacraments I could not live long. I thirst for the religious cult and at times I would like to enter some church, be openly and organically joined with the life of thousands of years. I would not want to set up a small sect, which oppresses personality and fails to attain universality. . . . For me religious life must above all be unselfish—it must have no power-loving plans. . . . The supreme uplift in religious life is a matter of contemplation and feeling, rather than of voluntarism. "Thy will be done." . . . I still feel that true transfiguration is bound up not only with the strong union of a few people in a society, but also with the discovery of new paths into the world, into nature, into man, to every human face in which by love we may see the idea of God beneath its repulsive covering crust. Are you searching for these ways? By inner experience I have learned that first of all one must destroy in oneself all self-esteem, all self-exaltation. Only then can selfless love for the world begin.

A few lines from the next letter show how Berdyaev's thought was already taking not merely a religious but a theological turn:

Both your and my situations are difficult and tormenting, and
I do not know where our tendencies will lead. I am profoundly
convinced of the truth of my faith, but am not so convinced of
my significance. The desire for a new life, for salvation, increases
with every day, but it appears that everything must be based on
self-denial. If there is no love in the heart,—and there is so little
love,—the heart is so lacking in love. . . .

One further letter, written the same year (1907), heralded his break
with past attitudes and the dawn of a faith that throughout the remainder of Berdyaev's life never doubted Christ:

Our relations now will not at all be what they were formerly. I
now stand on quite another ground, and have something quite
other in my heart. The question about you is a vital and a painful
question. If once I was not with you because I did not know
whether or not I was with Christ, and you did not know whether
or not I would be against Him, now I will not be with you but
rather against you, if I feel that you are against Christ, but I do
not doubt Him and never will. I doubted your nearness to Christ
and I suffer from this doubt. And still I cherish the, for me, precious hope that we will be together.

When they met in Paris at the beginning of 1907, there was an attempt at a reconciliation of their ideas. Hippius says "he was no longer
hesitating between the ideal of the Madonna and the ideal of Sodom"
but had not yet entered the church. For a time the two met every day
at one home or the other, but the more they talked (Hippius says
Berdyaev was inclined to polemics, even where they were not appropriate) the further apart they found themselves. A meeting of ideas
was evidently impossible, and they were never "together" again. The
Merezhkovskys were resident in Paris from the time Berdyaev arrived
in 1923, and they soon made another effort at understanding, but it
failed, and they never met thereafter.

# 8

## "SUB SPECIE AETERNITATIS"

In addition to Berdyaev's letters to Hippius, we have other comments of his on his significant spiritual evolution at this time (1906-7). It was brought about partly, he wrote, by his reaction against the prevailing atmosphere of the intellectual circle in which he moved in the capital. Out of this group, however, certain more spiritual figures began to emerge in the transition toward religious realism and religious faith among them Bulgakov, Frank, and the young Kartasheff. Berdyaev shared with them the "great hope that a continuation of revelation was possible in Christianity, a new outpouring of the Holy Spirit." He could not accept the pagan, magical elements in Christianity that many of the group were emphasizing, but with Bulgakov and Frank took the more spiritual way. They were already professed Christians and helped him to see that Christianity did not weaken his original social concern: "I became a Christian, not because I ceased to believe in man, his dignity and higher calling, his creative freedom, but because I was seeking a deeper and surer basis for this faith." There was one moment, one summer evening in the country, when he was walking in the dusk before a gathering storm and all at once "light blazed out in his soul." He insisted it was not what is usually known as conversion, for he had not been an atheist or agnostic when it happened and the inner contradictions troubling him did not vanish with that moment. But at least the summer of 1907 saw him well forward in his definitely Christian experience. He began reading the church fathers—Origen, Justin the Philosopher, Maxim the Confessor—and felt these works were of immortal significance in the religious history of the world. He felt himself more at home with the Greek fathers than with the scholastics. Again Dostoievsky captured his thought. He gave a public lecture on the "Legend of the Grand Inquisitor," saying that the Christ he had accepted was the Christ of the Legend, the Christ of the free spirit. Always thereafter, he added, any denial of the limitless freedom

99

of the spirit would have been a denial of Christ himself, an acceptance of the temptation of the Grand Inquisitor.

There are a few phrases, scattered through Berdyaev's chapter in the autobiography entitled "Turning to Christianity," that sum up his position as a Christian: "I confess a spiritual religion, I am a free Christian, who has not broken away from the church." Although he had never left the church, he felt at this point little appreciation of its traditional and liturgical riches. "I could accept religious history and religious tradition only as signs of something else which was taking place in the depths, as relative, instead of absolute." It was only later, in Moscow, that he began to feel the beauty of the ancient churches and the rich Orthodox services conducted in them. He came into this new appreciation almost like a child—but of course with quite a different development and state of mind. He contrasted his with the experience of Bulgakov, whose father and grandfather had been priests and whose entire childhood life was permeated by church forms and church tradition. But Bulgakov was a great stay for him in this period. As far as we know, Bulgakov had no idea yet of entering the priesthood, but his return to the normal life within the Orthodox Church helped show the way to Berdyaev. Another helpful friend of this period was Anton Kartasheff, one of the few men with whom he could discuss such matters. In a letter, Berdyaev wrote: "I am almost the only writer to defend the religious idea. Rozanoff is fading; Merezhkovsky no longer appears in public. . . . I find consolation with Kartasheff, who is nearest of all to me. We agree together in our thirst for religious gnosis."

His attitude was partially reflected in the life of Russia's intellectuals. By the end of 1906, the tastes of the "advanced" literati began to change. The political leadership had separated from the spiritual leadership, the latter retiring almost completely from civic life. In Moscow, a Religious-Philosophical Society had been organized. Several of the St. Petersburg group suggested a similar effort there. Berdyaev and Hippius both said the initiative was Berdyaev's; other sources consider Bulgakov and Kartasheff to have been the leaders, but at all events Berdyaev quickly joined. He saw he could not carry his own ideas against the Merezhkovskys, and the new group welcomed him. They recognized his talent but evidently did not expect new leadership. Berdyaev opened the Society with a lecture on "Christ and the World," a strong attack on Rozanoff's recent article "Of the Sweetest Jesus

and the Bitter Fruits of the World." Berdyaev said Rozanoff thought
not in logical but in physiological terms. The vivid discussion that followed may be imagined. It set the tone for the Society's further programs. Discussions often became disputes, albeit "on a high level"—
often "going into great mental refinement." Moscow circles claimed the
"refinement" often went too far. Stepun speaks for Moscow when he
claims that, in St. Petersburg, "religious and artistic problems were more
immediately and with more complexity interlaced with political utopias
and social dreams."[1] In good Russian style, these speakers went to
the bottom of problems. Berdyaev compared their approach to that of
French intellectuals at one of the famous "decades" of Pontigny. The
topic was "loneliness." They talked of the loneliness of Petrarch or
Rousseau or Nietzsche, but not about loneliness as a basic, "final
mystery in life." Berdyaev recalled the incident in Belinsky's life when,
after an all-night discussion, the great man protested: "We really should
not break up yet, we still haven't settled the problem of God."

The problem of God was the background of the activities of the St.
Petersburg Religious-Philosophical Society.[2] Here two tendencies began to appear. Berdyaev noted them in a letter: "How little has yet
been done to put the problem, to clear up the differences of opinion
between those who want to renew and reform the old church, and
those who seek a new revelation." The meetings continued for over a
year with the participation of "men of the highest level of intellectual
culture Russia ever saw." Whether Berdyaev's departure to spend the
winter of 1907-8 in Paris was a contributory cause to their decline is
not clear, but about a year later Hippius is writing: "In Petersburg we
found an officially permitted Religious-Philosophical Society. It was
contrived by Berdyaev, then he threw it over. Now it was barely stag-
gering along."[3] In summing up the values of the Society, Berdyaev
wrote that results were disappointing. There were no new revelations;
neither were there any church reforms—but it was of undoubted spiritual and cultural influence.

One notable phenomenon of this period of youthful renaissance was
the appearance of an entire gamut of new journals, initiated and op-
erated by individuals or groups to present their various lines of interest.
Diaghlieff's *World of Art* was "the first aesthetic journal, in the best
sense of that word, in Russia." There were *The Journal for Everyone,
Russian Thought*—in which Berdyaev published a number of articles
—and another, called the *New Way*, having the remarkable record of

nearly three years of existence when Berdyaev arrived in St. Petersburg. Its record was notable because of difficulties encountered in publishing any magazine under the tsarist regime—before 1905, at least. The essential basis was a small group of persons—small enough to avoid too great differences of opinion—with a more or less clear idea. How varied these ideas were may be gathered from journal titles of the period: *Torches, The Leader of the Muses, Quiet Thoughts, The Logos, The Way, The Demons, Sophia, Works and Days*. It might be any kind of an idea, although of course it could not be political. The second essential was permission to publish. This had to be obtained, often after prolonged and painful discussion, from the competent ministries. Next came the problem of funds. This meant finding a wealthy patron willing to spend money with hope not of profit but possibly of some personal credit—an "angel," in theatrical parlance. Although the intelligentsia, like Berdyaev, always seemed to have funds sufficient for themselves—their extensive travels, their comfortable scale of living—it seems never to have occurred to any of them that one might invest in a journal. There were practically no authors' honoraria; payment was made only to those actually in need. In this sense the initiating group might be said to contribute materially to the cause. The editorial offices were often in the apartment of the owner or in a building where some of its chief collaborators or personnel lived.

Those were material difficulties; on the nonmaterial side they were no less formidable. A responsible editor must be found. He was often known as the "sitting editor"—if anyone had to sit in jail for some alleged fault of the paper, it was he. And of course this man must be sufficiently in agreement with the purpose of the periodical to be willing to sign the copy and thus assume responsibility before the law. He had to pass all his copy through two censorships, the civil and the ecclesiastical. What the police censor passed might be cut by monks of the Alexander Nevsky Monastery. Added to this were the constant and inevitable differences of opinion of a generation of individualists that not only possessed no trace of experience at teamwork but not even the idea itself. No better example of such a periodical's troubled history could be found than that of the *New Way*, with which Berdyaev was to have his first journalistic responsibilities.

The "group with the idea" of the *New Way* centered around the Merezhkovskys. The journal was the outgrowth of a distinct novelty in the intellectual life of the empire at the turn of the century. A group had obtained qualified permission to conduct a series of "Religious-Philosophical Assemblies" designed to bring representatives of the liberal intelligentsia and the Orthodox Church together for free discussion of spiritual problems. These were two separate worlds, with almost no contact between them. The meetings continued for more than a year, attracting great public attention despite strict attendance limitations. They were chaired by the young Bishop Serge. The central theme invariably dealt with the intelligentsia and the church. Someone called these meetings "the only refuge for free speech in the empire." They eventually proved too free for the reactionary Pobiedonostseff, *Oberprokuror* of the Holy Synod, and were forbidden early in 1903. But the magazine set up by the group initiating the "Assemblies" was permitted to continue. Its previous numbers had carried full reports of the Assembly meetings, together with material fairly well dominated by the Merezhkovskys and Filosofov. A crisis arose within the responsible group, however. Pertsoff, the "angel" in this case, lost interest in the magazine and withdrew. Subject to sharp criticism in the press, the journal began to lose subscribers. One day George Chulkoff, poet-exile in Siberia, just returned to the capital, in a conversation with Merezhkovsky joined in the general chorus of fault-finding—whereupon Merezhkovsky suddenly offered him the job of secretary (manager), with the privilege of selecting the magazine's contents. It was typical of the Merezhkovskys that immediately after having turned the magazine over to this completely new collaborator they went on a long tour abroad. Upon their return Chulkoff met them with a plan for reviving the *New Way* by bringing into the editorial group some of the "philosopher-idealists" who were attracting public interest. The proposal was made and the "idealists" accepted. Berdyaev and Bulgakov, together with N. O. Lossky and S. L. Frank were among the new partners. The *New Way* published three numbers under the new editorial arrangement. But it soon became evident that the two groups were incompatible. A moment came when Chulkoff went over to the "idealists," and it was decided to indicate the change of policy by stopping the *"New Way"* and carrying on under another name.

Thus *Life's Questions* came into being, starting with the January, 1905, number under the direction of Berdyaev and Bulgakov, installed in spacious new premises. The official editor was N. O. Lossky. The "angel" this time was D. E. Zhukovsky, a close friend of Berdyaev. For

a few months the new journal flourished. It was no longer the mouth-
piece of one small group but "the meeting place of all new tendencies"
in thought. Actually, this was the first experiment in Russian history to
combine political agitation with metaphysics. Berdyaev and Bulgakov
published their articles. There were the strange, esoteric "poets" like
Andre Byeli, Alexis Remizoff, and Alexander Blok, politicians like Peter
Struve and Prince Eugene Trubetskoy, and others with still more radical
views. Boris Zaitseff, at present the dean of Russian writers, joined their
ranks after Lenin and Lunacharsky had put him out of their communist
organ *Pravda* because he was "too mystic." The task of bringing some
sort of harmony into this variegated group was made difficult by the
tragic period in which the journal began. The "Bloody Sunday" of
January 9, 1905, had touched off a wave of reaction expressed in increased police surveillance and a merciless censorship. To circumvent
this and contrive to print articles with the liberal content the editors
desired was no simple matter. It was an art, however, well practiced by
Russian liberals[4] of all periods, even on occasion in Soviet Russia today,
and Berdyaev and Bulgakov were adepts. Because their readers, also,
were well trained in reading between the lines, the widest reading public quickly comprehended the message. In that revolutionary year, the
editorial offices on Seventh Exaltation Street must have been a
bewildering place. Remizoff, liberated from Vologda about a year after
Berdyaev, went first to Kiev because he was forbidden residence in St.
Petersburg. He says Berdyaev met him like an old friend and inquired
how he might help him. As a result, Remizoff, now enabled by the
amnesty to return to the capital, was installed as "secretary"—which
meant office manager. Putting into such a position a man whose sole
interest and experience in life was word painting, and a man then half-
blind, is a comment on the practical sense of Berdyaev and Bulgakov.
Its results on the office organization may well be imagined. Remizoff
himself complained that it tied him to the office all day and gave him
no time for his writing. His first long article, the one he reworked
twenty times in Vologda, was published in *Life's Questions* on Berdyaev's insistence—other editors had insisted they could not understand
a word of it. There seemed always to be a milling crowd in the place.
Each new political event in a year filled with sensational happenings
brought chaos into the office: a subdued roar of voices, demands for
published protests, people signing petitions or "declarations." Alexander
Blok tells of his first visit to the offices. Climbing the stairs, he heard

someone shouting behind a door: "You are a mystical fighter against God." He knew this must be the voice of *Life's Questions*. Entering, he found Bulgakov engaged in a friendly dispute with the journal's backer Zhukovsky. The two disputants went off somewhere; the others in the room went on drinking tea. Hospitality there was of the essence. Boris Zaitseff and his wife, who lived in Moscow, always stayed in some of the rooms at the "big house" occupied by *Life's Questions* when visiting the capital.

*Life's Questions* was bound to be short-lived. Its history coincided almost exactly with that of the stormy year 1905. It had no central cohesive idea, and bit by bit it fell apart. First the Merezhkovskys quarreled with the new policies and withdrew. Others of the original multicolored contributors' group were eased out by Berdyaev and Bulgakov. Even those who continued to write for the journal were still searchers themselves and had not yet found a stable basis for their thinking. Added to this were difficulties of administration. Bulgakov still lived in Kiev and could come to Petersburg only occasionally. By his very temperament Berdyaev was unable to interest himself in anything like business administration. Remizoff was willing but hopelessly incompetent, and after a few months even Zhukovsky began to diminish his material support. Further, the waves of unrest and government repression tended to smother all creative work. Some of the contributors of *Life's Questions* fled abroad, others no longer ventured to express their ideas in writing, and the censorship became more intolerant than ever. Eventually funds ran out completely and the journal ceased publication.

What concerns us particularly in *Life's Questions* is its almost step-by-step revelation of Berdyaev's spiritual evolution. Writing of it a few years later, Shestov could say:

On the pages of *Life's Questions* there is unrolled the history of Berdyaev's conversion from a metaphysician to a believing Christian, a conversion which surprises us particularly by its impetuosity. Even for Berdyaev, it is too swift. He has become a Christian before he learned properly to pronounce all the words in the Creed. Evidently this metamorphosis has occurred on the threshold of consciousness. In his article "On a New Religious Consciousness," where for the first time he begins to speak of Christ, of God, and the like, he hesitates, stutters . . . in a word shows all the signs of one who has dropped into a strange and unknown region, where he has to move by guesswork.[5]

Despite the fact that Shestov, a believing Jew, may have missed some of the essentials of Christianity, his remarks here are a fairly accurate summary of Berdyaev's position at the time. What Shestov said about *Life's Questions* is equally true of Berdyaev's books. Like a series of photographs of a moving object, each reveals a position somewhat advanced over the one before it.

This is true of *Sub Specie Æternitatis*, which appeared in 1907. Neither of Berdyaev's two previous books had attracted a wide public, and this one made no large splash either—too many other voices were filling the air. One reason it made no greater impression was because the book is a reprint of twenty-three essays that had already appeared in various journals between 1900 and 1906. It is dedicated to "Li," Berdyaev's pet name for his wife Lydia, and as with most of Berdyaev's works it represents a personal approach to the problems involved. The opening chapter, "in place of an introduction," is entitled "About Realism." Here Berdyaev explains that in spite of the "apparent contradictions" among the articles, there is a real, inner unity and order in (his) thinking . . ." one desire, to decipher the meaning of life—life of the person and of the world." The book showed his gradual liberation from such powerful movements as marxism, kantianism, nietzscheanism, through idealism.[6] But, Berdyaev wrote, he could not stop with idealism; there was nothing creative in it. He went farther, "from idealistic absolutism to mystic realism." This meant religion. "All problems of being . . . develop into problems of religion, even social problems; . . . I cannot be a nihilist, cannot trade mysticism for mystification . . . hence I must build my . . . ideal for society on real-mystical, i. e., religious foundations."[7]

Berdyaev explains his spiritual movement away from marxism in terms that some otherwise intelligent thinkers have not yet discovered today, half a century later. "The dialectic theory of the necessity of social catastrophe is not only unscientific, logically inept, conflicting with the facts of life, but it is profoundly anti-idealistic"—this within a few years after marxism had been hailed by the mass of Russian liberals as the all-sufficient, scientific answer to every problem! Berdyaev went further; there was no possible connection, he insisted, between material operations like forms of production and exchange, and ideology, whether this be "the discovery of a scientific law . . . or artistic creativity."[8]

"You can talk of dialectic idealism, but not of dialectic materialism. . . . We must choose: either the historic process is a dialectic process, the self-revelation of ideas, and then there is within it a pitiless inner logic, or it is a materialistic process, and there is no logic in it, no reasonableness, only chaos."[9] Engels' theory of knowledge "is beneath all criticism, does not even make a serious attempt to put a base under dialectic materialism."[10]

Not only marxist materialism was to be cast aside, but positivism as well: "Positivism is incapable of reaching the height where it recognizes that freedom is above happiness and satisfaction, above the firm supports of life, perhaps above life itself . . . that freedom is God, that God is absolute freedom." Thus "freedom is equally a religious-metaphysical and a social-political idea,"[11] and the philosophy of the future will be a philosophy of liberation. It was time to cast aside such "evolutionary superstition, for ideology comes not by automatic evolutionary development, but by spiritual effort: ideology is the revelation of spiritual values that are of eternal significance, and are independent of any sort of evolution."

Materialism and positivism having been thus demolished, the book proceeds to Berdyaev's own thought of a new social order, the realization of which was to be considered quite apart from the question of political revolutions—which are facts occasionally encountered in history but having nothing to do with social development. The new society, like the new man, must come through an application of spiritual, not material, values. It will come, not as "some dialectic cataclysm, but as the appearance in world history of a new, great idea—the incarnation of all-human progress."[12] This must come out of a knowledge of eternal truth, truth that is "not human intellect, but super-human organism. And reasonable knowledge is the self-knowledge of Divinity, with which we commune in the intuitive-mystic act of knowing."[13] In contrast to the positivists and even the abstract idealists, the group for whom Berdyaev spoke "wants to unite ourselves with the eternally-existing God, to continue the millennial work of His creation."[14] In reply to the ancient argument that in such parlous times men should not be concerned with abstractions like religion, Berdyaev first asked what sort of religion? For him "religion must be concise, sensible, connected with living history, obliging us to living political action. I have no use for a religion which has no relation to all the fullness of life, to the process of history, to the future of human society."[15] To "scientists" who could not believe in God, Berdyaev offered a Christian apologetic: "No science can prove that miracles are impossible in the world, that Christ did not rise from the dead, that the Divine nature does not reveal itself in mystic experience . . . all this is simply outside science." In his own thought he had left all the old positions behind, and "from the false 'sobornost' of the marxists, from decadent-romantic individualism, I move toward the 'sobornost' of mystic neo-Christianity." Note the word "toward." This was 1906; Berdyaev could not yet say he stood on definitely Christian ground. Within a few months he had advanced still farther and could be writing to Hippius as chronicled in the previous chapter.

It is usually assumed that because Berdyaev had no church experience or religious contacts in his youth, his eventual Christian faith was developed out of his thought evolution alone. Some lines in an article written in Paris (Put No. 49)[16] give a different story: "Dostoievsky and Tolstoi had a special significance in my inner life. The ingrafting I received from them preceded the influence of German idealism and marxism." If this be true, it must be remarked that the "ingrafted" ideals remained dormant a long time before they began to grow.

Although Sub Specie Æternitatis did not create a wide sensation, some sharp criticism was voiced against it. Typical of the times was Shestov's review in Torches entitled "Praise of Stupidity": "We both agree in one thing, we both hate any kind of 'ratio' and over against it we set, Berdyaev his Great Reason, I, Stupidity. I write it with a capital as Berdyaev does his Great Reason." The reviewer proceeded to examine what Berdyaev "can do and say in praise of Stupidity." First the writer (Berdyaev) attacks good sense: ". . . he abuses and tramples on it—no other of our authors can take such a superior, scornful tone . . . and poor good sense . . . trembles, loses the thread, and does not know what to say in her own justification."[17] But here Berdyaev's "strange duality" began to be felt, and "the article which began so wonderfully, closes with a project of agreement between Stupidity and good sense, a bargain where all the profit is in favor of the latter. . . . Berdyaev softens and restores to good sense . . . at least part of its historically-recognized rights."[18] "What other writer," asked Shestov, "has the courage so openly to contradict the laws of logic? . . . Berdyaev says, 'it may be that the laws of logic which hold us in a vise are only an illness of being, a defect in being itself'—why 'may be'? better outright dogma: 'logical laws are only a disease of being,' and hence the conclusion: since logic is not obligatory for us, it would seem that the laws of nature both exist and do not exist, since miracles are not only possible but have even occurred . . . before the eyes of men."[19] Even then the basic question remained: ". . . where is the guarantee that what we have declared holy is holy also before the face of eternity?"[20]

Despite this gentle ridicule, Shestov and Berdyaev remained friends. Among Berdyaev's other friends of this St. Petersburg period was the Bishop Serge who had played a significant role in the short-lived Religious-Philosophical Assembly. Berdyaev was also on friendly terms with Blok and Byeli, the two leading symbolist poets, since despite the aggressive individualism, the "very great freedom of creativity" of these literati, "they did not wish to remain in this freedom but continued their searching for some connecting ties, some sort of organic culture."[21]

And all of this against a background of trouble in the country such as had scarcely been known since the "Troubled Times" of an earlier century. The newspapers carried a daily statistic on cholera in St. Petersburg: "Thirty new cases, thirty-six deaths, twenty-two recovered." There were detailed accounts of Jewish pogroms—daily lists of death sentences carried out in various parts of the empire. The *Evening Moscow*, on January 3, 1907, reported the execution of three men in Libau who had stolen fifteen hundred and sixty rubles and of another who had robbed a cabman. In preparation for the trans-Siberian journey of a well-known general, this poster was placed in all railway stations: "In case of any attempt on the life of General Rennenkampf or of those accompanying him, or of those responsible for his safety, all those held in jails as hostages will be immediately executed."

That summer, 1907, Berdyaev spent in the country. He was physically tired after the broad living of the capital and mentally weary and disillusioned by the "decadent" tendencies that seemed to be getting the upper hand. Eugenie says Berdyaev felt the St. Petersburg intelligentsia were busy with unimportant gossip while Rome was burning. This feeling is clearly indicated in his letters to Hippius quoted in the previous chapter. Besides, he seemed suddenly to have realized how his own thought had become centered on the purely academic, leaving aside the high social ideals with which he had arrived less than three years earlier. Berdyaev thought it a weakness on his part—a bit of the egoism of a cultured elite. While he had made the acquaintance of "many interesting people," he wrote, he began to feel the predominance of "an unhealthy, mystical sentimentality" that Russia had not known before. He had had enough of what he called "double-thinking." He never went back to St. Petersburg. That autumn he and Lydia left for Paris where they spent the winter, and when they returned to Russia it was to make their home in Moscow. His St. Petersburg friends felt it was almost desertion to the enemy. There was a sharp rivalry between the intellectual circles of the two cities. Hippius spoke of the poor taste of the Moscow editors of a journal, who refused a poem by Blok, and when Blok accepted the editorship of *The Golden Fleece*, Moscow's leading literary journal, Byeli was furious: "The Petersburgers are getting their own organ in Moscow?"[22] But it was like Berdyaev not to be concerned about what others thought of him. He had already broken with several of the groups with which he had been connected.

There has been considerable speculation as to why Berdyaev left St. Petersburg so suddenly and so finally. Was there some other more drastic break in relationships than those he mentioned himself, or was it just an accumulation of antitheses? Berdyaev hinted that his incapacity to fuse completely with any one group had annoyed many people, and that he had been made to feel this strongly. Kartasheff thinks it was simply a matter of Berdyaev having learned all he could in the capital and now wishing to experience another milieu. He had been in more or less intimate contact with "the totalitarian revolutionary thought of the Social Democrats, the new religious consciousness of the Merezhkovskys, the gnostic sectarianism of the anthroposophists, the Dionysian element spread all around,"[23] and although none of them had been able to capture him and compel him to renounce his spiritual freedom or his personal conscience, he had "known them from the inside" and thereby had enriched his own capacities. This was achieved partly by the very fact of his opposition to some of these movements, Berdyaev said, especially with regard to his spiritual evolution. The religious process going on within him had reached an advanced stage, and argumentation with the Merezhkovskys "greatly promoted my turning to the Orthodox Church."[24] His horizons were widened and his emotional life enriched by the three years in St. Petersburg. It had been a sort of broad postgraduate course, and Berdyaev himself was putting an end to it. A new chapter was to open with his relocation in Moscow.

# 9

## "THE PILLAR AND BULWARK OF THE TRUTH"

But before Moscow came an interlude in Paris. Eugenie Rapp and her husband had been living there while Eugenie worked at her sculpture. The Merezhkovskys also had been in Paris for a long period, so long says Berdyaev that they were out of touch with events at home and took an attitude toward them "from this beautiful distance"—which he found unacceptable. "The whole winter passed in stormy discussions" with them. Berdyaev was thinking along lines of spiritual renewal in the church, "in the sphere of prophecy," while the Merezhkovskys were still pursuing their idea of new sacraments in their own small group. Hippius recalled it thus: In January, 1908, "N. Berdyaev arrived from St. Petersburg, the same former marxist with whom I had spent so many late evenings in discussion . . . one of the 'idealists' to whom we had turned over the *New Way*."[1] She took pleasure in noting that while the *New Way* had lasted three years, its successor under Berdyaev's editorship, *Life's Questions*, survived only a few months; idealism was only a stage on the way to religion—in fact "only in marxism or in the church, could be joined such different temperaments as Berdyaev and Bulgakov." Hippius also came to know Lydia Yudifovna but could not understand the latter's "too-gloomy mood."

In April the Merezhkovskys returned to St. Petersburg after nearly three years abroad. About that time the Berdyaevs also returned to Russia but now established their home in Moscow. Berdyaev's time abroad was not entirely devoted to argumentation with the Merezhkovskys. He was interested in spiritual and social movements in France, especially the "modernist" trend just starting in the Roman Catholic Church. And in the spring before they went back to Russia the Berdyaevs, accompanied by Eugenie, made a trip to Rome. They installed themselves in a German pension and "did" the city. Berdyaev was untiring; he kept the two ladies sightseeing each day until, by nightfall, they were too weary to do anything but drop into their beds. Berdyaev "always had a book to read to rest his mind" and was particularly interested in early Christian art and history—the catacombs and the older churches. He was beginning to appreciate the "poetry of life of the Middle Ages and of the Renaissance," in contrast to the "unbelievable prose" Leontieff had found in European democracy.

The Moscow that Nicolai Alexandrovitch found was about halfway between the 1905 revolution and the great war. Much of the old order had been shaken by the revolution, but in a sense nothing had broken. Some of the intellectual energy that had been expended in struggle against the government had now turned to industry, agriculture, and business, and there was a marked rise in economic levels all across the empire, in cities and villages alike. As Tyrkova-Williams remarks, even the peasants were able to eat jam on their bread, not alone on one saint's day a year but every Sunday. In the cities, new fortunes made in industry enabled the rise of wealthy patrons of the arts without whose aid the cultural renaissance could scarcely have come to pass. The old aristocratic families carried on as usual in their great town houses and country estates, and Berdyaev found himself accepted socially as belonging to this circle. After the fierce revolt of his youth against all tradition he was now nearing forty, and a natural tendency toward more conservatism had set in. He came less to depend solely on his own intuition and undertook to consider the thoughts, even the theories, of others. The "synthetic" attitude of the group around Prince Trubetskoy and the V. Solovieff Society, where he was received as an equal, appeared more acceptable than it could have a decade earlier. But despite surface appearances, much of the old Russia had received a death blow to which the 1917 revolution merely added its coup de grâce. The poetry and philosophy of these years is full of a sense of decay and impending catastrophe. Byeli said the upper class was like an old lady alone in an old-style house and an old-style dress, solemnly proceeding with the antique ritual of morning coffee: "And so you, old Russia, proud and stagnate in your ancient greatness, every day, every hour in thousands of offices, palaces and great estates, are carrying out the old rituals . . . but look about you, and you will see the abyss beneath your feet."[2]

This consciousness of standing on the brink of an abyss but enjoying the sense of dizziness conditioned much of the intellectual life of Moscow, at Berdyaev's arrival. The great houses were open, hospitality was unlimited (one winter the whole Berdyaev family spent as guests in a Moscow friend's home while the plumbing in their own house was being repaired), and outwardly the life of the upper classes moved on as before. Nicolai Alexandrovitch became interested in the old city, where every paving stone was a bit of history, and in the old traditions, cultural and religious, of the Moscow patriarchal families like the Trubetskoys—especially the religious traditions. It was a new approach to the problems of religion, and Berdyaev made an effort to "restore the broken tradition" in his own life—although "acquire" would be a better word in view of his unreligious childhood and education; he said the very idea of tradition was alien. He began with new interest to read Solovieff, the slavophiles, and Khomiakoff. His small book on Khomiakoff was begun during the first year in Moscow.

Bulgakov, already living in Moscow, helped in this effort by bringing Berdyaev into contact with a group of religious thinkers around M. A. Novoselov, in whose "monastic" quarters regular meetings were held. This circle differed from the Moscow religious-philosophical groups in that its members were men like Bulgakov, already returned to the Orthodox Church, or faithful Christians who had never left it. They were rooted in the Orthodox traditions, regularly attended divine service, and made pilgrimages to the monasteries. Some had placed themselves under the guidance of an "elder," that very special institution in the monasteries of Russia immortalized by Dostoievsky in the figure of the *starets* (elder) Zosima. With this traditionalism, however, went a certain freedom of thought and an attitude of independence toward the Orthodox hierarchy. While he could not accept all their attitudes, "conservative with a strong monastic-ascetic leaning," Berdyaev had deep respect for their sincerity and piety. He sincerely wished to penetrate deeper into Orthodoxy. Once, urged by Bulgakov, he made an "experimental" visit to the Zosima monastery. He prepared for his visit by reading the early church fathers, particularly the collection of ascetic writings translated from Greek entitled *The Love of Good*—but could not enter fully into its teaching, which he felt was "the refusal of all creative upsurge." For his devotional reading he preferred the *Imitation of Christ* with its "noble sorrow, its bitter feeling of human life and destiny."[3] Interest in the elders characterized the newcomers, seekers after the reality of orthodoxy, rather than the traditional faithful folk who had never broken with the church, Berdyaev remarked. His first impressions of the monastery were unfavorable; the place itself, under damp snow, was dreary. As he entered the church he saw, to his surprise, the Grand Duchess Elizabeth Feodorovna and was reminded of the ties between monarchy and church he so sincerely deplored. His impression was strengthened when, after services lasting most of the night, he made confession to the Elder Alexei—famous now for having lived in complete seclusion and later as the monk who drew the final lot to choose a patriarch. In the conversation with Elder Alexei, Berdyaev "felt nothing spiritual" and nothing "spiritually instructive." "At any rate, it became clear to me that I do not belong among those who confide their whole wills to the spiritual direction of elders."[4] Even this most famous of the elders could not tell him what to do. He was willing to repent his many sins and thereby abase himself: ". . . but I could not abase my searching for a new spirit, my knowledge, my love of liberty." The negative incident, however, did not discourage Nicolai Alexandrovitch in his efforts to comprehend Orthodox spirit and doctrine, and contact with new friends like Novoselov, Father Paul Florensky, and Bishop Feodor, rector of the Moscow Theological Academy, played a significant role in his eventual decision to "re-enter" the church.

Not all the religious searching so characteristic of the intelligentsia of the time was as orthodox as the Novoselov group. Another, generally younger, group of seekers were attracted by the mystic and the occult. These were the symbolists Blok and Byeli and the group around a magazine called *Musaget*. In external circumstances *Musaget* was typical of the ephemeral magazines that sprouted in Moscow: a tastefully furnished headquarters where the office man served tea in white gloves; a great expenditure of money by a group of young literati with a wide variety of interests, who at nightly tea parties decided on the journal's program—extraordinary in both its cultural level and budgetary inviability. Within a short time, instead of one there were three magazines: *Musaget*, continuing its purely literary interests, *Logos*, an international philosophical journal, and *Orpheus*, dedicated to mysticism. None of these or the others like them pretended to be an ordinary commercial operation. There was no thought of serving a given public, of supplying a demand, even of a wide circulation. Some "angel" provided funds, and the periodicals carried on until their initiators changed interests or fell apart. The same was true of *Put* ("The Way"), a publishing house founded as a counterweight to *Musaget* and *Logos* by Berdyaev, Bul-

gakov, and Prince Trubetskoy. They represented the more conservative
—it is difficult to imagine Berdyaev having anything to do with con-
servatives at any time!—element in the Religious-Philosophical Society.
Stepun explains the difference between *Put* and *Musaget*: "The basic
question of *Put* was 'what is your belief?' while that of *Musaget* was
'are you a master at your profession?' "[5] And he quotes a conversation
with Berdyaev to show how *Put* differed from his own organ *Logos:*

> "For you," Berdyaev shot at me, "religion and the church are
> problems of culture, while for us culture in all its manifestations is
> an inner problem of the church itself. You want to come to God
> by philosophical ways—but I affirm that you cannot come to God,
> you can only proceed from Him; and only by proceeding from God
> can you come to the true, i.e. Christian, philosophy."[6]

Berdyaev and his colleagues made of *Put* a publishing house that not
only reprinted some of the best of the slavophile works, but issued many
new books, especially those of the members of the Religious-Philosophical Society. These included two of Berdyaev's own volumes, *Khomiakoff* and *The Philosophy of Freedom.* Owing to generous financial
backing, the publishing house was able to offer not a few writers of the
day the chance of seeing themselves in print—writers who otherwise
would have had difficulty placing manuscripts with a commercial publisher. Berdyaev found Moscow less tense than St. Petersburg, with a
deeper culture based on its old university and its stable traditions. If
the capital was like the lower house of a parliament, Moscow was the
senate. Even the Moscow method of conducting discussions was more
productive than that of Petersburg. Unlike the capital, Moscow insisted that every lecturer permit open discussion after his talk, and
whatever the problem, "of creativity, culture, the tasks of art, the building of society, of love,"[7] it was treated as a spiritual whole, with the
religious element placed at its center. Other leading figures Berdyaev
mentions in connection with the Religious-Philosophical Society were
Andre Byeli, V. F. Ern, B. P. Vycheslavtseff,[8] and G. A. Ratchinsky.

With most of these men Berdyaev was destined to have contacts in
later life abroad. Vycheslavtseff was for many years his colleague in
editing *Put* and other productions of the YMCA Press in Paris. Ratchinsky, a Moscow personality widely read in philosophy (although more of
a dilettante than a profound thinker), had usually been asked to chair
the meetings—he would talk too much otherwise, but as chairman he

was permitted only a résumé of the evening's discussion. With Berdyaev's arrival in Moscow, the meetings of the Society took on new life.
Byeli wrote: ". . . into the world of my thinking came Berdyaev . . .
a great personality, chivalrous and very vivacious. I liked his directness,
the openness of his thinking, his kindly smile, the sententious and always rather sad glance from his . . . shining eyes, his Assyrian
head. . . ."[9] It was a variegated group that met in the palatial home of
Margarita Kirillovna Morozoff, wealthy patroness of art and learning.
Not all members of the group were philosophers; many were "specialists" in other phases of culture, "from the apocalypse to the ballet."
And the themes for discussion were as varied as the speakers themselves. Stepun reported a lecture: "Of immanent transcendentism,
transcendent immanentism, and of dualism in general," by Yakovenko,
another member of the group. One wonders how the chairman summed
up the discussion of that one after Bulgakov, Berdyaev, and the solidly
traditional Prince Trubetskoy had had their say. One wonders, also, if
such endless philosophizing, so consistently pursued year after year,
could have taken place at that time anywhere but in Russia. Despite
its wide-ranging topics and the amateur quality of some of its "philosophers," the profound spiritual life of this group left its mark on
Russian, even European, culture.

   In the work of the Society, Serge Bulgakov had a strong directive
influence. Berdyaev called him "the central figure." As Berdyaev had
done in St. Petersburg, Bulgakov in Moscow gave the keynote to the
program. Whereas similar groups in western Europe tended toward
separation of theology from philosophy, in Russia the two were joined
in an original type of religious philosophy characterized by independence from scholastic traditions and church authority, and by great freedom of thought, with philosophy justifying religious faith and religious
experience providing bases for philosophy. Bulgakov was not a figure to
command attention in any group by his appearance, which reminded
Stepun of a village doctor. But when he began to speak—the deep-set
eyes flashing, the face, framed in long black hair, suddenly alight as
though by a slash in a curtain—his earnest thought revealed an independent and profound mind that carried its own authority. Although
Bulgakov had not yet taken orders, his thought at this period was more
deeply centered on religious philosophy than on economics, which was
still his formal occupation. His great theological trilogy was to be
written later in Paris, but an idea of the rich variety of his interests is

given by outstanding articles, one comparing Picasso with one of Dostoievsky's characters.

Another member of the Society who attained great prominence in
prerevolution intellectual Russia was Father Paul Florensky. Berdyaev
called him "mathematician, physicist, philologist, theologian, philosopher, occultist and poet."[10] After graduating from the university with
great promise as a mathematician, he had undergone a spiritual crisis
that resulted in his entering the Moscow Theological Academy and
eventually becoming a priest and a professor there. His brilliant book
*The Pillar and Bulwark of the Truth* still has great influence among
certain Orthodox circles, but Berdyaev was not impressed; in a long review he called it "stylicized Orthodoxy." Recognizing much that was
new and constructive in the book, Berdyaev felt that Florensky understood the Spirit as "moving backward rather than forward," that he
was "indifferent to the theme of freedom, and hence to the theme of
morality," and noted the strange fact that in a book purporting to be
an entire theological system, Christ is scarcely mentioned. Yet Berdyaev
concluded that Florensky was "one of the interesting figures of the
Russian renaissance."

These early years in Moscow may be considered the equivalent of
Berdyaev's completed university education. Because of his arrest and
exile from Kiev, he had not received a university diploma. If St. Petersburg equaled the completion of his undergraduate work, the Solovieff
Society in Moscow provided a postgraduate course. It was the period
when his philosophical ideas began to crystallize into something that
was his own. A decision had been reached in his religious life as well.
Although he still rebelled against much of the bureaucracy and dry
formalism in the Orthodox Church, he could now call himself a believing Christian and so declare it in a letter to Archbishop Antony.

The Berdyaev home in the Great Vlassov Lane—No. 14—in the
stylish Arbat quarter was the center of Berdyaev's activity during the
whole of his fourteen years in Moscow. The Berdyaevs, now a family of
three—for Eugenie had come to live with them in 1907—occupied the
*"belle étage,"* with some retired general on the floor above. After the
opening of the war had brought economic catastrophe to the Berdyaev
family, Berdyaev's father, ill and scarcely able to walk, was brought to
live with them until his death. Berdyaev's study, sacrosanct, was at one
end of the apartment. Here he worked and slept, emerging for his
meals, an occasional errand in the city, or one of the frequent "circle"

meetings. The walls were lined with books, the cream of his father's great library augmented by volumes he himself had been collecting ever since early boyhood. The lamp burning before the icon in the corner served a dual purpose, for until the later years in Paris, Nicolai Alexandrovitch could never sleep in a completely darkened room. The salon, furnished with a selection of beautiful antiques from Berdyaev's father's home, witnessed many interesting gatherings. Here the various—notably free—discussion groups Berdyaev so often brought together, both before and after the revolution, met around the samovar. Lydia Yudifovna, stately and gracious, aided by Eugenie, sometimes helped create the warm, informal atmosphere conducive to frank discussion; other times she would not appear at all. The tea table was always richly supplied with cakes and other confections, usually created by Eugenie, for it was a tradition that guests be served only home-prepared delicacies. Lydia's calm and poise provided the very spiritual corrective Berdyaev occasionally needed. Even when both Eugenie and Nicolai Alexandrovitch became excited over some disputed point, her slow quiet voice would help restore composure. An intimate friend once said Lydia always helped her husband view things "sub specie aeternitatis."

Even in the earliest Moscow days there was a slow stream of callers at the Berdyaev door. Berdyaev never turned any caller away but was not always a very vivacious host. If a visitor spoke quietly, Nicolai Alexandrovitch would continue the conversation politely, evidently wondering when the guest would leave. He particularly disliked it if the caller praised his books. But let him sense in the visitor an opponent and his entire manner would change—he became alert, witty, at once his brilliant best. On occasion, however, the argumentation would go a degree farther. One evening in 1914, just after the outbreak of the war, a small group of friends had gathered at Berdyaev's house—Bulgakov, V. Ivanoff, Byeli, and Ern, a promising young philosopher whom Berdyaev had befriended. For some reason Ern began to eulogise war in principle and the Russian generals and the Russian army in particular. Berdyaev argued that the only permissible war was a war of defense, and that it was criminal to praise murder. The dispute raged to the point where Berdyaev, moving toward his young guest, shouted: "I will not permit anyone in my home to defend violence and murder." Ern turned pale and left the house.

Teatime visitors were not the only guests at the Berdyaev house.

As in other Russian homes, there was always room for friends who spent days or weeks on their visits. Andre Byeli came for meals or to spend the night and, despite his instability, remained a friend of the family to the end of Berdyaev's life in Moscow. Berdyaev remarks how Byeli, who could never contradict anyone to his face, often took revenge for this in vicious articles caricaturing his host. After the appearance of such an article attacking Berdyaev, Byeli would not appear at the house for some time and then suddenly turn up for supper as though nothing had happened. One winter after three weeks at Ratchinsky's country place, Byeli spent six weeks in the hospitable "encampment," as he called it, of V. Ivanoff. Evenings, after the many guests at the "Tower" had left, Byeli would begin long conversations with Ivanoff, going on and on until the morning, when they would move into the host's study. There would be "long discussions about God, symbolism, the fate of Russia"[11] until at seven a servant would appear with a samovar and Ivanoff's favorite scrambled eggs, and at eight the company would be off to their beds.

The same type of hospitality reigned at "Babaki," the country place of the Trusheffs, where Berdyaev's mother-in-law maintained an establishment typical of the "small gentry." Babaki, near the village of Lubotin, about twenty-five miles from Kharkov, received its name from Catherine II who once passed that way and, noting the large number of "babaks"—a type of woodchuck—about the garden, decided the place should be so named. A long *allée* of great trees led from the village up toward the broad façade of the house. In the main body were the hall, the salon, a study, the great dining room with its round table seating twenty, and the family's bedrooms. In the wings were kitchens, servants' quarters, and guest rooms. Nicolai Alexandrovitch had his own study in a wing with windows overlooking the park, quite separate from the rest of the house. Remizoff was an occasional guest at Babaki and found the house full of guests, all entertained on a scale that "gave small consideration to expenses." Nicolai Alexandrovitch was very fond of Babaki. It reminded him of his father's estate, it fulfilled his dream of having a place with woods for his own, and it served as a sure refuge from the world. Some of the happiest days of his life were spent there, working in his study, riding across the fields, or taking long walks through the forest—alone or with Eugenie, for Lydia did not like tramping. Mme Trusheff insisted he should consider it his home, and he always had that feeling about Babaki. Here he could entertain his friends if he wished, but more important, he could "lay aside all worldly care" and, environed by the solicitude of three devoted women, be at liberty to think and write as it pleased him.

Eugenie recalls some characteristic experiences at Babaki. In contrast to what seemed to many his excitable nature, Nicolai Alexandrovitch managed always to maintain his *sang-froid* in emergencies. One autumn evening in 1905, when revolutionary unrest was sweeping the country, the family was sitting quietly before the fireplace when a frightened servant burst into the room. Eugenie goes on:

> "Mistress, fire! they've set fire to the stable." "Who did?" I asked. "Some fellows from the village, and then ran away," shrieked the servant. We all were disconcerted and surprised, because my parents had always been in excellent relations with the peasants. "What shall we do?—they'll burn the house too," shrieked my mother. It was late at night. The red flames lighted the windows—we all lost our wits, knowing that no one lived within two versts, and that help was to be had from nowhere. Only Nicolai Alexandrovitch was calm. "We must get the horses out. I'll go"—and within a few minutes was back and just as calmly said: "The horses are safe. We can't stop the fire, but the house is not in danger. Go to bed. I will guard the house." He took a revolver, loaded it calmly, and went out again.

It was a troubled year in the village as well as in the town. Eugenie recounts another incident:

> Once I was walking with Nicolai Alexandrovitch in the *allée* of our park, when he suddenly broke off the conversation, and with an angry shout rushed off toward the meadow. I saw a crowd of fellows and girls, getting up off the ground and running away, followed by Nicolai Alexandrovitch. To my question as he returned, he said, "They dared carry on their love affairs in broad daylight, in the sight of everyone. That's disgusting." The next day when we were lunching on the terrace, at the far end of the *allée*, there appeared a mob of village fellows with clubs in their hands. "Ni," exclaimed my mother, "run! They'll kill you!" (She understood that this was revenge for the scandal of the mob having been chased by one man.) But instead, Nicolai Alexandrovitch stood up and moved swiftly out toward the approaching crowd. The mob stopped. "Get out!" he shouted. Nicolai Alex-

androvitch's voice, usually quiet, in moments of anger would take on such power, almost inhuman, that it was difficult to stand against it. Brandishing their clubs, the men quickly surrounded him. I shall never forget that moment of deadly peril. Nicolai Alexandrovitch quickly whipped out his pistol [he says that despite his dislike of violence he always carried a revolver], fired a shot into the air, and the mob shuddered and ran away.

Not that Berdyaev lived in a state of war with the village. He liked the peasants and they in return liked his simplicity.[12] The servants adored him. The village barber, on one of his weekly visits to Berdyaev, remarked to Eugenie: "Nicolai Alexandrovitch comes from 'society' but still he converses with me." Berdyaev's relations with simple people were enriched by his contact with the changing population of a neighboring estate. The Tolstoian, V. A. Sheerman, had established a sort of colony for "seekers after God," be they also disciples of Tolstoi, or sectarians of one sort or another, or simple types "who had discovered their method of saving the world." Berdyaev seized this opportunity for new contacts and often went to talk with residents or visitors, or they came to him at Babaki, for long "spiritual conversations." Berdyaev took special interest in the individuals who had had their own personal revelation and came to expound it to him. Most of them, says Berdyaev, were religious anarchists like Tolstoi and more or less like himself. There were sectarians like the "Immortalists" with their conviction that because Christ had conquered death, a true believer in Him could not die. Berdyaev tells of one man who viewed time as the source of all evil and had a theory by which time, and hence death, could be overcome.

Nicolai Alexandrovitch's special friend among these "God-seekers" was Akimushka, an illiterate workman with a surprising talent for things spiritual and an acquaintance with the most difficult mystical themes. He was a sort of peasant Jacob Boehme, of whom of course he had never heard but whose profoundest mystical experiences were not unlike his own. Slightly younger than Berdyaev, he was small and thin, with bright blue, very myopic eyes like beads under his mop of fair hair. Akimushka would go on long walks with Berdyaev in the park at Babaki, and would sometimes stay for a meal, something any ordinary peasant would be most embarrassed to do. "These conversations with Akimushka are surprising," Berdyaev told Lydia. "We understand each other better than when I talk with the theologians."

There was something of St. Francis or St. Seraphim about him. He told how once, when he was walking alone through deep woods with nothing but a staff in his hands, a wolf, fangs bared, leaped out and faced him in the path. "And I stopped and said to him 'Brother wolf, why do you want to eat me? We are both God's creatures, both His children. You go your way and I'll go mine.' And he dropped his tail and went back into the woods, and I continued my journey." Berdyaev speaks of other striking personalities in this village, and recalls them as "the best people I ever met in my life." They made him ashamed, he said, of living in such favorable conditions for creative effort yet having done so little for the realization of a righteous life, compared with the spiritual achievement of these homeless wanderers.

If he got on well with peasants, Nicolai Alexandrovitch had even better relationships with animals. His life was dotted with instances when animals seemed to sense a special sympathy on his part. One day in the village Berdyaev noticed a stray dog—its fluffy white fur badly soiled, but evidently of a good breed of skye terrier—stopped to pat it and went on. That evening, as the family sat around the fireplace, there came a scratching at the door. Outside was the dog Berdyaev had saluted that day in Lubotin. How he had managed to pass the watchman and the dozen other dogs on the estate was a mystery. They kept the visitor until morning, when a peasant woman came and claimed him. The next evening the same experience was repeated. The dog ran directly to Berdyaev's study and refused to come out from under the desk. After this had happened several evenings, Berdyaev refused to give the dog to the peasant when she came for it. "He must be badly treated—I won't let him go." The woman insisted and Berdyaev lost his temper. It required the pacific offices of both Lydia and Eugenie to persuade the peasant to accept three rubles for her dog. Nicolai Alexandrovitch named the dog "Shu-shu," and it remained his favorite as long as he remained in Russia. Berdyaev wept when upon his banishment he had to leave it behind. Eugenie had not seen him weep since his father's death.

There is a charming picture of Berdyaev and his dogs during the terrible years of scarcity in Moscow after the revolution. When people fled the city, many left their pets behind, and it was painful to see the starving animals on the street. One day Lydia came home carrying a small dog, nearly dead from hunger, so dirty its color could not be ascertained. Berdyaev insisted it should be bathed. The only heat in the house was a small one-plate stove for which the only fuel available was antique furniture that had been brought in from Babaki. Soap came in parcels from abroad, and some had been saved for Shu-shu's toilet. "We can use some of that," Berdyaev said. "And hot water?" Lydia reminded him. "I'll cut some wood," he answered, and soon brought up from the basement enough furniture debris to make a fire. While Lydia and Eugenie were bathing the newcomer, Berdyaev supervised the operation "to be sure you don't get soap in his eyes." Some days later he remarked to Eugenie: "You know, when I go along the street with two clean dogs, everyone turns to look at me."

In the autobiography, Berdyaev speaks of his "passionate love for dogs, cats, birds, horses . . . especially for cats and dogs with which I have always had an intimate sense of nearness."[13] His love of animals was a reasoned part of his conception of the world—all of it God's creation. Without saying so, he seemed to accept the Orthodox doctrine of the Redemption as destined for the eventual sanctification of all creation. He explained it in one of the letters to Mme K:

> I do not like people who do not like animals; . . . this has a metaphysical meaning. Man is terribly guilty before the animal world and the whole cosmos: by man came the Fall. . . . Man is a cosmic being, also, and for me man has chief and central significance, but the fullness of human existence is revealed also, in relation to cosmic life, relation which cannot be purely utilitarian. Our concern for human suffering should not make us indifferent to the suffering of everything that lives.

Essentially timid with people, he unconsciously feared their displeasure at feelings he might express. But to his dog or cat he could give himself unrestrainedly, sure of acceptance. "With them he was relaxed and at peace," like many other animal lovers. In a letter to Lydia from Vichy he complained of so few dogs there. In another he wrote: "I have seen a dog film that increases my passion for dogs still more." During the occupation of France he once remarked that he did not love the Germans but could forgive them much because of their love for animals.

Doubtless the most famous animal in Nicolai Alexandrovitch's life was his cat "Muri," who graced the Berdyaev home at Clamart. An enormous black "beauty, very wise, a regular charmer," Berdyaev became very attached to him. Like the dog Shu-shu, Muri had adopted

Berdyaev. When the family moved to France, the two sisters made up their minds they would have no pets; arranging to leave them behind when the family traveled was too difficult. But a black kitten unexpectedly appeared, coming over the wall from a neighbor's yard. Each time it came Eugenie carried it back. "The lady says we should just keep the kitten," she told Lydia a few days later. When he heard their negative discussion, Berdyaev intervened: "Is it possible you don't understand that the kitten wants to live with us?" he asked determinedly. And Muri became a part of the family. Although Eugenie fed and cared for him, he "chose Nicolai Alexandrovitch as the object of his love." Berdyaev was as sensitive to its health, its comings and goings, as if Muri had been a child. If Muri fell ill a veterinary was called, and Berdyaev himself made sure the cat had its medicine at the proper times. If Muri was absent at bedtime, Berdyaev would not go to bed, and they would hear him at intervals going into the garden with his electric torch to look for the pet. Only after Muri was safely home would his master retire.

When they moved to a house in the rue du Moulin de Pierre, Berdyaev announced that he personally would carry Muri to the new home. The ladies reached the house first and were more and more disquieted as Berdyaev failed to appear. All at once he burst into the room: "A terrible thing has happened—Muri jumped out of my arms, and disappeared!" They dropped everything and went out to hunt— but to no avail. In vain Nicolai Alexandrovitch posted handwritten notices on all the telephone poles, offering a reward for Muri's return. Marie, the *femme de ménage* who sometimes helped with the housework, was hired to sit all day in the apartment they had just vacated, in hopes Muri might return there; days later, when all hope seemed lost, Marie came in, tears of joy on her face, carrying the cat. Eugenie says if Nicolai Alexandrovitch had suddenly inherited millions or won the Nobel Prize, he couldn't have been happier. Many visitors will remember Berdyaev with the great cat purring on his lap, and the animal "wandered into more than one passage in his books." Berdyaev wrote that in Muri's suffering before death, he himself experienced the suffering "of all creation, awaiting deliverance," and the death of Muri, "that charming bit of God's creation," was "the endurance of death in general." Unable to accept the idea of an impersonal immortality, he "demanded for himself eternal life with Muri."

Another experiment with pets in the Berdyaev home was unsuccessful. Once Lydia bought a canary that was occasionally let out of its cage to fly freely through the house. Then, as Eugenie tells it, the drama would begin. "Nicolai Alexandrovitch would drop his work to look out for the bird, running after it to see that it did not get entangled in the curtain or fall into the sink, or get outdoors into the frosty cold." The entire household was disrupted, and at last Lydia, who could not bear to keep the bird in its cage all the time, gave it to a friend.

Stepun has a vivid description of Nicolai Alexandrovitch in the earlier Moscow period:

> Not merely handsome, he is universally decorative. At moments when his noble head is still . . . and his face quieted in spiritual contemplation, he reminds you of some . . . portrait by Titian. In his burning eyes with their flashes of irony, . . . in his whole nature, there is something romantic. Berdyaev has beautiful hands and he likes gloves. . . . It is easier to imagine his ancestors as feudal knights riding proudly through the castle gates, than as the ruder Russian boyars.[14]

Another view of Nicolai Alexandrovitch at the time was given by an Orthodox priest who devoted sixty-two pages of his book on "Russian lay-theologians" to Berdyaev:

> Anyone who has had occasion, even from a distance, to observe Nicolai Alexandrovitch cannot but be captivated by the nobility of his person, the grace and animation of his manners and his speech, the affability of his address. He draws you involuntarily toward himself.[15]

# 10

## A DECLARATION OF INDEPENDENCE

In Moscow, as well as in the country, Berdyaev had frequent communion with sectarians and the "seekers after God." Out on the edge of the city, in a people's basement tavern called The Pit, he discovered regular Sunday gatherings in which a variety of original religious inquirers participated, and frequented their meetings until such were later forbidden by the police. He was practically the only one of the intellectuals ready to risk a cold welcome in this slum cafe, and pleased to be received as an equal—another searcher after truth. He was amazed at the high level of the conversations, the "mystic intensity, the complex and profound religious thought," expressed in a powerful imagery of language that made the literary tongue seem tame and pale. Here he met his friends the "Immortalists"; there were Baptists absolutely sure of their own salvation and the damnation of all the others; there were Tolstoians and schismatic Orthodox, beside any number of "seekers" who had, alone, found what for them was the truth. Considering a truth to be *the* truth, usually some Bible verse, they were narrow and intolerant. Berdyaev saw that "without contact with the thousand-year-old-roots," these bigoted sectarians could never achieve what they truly sought, and he argued strongly in defense of the Orthodox church. Nicolai Alexandrovitch soon discovered, however, that it was useless to contend with these people; they were not interested in his opinions. He was particularly happy in his relationship with these earnest people—all questions were for them, as for him, living questions, not merely theoretical problems for learned discussion. Eugenie states he never, on returning from The Pit, said "no one understands me," as so often happened when he came home from a meeting with his intellectual friends. He felt he had an extraordinary talent for understanding "the people." But a friend points this out as a misapprehension. Almost every *barin* like himself knew some

126

intelligent peasant, yet it did not mean all peasants were like this, or that the master really understood the peasants as a class.

In his contacts at The Pit Berdyaev was surprised to discover in these uncultured minds thinking not unlike that of Boehme, and ne began to reread this German mystic together with writings by Tauler and Angelus Silesius. He also read largely in the church fathers, Origen, St. Gregory of Nyssa, and St. Isaac the Syrian. The slavophiles and the recent book of Nesmeloff, *A Doctrine of Man*, began to influence his thought. One of the popular tendencies of this period of intense spiritual activity was known as "mystic anarchism," and for a while Nicolai Alexandrovitch thought it might satisfy him. But he devotes two pages in the autobiography to an explanation of why he could not be happy with that. Most of the mystic anarchists believed freedom to be an easy thing; he had always found it difficult to sustain.

About this time Berdyaev's attention was drawn to a popular mystical thought system, anthroposophy, and its leader, Rudolf Steiner. Although Berdyaev was already firmly established in his Christian faith, so many of his friends, including Byeli, were interested in anthroposophy that he wanted to know more about this, "the most interesting of occult tendencies so much in style" at the moment. Berdyaev says he was always interested in occultism but troubled by it; he could not deny *all* occult phenomena, but neither could he explain them. And he could not accept the occult in the form of religion. He was invited to attend a series of lectures by Steiner at an "anthroposophic lodge" in Helsingfors. The lectures he heard there were quotations from books he had already read, but they took on a new power under the magnetic oratorical gift of "Pastor" Steiner. His eyes exerted a personal magnetism that actually mesmerized many of his hearers. Berdyaev stayed through the lectures but was not "converted." Tyrkova met him on his return and inquired about his impressions of the "prophet." "Terrible," said Berdyaev, and to the question "Why?" "Black lightning shoots out of him." "Do you mean demonic power?" asked Tyrkova. "Just that," was the reply.

His passing interest in Steiner had led to contacts with an even stranger figure, one of his "emissaries," Anna Mintzlova. This strange person was for a time very prominent in the occult circles of the intelligentsia, and let it be understood that she had a special mission to gain adherents to the cult. She hinted mysteriously at a recent order under whose directions she had come to Russia. She succeeded for a

time in captivating Byeli and some of his younger poet-comrades. She
evidently desired especially to win Berdyaev, who first met her at V.
Ivanoff's, where she was living after the death of Ivanoff's wife. Conversation with her was interesting; she was highly intelligent, with a
"great art in approaching souls." But Berdyaev felt that her influence,
like Steiner's, was demonic. He describes a strange vision of Mintzlova.
He was lying half-asleep on a couch, looking at an icon in the opposite corner of the room with a lamp burning before it, when suddenly,
instead of the face of the picture, Mintzlova's face appeared, "with a
terrible expression" on it "as though she were possessed by some dark
power"; and it took the utmost exertion of spiritual force to make
the horrid image disappear. Byeli was one of the last people who ever
saw her. She was in a tormented state of mind and talked vaguely of
her unsuccessful "mission," for whose failure some secret powers had
condemned her to disappear. A few days later she separated from a
friend on a Moscow street and was never seen or heard of afterward.

The Mintzlova incident was not the only time that Berdyaev was
touched by some mysterious power. One day at the very end of December, 1913, when the Berdyaevs were living with Mme Grincvitch,
a tall stranger in a long black cloak called to see Berdyaev. He introduced himself as Dr. Lubeck, sent by the Order of the White Brothers
(Porret says this was a mystic Swedish lodge) to say they approved his
activity and were giving him their protection. Dr. Lubeck was still a
guest in the house New Year's Eve and on that occasion made some
startling prophecies, foretelling the war and the Russian revolution, all
of which the party found quite incredible. Still more so was Dr. Lubeck's prophecy to Nicolai Alexandrovitch: "You will be named professor of the Moscow University." "Impossible," smiled Berdyaev, "I
have no university degree." "You will soon see," was the reply. A
few years later, after the revolution (1920), Nicolai Alexandrovitch was
made professor of the university. Berdyaev was saddened when later,
in Paris, he learned that Dr. Lubeck had committed suicide.

Not as much writing was produced during this earlier Moscow
period as in Berdyaev's later life. Much time was spent in discussion
at various meetings, and there were periods of depression when he was
incapable of setting pen to paper. Nevertheless two books appeared—
with neither of which Nicolai Alexandrovitch was very happy later—
reflecting his thought at the time. The first, entitled *The New Religious Consciousness and Sociality*—"a youthful work, it is well that

it was never reprinted"—had actually appeared at St. Petersburg
before Berdyaev moved to Moscow, but it belongs in this spiritual period. In its "psychological preface," the writer stated:

> . . . I believe in intuition, subjective externally, but objective
> in its interior essence. . . . If they say my book is unproved and
> unscientific . . . they have neither proved . . . that what is
> demonstrated is the only truth. What if truth is regarded and
> seen, but neither deduced nor demonstrated?

The entire preface struck a very personal note. The young man said:

> Spiritually, I proceed from the fact that I am not a proletarian.
> . . . Aristocracy of spiritual descent . . . the inheritance re-
> ceived from my ancestors . . . imposes the duty of nobility.
> . . . Revolt against God is not noble . . . knightly loyalty to
> God is more beautiful . . . more noble. . . . The truth did not
> begin with me.

Characteristically, Berdyaev defined the targets of his revolt:

> This book is against three historic forces: . . . the old, dying
> church with its stagnant religious consciousness, . . . positivism
> and atheism, . . . and the false religion of social democracy;
> . . . [it is] against anarchic materialism, chaotic mysticism, and
> the social utilitarianism founded upon it.

Whereupon the thin volume proceeded to demolish these ideas, together with a few others, and went on to hint at what Berdyaev felt
the future might be like. It closed with a definite prophecy:

> In both the old church which has preserved holiness, and in
> worldly culture and society, invisibly accumulating a new holiness,
> there must come a conversion of cosmic character, a transition to
> the Divine-human way. . . . This conversion will not be a re-
> newal of the old, not a Lutheran Reformation, but something
> immeasurably greater: the changeover from a natural-human
> . . . to a divine-human order. The essence of evil is the deifica-
> tion of the natural, human element, apart from God: the es-
> sence of good is making human nature divine, in union with God.

Berdyaev's next writing attracted considerable notice. In 1909, a
group of seven[1]—most of them younger members of the Moscow

Religious-Philosophical Society—issued a symposium entitled *Milestones*. The slim volume went into five editions in almost as many months. It was at once a confession and a challenge. Warmly welcomed by many intellectuals and some liberal-minded church leaders, it was bitterly attacked by the materialists. For in essence the book was a public statement by these thinkers that the old a-religious philosophies, tradition of the intelligentsia, could no longer satisfy them, and that they were taking the way of religion. They called the others to follow. Nothing could have better pointed up the crisis faced by the intelligentsia. While the book was ideological rather than political, most of its authors were well-known members of the Cadet party and two of them, Struve and Izgoeff, founders of the Union of Liberation.

Because the seven articles were arranged alphabetically, Berdyaev's led off. Entitled "Philosophic Truth and the Truth of the Intelligentsia," it made a critical analysis of traditional attitudes of the Russian literati and advocated a return to truly Russian, Christian principles. In a note for the second edition, Berdyaev called *Milestones* a "spiritual reform effort." In effect it mirrored Berdyaev's own philosophical evolution. Russian thinkers, he said, had been content to accept European social philosophy and had concerned themselves too much with economic problems, to the exclusion of a creative philosophy of their own. There had likewise been too much concern with politics. "Interest was placed above truth, the human above the divine." The intelligentsia, since the 1905 revolution, had awakened to western philosophy but had actually been concerned with it only insofar as it served the interests of the proletariat. This revealed "our lack of culture . . . our feeble consciousness of the unconditional value of truth, and our mistakes in moral judgment."[2] A lengthy criticism of the Russian "distortions" of positivism and marxism contained the strangely prophetic statement: "Russian marxism . . . had an extraordinary faith in the . . . possibility of arriving at a socialist end in Russia, even earlier than in the west." Berdyaev did not shrink from naming names. He praised Lossky and Prince G. Trubetskoy as constructive thinkers, and while Rozanoff and Merezhkovsky were "notable mystics," he decried their "anarchic denial of philosophical reason." Even Struve came under Berdyaev's critical scalpel, and Lunacharsky was sarcastically called " 'a philosopher' of the social-democrat-intelligentsia." The "radical reform" so urgently needed in the thinking of the intelligentsia could come only by recognizing its past faults, by repentance, and by taking responsibility for future development: "Then a new soul will be born in the intelligentsia."[3] An indication of the impact of *Milestones* on the thought of the period is afforded in a bibliography appended to the fifth edition. It lists 217 published articles about *Milestones* within the year it appeared. The symposium attracted attention abroad as well as at home. In his European exile, Lenin devoted two public lectures and an article to it. He called it "the encyclopedia of liberal renegades." The *Great Soviet Encyclopedia* nearly fifty years later devotes more than half a page to *Milestones* as "the most complete expression of counter-revolutionary renegade opinion against which the Bolshevik-Leninists waged consistent and stubborn war."

It is a little-known fact that a second, similar symposium was prepared and printed in 1918, by almost the same group of thinkers. In a free country it might have had the same bombshell effect as did *Milestones*. Where *Milestones* had been criticism of the Russian intelligentsia, the new volume, entitled *De Profundis*, was an effort at philosophical assessment of the bolshevik revolution.

The fate of *De Profundis* was determined by the stormy movement of affairs in Russia. It came off the press in the autumn of 1918, just as the wave of terror following the assassination of Uritsky was mounting. This was evidently no time to publish such philosophical criticism of the regime, and the entire edition remained in storage in the shop where it had been printed. There it lay until 1921, when the Kronstadt mutiny roused the anger of workmen everywhere. At that time the workers in the printshop took it upon themselves to start the distribution of the small book. Most of its authors were already in emigration, but only the date 1918 on the cover saved the rest, including Berdyaev and Frank, from the angry reaction of the government.

One of the many protests against *Milestones* came through an open letter from Archbishop Antony of St. Petersburg. The letter, while approving the new religious tendency among the intelligentsia, disagreed with part of their thesis. Berdyaev was quick to respond, and in the *Moscow Weekly*—August 18, 1909—he published an open letter to the Archbishop. It began with a confession of faith—the first public statement, so far as has been discovered, that Nicolai Alexandrovitch considered himself a loyal member of the Orthodox Church: "By intricate and tortuous ways, I have come to faith in Christ and in His Church, which I now consider my spiritual mother." But if he was a loyal member it was more in the role of "loyal opposition," for he continued with a violent attack on the shortcomings of the church's hierarchy. He even used the biblical term "abomination of desolation" and said he could not forget either the hindrances he encountered on his own way to faith or "the lot of those who have been unable to overcome the hindrance."

The second book of this period, which Berdyaev later termed only a series of preliminary studies, was *The Philosophy of Freedom.* It was notable, however, for being one of the earliest in our modern world to define existentialist philosophy. Berdyaev always insisted that his existentialism differed from most of the modern philosophies parading under its banner. He urged that philosophy turn its back on the rationalism so characteristic of this age and "become a function of the religious life." These ideas, first sketched in this 1911 volume, were further developed in later books written in Paris. *The Philosophy of Freedom* encountered less violent criticism than had *Milestones*; in fact it was treated with an indifference much harder for Nicolai Alexandrovitch to endure. There followed a period of depression, with deep soul-searching and again the presentiment of impending catastrophe. Berdyaev spent much time at Babaki. He was inwardly consolidating the spiritual position achieved after so much inner conflict. For the next four years he wrote almost nothing; it was as if he was waiting for new light—new divine leading.

He was still in the "slough of despond" when in autumn, 1912, he and Lydia, accompanied by Eugenie, went to spend a year in Italy. Unlike other Russians who habitually spent several months of each year in Italy, Berdyaev was unacquainted with that historic land except for Rome. He had not been deeply impressed by Rome, and on this visit they went first to Florence. To how many thousands of travelers, particularly those in search of spiritual treasure, has the city on the Arno imparted a new sense of beauty! He found himself in another world. And Florence had its way with Nicolai Alexandrovitch. He was captivated by everything in the city. Long hours were spent in the museums and churches, where sculpture interested him less than painting.

Florence marked one more turning point in Berdyaev's life. These months gave him a new comprehension of the Renaissance and its philosophical, even theological, significance. He saw that the Renaissance, instead of being a simple return to antiquity, was caught between the purely classic and a deep-rooted Christian feeling, and that because

of this inner conflict, the inability to cast off Christian influence, the
Renaissance had failed to achieve a complete triumph.

The few centuries of the Renaissance (fourteenth, fifteenth,
sixteenth . . .) are marked by an intensity of man's creative
powers never before witnessed. But there are several renaissances,
and it is important to distinguish among them. There is the early
Renaissance, the trecento—all tinged with Christian color. It
was preceded by the sainthood of St. Francis of Assisi and the
genius of Dante. Mystic Italy, the source of the early Renaissance,
was the highest point of all western history. It was in mystic Italy,
in Joachim de Floris, that the prophetic hope of a new world-
epoch of Christianity was born, an epoch of love, an epoch of the
spirit. These hopes nourished the creativeness of the early Renaissance, which was through and through Christian in its tendencies. . . . But the hopes of mystic Italy were ahead of their
times. Man was as yet unable to realize that towards which St.
Francis and Dante traveled by different ways. . . . The great rise
of man in humanism was yet to come. The Renaissance of the
fifteenth century . . . revealed the struggle between the Christian
and the pagan elements in man. . . . The art of the quattrocento
is beautiful but painfully divided: in it Christianity encountered
paganism, and this encounter deeply wounded the spirit of man.
The Florentine art of the quattrocento strove towards classic
perfection of form and made great gains in this direction. But
we may trace in it also marks of Christian romanticism—a transcendent longing which did not permit of classic perfection.

Berdyaev concentrated much of his thought on the quattrocento
and on the work and character of Botticelli in particular:

The tragic fate of Botticelli . . . gives us a key to unlock the
secret of the Renaissance. . . . Botticelli is the most beautiful,
the most deeply moved, the most poetic artist of the Renaissance,
and the most divided and unsound, one who never attained classic
completeness. In the trembling soul of Botticelli the quattrocento
passed over from Lorenzo the Magnificent to Savonarola. . . .
In the whole lifework of Botticelli there is a sort of fatal failure:
he did not realize either the aims of the Christian Renaissance or
those of the pagan Renaissance. . . . In Botticelli there is revealed how the dream of the Renaissance was unrealizable, in-

capable of fulfillment. *The secret of the Renaissance is that it
did not succeed. . . .* In the great failure of the Renaissance lies
its greatness.

During their year in Italy the Berdyaevs spent some time in Rome,
which Nicolai Alexandrovitch felt was lacking in spiritual inspiration.
He appreciated the baroque fountains more than St. Peter's and remarked that baroque was an attempt to unite Catholic reaction with
the pagan Renaissance in the service of the Jesuit Church. A pilgrimage to Assisi proved disappointing also. It was Florence that
marked a new transition in his spiritual experience. He had a sudden
new vision of the whole of the world's history, human and divine.
God created man to be himself a creator. Man realizes his highest
capacities in answering God's creative love with loving creativity of his
own. In previous books and articles we can catch glimpses of Berdyaev's emerging philosophy, but here in Italy he saw a complete
picture. The disparate pieces of earlier thinking suddenly fell into an
integral pattern, and in a movement of inspiration amounting to
ecstasy he began to write. The result was one of the most important
books of his life, *The Meaning of the Creative Act.* Written, as he
said, "in one single movement, . . . the highest point of creative
ardor," it is fairly bursting with brilliant ideas, ranging over such a
broad scope of human life and thought that many later books were
necessary to develop them to the full. The fundamental idea of creative freedom, and man's religious vocation in the world, seemed to
explain much of life's mystery and give an insight into the future. A
coherent religious philosophy that, as might be expected, "differed
from the dominant tendencies" was now presented for the first time.
Here Berdyaev was no longer merely writing comments on the theories
of Rozanoff or Merezhkovsky, or even of Khomiakoff. It was his own
first confession of faith. Written as it was in one sweep of intense
energy, without thought of (or time for) research, the book was un-
even, somewhat "dated" in its polemics against other now almost
forgotten thinkers, and bounding with a youthful optimism that later
years proved to be immoderate. Throughout his lifetime Berdyaev
was unwilling to have *The Meaning of the Creative Act* reprinted,
wishing first to make revisions. He did a certain amount of re-editing
for a German translation published in 1927, and after his death it was
decided to proceed with English and French editions.

That element in the book which Nicolai Alexandrovitch later considered "too optimistic" centered on his concept of the three epochs of human history: the epoch of the Law, the epoch of Redemption, and the epoch of Creativity. The Law is represented by the Old Testament and the Redemption by the New; the epoch of Creativity, giving fulfillment to both the preceding ones, Berdyaev conceived as just about to dawn. In another approach, Berdyaev said these three epochs corresponded to the three Persons of the Trinity; "the creative Act is not in the Father nor in the Son, but in the Spirit, which is why it surpasses the bounds of both Old and New Testaments," he wrote—for the essence of the Spirit is Divine-human. Man has exhibited great creative activity in the past, but it was not religious creativity, such being possible only in the Spirit—in the realization of the Orthodox idea of man's becoming divine—as a response to God's redemptive act in becoming man. That this third epoch would some day dawn on the world Berdyaev never doubted. Neither the suffering of war, revolution, nor the sorrow of exile could alter his faith in man as co-creator with God. "We shall have to pass through a period of darkness before the new light beams out," he wrote in 1926, but "I still believe that God calls men to . . . a creative answer to His love." Although earlier writers had hinted at it, Berdyaev's idea of three epochs was original. St. Gregory of Nyssa possessed the idea in embryo only. Joachim de Floris approached it somewhat more closely.[4] Kartasheff says none of the church fathers seem to have considered the possibility of further revelation following that of the New Testament.

Begun in Italy, the book was finished somewhat more than a year later but published only in 1916. If his earlier works had not attracted much attention, this one resounded throughout the entire Russian intellectual world. It was not merely abstractly philosophical; it went straight at problems of conduct that troubled many hearts. Others had felt the need of comparing St. Seraphim the hermit, whose ascetic mysticism affected the entire spiritual life of Russia, with Pushkin, one of the greatest poets Russia—or the world for that matter— has produced, but no one had so clearly stated the case previously: "St. Seraphim created nothing but himself, and by this alone he transfigured the world. Pushkin created . . . immeasurable values for Russia and the world, but . . . destroyed his soul in the creative outflow of his genius. . . . Wouldn't it have been better . . . for the purposes of God's Providence" . . . if there had been two saints instead of a saint and a genius? Berdyaev asked. He then answered his own question: "For God's purposes in the world, the genius of Pushkin is just as necessary as the sainthood of Seraphim."⁵ To this challenge to the traditional church, Berdyaev added others. In the matter of erotic love the church had gone astray, he said. "Christian love . . . has become . . . complete abstraction, bodiless and bloodless. Christian love has not yet been revealed . . . in the religion of redemption; . . . its revelation demands a creative act."⁶ So too, as concerns morality: "Traditional Christian morality does not spring from the Gospels . . . but from extra-Christian . . . sources. . . . Man cannot live in this world and create new life, using only the morality of conflict with his own sins." Consequently, "he is powerless to accomplish anything."⁷

No wonder the book brought down upon his head in almost unanimous thunder a majority of Russia's prominent thinkers. It was too "different from the dominant tendencies" not to be violently attacked. The assault came, first, from among his friends. Bulgakov called it "a demonic book." Rozanoff at first took the line of ridicule: "Berdyaev calls Russia, and I suppose all of us, to religious creativeness, religious heroism, religious greatness. . . . I fear that this is not to be the lot of Russia." Two months later Rozanoff was writing more seriously, but just as negatively, of "that huge book"; he regretted his unfavorable criticism of Berdyaev's "appeal for religious creativity, religious heroism, or at least religious activity. . . . We Russians, in religious and spiritual matters, are still in the first reader. We haven't learned to think . . . what kind of heroism is possible here? Berdyaev has been overhasty in talking of heroism; . . . let this creativeness shout about itself once it has begun to act."

Rozanoff was kinder than most of Berdyaev's critics. Frank was more direct, if more pontifical. In his review of *The Meaning of the Creative Act* he deplored a situation "where philosophy is openly identified with poetic inspiration, religious faith, or moral homiletics as in the case of Nietzsche for instance, who sees in the philosopher not the seeker after truth, but a legislator of values. Here is real philosophical falling into sin. This is genuine philosophical decadence."⁸ A few months later a Moscow annual of philosophy carried another sarcastic review. Its author, one Lundberg, ridicules the tasks Berdyaev has set himself: "First the salvation of society, then the proletariat, next the salvation of mankind, then idealism, and now salvation and division into two parts of the cosmos, by free creativeness. . . . Neither angel nor demon could think up such tasks, not to mention their solution; . . . a pitiful attempt."[9]

Lundberg's comments were not wholly unjust. Nicolai Alexandro-vitch's ideas had grown as he worked with various groups, learning what each had to teach him before moving on. The Meaning of the Creative Act signaled his departure toward a position all his own. Lundberg represented the extreme in criticism of the book. Practically all Berdyaev's critics, however, would have agreed with a review of the English translation appearing forty years later: "We may reject or accept Berdyaev's philosophy, but we cannot ignore it. . . . He does not evade the current problems and moral issues that challenge mankind."[10]

Returning to Moscow from Italy, Berdyaev did not resume life as it had been before he left. More than most Russians he was burdened with the vast malaise preceding the great war. He no longer fre-quented the meetings of the Religious-Philosophical Society. The Meaning of the Creative Act, on which he was still working, had set him apart from many in the group. Most of his contacts seem to have been with friends who came singly, or as participants in the dis-cussion evenings at his home. Usually they discussed spiritual prob-lems, but the mood of the time brought them inexorably to political and social applications. It was a time of intense but unquiet living, with constructive activities in the literary and artistic spheres played off against a precarious and reactionary political situation. Moscow was beginning to widen its cultural interests to include western Europe. New translations of western literature—the German mystics, the Greek classics—appeared. The new Art Theater presented Hamsun, Ibsen, Maeterlinck, and Strindberg along with Shakespeare, Schiller, and Molière. Sarah Bernhardt and Duse, Moissy and Salvini were appear-ing on other Moscow stages. Chaliapin and the music of Mussorgsky seemed to equal anything the west could produce. That was the posi-tive side. The Balkan War, begun with such enthusiasm for liberating Orthodox brethren from the Turkish yoke and replacing the crescent with a cross over the domes of St. Sophia, had ended in Russia's prac-tical withdrawal, both physical and moral, from the entire peninsula. A distracted and incompetent government attempted to fight rising discontent in Russia with such hysterical measures as anti-Semitic riots and the world-gripping Beilis case. There were reports of cor-ruption and perversion at court and among the hierarchy of the church.

Against this background life in the Berdyaev home continued, and
Nicolai Alexandrovitch spent it in communion with his friends. There
was Father Abrikosov, leader of a Roman Catholic group through which
Lydia later became converted. The deeply spiritual and ascetic life of
the group impressed Berdyaev. He called them real wrestlers of the
spirit. There were others, men destined to play important roles in
the Soviet government: Lunacharsky and Bonch-Bruevitch—although
these came rarely—and the talented Vladimir Ern, avowed foe of the
Neo-Kantianism of the Logos group, and Bulgakov and Florensky, both
concerned with the Sophiology that Berdyaev could not accept. Such
a range of talent! One thing the Russia of that time did not lack was
men of great endowment. And not only men. There was Eugenie
Herzig, "one of the most remarkable women of the beginning of the
twentieth century," whose "intimate conversations" with Berdyaev influenced his thought and helped assuage his sense of loneliness; and
Margarita Kirillovna Morozoff, in whose beautiful, spacious house
especially built to accommodate them, the philosophical "salons" for
which she was famous met together. She had an ability for uniting the
"most ununitable people" and was largely responsible for the friendly,
"culturally polite" tone of Moscow discussion groups.

Just before the outbreak of World War I, Berdyaev's growing dissatisfaction with the church administration reached a climax. A quarrel
among Russian monks on Mt. Athos over a new sect developed into
open hostilities and what appeared to be a mutiny against established
authority. It was typical of the "jumpy" government that a torpedo
boat be dispatched from Sebastopol at the request of the Holy Synod,
and sailors manhandled the refractory monks. Berdyaev says he had no
special sympathy for the monastic sect in question but was revolted by
church recourse to force. His article about the affair, "Quenchers of the
Spirit" (in Russkaya Molva, August 3, 1913), was immediately confiscated. It was a blistering attack on the Holy Synod, a wild mixture
of Christian theologizing and the rudest of polemics. If, as Berdyaev
stated in the article, Archbishop Antony had "burst out with abuse
more worthy of a cabby than a prince of the Church," Berdyaev himself was little milder. His first fire was directed at the hierarchs forming the Holy Synod, who converted the "heretical" monks to "the true
faith of the Synod by the aid of bayonets" and hence were "a thousand
times worse than soldiers or policemen. . . . Our bishops," he affirms,
"are incapable of going into such questions, for which only mystics

. . . and men of higher contemplation are capable. . . . The bestial action . . . reveals a hitherto unheard-of decline of the church, its ultimate humiliation." Then from persons, Nicolai Alexandrovitch turned his wrath on institutions: ". . . the Holy Synod, respected by no one, whose canonicity is even doubtful . . . the voice of the visible, and perhaps only the apparent church . . . fears spiritual life as it fears the fire. . . . The very lowest, swinish, materialistic life is dearer to the Synodal church than the higher, spiritual life." His attack was climaxed with: "The Synodal church is not the true Church of Christ . . . [its] paralysis has already become rigor mortis . . . it stinks like a corpse and is poisoning the spiritual life of the Russian people."

This was not the first time Berdyaev had openly challenged the official church. Beside the letter to Archbishop Antony in 1909, there was a still earlier, more fundamental—though less violent—outburst. In 1907, an article (*Vek*, May 6, 1907) entitled "Nihilism on Religious Soil" had stated flatly that "Orthodox Christianity is a doctrine of individual salvation, salvation in heaven, of separation from the world which is all infected with evil. . . . Orthodoxy does not believe in the Kingdom of God on earth. . . . Servility is blessed by our Russian Church, just as courage . . . and impulses toward the high and distant are condemned." These earlier attacks had been officially overlooked, but with "Quenchers of the Spirit" the Synod's wrath overflowed. Berdyaev was at once arrested and charged with blasphemy, an offense automatically punishable with life exile to Siberia. His lawyer said the case was hopeless but, thanks to the war, was able to drag out proceedings until the revolution annulled all pending cases. Without the revolution, Berdyaev knew, he might have spent his remaining days in Siberia rather than Paris. It was a typical Berdyaev gesture—risking lifelong exile for the sake of some dissident monks in Greece of whom he had scarcely heard until the crisis arose.

# 11
## WAR, REVOLUTION, BANISHMENT

The outbreak of war in the summer of 1914 found Russia unbelievably unprepared, both physically and morally. The general sense of depression resulting from the Russo-Japanese War and the crushed 1905 revolution had deepened, among the intelligentsia, to despair—"we're headed for ruin, and nothing can be done about it."[1] Blok wrote a poem "We are the Children of Russia's Terrible Year," but among the elite, despite pervading unrest, there seems to have been no realization Mars was at the gates. They knew matters were in a very bad way at court and in the government. The vacillating, kindly Tsar, dominated by his iron-willed but overcredulous Tsarina, was a mere figurehead. In the church's Holy Synod there were not a few unholy men. The clergy in general was untrained for educative contact with the people, and most of them felt they were doing all that was expected. If there was a sermon, "it spent itself mostly on how a person got into the Kingdom of God, and touched very little upon how he should live worthily on earth."[2]

The army was not much better off. Its officers, after finishing an excellent military schooling, were all too often permitted to drowse away the days at their regimental posts. The average officer seems to have believed "the essence of making war was in bravery, daring, the readiness valiantly to die, and that all the rest was not so important."[3] Top brass proficiency is illustrated by what happened when Grand Duke Nicolai Nicolaevitch was named commander-in-chief. Russia had declared war July 20. The Tsar waited three days before naming a commander. In the Grand Duke's family the 25th and 26th were given to a silver wedding celebration, and because the 27th was His Royal Highness' birthday, they took a day to celebrate that. In the course of the day it was announced the commander-in-chief would proceed to headquarters on the 31st. By then the war was a week old!

With the nonmilitary leadership and the populace in general

the situation was somewhat better. Despite some pessimism there was an upsurge of popular patriotism, with orators thundering speeches in street demonstrations. Most of the intelligentsia continued their usual living, in cities that were doing the same, with restaurants and theaters crowded. The new recruits drilling in the streets were almost the only change in the normal scene. Some writers turned to the war for their themes. Extremists began to wonder how they could use the war for liberation from the monarchy. Hippius in a letter to the St. Petersburg Religious-Philosophical Society sought to demonstrate that "any war is a debasement of the general human levels," but in the two evenings of debate following, Kartasheff and others urged "religious acceptance" of the war. The intelligentsia, always idealistically inclined, tried to justify the war with some purpose higher than mere politics or economics, and "war to end war" and similar slogans began to be heard. One to another they passed on Rasputin's latest "prophecy" of victory, "with the Russian fleet in Vienna." Cabinet ministers changed rapidly. On the front, some Russian trenches were held with one rifle for five men and almost any wound was mortal for want of adequate medical attention. At court, patriots tried openly or by intrigue to separate the Tsar from the Tsarina and her baneful influence. The entire kaleidoscopic situation was more like some fantastic novel than anything imaginable in real life.

In all this overture to the tragedy, and throughout the war as well, Berdyaev played a listener's part. His theoretical view of war was a deduction from his basic doctrine of the freedom of the person. War meant that society takes over much of the individual's liberty, and good could not be wrought by evil means, although he shared the view of most intellectuals that this, a defensive war, was justified. Nicolai Alexandrovitch took no part in the *Zemstvo* and Red Cross activities in which a majority of civilians were engaged. His writing at the time did not ignore the war—although it is mentioned only incidentally in his autobiography. We know of only ten articles published in 1914. After that, under economic pressure owing to the loss of income from his estate in Poland, there was a constantly increasing flow of writing: thirty-four articles each in 1915 and 1916, and fifty-five as tension mounted toward the bolshevik revolution of 1917. Yet even here the themes were mostly abstract: "War and Renaissance," "Of Man's Slumbering Powers," "Nietzsche and Modern Germany," "The Justification of Love for the Fatherland," "Authority and Responsibility." Reading most of the prerevolution articles, one would never

know that Rasputin or Pobiedonostseff or even the Tsar existed. But
Russia existed, and Berdyaev wrestled with the angel of her future.
Some of his letters to the editor of *Birzhevie Vedomosti* indicate that
he had the usual author's difficulties. In 1916 (April 13), Nicolai
Alexandrovitch was writing:

> I urgently request the editor to inform me at once if this article
> is to be printed, and just when. If my article cannot be printed,
> then . . . return it to me. . . . I must say that such a long de-
> lay with no explanation of the reasons is very inconvenient. . . .
> Articles for a newspaper presuppose quick publication. There
> should be a serious reason for not publishing. Note that my ar-
> ticle "On Conservatism in Russia" has been lying on your desk
> since August.

Somewhere during this time Berdyaev produced the remarkable little book *The Destiny of Russia*, partly reprinted essays, partly new
work—published in 1918. The book, the last of Berdyaev's works to
be published in Russia, surveys the Russian character and the place
of Russia in the postwar world, together with some commentary on
Russia's allies France and Britain. There is a penetrating chapter on
"Holiness and Honesty" where Nicolai Alexandrovitch begins by saying: "The Russian does not have a sufficiently strong consciousness
that honesty is obligatory for every man." Through long generations
the Orthodox Church has extolled humility as the supreme virtue. As
a result, other equally important virtues have been lost sight of, and
too little attention has been given to moral improvement. "If he is a
religious man, he thinks God will do this for him. If he is an atheist,
the social milieu will attend to it." In consequence the average Russian's attitude is: "Better humbly to sin, than proudly to attain perfection."[4]

In a chapter on "The End of Europe," Berdyaev's universalism becomes evident. This was the end of Europe's monopoly on culture.
Out of the war must come some sort of international, or supernational,
collaboration. One of Berdyaev's delightful self-contradictions occurs
in this section when he declares that Britain's mission in the war is external while Russia's is internal. Russia surely was not imperialistic, yet
"a Russian Constantinople should be a center of union for East and
West!"[5] The effect of his prewar visits to France, one learns, was: "In
modern France one feels an uneasiness, a weariness from its . . . history in which so much that was great and historic was accomplished;

. . . we feel exhaustion here." He takes a pass at the French in prais-
ing their capital city: "Paris is a being higher and more beautiful than
the modern, bourgeois Frenchman."[6] Written during a war that already showed signs of turning out badly for Russia, the slim book gave
evidence of Berdyaev's profound love and understanding for his country and his optimistic view of the future.

If during the first years of the war little action on Berdyaev's part
was evident, it was somewhat different when the revolution came. Conditions in the country deteriorated further. Prewar prosperity had
continued by inertia through the first year and more, but now there
was a serious decline. Revolutionary propaganda was seeping to the
armed forces. There was hunger in the cities. Miliukoff says[7] the first
two months of 1917 might be considered either an epilogue or a prologue; everyone awaited great events, but no one seemed to have anything but a vague premonition of what they would be. A wave of strikes
swept the country, then mutinies began in city garrisons. Under pressure the Tsar abdicated, the Duma was dissolved, and the cabinet
disappeared. On February 28, 1917, in the place of a government and
a philosophy of state there was a void. The revolution had begun.

To most of the intellectuals the change was neither unexpected nor
unpleasing. Monarchist sympathy had been an almost unforgivable
crime. To the man in the street, however, it was a cataclysm. One has
only to read Russian novels of the turn of the century to appreciate how
the thinking of all Russia centered on the Tsar and his family. The
monarch had been regarded with a quasi-religious veneration that was
well expressed by a young officer at the moment of the regime's collapse: "In my life there have been two holy things—God and the Tsar.
Now there is only God."[8] Of all the intelligentsia, Berdyaev was perhaps the least overcome by events. For more than a year he had been
participating in closed meetings of left wing intellectuals. The group
did not include "the extremists," but among its participants were future Soviet dignitaries. Although he took an active part in discussions
and sometimes chaired the meetings, Berdyaev felt he did not belong
with this group—and was unable to play a constructive role in the
swift-moving events.

Like many of his associates, Berdyaev had foreseen the revolution. He
possessed a somewhat clearer idea than most of what might happen
when it came, although many elements in its development astonished
him also. He never believed in the idyllic revolution anticipated by
many of his friends; he realized it would initiate a regime of oppression

and crush individual freedom. It began mildly enough. But while blood-less at first, early 1917 was a time of increasing malaise. Berdyaev called it a nightmare summer, and the autobiography gives a picture of his indecisive running about, attending meetings but taking part in none. In later years he said he could not accept the theory beloved by many émigrés that evil elements imported from abroad had caused the revolution. The old regime was not overthrown, it decayed and fell apart. Through the past decade Nicolai Alexandrovitch had watched the increasing separation between "idealists" and "materialists" among the intellectuals, and with real suffering had seen how the idealists gradually lost almost all interest in social reform while the materialists ceased to advance spiritually. When the revolution broke, they were still standing by their early positivist and humanist guns. In contrast to France, where an intellectual elite had provided the active revolutionary leadership, the men who made Russia's revolution were still living with outdated ideas of the sixties—Chernishevsky and Marx instead of Solovieff—a thoroughly utilitarian philosophy with neither knowledge of nor interest in the newer cultural movements in Russia or western Europe. The Russian revolution "took place under the sign of nihilist enlightenment, materialism, utilitarianism and atheism."[9] The grad-ually widening breach between the "elite" and the people had become a chasm in which Russia's brilliant renaissance was swallowed up.

Each day's news of the war was worse than the one before. Russian death tolls equaled those of all the other allies together. Production disorganized by excessive mobilization was hampered still further by a transportation system on the verge of collapse. The blood of Ber-dyaev's martial ancestors boiled as soldiers began to demobilize them-selves, and he was surpised to find himself sympathizing with the gen-erals. Disorder in the country increased, with a dozen different left-wing political groups struggling among themselves for power. There were political meetings in almost every city block. One day a friend of Berdyaev met an acquaintance on the street. "You should have been at our meeting last night," he said. "A professor spoke, and proved conclusively that the monarchists are right." The "professor" was Nicolai Alexandrovitch, fighting as usual for the minority.

As the government shifted increasingly toward the left, the estab-lished church began to feel its heavy hand. To meet the new situa-tions the church held a *Sobor* or Great Council in Moscow in August, 1917; over half of the assembled 564 delegates were laymen—the first such gathering in two hundred years. Through his friends, especially

Bulgakov—with whom he had attended some of the preparatory meetings—Berdyaev kept in close touch with its deliberations. These continued through the bolshevik coup; a patriarch was elected with gunfire clattering in the streets.

Nicolai Alexandrovitch had more than a passing acquaintance with
Tichon, the new patriarch. When Berdyaev left Russia, Tichon gave
him documents for Metropolitan Eulogius in Paris. Berdyaev criticized
the *Sobor* for being so concerned with reorganizing the church administration that it failed to deal with "the religious problems which
had tormented Russian thought of the nineteenth and beginning of
the twentieth centuries." Considering the gigantic civic changes to
which the church had to adapt itself and the fact that it was convened
in such uncertain times, with the communist seizure of power practically forcing adjournment, Nicolai Alexandrovitch's criticism was
probably too severe.

Even if he were not fully satisfied with it, the church was almost
the only part of Russian life that seemed to be doing something constructive. All about was dissolution. Even the faces of the people
seemed to change. Returning one day from town, Berdyaev told with
emotion how he had watched a company of soldiers marching past.
"I could not recognize the faces of our soldiers. They were always
good-natured, with shining eyes and a springy step—and now all at
once they have somber, stern faces with sharply cut lines, and a heavy
tread, as though they were trampling someone down." He noted the
same change in the faces of former friends who had thrown in their
lot with the left. They no longer resembled the intellectuals he had
known, the men who for decades had been "preparing the revolution."
Gone were the beards; the left flank was clean-shaven, like the groups
of sailors going about the streets in trucks. The "new anthropological
type" had lost "the kindness, the vagueness . . . of former Russian
faces," and instead there was a mixture of cruelty and energy—product
of a long disastrous war. He saw it in the faces of members of the ill-
fated Council of the Republic. Delegated by the Union of the Liberal
Professions of Moscow, he had gone to Petrograd (the name had been
officially changed at the outset of the war) for those futile meetings.
Here were many old friends whose lives had been spent in prison or
exile, now grasping for the government of the state. The change in
his former associates—their looks, their manners—so revolted Nicolai
Alexandrovitch that he would not speak to them.

Trotsky demonstratively walked out of this Council meeting, to call the proletariat to take over. What Porret calls "the passover of the communist religion" was at hand. With the Soviets in power and many of the less radical leaders in hiding, Berdyaev watched ever coarser and more violent application of the idea that the end justifies any means. He railed against the bolshevik regime; while Nicolai Alexandrovitch believed academically that world history, along with epochs of steady development, seemed to be fated to advance sometimes by sudden leaps which are revolutions, he detested the coarseness and cruelty of this fresh example.[10] The bolsheviks were not only crushing man's freedom, they were grinding down man himself, and "the idea of mankind crowded out the idea of man."[11]

Eugenie gives a typical glimpse of Nicolai Alexandrovitch in the first days of the revolution. Rumors reached Moscow that uprisings had begun in Petrograd, and the Berdyaevs joined a great crowd of people moving through the streets toward a government office. The atmosphere was electric. In front of the building the soldiers on guard already had guns cocked to fire on the steadily advancing, threatening crowd. Berdyaev elbowed his way to the front, marched across the intervening space, alone, and harangued the soldiers, urging them not to fire on their fellow citizens. A few months later any man in such a position would have been felled by an officer's bullet. The astounded officer heard him through, gave a command, and the men lowered their rifles—and the crowd dispersed without further incident. It was characteristic of the entire revolution that action often was fatally determined by someone's talent for oratory. Berdyaev was not impressed by the oratory; one day he gravely offended Byeli by laughing at his enthusiasm for Kerensky.

He had still less illusion about the bolshevik revolution. It was barely two months old when he wrote in *Russian Freedom:*

> The Russian revolution has turned out to be a consistent application to life of Russian nihilism, atheism, and materialism—a vast experiment based on the denial of all absolute spiritual elements in personal and social life. . . . The bolsheviks are the final Russian nihilists. . . . Russian nihilism is possessed by a thirst for equality at any price. This . . . leads to the destruction of all values; . . . in it is the spirit of non-being. But being was conceived in inequality, . . . in individual differences, "the elimination of all qualitative differences" (a quotation from the then

newest communist slogan), would be a return to primordial non-being, which is complete equality.

For those accustomed to ruthless communist extermination of all opposition it seems incredible that Berdyaev could have published an article containing those words, and still less credible that he could have lived and worked under the bolshevik regime five years thereafter. "The application to life of Russian nihilism" had not yet become fully consistent during the first few months of Lenin's rule.

Berdyaev experienced the catastrophe as a part of his own personal destiny; he said the revolution took place within himself. Strangely enough he felt better after it had reached its crisis and the bolsheviks were in the Kremlin. Instead of the passive attitude of the prerevolutionary years, there now appeared a period of "great activity"; he "gave many lectures and speeches, wrote much, disputed." Kartasheff noted the surprising fact that after 1918, when he was already an outlaw hiding in friends' homes in Moscow (among them Berdyaev's) he could still attend the meetings of various philosophic "circles"—including that around Prince E. Trubetskoy, where of course Berdyaev would be holding forth. As the communist grip on the country tightened, Nicolai Alexandrovitch could see ever more clearly the totalitarian oppression it was becoming, and his anger increased. In reply to friends who still believed in the coming reign of freedom and justice he would sometimes break into denunciations of the evil forces at work, with the result that in influential circles he gained the reputation of a reactionary. He watched the communist party, directed by Lenin—the only man with a definite program and the ruthless will to force it upon the country—slowly tighten its clutch. Berdyaev had known Lenin in the prewar "liberation" movements. They probably met again during the Kerensky regime. Nicolai Alexandrovitch never knew Stalin. With the Cheka the first signs of a police state appeared—a pervading sense of insecurity and the now familiar pattern of midnight arrests. Early in 1918, Berdyaev wrote a passionate protest against the Soviet regime. *The Philosophy of Inequality* could be published only after his arrival in Berlin four years later. "The revolution is completely negative," he cried. "The egalitarian cult is beating down to a dead level all the peaks of culture. There is no place for an elite, no possibility for genius to express itself. Equality is a metaphysically empty idea; . . . social justice must be built not on this, but on the recognition of the dignity and worth of every human person." In his autobiography

Nicolai Alexandrovitch called this work "a very emotional book, reflecting a stormy reaction" to the events of those days, "unjust in
many ways"; but basically it was true—he was defending freedom. In
the midst of political and social catastrophe he could discern the
deeper, spiritual crisis.

If Lenin called Berdyaev a renegade, what Berdyaev said about those
of his friends who "adapted themselves" to the new regime was
equally expressive. When he heard that his old friend V. Ivanoff had
dedicated a poem to Kameneff, he flew into a rage and never spoke to
him again. After he had repeated this performance with Gershenson,
the latter used jokingly to warn others not to pass Berdyaev's street:
"He might be firing from the window." It was a time of confused contradictions. The authorities gave Berdyaev a document protecting his
house and his precious library from police intrusion, and then arrested
him. Nicolai Alexandrovitch continued his active hostility toward the
regime, yet accepted a double food ration, given for some reason to a
group of twenty prominent writers who were promptly nicknamed "the
twenty immoratals." This move was probably due to Lunacharsky, who,
during the early part of the communist regime when some of the old-
line "intellectual" revolutionaries were still in power, repeatedly used
his influence to ameliorate the lot of former friends. A time was approaching when the police would be asking servants "what does your
master think," and when in the treatment of their political adversaries
the Bolsheviks would no longer distinguish "between actions . . .
committed in fact and those . . . which should have been committed
as a consequence of . . . opinions"—as Koestler says. In the course of
a grandiose celebration on the occasion of the first anniversary of the
bolshevik revolution—October 25, 1918—Lunacharsky issued an appeal to all writers to serve the new regime. In the enthusiasm of the
moment many accepted. Berdyaev refused. Whether or not his refusal
had anything to do with it, Berdyaev together with Lydia and Eugenie
were compelled shortly after, in the new universal obligation to labor,
to clear off the tracks of some marshaling yards in the dead of winter.
Rising mornings at five, in twenty below zero weather, they had to
stand in line for roll-call, after which they were marched by guards
with fixed bayonets out to work lasting until dark, often with nothing to eat until, barely able to stagger home, they could prepare something on the small stove that was the only source of heat in the
apartment. Nicolai Alexandrovitch did not rebel against disciplinary
measures—he merely remarked that the principle was badly applied.

Through these years Berdyaev wrote steadily. During a three-day cannonade at the time the communists were crushing the last "white" resistance in Moscow, he left his study when the maid—the keeping of servants had not yet been forbidden—screamed with fright, long enough to scold her for becoming excited. Once when a dud shell crashed into the apartment on the floor above and the family had to rush for the cellar, Nicolai Alexandrovitch waited to look around for the dog before following them himself. In one of the letters to Mme K, he could write: "I dislike intensely fear or fright, and have never experienced either in the least degree, even when I faced Dzerzhinsky in the *Cheka*." During the four years between 1918 and 1922, four books were written, the two already mentioned and *The Meaning of History* and his *Dostoievsky*. All but one had to wait for publication until he was sent abroad. Beside his writing Nicolai Alexandrovitch gave many lectures, to a variety of audiences. One of the largest was at the Anarchist Club—the communists snuffed out the anarchist organization only late in 1918—where a public debate had been announced. The topic was "Christ," and Berdyaev was invited. One of the few detailed accounts in the autobiography of personal action tells of this meeting. The crowd had given excited accord to horrible statements about Jesus and his mother, and anyone who questioned the "scientific" facts adduced would risk the active disapproval of this largely uncouth assembly. Berdyaev felt a sudden inspiration and made "the best speech of his life." It later served as the basis for his famous essay "The Worthiness of Christianity and the Unworthiness of Christians." He lectured under government auspices in an institution whose name, characteristic of the times, was The State Institute of the Word. After he had spoken on science and religion to a very large audience, mostly Red Army soldiers and workmen, some of the men walked home with him, continuing the discussion. The lectures and discussion of this stormy period provided material for several of Berdyaev's later books. The preface to Berdyaev's *Dostoievsky* states that the seminar he conducted in Moscow "at a time when it is stylish to deny the importance of ideas and suspect their value"[12] caused him to collect his thoughts on the great writer and resulted in the book. At every lecture communist censors sat in the front row, and as usual Berdyaev wasted no words in expressing his opinion. When Eugenie urged him to be more careful he gave a characteristic reply: "It would be better to be honest and die before a firing squad, than to be careful and die in your bed."[13]

Incredible as it may seem, Berdyaev organized his own lecture courses. Some were conducted in private homes, but there was also the almost-official Free Academy of Spiritual Culture, which he initiated in the strained atmosphere of Moscow and with the consent of a governing clique whose life doctrine affirmed there was no such thing as spirit. The institution lasted three years, until Berdyaev's banishment in 1922. Although no public advertisement was possible and news of the lectures could be spread only by word of mouth, they were very popular—here was one remaining center where people could speak freely. The lectures were so popular that on one occasion the building manager feared the floor of the hall would collapse. At another lecture, on "Theosophy and Anthropology," Berdyaev arrived to find the courtyard so crowded he could not gain entrance to the auditorium— despite protests that he was the speaker. Stepun gives a vivid description of the meetings: "In the tense mood of those gathered here one felt . . . the impelling necessity not to speak . . . superficial and empty words. . . . In Berdyaev's lecture were those spiritual, objective . . . words about the most important things in life that we all expected from him."[14] One series of lectures was given in the building of the State Alcohol Administration, and some enemy took occasion to write an article for Pravda complaining that religious lectures were given on government premises. This led to Berdyaev's being called to the Cheka for an explanation. He smilingly recounts how, when he exhibited a letter from Kameneff showing the Free Academy's proper registration with the Moscow Soviet, the investigator had the utmost difficulty understanding what "spiritual culture" was. As the lectures continued into their third year and would-be totalitarian authorities turned the screws ever tighter, the audiences at Berdyaev's lectures increased. He never ceased to believe the communist regime could be reformed from within, and although later years refuted his hope, the experience convinced him that thirst for freedom of thought would never be entirely suppressed in human life.

Nicolai Alexandrovitch participated in another public protest against the government when word spread abroad that a proposed church procession forbidden by the authorities would take place nevertheless, and what might have been a normal, quiet affair took on the dimensions of a demonstration. It was rumored the procession would be dispersed by gunfire, and the few hundred persons who decided to follow Patriarch Tichon and the church banners were advised to take what might be their last communion before the hour of crisis

Nicolai Berdyaev in 1934, at the age of sixty.

The Berdyaev Coat of Arms. The upper half of the shield bears three silver spearheads on a red ground; the lower half, a silver castle against a blue backdrop. The crown-topped helmet with three plumes was usual for the nobility. In 1598, 1706, and later, the Tsar granted estates to the Berdyaev family in recognition of loyal service to the throne.

Marie-Gabriel, Count of Choiseul-Gouffier (1752-1817), Berdyaev's great-great-grandfather, founder of the Russian branch of the family. At the age of thirty he was a member of the French Academy; at thirty-two, French Ambassador at Constantinople. Following the outbreak of the French Revolution he fled to Russia, where he became the confidant and counselor of Catherine the Great.

Princess Alexandra Sergeevna Kudasheff, Berdyaev's mother. Educated in Paris like most of the Russian gentry of the time, she always spoke French and never learned to write good Russian.

Alexander Michaelovitch, Berdyaev's father, in a photograph taken before he was twenty, the age at which he became the first man in five generations of his family to retire from military service. "Owned 960 souls in the Province of Kiev."

Berdyaev at twenty-seven (1901) while he was in exile at Vologda.
His first book was published that year. "*I was always in the opposition and in conflict. I revolted against aristocratic society,
against the literary world, against communism.*"

Berdyaev married Lydia Judifovna Trusheff in 1904; this portrait always hung in his study. *"He loved her with a beautiful and ethical love."*

Eugenie Judifovna Rapp, Berdyaev's sister-in-law, in 1955. A member of Berdyaev's household of forty years, she was *"one of the few people who have understood me. . . . I am greatly indebted to spiritual dialogue with her."*

The Berdyaev homes for forty years. At left, the archway leading to the apartment house at 14 Great Vlassov Lane, Moscow, where the Berdyaevs lived from 1907 until his banishment in 1922. At right, the street entrance to the house in Clamart, near Paris, purchased in 1924 with a legacy left him for the purpose by an English friend—one of the "miracles" of Berdyaev's life.

Berdyaev in his early years abroad. At left, in an enlargement from a group photograph taken in 1923 of the Presidium and professors of the Russian Scientific Institute in Berlin. At right, returning from one of the long walks with students which followed his lectures at the Russian Student Christian Movement Conference at Montfort L'Amaury, France, in the summer of 1930.

Berdyaev at seventy-four, in a photograph taken about two months before his death.

arrived. Berdyaev took communion with his friends. Instead of a few hundred persons the procession grew to thousands, which apparently so impressed the police that the long route of march was covered without incident.

Beside Nicolai Alexandrovitch's public activity, his apartment, its patriarchal furniture and the portraits of ancestor generals undisturbed, became a center of further spiritual activity—the only house of the kind in Moscow. There was a meeting every Tuesday evening with attendance of twenty or more, for discussion of topics too "hot" for handling in public. There were "regular" members like Ratchinsky, and new faces each time. One fairly constant attendant was Olga Kameneva, sister of Trotsky—which probably explained the lack of police interference. Even then the authorities exhibited an astounding tolerance, for Berdyaev insisted on speaking as freely as ever. And when he made statements like those in his book on Dostoievsky: "Godless freedom cannot fail to give rise to limitless despotism," or how Dostoievsky "knew that the revolution would not end in freedom, . . . that a movement had begun toward the final enslavement of the human spirit,"[15] they certainly did not pass unnoticed by the men in the Kremlin. One member would read a paper, and the group would discuss it. People of all opinions came—of the extreme right and the extreme left, anarchists and Old Believers—to sit in their overcoats in an unheated salon throughout the long evenings of debate. Subjects varied as much as participants. At one meeting Berdyaev would ask what topic should be discussed at the next and who would like to present it. This was the only program preparation.

Eugenie, ever the efficient hostess, served a hot drink made with birchbark instead of tea, and cakes made of grated carrots. She recalls how, for one especially large meeting, someone provided a real cake that had to be cut into more than fifty pieces to give each guest a taste. An indiscreet article in a Paris paper by one of the participants in these "Tuesdays," proving thereby that freedom of speech still existed in Soviet Russia, was probably one of the contributing causes of Berdyaev's eventual arrest and imprisonment. In defense of the authorities it must be said that Berdyaev and some of his friends, among them Muravieff and one of the Trubetskoys, belonged to a secret group maintaining contact with the "rebel" General Judenitch. A new member admitted to their small circle turned out to be a spy, which resulted in the arrest of all the men in the group.

Six weeks Berdyaev sat in solitary confinement in the *Cheka* prison

before being summoned one midnight for interrogation. Endless stone
corridors, dimly lit, led finally to a level where there were carpets on
the floor, and he was ushered into a large, richly furnished office. The
man behind the desk was a stranger with melancholy eyes of a dim
gray, and courtly manners. "My name is Dzerzhinsky," he said. It was
the name peasant women used to frighten their children—the organ-
izer-in-chief of the dread *Cheka*. On the way in, Berdyaev had decided
not to wait for questioning but proceed at once with a statement of his
position. So instead of stammering with fright, he replied: "Please
note that I consider my dignity as a thinker and writer demands that
I tell you, plainly and directly, what I believe." Dzerzhinsky seemed
not surprised: "This is what we expect of you," he said. Whereupon
Berdyaev "gave him a whole lecture, for forty-five minutes." Beginning
with an assertion that he was not a politician, Nicolai Alexandrovitch
explained the "religious, philosophical, and moral reasons" why he
was opposed to communism. The inquisitor heard him out with only
an occasional interjected remark, then tried to secure information
about other people. Berdyaev knew the *Cheka's* principal source of information was individuals held under arrest and had decided in advance
not to speak about persons. His previous experience helped him dodge
most of the questions, and for one Dzerzhinsky himself gave the answer. Evidently pleased with his guest, Dzerzhinsky terminated the interview by telling Berdyaev he was free but must not leave the city
without special permission. Turning to his assistant, he asked that "in
view of the danger from thugs in the street so late at night" Berdyaev
be taken home by car. It turned out that no car was available, but
Nicolai Alexandrovitch, with his luggage, was delivered to his door by
motorcycle. It was like Berdyaev that after such evidence of the great
man's favor he did not alter his opinions of him. One day when they
met on the street and Dzerzhinsky politely raised his hat, Berdyaev
refused to return the greeting and turned aside. This might have meant
immediate arrest, but fortunately no ill resulted from Berdyaev's insult-
ing gesture. He had no further dealings with Dzerzhinsky.

Berdyaev was acting president of the All-Russian Society of Writers.
This organization was another of the inconsistencies of the time; although its constitution stated "no communist may become a member," the document was approved by the government, which gave the
society the former home of Hertzen for its headquarters. The Society
still meets today in the same building; whether or not its constitution
has been amended is not known. Nicolai Alexandrovitch frequently had

to represent the Society's interests before the authorities, usually in an effort to have some member released from prison. He did not mention having to report to any of the "mighty ones" on his activities as professor at Moscow University. He was elected by the University itself and throughout the academic year 1920-21 delivered a course of lectures, thus fulfilling the prophecy of the mysterious Dr. Lubeck. In Soviet Russia today it would be as impossible for a man without a degree to hold such a position as it was under the Tsar.

After his release from prison Berdyaev carried on with another enterprise, the extraordinary Authors' Bookshop. In those early days, when the communists were still learning how to be a totalitarian state, the government permitted some members of the Writers' Society to maintain a shop for the sale of their own works. These were handwritten manuscripts of fifteen to twenty pages each, copied with the aid of carbon paper, and sold at what then seemed high prices. M. A. Ossorgin was director of the establishment. (There was one other in Moscow.) Zaitseff had been hired as a salesclerk "to keep him from starving"; Byeli, Berdyaev, and others sold their manuscripts. Berdyaev also was a "salesclerk"—at least he stood behind the counter on occasion. Ossorgin used imperial banknotes to bind his manuscript, which the others thought almost unfair competition.

Most of the writers were in the same situation as Berdyaev himself. The war and revolution had cut off all his regular income, and the general confusion of an anti-intellectual regime made regular employment impossible. The only time in his life Berdyaev suffered actual want was during the four years after the revolution in Moscow. This bookshop, even if it sold very few books and made a still more meager profit, became a regular club. Despite the favor shown them, most of the writers took a dim view of the new government. The shop served the need for a center where friends could meet and be sure of a sympathetic atmosphere in which to discuss current events. Nicolai Alexandrovitch was not the easiest of partners to get along with. One day Zaitseff, working on the second floor, heard a sudden quarrel in the shop below. Quite oblivious of the customers standing by, Berdyaev was pouring invective on Professor Zhivigetov, a "fellow salesman," shouting and stamping his feet. Soon he broke off and came raging up the stairs. Here he strode back and forth across the floor, hands clenched behind his back, muttering to himself. After a while he went downstairs again and asked the colleague's pardon. It later appeared that when Berdyaev had casually told the other man he was going

across town on an errand and would be absent most of the afternoon,
the other had mildly reminded him that today was Berdyaev's turn to
tend the shop. The idea of being on the same level as a mere clerk had
seemed to Nicolai Alexandrovitch so preposterous that he lost his
temper.

For any but the highest Soviet dignitaries, life in Moscow in the
immediate postrevolution years was difficult. It is notable that Berdyaev never referred to this in his autobiography. There was a
scarcity of everything. Byeli told how he had to wear his shirt Russian
style over his trousers to hide "the indecent state" of the lower gar-
ment. Food was obtainable only by barter with peasants who brought
it to the markets. There were long queues before every sort of shop—
except the authors' bookstore. This was hard enough in summer, but
in winter it was terrible. In the Berdyaev house the temperature
rarely rose above freezing. Eugenie had somehow arranged the trans-
port of furniture from Babaki, and chopping this up bit by bit, they
heated with one small wood stove that could be moved from room to
room. "It was hard to see my father's great oaken armchair broken
up," she said. In the mornings when Berdyaev was writing, the little
stove stood in his room. But it had to be used for cooking as well,
and was moved out in time to prepare the one hot dish of the day.
Nicolai Alexandrovitch insisted upon doing the heaviest work about
the house, himself chopping up the furniture and carrying out refuse.
All the plumbing froze during the heatless winter and by spring the
cellar floor was coated with ice that had to be chipped up and carried
out. For one as squeamish as Berdyaev and as hypersensitive to odors,
this was a job demanding real heroism. He completed the task
swathed in an old dressing gown to protect his clothing from chips of
the frozen mass. In every way, Eugenie recalls, he was as helpful as
possible. About one matter, however, he was apologetic but firm; he
must be undisturbed during his hours of writing.

Some of Berdyaev's left-wing acquaintances felt he disliked the
Bolsheviks as much for their coarseness and lack of culture as for their
politics. Berdyaev insisted it was on spiritual, not social, grounds that
he decried the revolution. Freedom, he believed, is aristocratic rather
than democratic—men, as the Grand Inquisitor said, are trading
freedom for bread; food for the spirit is bartered away for food for
the body.

Berdyaev's article "Quenchers of the Spirit" had expressed his
dislike of the "official" church. He was perhaps unfairly disappointed

at what he called "ecclesiastical orthodoxy"; the revolution had been almost incomprehensible for an organization existing under the control and protection of the monarchy. Later, with Orthodox Christians—lay and clerics alike—facing persecution and terror unflinchingly and a list of martyrs probably unsurpassed in history, he came to have another opinion. One encounter shortly before he left Russia was particularly influential in forming his new impression of a church that had been tried as by fire—the contact with Father Alexis Metcheff, who became Nicolai Alexandrovitch's confessor about this time. A remarkable and radiant personality, Father Metcheff was widely revered for his saintly life and unusual talent for discerning the needs of those who crowded around his doors. At the close of each liturgy, crowds including Red Army soldiers and officers would wait for him to come out of the church. Unable to speak personally with each one, he would pick out those most in need of spiritual guidance. The people said he was clairvoyant, so unerring was his choice. Returning home from his final talk with Father Metcheff, Berdyaev told with amazement of his impressions: "Father Metcheff rose to greet me. He was all in white, and it seemed to me that he radiated light. I told him how terribly painful it was for me to leave my fatherland, and he only said: 'You must go—the west must hear your word.'" In Father Metcheff Berdyaev found again his full communion with the Orthodox Church. Eugenie says he considered Father Metcheff a saint.

During these four years of deprivation and disorder, the Berdyaev family had for the first time in their lives, been unable to leave Moscow for a summer in the country. Let Eugenie tell the story:

> In 1922 we happened to learn that in the village of Borvikha, near Moscow, a peasant would rent his hut for the summer. We . . . decided to go. Ossorgin,[16] who also passionately loved the country, joined us. It was inconvenient for private persons to travel by train, so we hired a cart, loaded it with mattresses and blankets and bags of salt. The peasants would sell nothing for money and food could be had only by bartering. All our silver and valuables had been traded away during the first year of the revolution, but for salt and matches I got from the Soviet institution where I was compelled to work, one could obtain milk, eggs and bread. The cart loaded, Nicolai Alexandrovitch picked up his favorite dog Shu-shu, intending to walk the thirty kil-

ometers, and the procession started. The village was charming—
on the bank of the Moscow River with golden sandy beaches
and rolling hills on one side, and a mighty age-old forest on the
other. Somehow we managed to get ourselves installed under the
low-beamed roof and began a quiet life, a rest from the nightmare
when every day there was firing in the streets, and any day the
secret police might burst into the house, to arrest Nicolai Alexandrovitch or requistion something or other. . . . After all that,
our life here among the fragrant pines seemed like a dream.
Mornings, we breakfasted on the tiny porch, drank a muddy
beverage we called coffee, and milk, which was a great rarity in
the city. After breakfast Nicolai Alexandrovitch would go to his
writing in a room barely large enough to hold a small shaky table.
Sometimes Ossorgin would tell him "you are wasting your time
at writing. Soviet citizens ought not to spend time thinking; it's
a bourgeois relic. The Party does the thinking—let's go fishing."
We all rested after lunch and met again at five for tea. Of course
it was not real tea; we made it from dried carrots or birchbark.
Sugar was a very rare article, but Nicolai Alexandrovitch received a little in his special author's ration. Tea-time was the
gayest of the day. We read our two newspapers—*The Cock*,
edited by Ossorgin, and *The Turkey*, published by sister and me.
Each accused the other of departure from the "general line" and
made fun of the Bolsheviks' decrees. We would laugh until we
cried. After tea we would walk in the woods, sometimes gathering mushrooms. Evenings Nicolai Alexandrovitch would sit again
at his work. . . . So our hungry, happy days passed.

Toward the end of summer Berdyaev decided to go to Moscow "to
see what was happening." The one night he spent in his home he was
arrested. After a week in prison he was called before an official who
read him an order—of perpetual banishment, not to Siberia but outside Russia—and he was made to sign a statement recognizing that
if he should return he would be shot. He was then set at liberty
pending actual deportation. He soon learned that he was not alone
in this situation. A group of "writers, scholars, [and] social workers
who were recognized as hopelessly inconvertible to communism"[17]
were likewise to be deported. This was one of the few occasions in the
entire history of the Soviet government when such persons were permitted to leave Russia. It was rumored Trotsky had insisted upon

this form of punishment rather than execution. Lunacharsky's influence seems more likely. No one knows the actual reason—perhaps the Kremlin dared not "liquidate" such well-known persons, whose only crime had been idealogical disagreement with the established religion of Marx and Lenin. One probable factor was the Geneva conference under way at the time and the Kremlin's desire to avoid an unfavorable impression abroad.

To Berdyaev the decree of banishment was like a deep wound. He was proud of the fact that through these five years of demonic pressures, when so many of his former friends had "adapted" to the new regime, he had never wavered in his "moral irreconcilability." Although on several occasions he had been offered the possibility of leaving the country, the idea had been curtly refused: "I was born a Russian. My country is suffering. I ought to stay with my country." For despite his constant criticism of the government and state church, Nicolai Alexandrovitch loved Russia as deeply as any man could. "Without love of country," he wrote in 1915, "a man is unable to create."[18] He loved Russia as much because of, as in spite of, her "most monstrous contradictions, her puzzling antinomies, her mysterious elementalism." Neither was he blind to the serious defects in Russian character. Russia "is so heavy, inert, lazy, . . . accepts her life so submissively. . . . No one of our classes wants to rise—aristocracy, merchants, peasants, the clergy, the bureaucracy—all prefer to remain . . . like everyone else."[19] "The Russian people lack ambition. As in the traditional prehistoric days when the Russians invited the Variags to come and rule them, the Russia of today," he said, "is a maiden awaiting a fiancé, a master."[20] That was before the revolution; he was anything but happy when Lenin assumed the master's role. But to the end of his life he never lost his faith in the special mission of the Russian people, which through the centuries had believed that the Kingdom of God is realizable on earth. He saw Russian communism as a distortion of the Russian messianic idea. And in the midst of World War I he sensed the nearness of a new day: "The present war ought to close on a . . . great union between west and east . . . Russia is being called to play a defining role in the life of mankind."[21] "Russia is called to be a liberator of the nations"[22] but liberator on a spiritual basis, not the "liberation" Stalin brought to Hungary and Czechoslovakia. "The Russian people, with its age-old idea, does not like the building of this earthly city, and is yearning toward the Coming City, the New Jerusalem. But the New Jerusalem is not separate from the colossal Russian land. The New Jerusalem is related to that land, and that land will be a part of it."[23]

There was a further reason why Berdyaev regretted having to leave. He was completely out of sympathy with the emigration, now centered in Berlin, and forcsaw difficulty in getting on with its members. There seems to have been some latitude in the expulsion order, for Kuzmin-Karavaeff reports considerable discussion among expellees as to whether they should leave at once or wait further developments. Berdyaev was leaving now: "Don't you realize that if we wait too long, we shall arrive in the midst of the social revolution in Europe?" The G.P.U., recent successor to the *Cheka*, volunteered to arrange German visas. The Germans, on their part, let the G.P.U. know that Germany was not a country to which political undesirables could be deported. If the expellees themselves requested visas, these would be granted. To the Berdyaevs, the Germans were most helpful. Visas were granted as requested—after it was too late to catch the less comfortable of two steamers. They also forwarded some of Berdyaev's manuscripts and notes via diplomatic pouch.

In the Berdyaev household there was much anxious discussion. How many should leave? Eugenie and her mother felt that four persons would be an intolerable burden on Nicolai Alexandrovitch, but Berdyaev insisted the family not be separated and secured German visas for all four. Exiles were permitted to take only two or three suitcases apiece, containing only personal belongings—no letters or photographs, not even the family icons. Together with wives and children, it was a convoy of seventy persons that armed guards escorted to the train for Leningrad. In that city, during the day or two before the steamer sailed, the Berdyaev family stayed with their friends the Losskys—who were scheduled to leave on the same boat. Other friends of Berdyaev accompanied him on the journey.[24] Like him, many were to attain greater prominence abroad than they had at home—Bulgakov and Frank in Europe, Sorokin and Lossky in America. Because the only ships left to the Germans after the great war were old hulks none of the Allies wanted, the *Oberbürgermeister Haken* was far from being a luxury liner. Families were lodged in cabins of a sort, and the single men slept on deck. The families took their meals in the dining-salon while bachelors ate with the petty officers. Lydia told one of the men they were fortunate, because mealtime gatherings in the salon were frequently marred by quarrels among the exiles.

These exiles departed "not knowing whither they went." They knew the German authorities would provide some kind of living space in Berlin—this had been promised, but where and how they had no idea. Eugenie, whose employment in a government office in Moscow had helped support the family, planned to look for work in Germany. They could have no other plans. It was a tragic moment as the steamer passed by Kronstadt and Berdyaev stood at the rail overcome with sadness, catching his last glimpse of Russian land. Sensing his intense spiritual pain, Eugenie touched his arm and said: "Ni, maybe we *will* return." "Never," was the reply, and once more a Berdyaev premonition would be confirmed by history.

# 12

## BERLIN

When the train bringing the seventy Russian exiles from Stettin arrived in Berlin, they were met by official representatives of the government. The socialist government seemed to give special attention to the Berdyaev family. Two large rooms in Frau Dehme's apartment, 31/32 Ranke-Strasse, had been prepared for them. The landlady was disagreeable, permitting their passage through her living room to their own rooms only on a strip of old carpet laid over the rug. For people with no fixed income, food was scarce. Mme Kuskova, who—after she and her husband were saved from a firing squad through the intervention of Hoover and Nansen—had also been banished, arriving in Berlin in June, before the Berdyaev party, tells how Berdyaev used to come to her apartment. "There was a dish of raw sugar on the table, and he would eat it in huge spoonfuls. I sometimes wondered if he came to us just for that sugar."

German officialdom was more cordial than the émigrés. The German Red Cross and the Society for the Study of Eastern Europe gave a splendid reception for the newly arrived exiles. There were speeches of welcome, and replies by members of the group. Berdyaev was not one of the speakers, probably because he could not share the "black vs. white" attitude of some of the orators toward the Soviet Government. To Nicolai Alexandrovitch, who had frequently visited Berlin before the war, the postwar city was depressing. Streets were full of wounded veterans, millions of men were unemployed, and rampant inflation added to the misery. Even the government representatives whom Berdyaev met at functions given in honor of the exiles these first few weeks seemed gray and uninteresting.

Berlin was already the intellectual center of the million-and-a-half widely scattered Russian émigrés—with many organizations, several publishing houses, and much political activity. But the émigrés in Berlin would have nothing to do with the new exiles.[1] The fact that this small group had elected to remain in Russia when a million others had fled abroad had not endeared them to the mass. Word went around that these newcomers were not exiles but really Soviet agents, sent to undermine the solidarity of the emigration. Solidarity was a poor word for this or any other emigration, whose members were doomed to carry their quarrels with them and be subject to continuous fractionization until all strength was exhausted. Even some of Berdyaev's friends soon were fighting him. Struve, who a short three years before had been hidden in Berdyaev's home after his escape from the dissolving army, was now a leader of the main stream of thought that advocated armed intervention to overthrow the Communist regime. When Berdyaev argued against a military adventure— saying Bolshevism was a spiritual, almost a religious movement, and could be countered only by spiritual means—no one understood him. He appeared to be actually sympathizing with the tyrants in the Kremlin. He called a meeting in his home of the "very tops" of all the émigré groups, and argumentation rose to such a pitch that Frau Dehme threatened to call the police. Berdyaev told them they were almost as much opposed to freedom and caught with "elementary ideas" of political and military action as were the Bolsheviks. Many of them even hoped for a restoration of the monarchy. All this was past, he said, and history could not be moved backward. If he had sometimes felt lonely in Russia, it was a sensation less strong than his near-isolation from the Russian population of Berlin. This divergence put an end to Berdyaev's close contact with Struve. During the late war their common hatred of Hitlerism and what it stood for brought them again into partial sympathy. When later Berdyaev was hospitalized after his operation, Struve called on him, and after his recovery Berdyaev returned the call. Apart from these two contacts, they never met again.

The exile group at once proceeded to organize things for themselves. Berdyaev had more knowledge of Germany than most of the Russians, spoke the language easily, and quickly oriented himself in the German scene. This helped advance their projects. Already existing associations were largely political; the new exiles set up cultural institutions. Before 1922 was over, the Russian Scientific Institute had been founded, staffed almost exclusively by members of the exiled group, and aided by the German government. Four courses of study were offered: agronomy, economics and statistics, law, and "philosophical-spiritual." Berdyaev became dean of the Institute and gave courses in ethics and the history of Russian thought. The initiative for starting it was not his own, however, and Berdyaev shortly lost interest.

He was more attached to the Religious-Philosophical Academy, which was his own idea. In contemplating exile while still in Moscow, he had hoped to set up a group which in a free country could continue the work of Moscow's Solovieff Society. Materially provided for, Nicolai Alexandrovitch was able to devote full attention to the Academy and other social activities.

If the older folk among the emigration would have none of him, Berdyaev turned to youth. Within a few months after his arrival in Berlin, a group of intelligent young people was meeting fairly regularly in his home to discuss religious and philosophical topics. Among the score or more who came were not only his friends but some of his sharpest critics. Eugenie recalls some of the participants: Smolitch, Babitch, Vera Chulkova, Sophie Shidlovsky, Lunin, Pianoff, Fidler, Sliousberg. Although Berdyaev asserted he was not and did not wish to become a teacher, from his early days in Berlin until his death he always had around him a group of younger men and women who were attracted by his brilliant discussions of life problems. Many remained his disciples, in the sense of sharing his message with others. After an opening talk at such meetings, Berdyaev would ask for questions. The group soon discovered that if he were merely answering a question Berdyaev was "rather dreary," but if anyone started an argument with him, sparks began to fly. In general, Nicolai Alexandrovitch was inclined to dodge direct questions, much preferring debate. He found real satisfaction in these meetings with young people, and they were continued in Paris. To many participants the meetings opened a new view of life. One of them reports: "he swept us all off our feet." Several found their way back into the church as a result of their contacts with Berdyaev. Former members of his study circles have always formed the motive center for moral support of Berdyaev's ideas. A result of their activities is the present Berdyaev Society.[2]

One of the young men near Berdyaev was V. N. Ilyin. He had arrived in Berlin from Constantinople about the time the Berdyaevs came. Eugenie noticed the poorly dressed young refugee in church and, after conversation with him, told Berdyaev about him. Nicolai Alexandrovitch invited Ilyin to the house, and the young man became a constant attendant at all Berdyaev's "circles" and public lectures. He recalls his first impression of Nicolai Alexandrovitch at a meeting (1923) of the Religious-Philosophical Academy, on the occasion of the three hundredth anniversary of the birth of Pascal. A friend in Moscow had written of the astonishing contrast between Berdyaev's dandified exterior and the profundity of his thought. Ilyin noted the flashing eyes beneath a shock of black hair—"the look of a grand seigneur"— and the clarity and vigor of the speech, the love for sharp expressions and paradoxical turns of phrase. He became a close friend of the Berdyaev family in Berlin, often spending whole days at their house "eating, drinking and conversing." Nicolai Alexandrovitch was very kind to him, helping in many ways, although always too tactful to offer direct pecuniary aid. Ilyin achieved the distinction of being the only person outside the family who might enter Berdyaev's study while he was at work.

Ilyin tells one revealing incident of those Berlin days. At an Academy meeting, the speaker closed his lecture on Descartes with: "Descartes, Christ, Socrates, and other great thinkers agree with me." Berdyaev challenged him immediately: "I have just heard something monstrous. You called our Lord Christ a 'great thinker.' He was not a great thinker, but God, and the Saviour of the World." While most of the group meetings in Berlin were unmarked by special incidents, there was one that caused talk throughout the city. Some of the young people had not yet accepted Berdyaev's Christian position, while others, in keeping with the reactionary atmosphere of the emigration, took an almost "black hundred" view of the place and function of the church. As a result of discussion on these matters, it was agreed to invite Metropolitan Eulogius[3] to meet the group. The meeting took place in the Berdyaev apartment. Of course there was tea—real tea was one of the luxuries of Berlin—and Berdyaev, after greeting the Metropolitan, spoke at some length on the importance of Christian organizations of youth at a time when anti-Christian forces were well organized and aggressive. Then one of the members spoke in the name of the group. Beginning with effusive praise of Orthodoxy, he proceeded to attack the Roman Catholic Church, concluding with an appeal to the Metropolitan: "We call you, Your Eminence, to use your bishop's staff like an iron rod to destroy those wolves in sheep's clothing who have come among us and are stealing your flock." The wise Metropolitan listened to this admonition with his quiet fatherly smile, and although Berdyaev's face was white with repressed anger, nothing further was said on the matter. But as the Metropolitan was being ushered out, Berdyaev passed the word for the young people to remain. Then he turned on the offending member. His voice was harsh and imperious: "You

insufferable boy—you not only permit yourself to instruct the Metropolitan as to what he should do, but in a home where the hostess
belongs to the Catholic Church you presume to speak in such a coarse
and indecent tone about the Catholics. I demand that you apologize
immediately to my wife and then leave this house!" To the rest he
said: "We must always take a Christian attitude toward all Christians
of whatever confession."

Other personal contacts were of considerable importance to Berdyaev
at this period. The "iron curtain" had not yet fallen, and there were
meetings between émigrés and Soviet writers. Nicolai Alexandrovitch
also made full use of the possibilities in Berlin for contact with western
thinkers. He was greatly attracted by Count Keyserling, whom he considered "one of the most brilliantly endowed thinkers of the west."
Their meeting in Berlin began a lifelong friendly relationship. Berdyaev
could not agree with the German philosopher's "indefinite dualism of
the spiritual and the telluric," the latter "not subject to any moral
element," or "his spirituality, more Hindu than Christian."[4] But
Keyserling—already acquainted with some of Berdyaev's books—
showed him great attention, helped arrange for a German edition of his
*Meaning of History,* and even wrote a preface for it. Berdyaev had
looked forward to meeting other Germans who were making headlines
in the world. They did not always live up to his expectations. Of
Oswald Spengler, whose startling *Decline of the West* had attracted
world-wide attention, Berdyaev reported only that he "looked very
bourgeois." Acquaintance with Max Scheler was equally disappointing.
Berdyaev had found some of his own ideas in Scheler's books, differently expressed but basically the same, and had looked forward to
meeting a kindred spirit. The first meeting—and Berdyaev did not
record another—was unsatisfactory. Scheler seemed to have departed
not only from Catholicism but from Christianity as well. His conversation was rich in ideas, but Berdyaev could discern in him "no central
idea of life."

One of the members of Berdyaev's youthful following in Berlin was
F. T. Pianoff, long a leader in the Russian Student Christian Movement. Matured beyond his youth by the bitterest last-ditch fighting
against the bolsheviks in Moscow, he had left Russia in 1918. Pianoff,
acting for the North American YMCA, called shortly after Nicolai
Alexandrovitch's arrival from Russia. He was impressed by Berdyaev's
noble figure despite the very disorderly rooms of the cheap Berlin lodging. Berdyaev had never heard of the YMCA. From their first conver-

sation Pianoff had the impression of a handsome, friendly, rather naive grown-up boy. Out of this first meeting grew a friendship lasting throughout Berdyaev's life. Pianoff found that Berdyaev could be easily imposed upon by unscrupulous people wishing to use him. But when Pianoff attended Berdyaev's first lecture on what Russia had to give the world and what the west could offer them, he was deeply impressed both by the man's brilliant mind and his spiritual power. This meeting, attended by nearly a thousand persons representing all political colors in the Berlin Russian colony, may be said to have been the origin of the Religious-Philosophical Academy.

In this connection the ephemeral existence of another philosophic association is worth recording. Before the exile group reached the west, there had been launched in Berlin a Union of Russian Philosophers under the aegis of Professor (now Archpriest) V. V. Zenkovsky.[5] The appearance on the scene of Berdyaev's Religious-Philosophical Academy, whose faculty was made up almost entirely of members of the exile group, emphasized the division between exiles and émigrés. Two philosophical societies were manifestly unnecessary, and the American YMCA—backers of the new one but desirous of serving all Russians abroad—made an effort to merge the two. Berdyaev took the position that he could not collaborate with a group of émigrés, however, and nothing came of the attempt. What with Berdyaev's brilliance and the support of American capital, the earlier organization soon faded. Relations between Zenkovsky and Berdyaev were strained from then until Berdyaev's death, with responsibility shared by the two men probably in equal measure.

In its November-December (1922) number, the *New Russian Book*, a monthly magazine published in Berlin, carried an important news item:

> The formal opening of the Religious-Philosophical Academy in Berlin, organized in connection with the American Young Men's Christian Association, took place on December 1 (1922). The hall was crowded. The meeting opened with an address by Nicolai Alexandrovitch Berdyaev "On the spiritual renaissance of Russia, and the aims of the Religious-Philosophical Academy." The speaker's basic thought was the crisis of humanism. Berdyaev called for the union of Christian forces of the west and the east. Then Professor Frank spoke of the essential unity of philosophy

and religion. . . . Professor L. P. Karsavin spoke on the religious understanding of history.

The following courses are offered in the Religious-Philosophical Academy: Professor G. P. Eichenwald, "Philosophic Motives in Russian Literature"; N. A. Berdyaev, "The Philosophy of Religion"; F. A. Stepun, "The Essence of the Romantic"; L. P. Karsavin, "The World View in the Middle Ages"; I. A. Ilyin, "World View and Character" and "The Philosophy of Art"; S. L. Frank, "Greek Philosophy" and "The Bases of Philosophy"; V. E. Sezemann, "Ethics"; N. S. Arsenieff, "The Antique World and Early Christianity."

This notice was a mild reflection of the facts. The crowded hall contained the intellectual elite of Russian Berlin. Metropolitan Eulogius was present. And as might have been expected, Berdyaev's lecture was a sensation. Instead of a tirade against the revolution and the bolsheviks, without which almost no speech was made in the emigration circles of the period, he spoke of their common guilt for what had taken place in Russia and called for new cultural and religious forces to oppose and replace communism. As time went on, many of his listeners accepted the truth of his charge that "all were responsible for all," but at the moment it was too strong medicine for most of them to take. He was, as usual, left very much alone.

He was not idle in his loneliness. He continued the habit of spending long hours at his writing. He browsed widely in the state library and reread many of the books he had been unable to bring with him from home. And in the course of his writing, without intending to do so, he produced a "best seller." He called it "an etude." The small book has been translated into a dozen other languages and has perhaps been read by more people than any other of Berdyaev's works. Its title was *The New Middle Ages*.[6] With the great war, man had reached the end of an epoch, Berdyaev wrote in 1923. Although the "war to end war" was over and the League of Nations, with men beginning to think in terms of one world, was a promising infant of three years, the whole of eastern Europe was in ruins. Even Germany, almost undamaged materially, was bankrupt and poverty-ridden. But Berdyaev was looking beyond these difficult times:

> The processes moving toward the elimination of national isolationism and toward the formation of a world-unity, I have called the end of modern history, of its individualistic spirit, and the

beginning of a new Middle Ages. This is to be looked for, but our time will not see the world-brotherhood of man. The road just ahead will be dark and weary: mankind must pass through a period of difficulty before the new day dawns. We are now entering a second Middle Age in history.[7]

The Middle Ages were in their way creative times. Mistakenly called the Dark Ages, they represented in actuality a slow accumulation of the spiritual forces that blossomed into the Renaissance. What was really great in the Renaissance, Berdyaev wrote, was the Christian spirit, guarded and developed through the Middle Ages. From the seventeenth century until now, man had been relying upon himself, with the rise of humanism and the development of science and technics. This experience resulted in something near spiritual insolvency, Berdyaev declared, and the communist revolution in Russia was an excellent illustration. "The Russian revolution has realized what Dostoievsky foresaw." Dostoievsky pointed out that the basic question in the socialism of his day was spiritual, not material, and proclaimed that Russia could not be saved by an atheistic social program but only by spiritual reformation. In several of his books Berdyaev developed the idea of the despiritualization of man in our modern world. With the Russian revolution, mankind had reached an era of near-bankruptcy in spiritual values. While man had entered the Renaissance with a new spiritual vigor developed in the quiet of the Middle Ages, modern man brought a weary spirit—a tragically debilitated faith or none at all—into the epoch now beginning.

And just as the salvation of Russia must be a spiritual process, so must the redemption of the modern, humanistic world. As in the first years of the Russian catastrophe he had called for a new spiritual awakening—an aggressive forward movement by the forces of Christianity— Berdyaev now challenged the entire western world to do battle against the powers of darkness. Instead of being coffered off in a small sector of life, Christianity must again permeate the whole, as in the Dark Ages when religion was culture and social order and the pervasive element in man's thought. Berdyaev did not mean, here, the dominance of an organized ecclesiastical authority. The boundaries of the real church are far wider than people think, and its life reaches out invisibly to encompass all civilization. But this would be in the future. The world must pass through a dark period; the struggle will be long and arduous.

A new Christian chivalry must be born, aligning the efforts of man the creator more closely with God's. Night was closing in, but Russians could and must struggle toward a new day.

This small book, the first of his works to be translated from Russian, brought Berdyaev to the attention of thinkers all over the world. It was probably responsible for an invitation (1923) to lecture in Rome, where Professor Lo Gatto, an old friend of Russia, was concerned with an Institute for Eastern Europe. Berdyaev, discovering that his books had preceded him, was at once invited to lecture for numerous bodies. Letters began to reach him from all over the world, and he realized his audience was far wider than he had imagined. He was encouraged to seek publishers for other books, two in manuscript that he had been able to get out of Russia, and another, produced during the Berlin period, entitled *The Meaning of History*. Although the YMCA Press already existed, only one book, *Dostoievsky*, was published by that house—of which Berdyaev was soon to become editor-in-chief.

Unhappily, fame did not improve Berdyaev's fortunes. The year 1923 saw the final collapse of the German currency. The modest stipend Berdyaev received from the YMCA was soon outdistanced by mounting costs of living. About this time Berdyaev wrote his old friend Shestov, then in Paris, asking about the possibility of locating in France:

> It is difficult and unpleasant to make an appeal to the French for myself. You should take up the question for a small group of philosophers, together. . . . We have remained in Berlin because it was the cheapest city in Europe, and here was concentrated the largest number of Russian young people. Now everything has changed. Berlin has become the most expensive city in Europe and Paris has become the Russian center. . . . Our income is . . . reduced. The situation of the Scientific Institute is hopeless: The Religious-Philosophical Academy has a pitiful budget. . . . Russian publishing houses have stopped publishing in Berlin. I feel that the Berlin period of our life is closing and the idea of a move to Paris comes into my mind. We may be able to transfer at least part of the Religious-Philosophical Academy to Paris but . . . it will be necessary to seek other means of earning money. . . . Could something be obtained from the French government, at least for a small group of exiles? . . . I ask your counsel and your help.

As it turned out, neither the French government nor French educational institutions were able to offer material assistance, and Berdyaev never could forget it. On several occasions he compared the friendly reception he had received from official Germany with the "cold shoulder" shown him by the French government. His criticism of France was not altogether just; in Germany a social democrat government was closely related to the new government in Russia, and Berdyaev was labeled a socialist. France was still struggling to recover from the devastation of war, and already had masses of refugees—not alone Russians—with which to deal. A majority of France's intellectual leaders knew nothing about the new Russian prophet who had so excited Berlin. It was only after he arrived and could make personal contact with some of France's Christian thinkers that *The New Middle Ages* was translated into French (1926). Thus both materially and morally the French were unprepared and unable to help Nicolai Alexandrovitch, and this he should have understood.

A crowd of "more than fifty" saw the family off for Paris, among them many of the young people with whom Berdyaev had made friendships in his short two-year stay in Berlin. The group of four stowed their meager luggage in the racks of a third-class carriage—none of them had ever traveled in anything but first-class before—and were off for Paris, hearts heavy at the close of an important chapter in their lives. Berlin had been Berdyaev's introduction to the west. Like many other people, he had discovered that visiting a country as a tourist and residing in it are two different things. In the autobiography, Berdyaev devotes a page to what he had brought with him from Russia and how his Berlin experience affected his thought. As a Russian he had been a universalist, thinking of universalism as distinctive to his homeland. Out of the travail of the revolution he brought an eschatological sense of historic destiny that he found few thinkers in the west sharing. With it, he brought a conviction that communism develops largely because organized Christianity fails to solve certain problems—indicating a crisis in world Christianity. He was deeply conscious of the conflict between the individual and society—between personality and world harmony—conflicts that he saw to be unsolvable within the confines of history. But despite this somewhat somber philosophical cargo, he also brought to the west his confidence in the dawn of a new creative epoch in Christianity. For a quarter of a century, in Paris, he was destined to communicate both his pessimism and his hope to thinking men and women around the world.

# 13

## PARIS IN THE FALL

After arrival the family spent a few days in "a modest hotel" (how "modest" a Paris hotel can be!), but thanks to Prince Nicolas Trubetskoy they soon found three small furnished rooms in suburban Clamart, on the ground floor of a house set in a small garden. Both the garden and the forest of Clamart pleased Nicolai Alexandrovitch immensely. They reminded him of his homes in Russia, and whenever he could, he walked or rode his bicycle through the woods at Clamart. Passionately fond of the outdoors, he could scarcely name a tree and never was interested in the species or name of a new flower—although he had a marked preference for roses. For him, most of the world's flora was either roses or not roses. Berdyaev loved nature, but not all of it. Once when taking a rest at Brides-les-Bains in the French Alps, he wrote: "The mountains are not my element, neither is the sea. I like the country, the broad grain fields, woods, meadows, lakes, the linden groves. I imagine heaven must be like that. I regret that I cannot spend most of my life in the country." Lydia did not share his feeling. A year after the previous comments, he was writing her: "It grieves me that you do not share with me this love for . . . life in the country."[1]

They lived four years in the house at No. 2 rue Martial-Grandchamps; then the house was sold and the family had to face the terribly difficult housing problem again. One day at the market, Lydia heard of a vacant house for rent at 14 rue de St. Cloud. Always in straitened circumstances, for them the problem of furnishing a three-story house was almost baffling, but they had to leave the first residence by the end of the month, and Eugenie, greatly against her will, asked a Paris relative for a loan. This in hand, the two ladies spent days at the famous Flea Market collecting the cheapest furniture they could find, regardless of its state of disrepair. They repaired and reupholstered these things themselves and so collected the most essential items. The house was "very comfortable, with central heating, and a

large study on the second floor for Nicolai Alexandrovitch," and here
they spent "the happiest years of their life in exile." But toward the
end of 1936 the rent was suddenly raised to a figure the Berdyaevs
could not possibly pay. By that time the housing shortage in France
was such that to secure any apartment, cheap or "de luxe," it had to
be purchased outright—and the necessary outlay was enormous. The
two women were beside themselves with anxiety. Berdyaev, "as usual
in a catastrophic situation, was calm."

Then a miracle happened. Reading his mail at the breakfast table
one morning, Nicolai Alexandrovitch remarked: "I can't understand
why some notary in Paris wants to see me. I have no reason to deal
with notaries." He went to call on the notary, and the two sisters
could not imagine what gave him such an exultant air as he opened
the gate on his return. "Imagine," he said, "Florence has left us
money to buy a house." Then they recalled a remark once made by an
English friend, Mrs. Florence West[2]: "I wish you might have your
own home; life in exile is so difficult." "How strange," Berdyaev remarked, "here I am suddenly a man of property." "And thank God,"
Lydia replied, "without your 'property' we would soon be on the
street." Shortly afterward the Berdyaevs were installed at 83 rue du
Moulin de Pierre in Clamart—and the home was established which
has been, ever since, a place of pilgrimage for seekers of the truth from
many lands and races.

Hundreds of such pilgrims remember the green-painted grill that
opens into an extensive garden, its once-formal flower beds long neg-
lected, its roses and other vines a jungle closed in save for a swept
path or two. It would never have entered Berdyaev's mind to take a
hoe or pruning shears and clean up the garden. Besides, the ladies
liked it that way. They felt it reminded them of their old Russian
garden. "After all," they argued, "this is no Versailles."

One goes up curving steps to the small porch overgrown with vines,
and to the door, which was apparently never locked—the bell was
permanently out of order and one had to call out to announce his
arrival upon entering. Doors on either side of a corridor lead directly
from the entrance to Eugenie's room on the right and a dining parlor
on the left. Behind the parlor is a small kitchen. The corridor angles
past a curving stairway toward the "big salon"—so large that it has
recently been transformed into an Orthodox chapel. The furniture is
what still remains of the Flea Market purchases, most of it somewhat
decrepit. Next to the kitchen door in the dining parlor is a square

table, its dark red cover adorned by a lace doily. There is a divan against the opposite wall under the icons in the corner, with a lamp usually alight. For years, from the outset of the war, the only heat in the house came from a small stove set in the back corridor stairwell. Eugenie has lived through entire winters with the temperature around 50 degrees Fahrenheit. Recent repairs to the old central heating plant have made it possible to keep the two-story house reasonably comfortable.

Berdyaev strove with all his might to make an ideal home but never felt he succeeded. How seriously he took the task is evident in a letter to Lydia:

> We give so little consideration to our common life, are too much absorbed in ourselves. We have not transfigured our lives, have not subordinated our way to the Christian way, the way of union in one Christian love. I know that way is hard, it presupposes a tormenting reworking of our lives, of our everyday communion with each other.

Spinka, author of Berdyaev, Captive of Freedom, says Berdyaev was not easy to live with; Eugenie asserts the opposite is true, and that Nicolai Alexandrovitch was considerate and as helpful as his small practical capacities permitted. That these were not extensive is evidenced by Eugenie's remark that if he tried to fix something he was sure to spoil it; consequently they never sought his help save in emergencies. One day in Moscow when Lydia was ill and Eugenie busy with something else, she casually asked Nicolai Alexandrovitch if he would start a fire in their small stove.

> It was a very ordinary kind of stove. Ni stood in front of it, a look of bewilderment on his face. "How do you open the door?" "Turn the knob," I said. "But how do you turn the knob?" "With your hand, of course." "It's strange but it won't turn!" . . . and I interrupted him by turning the knob myself. "And what next?" he asked. "Put in the paper and then the kindling, and after that has started, put in a little wood." "But the wad of paper is too big to go through the door—what should I do?" With that I said: "Ni, you'd better go back to your writing"— and I built the fire myself.

One day the light over Berdyaev's desk went out while he was writing. This was most disturbing. "Genie, I'll go out to get the electrician!" A young woman staying in the house heard the remark. "It's only a fuse," she told him. "If you have a stepladder, I can fix it." This she did in the briefest time. Berdyaev was carried away with surprise and admiration—that anyone, and a woman at that, could repair electrical apparatus! Although he was not often asked to serve as handyman, Berdyaev occasionally did the family marketing. On such occasions every detail had to be discussed—was the butter at Hauser's better than at "Maggi." This might last half an hour. And often, standing at the already opened door, hat in hand, the inevitable scarf wound about his neck, Berdyaev would turn back: "Now, Genie—maybe after all it would be better to buy at Hauser's."

Normally Eugenie did most of the marketing, Nicolai Alexandrovitch being interested only in purchases of milk, butter, and wine. He bought good wines at the Nicolas store nearby, and in the French style there was always wine on the table, though Berdyaev drank sparingly. Unlike most Russians, he never took vodka; he thought it vulgar. Despite his personal fastidiousness, Berdyaev would uncomplainingly carry an old sack when he went marketing, and people would notice the contrast between the well-dressed man, with his fine tie and perfume, and the dirty bag full of bottles, milk cans, or parcels.

At his writing he demanded complete isolation. But he always shared his thoughts and experiences eagerly with the family. Returning home from a lecture or meeting, he would call from the door: "Now, I'll tell you all about it—please listen attentively." From a journey he would write home asking that no visitors be in the house when he arrived. "I want that just we three should be together, so I can tell you all I have been living through." He would discuss with them the plan of a new book or read an article he had just written, asking for their comments and often agreeing with their criticisms. In view of his almost total incapacity to speak of anything personal to others, this need to pour out everything to his wife and sister-in-law is notable. Eugenie thinks it a reaction from his lonely youth. Sometimes Eugenie would interrupt his detailed recital with: "But what you're saying isn't interesting at all." To which Nicolai Alexandrovitch would reply: "On the contrary. I'm telling this in a very interesting way."

It was part of his boyish nature that Nicolai Alexandrovitch loved holidays, particularly their outward expression. Despite his general feeling that things material were unimportant, he was a great stickler for the exact observance of rites and customs, particularly those about Christmas. No food should be taken on Christmas Eve until the first star appeared in the evening. Then the Christmas tree could be lighted and supper served. Although there were no children in the house, they always had a Christmas tree. Once in Italy, where pine was not available, he produced a branch of mimosa with small candles affixed to it. Mme Klepinin recalls one Christmas when she was a guest for supper. Lydia had worked wonders with house decorations made from the simplest materials, and served as master of ceremonies. Each person had been asked in advance to bring a small gift and a literary contribution—verses or a story. That night Berdyaev talked on "Love is Born," while Lydia read a story she had written on "Venite Adoremus." As in all Orthodox households the "feast of feasts" was Easter, and Berdyaev always insisted upon all the proper accoutrements. Once during the German occupation, when it was impossible to have the traditional "pascha" cheesecake, he said it was no holiday. One winter during the worst scarcity of wartime, a package came from abroad containing among other things pure white flour. Berdyaev decided to guard it in his own room until Easter—"the women might use it up before." His cry of dismay resounded through the house when, on going to get the flour, he found that mice had eaten both it and part of his best hat, under which it was hidden. One year the Berdyaevs rented a room to two young women, and Nicolai Alexandrovitch was certain there would be difficulty with strangers in the house. The two knew of this and were most careful not to disturb him when he was at his desk. After a short time, Berdyaev told them how relieved he was and invited them to the Sunday evening meetings in his salon.

Mealtimes were enriched by Berdyaev's conversation, although sometimes it seemed more of a monologue. He ate rapidly to have more time for talking. "Genie, you be quiet. I'm telling such interesting things." Berdyaev's favorite meal was breakfast, when he would recount new ideas that had come to him in the night, his plans for writing, what lectures he had to prepare. Often he would discuss a meeting attended the previous evening, but other times, especially if the meeting had been stormy, he might never mention it. Berdyaev was always interested in the news of the day, particularly the crime news—a child abducted, or a shopkeeper murdered. He had written in his *Dostoievsky*: "The study of the limits and boundaries of man's nature leads to the study of the nature of crime."[3] The reverse is also true, and when Berdyaev would comment on the latest crime he always tried to imagine the human values and stresses behind it. Nicolai Alexandrovitch was clever at discussing and describing the characteristics of people they all knew, and sometimes would outline these with a twinkle in his eye—but with words of kindly affection rather than judgment.

Discussing the qualities of different nations, he usually had a good word for the French and the Italians. From a conference in Hungary (1928) he wrote "What a blessed country is France! It is easier to live there than in any other land." And during his 1938 visit to Riga: "I have also been feeling that I can live only in Paris, and that France is my second fatherland." He esteemed the English for their aristocratic traditions and love of liberty but found misleading the "humor by which they express their admiration." Instead of spiritual depth he thought there was "much that is childish and naïve," and "feared they would not understand what I am going to say about marxism." Since most of his contacts with Britain were in Student Christian Movement conferences, it is not surprising that he thought the English "extremely pious and prayerful." He did not care much for the Poles, although he certainly had Polish blood in his veins. Yet he was no chauvinist. Writing from Warsaw to Lydia (1927) he spoke of his newly acute "love for Russia and at the same time for France, with her great and refined culture. I am an enemy of chauvinism, and cannot even call myself a nationalist. But there is something other, deep and eternal in the God-created image of a people, and one must be true to this, as to the eternal image of every single person."

The Berdyaev table was never richly laden except on holidays or if special guests had been invited. Berdyaev preferred a vegetarian menu, eating meat only once a week. He dreamed of living on a strictly vegetarian diet like Tolstoi, but only managed it for a period of about seven years. In France, Eugenie says, they always had to live on such a modest budget that a vegetarian table was impossible.

When he was not writing or talking, he was reading. He read in his study, in bed, even in the bath. He was usually engaged in about seven books at a time, and these were piled neatly on a table beside his bed. He would never read books or articles about himself. His usual method in reading was to underscore portions that interested him, although he occasionally made notes. Unable to buy all the books he wished to read, he had an arrangement with a French publisher who permitted him to borrow books and then return them, underlining and all, if he did not wish to purchase. Nicolai Alexandrovitch could not bear reading aloud if he was supposed to do it, but he enjoyed being read to. Lydia had an especially pleasant reading voice, and many evenings were spent in her room, where the reading took place. After Lydia's

health failed, it was Eugenie who did the reading. They would read
a while, then stop for discussion. Nicolai Alexandrovitch in his armchair, Muri purring on his lap, would relax with an after-dinner cigar
and, like a child, visibly enjoy the reading of his favorite classics. He
liked good cigars—holding a cigar in his hand helped overcome the
tic, he felt. He greatly missed cigars during the war, and was grateful
when Helen Lowrie brought him some on her first trip from Switzerland to liberated Paris. Russian classics, or Greek, or English in translation, Tolstoi and Dostoievsky, were read and reread. Among the
English writers he enjoyed especially were Dickens and Shakespeare.
Berdyaev usually chose the reading. He would agree to listen to a
modern novel only under pressure—but then follow with close attention
and offer penetrating comments—on Faulkner or Greene, Sartre or
Blanchot. Often there would be a sudden interruption: "Just a minute, I'll be right back. You can go on reading. I've just had a very
important idea." This never failed to annoy Lydia. "I don't understand
why I should read if you don't listen." "But I do. How is it you still
don't comprehend that at the same time another process is going on
within me?" He was never interested in cards or parlor games. For
most of the Paris years there was less time for evenings at home than
there had been at Babaki or even in Moscow.

In Paris, Berdyaev's daily schedule was carefully planned and strictly
adhered to. He demanded his meals, even his tea, exactly on the minute set for them. Coming downstairs in the morning, watch in hand,
he would ask: "Genie, is coffee ready?" After breakfast he usually went
back to his study, although occasionally he would go out for shopping
or to the postoffice. After lunch he usually napped for an hour; then,
because there were always letters, from the most varied correspondents
in all parts of the globe, he would groan and begin writing his replies.
The afternoon, too, was his favorite time for receiving visitors—he did
not like callers in the evening. But no one who came to him for counsel was ever turned away. He usually took a promenade in the forest
about midafternoon, either by bicycle—until in later life his doctor
forbade it—or afoot. He preferred to walk alone—the most interesting
thoughts occurred to him then. In Clamart the family budget permitted
one visit to the cinema each week. Nicolai Alexandrovitch loved to go.
Eugenie could not see why, for half the time he was so occupied with
his own thoughts that he would lose the thread of the story. "Why
did he kill him?" he would whisper to Eugenie. "Why do you come
to the theater?" she would ask in reply. The film seemed to be a matter

of indifference to him. Once, sent by Lydia to study the posters in front of the cinema, he recommended their going. "It ought to be interesting," he reported, "shows the sea and great cliffs." The film, set on a convict island, turned out to be such a blood-and-thunder piece that the ladies could not sit through it. On the way home they took Nicolai Alexandrovitch to task: "Couldn't you see by the poster they were convicts?" "No, I thought they were sailors, or something," was the answer. The moments in the cinema when Berdyaev's mind was on something else were often highly productive. One of his books was conceived during a cinema performance.

Living with Nicolai Alexandrovitch was not the usual family experience. He was almost never quiet. One sensed the storm raging in the depths of his being—with all the atmosphere around him electrically charged. But there were also times of calm when the tension in Berdyaev's spirit relaxed, and then he would become a witty, joking companion. Life with Berdyaev was not at all the ordinary movement "in a close circle, with everyday cares and ennuis, but life in a broad, limitless world." It is not surprising to learn that Ni, as he was always known in the family (and nowhere else), was not the only sometimes difficult one. Li—poetess and mystic, was not always the calm balance wheel for her husband suggested by her valuable role in group participation. Berdyaev protested against her tendency to live apart.

> In your life there is a temptation, an illusion, to which you are subject: the absence of contact with others and an unwillingness to share their daily life. This can become a refined form of egoism. I have always thought that man was put into life with these or those other people not by accident.

An earlier letter penetrates Lydia's character more deeply:

> And now about you, my friend. Your temptation and error are connected with time and space. You seek another life, and in this you are right. This is the positive side in you. But . . . you tie up this new life with . . . a change of apartment,[4] city, the people around you. You speak of disliking what you call our "family" life. But first, our life very little resembles the usual traditional "family" life. And chiefly you forget that beside this so-called family life, into which you could breathe another spirit, and change it into a fraternal life, there is only a convent, a commune, or life in hotels . . . least of all like a Christian life. My tempta-

tion lies in concern for the future, yours in your unwillingness to understand and feel that another, better, new life must first of all begin with inward and not outward attitudes toward everyday life, which is our common burden. . . . It tortures me that you so often curse our life, sent us by God, instead of trying to lighten it. Think about this seriously, my dear one, as I think seriously about my temptation.

Eugenie says her sister was unhappy, even depressed, because she could not live "her kind of life: to sit alone and read the Psalms. Nicolai Alexandrovitch and I could not live that way."

Although some who have seen her poems feel they deserve publication, Lydia always refused to have them printed. "I have too high an opinion of art," she insisted. It was one of Berdyaev's unfulfilled wishes to issue at least a small volume after her death. But this attitude of reserve did not apply to Lydia's faith. Converted to Roman Catholicism during the revolutionary years in Moscow, she felt it her duty to try to bring her sister also into that church. She never tried to convert her husband; Eugenie says he never considered belonging to the Roman Church. In the sometimes stormy arguments between the two sisters on religious or confessional questions, Berdyaev would smilingly refuse to take sides.

The story of Lydia's conversion to Catholicism is interesting. In childhood she had a religious experience in the Orthodox Church, normal for a girl of high spirituality. Later, like most of the intelligentsia of the period under the influence of revolutionary "free-thought" ideas, there was a time when she had no apparent religious life and no relation with the church. Subsequently, she resumed her earlier attitudes, and regularly attended services and took communion in the Orthodox Church.[5] The revolution shocked her deeply. She felt that if the Orthodox Church had been "a real church," communism could not have captured Russia. In communism itself she saw only evil and negation. Her disapproval of the Orthodox extended to all churches, and she frequently made derogatory remarks about the Catholic Church. She said it was unattractive, cold, and formal. There was more religion in the Orthodox Church, she thought. But once, from Paris, where she was working at her sculpture—about 1905-6—Eugenie sent Lydia a book on the life of St. Therese with the remark that reading it would show her some good in the Roman Church. A dozen years later, during the terrible deprivation of the postrevolutionary period, Lydia fell ill. Pneumonia developed, and in a heatless house, with neither physicians nor adequate medicines available, the situation was grave. One night Lydia had a vision of St. Therese, who told her to join the Roman Catholic Church. Lydia "was not disobedient to the heavenly vision," and with some difficulty found a small Roman Catholic group in Moscow, led by a priest named Abrikosov. When she consulted Nicolai Alexandrovitch about the matter, he made no objection. Everyone must find his own way, he said, and he refused to make a decision for another. With Father Abrikosov's blessing, Lydia entered the Roman Church.[6]

She was not a person who could admit compromises in matters of politics or religion. For her the Roman Church was perfect, and she resented it if Eugenie or Ni ventured to criticize any phase of that church's life. That this was not rarely the cause of family discord is evident from some of Berdyaev's letters to her:

> Your last letter grieved me. . . . All my spiritual effort, all my good intentions, have come to naught. You are not agreed with me in anything. Lord! how sad life is, and how unhappy people can be; . . . how I wish for at least a little joy. The spirit of division, of fanatical exclusiveness . . . brings me to despair. You say, you can admit brotherly relations with me, because in your estimation mine is a Catholic spirit. But I think that mine is neither a Catholic nor an Orthodox (of course not Protestant) spirit . . . but rather a spirit oriented toward the super-confessional (not inter-confessional) epoch of Christianity. . . . you should shun, my dear child, the ways of alienation, of coolness toward the world of men. But you will not listen to me. You think you should hearken only to the priest. And yet I hope that this letter will not be in vain; . . . deep within me there move both a torturing pity and a sympathy for which I cannot find expression.

A few years later he is writing in a more persuasive tone (Vichy, 1929):

> We must make a friendly effort to change the spirit of our home for the better, to create a happier atmosphere, more light and free. Let us be more considerate, patient, bear each others burdens.

And a year later (Vichy, 1930):

> At home things are not always well. We are not always at peace. You, my dear, are not satisfied with our life, express your distaste for our house. This torments me, and creates unrest in life. And I so long for cosiness and quiet, peace and love.

Lydia's uncompromising attitude faded toward the end of her life, and in the last two years she declared that she was no longer a Roman Catholic but belonged to the "church of the Holy Spirit"—not any more feeling herself separated from the other two. Henceforward there were no more acrid controversies about religion in the Berdyaev house. Spiritually, she had passed beyond the boundaries of earthly separate churches, and felt her priest was right when he assured her that her mission was to live in the "church of the Holy Spirit." When she died, the first requiem said over her body was Orthodox, and both Orthodox and Catholic priests participated in the funeral ceremonies. Yet all differences, even as fundamental as those of religious confession, could not blur the fact that between Ni and Li there was a deep and profoundly spiritual love.

Berdyaev's study in the house at Clamart has been left almost unaltered since he died at his desk, in 1948. It is a squarish room on the second floor with windows on two sides, all its walls lined with bookcases, and a desk in the middle facing the south window. A couch in the corner away from the windows, and three chairs, make up the furniture. On the desk, at the left, stands a small electric lamp with an ordinary green glass bell shade. At the back of the desk is a row of small drawers for letters or notes, with some books piled on the top. In the middle one sees a double inkwell of bronze with a pile of pens, pen nibs, and a penknife in tiny general disorder. A desk calendar still shows the last day of Berdyaev's life, the 23rd of March. At the right side of the desk are three piles of books, with another at the left side near the lamp. Two rounded, fist-size stones that Berdyaev had picked up somewhere on his walks and used as paper weights complete the desktop furnishings. The pictures on the walls are all portraits, mostly of Russian writers: Dostoievsky, and Tolstoi, Fedorov and Gogol— with Boehme, Baader, and Nietzsche to keep them company. A photograph of his mother (reproduced in this book), one of his nephew, and one of his old friend Shestov, complete the list. Berdyaev himself hung the pictures. The chair in which Nicolai Alexandrovitch died is a simple bentwood armchair with a cane seat. One of the books is a large, well-thumbed Bible, with many places marked. For his marking, Nicolai Alexandrovitch used a vertical line in the margin, with an occasional crossmark at the end of some special verse. In the later years of his life, he said: "Now I'm reading the Bible quite differently than ever before, with a new special attentiveness."

Save for its now dingy wallpaper, the small room adjoining the study, where Berdyaev slept, might be a monk's cell. There is room for a bed, a chair, and a night table beside the bed. On the table lies a prayer book, together with an icon given him by Father Metcheff on his departure from Moscow and the seven books already noted—what Berdyaev happened to be reading at the time. The few hundred books filling the shelves around the study walls form a library that it would be unjust to compare with those of scholars like Freud or Dewey, who had spent most of their lives in one place and whose library catalogues undoubtedly reflected the owners' tastes and interests. What Nicolai Alexandrovitch had in his library represented what he had been able to buy, mostly secondhand, out of a budget always too meager for the family's use. Berdyaev's exceptional position among the émigrés, a literary man living on a salary plus his royalties, gave him the quite undeserved reputation of being well-to-do. Sometimes books were sold, not bought—volumes of biographical novels for instance, of which a considerable number still rest on the study shelves. But some books do indicate Berdyaev's tastes and interests. There are Nietzsche, Tolstoi, some of the church fathers, Windelband's history of philosophy, and modern writers like Maritain and Barth—books mostly of Russian, French, and German writers. There are few books in English; Berdyaev had only a slight knowledge of that language. There appears to be no formal system of arrangement by subject and content on the shelves, although Berdyaev always kept his books in the same places and was fearful of alien hands disturbing their order. In one of the letters to Mme K, he wrote: "I love order just because in the depth of my being chaos moves darkly. But this is mental-physical chaos: the spirit in me is always stronger." He resisted any attempted invasion. "Ni, get out of your study, we've got to clean it," Lydia would announce. "But not today," he would complain. "Well, you can't live in the midst of dust like this." "If you absolutely must—only for goodness sake don't touch the desk or the books—my whole day's work will be spoiled," he would plead as he reluctantly left the room. "All your dusting is only a prejudice, nothing more." Members of the household were really afraid to do much to the bookshelves, but once a house guest, during Berdyaev's absence in Vichy, spent three days carefully going over shelves and books that had evidently not been touched for months. With fear and trembling she told him of it upon his return, but he only said he was very grateful.

In Berdyaev there was a great deal of the artist but little of the Bohemian. He even derided bohemianism in others. Ilyin, who was for a time almost a member of the family, says he never saw Berdyaev in pajamas; even for breakfast he was always well dressed. His sense of order prevailed in his sleeping room as well as in his study. His clothes were always laid on the same chairs, his shoes set in the same place, even the blanket on the foot of his bed was always folded in the same way. He had done this so often, Eugenie says, that it had become entirely automatic. He could have dressed in the dark, if necessary, knowing just where each piece of apparel lay. Perhaps this sense of undisturbed order was the reason for the torment Berdyaev experienced in packing for a journey. The household would be upset for several days while he decided what should go into his luggage. How completely he prepared for travel was evidenced one time in London when he asked Pianoff to act as his interpreter at the barber. Berdyaev had brought with him his own razor and shaving brush and insisted upon the barber's using them. In thinking about a forthcoming journey Berdyaev was always pessimistic—he might miss the train, might lose his tickets, the weather might be bad. What would happen to Lydia and Eugenie in his absence? Would he have trouble with the customs? He considered it "revolting" that every traveler at an international border should evidently be "considered a priori a criminal." But in one item he was always, quite illogically, an optimist: when setting out on a journey, or even for a meeting, he nursed an almost boyish certainty that he would meet supremely interesting people or have some other interesting experience.

In the home Nicolai Alexandrovitch was very solicitous for the welfare and especially the health of other members of the family. His wife and sister-in-law always tried to conceal illnesses from him, for he would "become desperate," call a doctor at once, demand that his minutest orders be carried out, and insist on taking temperatures himself to make certain nothing was being hidden from him. He would surround the invalid with exaggerated solicitude—as long as he could do anything to help. But if there was hopeless suffering, Nicolai Alexandrovitch could not bear it; he simply ran away. When Lydia, on her deathbed, cried out with pain that could not be assuaged, Berdyaev would leave the house, hands over his ears. He could not passively endure the suffering of others. If he himself became ill with a cold or anything mild he would take quantities of medicine—the family spent a small fortune on medicines—and be greatly disturbed. As with other tests of courage, the milder things frightened him the most. Berdyaev insisted this trepidation was not a fear of death, at least for himself, but just that his "strongly developed imagination was directed toward the worst side."[7] "In my imagination I have lived through more misfortunes, suffered with greater acuteness, than ever in reality."[8]

As in not a few families, Russian or American, there were worries over finances. From Cauterets in the Pyrenees (1926) Berdyaev writes Lydia:

> I am delighted to return home, but a series of definite questions clouds my pleasure: about our apartment, about our finances. I do not feel any stability in our life, no firm base. . . . And this is very hard, especially for a philosopher, helpless in life.

And again, years later (1933) he is writing his wife:

> My joy at returning home is poisoned by the thought that unpleasant business will begin at once. The dollar continues to fall. We shall have to cut down a lot of our activities. This constant worry and struggle is wearying. I do not think I will have to work any more, but only more efficiently.

He longed to be free of economic worry. He wrote (Vichy, 1933):

> Your last letter has greatly upset me. Again I feel your dissatisfaction with our life. Sinful man that I am, I dream of some elementary security for the last part of my life, of greater independence. I would like to have only to lecture, edit the journal [Put] and, most important, to write my own [thoughts].

Despite these concerns, Berdyaev's was in many ways a sheltered life. He called it "being one of the privileged few," but conditioned this by saying his privileges did not include wealth or power. Wealthy he never was, yet except for the period of war and revolution in Moscow he always had an assured income, even if it was sometimes small. Until the war ended payments from his father's estate in Poland, he apparently never had to give money a thought; it was always there, for whatever he wanted to do—travel, publish a collection of his articles, dress

in the height of fashion. Even in the famine time, 1917-18, he had
been one of the twenty "immortals" who received double food rations.
It was a privilege shared only by a handful of the enemies of the Soviet
regime that he was banished and not executed. Wherever he went, the
way seemed to open before him, to activity made possible by assured
material support. He himself thought it a matter of providential guidance—"that Higher Power which has guided my life."

Even in exile this was true. Only a brief time after his arrival in
Berlin, the North American YMCA arranged to support him, the
only man in the emigration given such effective attention. Berdyaev
was made editor-in-chief of the YMCA Press, now the largest publishing house of Russian books outside the Soviet Union, and held this
post to the end of his life. Even during the German occupation of
France, the YMCA managed to transmit funds to him. Porret tells of
this contact—so important in the last twenty-five years of Berdyaev's
life:

> There were some secretaries of the American YMCA in Berlin.
> They knew Russian and wished to be of use to the émigrés . . .
> to create a spiritual atmosphere. This was not a movement to
> evangelize the Russians. . . . The Americans knew the Slavic
> soul, respected the Orthodox faith, and strove to deepen relation-
> ships without detaching the Russians from their church. Them-
> selves Protestants, they undertook in a truly ecumenical spirit a
> magnificent, unselfish task, full of comprehension and tact, that
> . . . created vital centers throughout the emigration, turning an
> uprooted youth to the Christian life.[9]

But an assured salary from an American institution did not entirely
free Nicolai Alexandrovitch from financial concern. He might have
been describing himself when he wrote of Leontieff:

> Material need plagued his whole life . . . a great trial for his
> aesthetic spirit which demanded plastic beauty in his surround-
> ings, for his incapacity for any sort of breadwinning profession.[10]

In Berdyaev's case it was not his own personal lack, but the inability
to provide adequately for Lydia and others near and dear. The house
was never properly heated, and Lydia suffered from the cold. She was
passionately fond of the sea, but there were no means to send her to
the shore on vacation. The two women in the house were unac-
customed to the heavy housework they now had to do, and it pained

him to observe their fatigue. He was incapable of helping with the housework or of providing a fulltime servant. He practically never had any money in his pocket. He would come into the YMCA office, and at the close of a committee meeting remark quietly with his appealing smile: "Donald Ivanovitch, I need money." And one always found a reason to make an "advance" on some project or other. He would never accept more than was actually due him, even though he received it somewhat ahead of time. Mme Trusheff, Berdyaev's mother-in-law, had a poor opinion of his business abilities and once asked an intimate friend to look out for the family's finances after her death.

In home finance, however, Berdyaev tried to keep order. He would carefully budget his anticipated income, and the family would be instructed to live within it. There were times when he criticized the ladies sharply for not having done so. Berdyaev kept all the bills—light, power, water, etc.—in excellent order. But unfortunately the budget did not take into account the ultragenerous aid to others less fortunate to which the family was addicted. Such aid might be in the form of a loan, medicine purchased for the sick, or the actual feeding of perhaps half a dozen unsuccessful writers or journalists. It was the way they had always done in Russia! Much of the family's perennial penury resulted from just that attitude. As Berdyaev wrote of Leontieff: "He did not completely renounce the aesthetics of life . . . and found place in himself for contradictory elements."[11] Berdyaev explained his love of perfume by an "extraordinary squeamishness about odors" that had compelled him to pass half his life holding his nose. He liked good clothes, and in Moscow, even when he went "slumming" to the Pit, was always elegantly dressed. In Paris, however, he was not extravagant in this respect.

People who knew Berdyaev in earlier years had perceived an inconsistency between his social passions and his aristocratic attitude toward other, less privileged individuals. This was greatly overcome as he matured, but never altogether. From one of his journeys he wrote Lydia (Warsaw, 1927): "I dined with the brother of Count Ratchinsky, in a regular palace. Imagine, I feel better in aristocratic society than elsewhere." As he says of Leontieff: ". . . without Leontieff's aristocratic instincts, his destiny is incomprehensible and his world-outlook inexplicable. Try as he would he never really came to like 'the ordinary residents of this dreary world.' " One friend asserts that Berdyaev was interested only in his peers, others who could stand up to him intellectually, or the very poor and downtrodden, while the entire middle

of the social gamut did not touch his thinking. He said he could not
endure the bourgeois mentality.

Berdyaev took a fully reasoned view of his unconquerable aristocracy.
He quotes Versiloff, in the Dostoievsky novel *The Adolescent:*

> I cannot help respecting my noble family relations. Through
> centuries there has developed in Russia an unprecedented, higher
> culture, which you will find nowhere else in the world. . . . It
> contains in itself the future of Russia. Perhaps there are only a
> thousand of us . . . but the whole of Russia has lived up to now,
> in order to produce that thousand.

He did not quote this with 100 per cent approval, however. He
agrees that aristocracy founded on wealthy families and inherited rank
have not seldom produced useful results, but he argues for an aristocracy of the spirit, even in the most democratic society. Without an
elite there can be no cultural progress, no creative effort. The old
aristocracy of race and heraldry is doomed; the spiritual aristocracy to
succeed it must have far different characteristics. Instead of pride,
there must be magnanimity and readiness to serve. Instead of demanding for itself, it must give itself to the service of others. The new
aristocracy must be a wise steward of the gifts God has given it.

To this last principle Nicolai Alexandrovitch was faithful. It was
illustrated in his generosity toward all those who came to see him or
wrote him for advice. Although he disliked letter writing, he tried never
to leave a letter unanswered. As his fame spread, they came in all
languages and from all corners of the globe. One day a letter arrived
from a young man in Australia—he was considering suicide and asked
Berdyaev's advice. Nicolai Alexandrovitch went straight to the cable
office and wired: "Don't shoot yourself. Letter follows." He never
dated a letter or manuscript; consequently the dates of papers in the
Berdyaev Society files are often only approximate. He never kept copies
of his letters, hence the almost complete absence of his side of a rich
and varied correspondence. The one important exception is the packet
of letters to Mme K found among his papers—which that lady must
have returned to him in exchange for her own. Another way he gave
richly of himself was in the "at homes" and more definitely organized
meetings that had characterized life in Berdyaev's circle from earlier
days in Moscow. The haphazard evening gatherings could be somewhat chaotic insofar as discussion went, but if there was to be a regular meeting, it was carefully organized and an informal invitation

giving the agenda sent out. Even for an "at home" Eugenie and Berdyaev would plan to confine the conversation to some general theme, and the company was rigidly held to it. Berdyaev disliked gossip intensely and would not have any in his home.

Berdyaev's devotional life was as well ordered as his hours of writing. On the table at his bedside lay a small, well-thumbed Orthodox prayer-book that he used for his morning and evening devotions. He would take time during a busy day for meditation. His regular reading of the Bible is reflected in his written language; *The Spiritual Crisis of the Intelligentsia*, particularly, is full of Biblical references and images. In a letter to Lydia he once wrote: "I pray to God, sometimes with passionate ardor, asking His merciful aid. I have my moments of mystical contemplation and communion with God." The breadth of his prayer interest appears in a remark about Boehme: "I always remember him in my prayers, together with Dostoievsky and some of my other favorite writers."[12] His religious life was not dependent upon churchgoing. Nicolai Alexandrovitch was not an every-Sunday attendant, but usually went to church on the dozen "great holidays" of the Christian year and made his confession and took communion during Lent, as do most Russian Orthodox even if they do not regularly attend church otherwise.

If Somerset Maugham could say ". . . to write was an instinct that seemed as natural to me as to breathe,"[13] Berdyaev might truly have said that for him writing was a passion. It was more than that, it was an obsession. He began writing in his teens, and there never was a time after that when writing was not his chief interest and occupation. He often said he had to write or he would burst. An inner voice, he said, told him what to write, and he obeyed. "The most positive content of my life," says the autobiography, "is creative thought, writing. I cannot imagine myself without the idea for a new book."[14] "He never for a moment could be passively receptive to the ideas of others," Eugenie states. "Nicolai Alexandrovitch's spiritual life was an uninterrupted creative current." This did not hinder his interest in the ideas or words of others, or in world events. He rejoiced at every new book or article he read and every rewarding personal contact; then something was immediately added, and a Berdyaev idea came forth. His critics sometimes alleged that his was an eclectic rather than an original philosophy, but this was only partially true and only insofar as the thought of a Boehme or Dostoievsky received a new "Berdyaev" carom to clinch the thought as his own.

He had to write, and he could write under almost any circumstances. As a matter of principle he wrote all morning and often again in the evening. He could go on with his work in Moscow throughout the bombardment of the Kremlin, when shells were screeching over his roof and he made the two ladies sit in the corridor away from windows. During the tragic summer of 1940, in the crowded pension where the family stayed, the only desk available was in a corridor with people constantly passing by; he wrote every day, just as though he had been in his own quiet study at Clamart. Chapter seven of the autobiography was written at that time, when "whole worlds were being demolished." Hippius tells how Merezhkovsky could write only in his study; even the silence of the Bibliothèque Nationale in Paris was not quiet enough for him to work. Berdyaev, on the contrary, would continue his writing even when the house was upset in the process of moving—almost sitting at his desk in the moving van.

Nicolai Alexandrovitch regretted that Khomiakoff had "no discipline—did not feel writing to be his chief calling, the purpose of his life." If, in contrast, Berdyaev knew writing was his chief purpose, it must be admitted that he had little discipline. Like Maugham, he "did not stop to consider if I wrote well or badly." He wrote in one upsurge of energy. "It sometimes seems as though someone else were writing, not I," he told Eugenie. He wrote so fast that many words became mere signs, not for single words only but for whole phrases, and he had to recopy his own manuscripts for the printer. He never had a secretary, and one is conscious of the terrible consequent waste of the time and energy of a genius. Often, when he would be unable to read his own script, Eugenie was called in to help. And Eugenie had to consult three other friends of Nicolai Alexandrovitch when, after his death, she was preparing his last manuscript, The Realm of Spirit and the Realm of Caesar, for the publisher.

This writing speed was one reason his books contain few quotations. The necessary data were in his memory, says Eugenie, and there was no time to look up references. His was not the patient researcher's type of mind. If Khomiakoff says that he did not like research in preparing his books, always quoting from memory and therefore occasionally making mistakes, Nicolai Alexandrovitch was like that also. The researching critics have not yet combed Berdyaev's books looking for errors, but there are at least three in the autobiography, one a probable slip of the pen, the others mistaken dates. He wrote once for all. He never could understand people who rewrote or corrected their manuscripts. His thought flowed so fast there was no time to consider what the book would be like. One of the characteristics of Berdyaev's style is long paragraphs; in his *Dostoievsky*, for example, there are paragraphs six or even ten pages long. He said he recognized as a serious defect his inability to analyze and develop his ideas, but they came so fast it sometimes made him dizzy. And although he acknowledged it as carelessness, Berdyaev handed his manuscripts to the printer unedited. Incidentally, he never worried about a publisher's deadline. In the YMCA Press there was never, for him at least, a precise date of delivery—although his manuscripts were always ready before the time they were expected.

In view of this fervid pace of writing, it is not surprising that there are repetitions. Stepun says Berdyaev's books were not constructed but "spurted out." Writing under inspiration, his thoughts occasionally overlapped. Yet even where a similar idea recurs, the careful reader discovers some fresh touch that renders it more vivid. There are contradictions as well—not only due to views that have changed with the years, but frequently within the same book because of a different approach in a later chapter. An author more careful of his reputation might have eliminated these before the book was printed, but Berdyaev did not care what the critics would say (he called it an "abnormal indifference"), and by the time a given book was off the press, he had lost interest in it—his thoughts deep in the preparation of his next. "He not only lost interest, but even forgot the existence of some of his books. On occasion, he would find some earlier work and with surprise in his voice would ask: 'Did I actually write this? It's really not uninteresting.'"

That he made no formal outline for a new book does not mean complete lack of preparation. Sometimes he seemed to think in chapters, or even in terms of an entire book. He once said that if you roused him from a deep sleep and proposed a topic for a lecture or an article, he could give it "immediately." At breakfast he would occasionally remark: "I have to write an article on . . . " (some particular subject). And at luncheon he would announce: "Well, the article is finished." The whole of *The Meaning of the Creative Act* seems to have come to him in one moment. At other times the germinal idea had to be brooded over before the swift writing process began. Eugenie could always tell when a new article or book was under way. He would be lost in meditation and give wrong answers to questions. "The atmosphere of his study would change—one felt a strange sort of energy, and stopping outside the closed door, one had the feeling of contact with an electric current." Berdyaev said the birth of a book cost him as much pain as the birth of a child. But even this longer, preparatory process was all within himself. He never read books on the general subject he was pursuing at the moment. He said it cramped the freedom of his own thinking. His reading provided not so much a source of ideas as a kind of mental catalyst, and his own experiences—spiritual encounters in particular—contributed more to his philosophy than could even the most philosophical of books. To her question "How do you keep in your mind all the books you read?" he told Eugenie: "My memory always retains what is necessary for my inner life or for my work, and the rest fades away."

All his own thoughts, however, were immediately noted down no matter what the circumstances. Lydia was subject to fainting spells, especially before a thunderstorm, and this always upset her husband greatly. Calling a doctor, he would sit by Lydia's bed, beg her to take her medicine even when she was unable to swallow, and then all of a sudden say to Eugenie: "Don't leave her for an instant, hold the hot water bottle. I'll be right back. I must just write down an important idea." Most ideas seemed to come to him like that—"a flash of lightning, a sudden inner light," he said. *The Destiny of Man* came to his mind, practically entire, during a Diaghlieff ballet having no relationship whatever to man's fate. He rarely read reviews of his own books. Sometimes he would hand Eugenie a pack of reviews, asking her to read them and let him know "if they contained anything interesting."

He was often critical of the books of others, particularly of modern novels. "I am surprised," he would say, "at the poverty of subjects in modern novels. Life is so rich, especially now, and offers so many subjects for novelists." "If you were writing a novel, what subject would you choose?" he was asked. He thought awhile, then replied: "Man in his conflict with the new social order now being born."

Once a book was written, Nicolai Alexandrovitch was usually dissatisfied with it and thought he could do a better one. He rewrote *The Philosophy of the Free Spirit* for a French edition[15] and said he could improve it if he reworked it a second time. This work received the Académie Française prize in moral and religious science. That he had little time to meditate on the qualities of past works is evident from the list of titles produced between his arrival in Paris—1924—and the outbreak of the war. These are listed in the Bibliography, but it is interesting to note that during the fifteen years 1924-1939, nine new volumes

appeared, among them the 320-page *Destiny of Man, an Essay in Paradoxical Ethics*—beside over sixty articles in *Put* alone. The last book
published before the war *Slavery and Freedom*, has been called "the
most profound, the most splendid, and the most satisfying of the books
of this great thinker." But it was a smaller volume, published in 1934,
that caught the world's imagination as had the earlier *New Middle
Ages*. *The Fate of Man in the Modern World* is an excellent example
of Berdyaev's talent as a prophet. In the autobiography he recognizes
this: "I have a great gift of understanding at once the connection of the
separate and partial with the whole, with the world's meaning."

# 14

## IN AND OUT OF ORGANIZATIONS

Writing nine books in fifteen years, beside scores of articles and count-less lectures, would be a notable record for any man. In addition, as he had done in Berlin, Berdyaev gave considerable time to students and other young people. Up to a certain moment he was much in the af-fairs of the Russian Student Christian Movement. The youthful group gathered around him in Berlin had not been the only one in the emi-gration. At about the time of Berdyaev's arrival there, student "circles" were springing up elsewhere. While taking somewhat different lines of study, these groups had essentially one purpose. The young people of the emigration were seeking a spiritual foundation for their lives—so completely disrupted by the revolution.

In a way these groups were a continuation of student Christian as-sociations which, under the inspiration of Dr. John R. Mott and Baron Paul Nicolai, had existed in Russia before the revolution for fifteen years. Many Christian intellectuals in the emigration gave their active support, among them Bulgakov, Berdyaev, and Zenkovsky. Correspond-ence and some visitation among the groups led to the first of a series of conferences that continues to this day. It took place at Prerov in Czechoslovakia, and one of its results was a formal organization em-bracing all such student associations in the emigration, the Russian Student Christian Movement Outside Russia. Supported financially and morally by the World's Student Christian Federation and the YMCA, the movement spread until, by the advent of Hitler, it registered mem-bers in many European countries and the United States. At the Prerov conference, Nicolai Alexandrovitch was very approachable as always, met all students on a basis of equality, and never let them feel a dif-ference between themselves and him. His participation in the confer-ence will long be remembered for his brilliant debate with Martzinkov-sky on the real meaning of "interconfessional." The word "ecumenical" had not yet come into general use. Whereas Martzinkovsky sought an effacement of all confessional differences in the Movement, Berdyaev argued that true interconfessional collaboration was most profitable when each member lived his own faith to the fullest.

The headquarters of the Movement was in a building in Paris, at 10 Boulevard Montparnasse, leased by the YMCA as a center for its activities in the Russian emigration. Once a meeting was announced at which Berdyaev's latest book would be the object of a "literary debate." As in Vologda, when invited to a public criticism of himself, he did not attend. Nicolai Alexandrovitch continued to be one of the active leaders, but was gradually identified with the "liberal" wing of the Movement. A student movement is a procession, personalities changing with the years. This is partly the reason for Berdyaev's complaint that while in earlier years they had heard him gladly, there came a period he calls reactionary, when he "had to act in a foreign milieu, hostile to philosophical thinking, to freedom, to spiritual creativeness, to social justice."[1] The first generation in the Movement were men and women who had fought in the revolution or come under its immediate shadow, and they understood the need for new thinking that Berdyaev preached. A few years later the pendulum of opinion began to swing the other way. Reactionary Orthodox hierarchs in Karlovtsi, Yugoslavia, called Berdyaev a modernist, even a heretic, and some of the Russian young people went along with the conservative view. This "right" wing moved toward a "monarchist" position, and there was talk of boycotting Berdyaev's lectures on the charge that he was not Orthodox. Learning of this, Berdyaev wrote a sharp letter to the Movement's president, Professor Zenkovsky, and had no further official relations with it. He began giving his lectures in the premises of a social center organized by Mother Marie and others of the liberal wing of the Movement, instead of in the Movement's headquarters as hitherto. It is interesting to note that when, as so often happened, there was a break between Berdyaev and another person or an organization, the initiative was usually his. Almost never was it a case of being pushed out; he walked out. A small group of students eventually followed Berdyaev, continuing to meet for years thereafter. Toward the end of his life he became aware of a younger student generation more sympathetic to his ideas, and believed that "in them a new Christian world is preparing."[2]

One of the things attracting students to Berdyaev was his broad erudition. While philosophic and religious problems, with an occasional immixture of politics, dominated most of his thinking, he was—like most of the intelligentsia—well read in many other phases of culture. These interests came into his books and lectures, and particularly into his relations with young people. The influence of Florence and the Renaissance upon his thought has been noted in Chapter X. To him art was something very important, as witnessed in *The Meaning of the Creative Act* with its extensive passages of what may well be termed art criticism. "I see the meaning of art," he wrote, "in that it leads us into another transfigured world."³ For him beauty was to be more than passively enjoyed. He said he created it for himself in creative appreciation and imagination. Nicolai Alexandrovitch had strong likes and dislikes among the world's artists. Leonardo "always moved" him; Botticelli he "loved very much." He disliked the Roman renaissance of the sixteenth century. He liked painting better than sculpture, although here again he had his own strong opinions. Once in Florence, standing before a Donatello statue, his argument with Eugenie became so heated that a small crowd gathered. Nicolai Alexandrovitch recognized the "prophetic presentiment" in art, and said he loved art for this essential. Writing to Mme K about modern art, he recalls how thirty years earlier, in his article on Picasso, he had said "the integrity of man's image disappears" in modern art, and "futurism was a mixture of man with machines and things." Art has lost beauty. Once the chief object of art was man—in ancient Greece, in the Renaissance, in the nineteenth century. Now art is becoming dehumanized, along with man, in the modern mechanized world. "The sense of art as the forerunner of life's transfiguration has been lost."

Unlike Merezhkovsky, who "did not understand or like music,"⁴ Berdyaev was very fond of it. Once he wrote: "The supreme moments of my life are connected with an interest in music." He enjoyed soft music on the radio when he was writing. He had no musical ear and never attempted to carry a tune, yet "music stirred the depths of his being, overcoming any mood of depression." Characteristically he explains: "It is not so much that I plunge into the given music, as that I experience a creative upsurge of my being."⁵ Music, he felt, provided compensation for his own lack of lyricism. Russian folk songs always moved him deeply. He said they expressed the Russian soul better than anything else. Nicolai Alexandrovitch enjoyed symphonic concerts. His favorite western composers were Bach, Beethoven, and Wagner. Among the Russians he preferred Mussorgsky and Tchaikovsky. He was not fond of opera and disliked ballet; was ballet too physical a form of expression?

He enjoyed poetry, especially the Russian. Writing poetry was not one of his own means of creative expression. Of Russian poets his favorite was Tiutcheff; he loved Baudelaire and Verlaine among the French, and Shelley and Goethe for the remaining west. Mme K must have written poetry, for in one of his letters to her he says: "You love poetry, but you do not understand that great creativeness, yes any true creativeness, is impossible for one's own sake: you can create only for the sake of God. . . .Creativeness is always sacrificial. Creativeness which does not pass through sacrifice is emptiness." He felt that literature as well as art was prophetic in the revelation of a given epoch. And he noted with anxiety how most modern novels seemed to deal with abnormal or partial men—fragmented personalities—fearing what this might mean for man's future.

Beside the Student Christian Movement, another institution where Berdyaev had significant contact was the Orthodox Theological Institute of St. Sergius in Paris. Founded (1925) by Metropolitan Eulogius because of the disappearance of all theological schools in Soviet Russia, it was the only Russian institution of higher theological learning anywhere. In the course of the years it has come to be recognized as one of the principal pan-Orthodox schools in the world. Financed only partly by Orthodox sources, it owes its existence and continuing fruitful work largely to the support of various non-Orthodox churches.

St. Sergius was staffed with some of the best theological minds of Russia. Of the few who were left in the Soviet Union, most had perished before theological schools were once more possible there. Leading figures on the original St. Sergius faculty were Bulgakov and Kartasheff, Berdyaev's old friends from St. Petersburg days. From the first, the school based its policies on the decisions of the Moscow *Sobor* of 1917-18 and soon established the reputation it still has for liberal study within the dogmatic limits of the Orthodox Church. Berdyaev was invited to join the new faculty also. As the most widely known Russian Orthodox thinker, this was only natural. But he declined. He explained that while he was a believing member of the Orthodox Church and regularly took its sacraments, he nevertheless felt he was too independent in his own thinking to be a regular professor of the Institute. He agreed to give occasional courses if desired and, during its first years, did deliver some lectures there. Personal tension between himself and some of the St. Sergius faculty, together with his absorption in other interests in Paris, militated against his continued participation; although he lived in the same city as the Institute for a quarter of a century, it is barely mentioned in his autobiography.

Two crucial incidents connected with St. Sergius must be recorded. The first centered on Bulgakov. Berdyaev says that in Bulgakov's theology there are considerable philosophic elements, and is inclined to consider him a religious philosopher rather than a theologian. Bulgakov was an exponent of Sophiology, a none-too-definite theological concept concerning divine immanence in the created world. Although Berdyaev could not fully accept this doctrine, expounded in three of Bulgakov's monumental volumes, he approved it in general as evidence of "creative thought in Russian orthodoxy." Some less liberal portions of the church thought otherwise, and an enemy of the Institute sent a denunciatory letter to Moscow. Acting on this, and apparently without having read Bulgakov's books, an edict signed by Metropolitan Serge for the Holy Synod (1935) declared Bulgakov's teaching heretical. Berdyaev was incensed at this and wrote a resounding reply in an article entitled "The Spirit of the Grand Inquisitor." He was not especially in agreement with Bulgakov on the new theory under dispute, but he gave himself fully in defense of his friend's right to state it. As always, Berdyaev universalizes the case. It is more than a dispute about Sophia, he says; it touches "the fate of Russian religious thought, of freedom of conscience, of the very possibility of thought in orthodoxy."[6] The brief article bristles with denunciatory phrases: "ecclesiastical fascism which is worse than political fascism"; the Metropolitan's ukase stems "from the religion of the Scribes and Pharisees"; "the synod assumes an infallibility superior to that of the Pope—wants to institute the Catholic practice of the Index." Berdyaev adds insult to injury by asserting that "the Orthodox clergy and monasteries lack culture and education," remarking in conclusion that "this obscurantist violence to theology . . . is on a very low level of thinking." The article at once plunged Berdyaev into hotter water than that in which Bulgakov had been immersed by the Metropolitan's declaration. Many of his friends, even those in the liberal section of the Russian Student Christian Movement, attacked him for insubordination to the authorities of the Church. His expulsion from the Student Christian Movement was urged. At a meeting of the Movement, several speakers made this and other accusations in his presence. Berdyaev listened quietly until they had finished, then thundered down on their heads with such an eloquent defense of liberty in orthodoxy that all the accusations evaporated. There were other severe disagreements between Berdyaev and the Movement, but they never tried to arraign him in formal judgment again.

The other incident concerned Professor G. P. Fedotoff, another faculty member at St. Sergius. Whereas in defending Bulgakov, Berdyaev had been defending the St. Sergius' faculty, this time he was attacking them. Professor Fedotoff was known for his "liberal," leftish sympathies, and his writings on political themes and happenings had worried those responsible for the Institute, including Metropolitan Eulogius. When an article appeared defending "Passionaria," famous in the Spanish Civil War then raging, public indignation was aroused. The conservative Paris paper *Vosrozhdenie* ("Renaissance") published editorials and letters denouncing Fedotoff's stand. Formal addresses of protest against Fedotoff as a professor of the Institute were circulated in some of the churches. Under this pressure, the faculty council of St. Sergius addressed a letter to Fedotoff asking him to consider the best interests of the Institute before writing further articles. Fedotoff replied that he did not feel the faculty council had a right to judge his actions—then apparently went straight to Berdyaev to complain. In a typical Berdyaev reaction, Nicolai Alexandrovitch, without consulting the other side of the controversy, sat down and wrote a scathing attack on the Institute: "Is There Freedom of Thought and Conscience in Orthodoxy?"[7] He struck straight at the question of principle. The case "shows a lack of courage, and servile feeling, which, alas, are very traditional." This was really unfair, for most of the Institute's critics considered it too liberal. "The condemnation of Fedotoff was a political act, compromising the institution and casting over it the shadow of reaction. . . . Conscience has been transferred to the collective, just as in communism," Berdyaev declared, and that dart must have struck deep, for if the entire St. Sergius group including Fedotoff hated anything, they hated communism. Berdyaev seized on one phrase in the letter to Fedotoff:

> It is demanded of Fedotoff that he be "national-minded;" the world is being drenched in blood by the action of "national-minded" people . . . who would gladly destroy every liberty, reckoning not in the least with the dignity of man, and would probably show as much cruelty as has been shown in Spain. . . . It is all too evident that they are trying to change the Orthodox in the emigration into an obedient arm of religious-politics.

Again there were violent arguments among the émigrés. The majority was on the side of the Institute. The faculty felt that in view of the personalities involved, the situation was not unnatural. As Berdyaev

had not joined the staff of St. Sergius, he was at liberty to speak his
mind. The staff there never felt spiritually separate from him, but
Berdyaev's hasty article marked the end of his personal relations with
the Institute. He never entered its doors again until he came for Bulgakov's funeral.

Berdyaev's fleeting experience with another organization is sufficiently characteristic to be noted. About the time Berdyaev arrived in
Paris he was asked to become a member of The Fraternity of St. Sophia. Named for a similar organization then existent in Russia under
the patronage of Patriarch Tichon, its basic idea was the union of all
Christian (Orthodox) intellectuals. For an individualist like Nicolai
Alexandrovitch, acceptance of the discipline of a fraternity would be
very difficult, but he felt he should enter the group out of a sense of
solidarity. Apparently it carried on for some time without a formal constitution. Try as he might, Nicolai Alexandrovitch found he could not
go along with the new organization; he agreed with its purpose, but
its methods and forms of action were alien. To the taking of communion in a body on a fixed date and to other portions of a ritual that
many of his friends accepted without difficulty, he found it impossible
to gear his spiritual life. When the new constitution for the fraternity
was being adopted, he wrote Prince Trubetskoy that he could not become a member. "He reserved the right to be himself," says Kartasheff.

When Berdyaev moved from Berlin to Paris, the Religious-Philosophical Academy had moved with him. As a matter of fact, most of
the leaders of Russian thought participating in the Academy in Berlin
eventually came to live in Paris. As in Berlin, Berdyaev dominated the
Paris organization. Under his guidance a many-sided lecture and seminar program was carried on for years, almost up to the outbreak of
World War II. Speakers from almost any intellectual milieu were invited, save "monarchists" and communists. For years it was one of the
main centers of Russian intellectual life in Paris. Berdyaev's lectures
naturally set the tone. Various friends will recall some particularly brilliant performance—"On Tolstoi and Dostoievsky," or "Anti-Semi-
tism" (he was against it). One who heard that lecture tells of his "un-
forgettable impression. Berdyaev was in a sort of ecstasy. The hair
seemed to rise around his head. He was like nothing more than an Old
Testament prophet."

The Religious-Philosophical Academy multiplied its outreach by
publishing *Put* ("The Way"), a periodical organ of "Russian religious
and philosophical thought" appearing approximately once every quar-

ter.[8] Launched in 1925 (the autobiography mistakenly says 1926), it continued until the war closed down all Russian cultural activity in France. Like the Academy, this project was made possible by the YMCA under the leadership of Dr. Mott, "a man of strong character, a remarkable Christian worker, . . . and a great friend of Russians and the Orthodox Church."[9] Although Berdyaev was its editor, it was not "his" organ. This would have been out of line with its purpose—"to provide a place of expression for creative thought on the basis of orthodoxy." Berdyaev says all shades of authors were admitted to the pages of *Put* save those "clearly obscurantist and maliciously reactionary." Even authors with whom Berdyaev had serious personal differences had their articles published. Although it was not a fighting magazine, it printed some of Berdyaev's most militant articles. Now a bibliographical rarity, the sixty-one numbers of *Put* have preserved some of the finest thought of the "cream" of the emigration. Among the more than one hundred thirty writers who contributed through the years are not only Russian Orthodox clergy or laymen, but men of other confessions like Jacques Maritain and Paul Tillich. As Berdyaev said on the magazine's tenth birthday, it was the one intellectual journal in the world spiritually grounded in Russian Orthodoxy. Stepun says: ". . . doubtless future historians of the emigration will discuss the large influence of *Put*." Berdyaev also contributed to a literary magazine of leftist tendencies, *The New City*. This was not his creation, as has been reported, but was started by Fedotoff and Fundaminsky.

The Paris period began Berdyaev's ecumenical contacts, first through the World's Student Christian Federation and then on his own initiative. He spoke for various student conferences, like the meeting at Eigen—in Austria's beautiful Ennsthal—in May, 1927, with its idyllic setting of blossoming apple orchards against snow-covered mountains, and later in the French Student Christian Movement retreat house at Bièvres, near Paris. At these meetings he had contacts both with Roman Catholic and Protestant leaders. There were numerous other meetings, often at 10 Boulevard Montparnasse, where personalities like Marc Boegner and Wilfred Monod could be seen. Some gatherings occurred in series, such as the "decades" of Pontigny,[10] and Berdyaev was pleased to find sympathetic hearers in every group. From the start he had to combat a tendency on the part of the non-Orthodox to consider him a spokesman for the Orthodox Church. He always disclaimed any such role and finally persuaded most of his audience, including the Romans, that he was to be considered only "an individual Christian philosopher." For the Anglicans, with their century-old longing for closer relations with the Eastern churches, his was so acceptable a message that they wanted it to be the voice of Russian Orthodoxy, and some there are to this day who so believe.

Toward the end of the twenties, Berdyaev felt that interest in these interconfessional gatherings was declining and decided to start some of his own. He had long had an acquaintance, which developed into real friendship, with Jacques Maritain—that "modernist in a Thomist cloak"—and proposed to him a series of meetings to be held in the Berdyaev home. Maritain agreed, on condition that no Protestants be included, and for several years periodic meetings were held—at first on theological, later on mystical themes—with some of the finest minds of French catholicism participating: Father Laberthonnière, Gabriel Marcel, Étienne Gilson and, later, Emmanuel Mounier. Their discussions were of great interest, but again Nicolai Alexandrovitch found that he was not fully understood. He never wanted to have people agree with him and follow his teaching, he says, although he did hope they would understand him. Yet he never was able to "make them feel his central theme," and then would come the bitter experience of people discerning in him "a man from another world . . ." who apparently "had no need of them or even of anyone else, although he was always ready to enrich his knowledge."[11]

Out of these meetings blossomed the French social-religious journal *Esprit*, widely influential in liberal circles. Berdyaev attended the meeting (1932) at which it was organized, and his astute "The Truth and Falsehood of Communism" appeared in its first number. It is a document every Christian of today should read. But even though he had quite a following of French Catholic youth, he felt a great difference between them and himself. Nicolai Alexandrovitch realized with regret that these young people did not appreciate what he considered his deepest themes: "uncreated freedom, God's need for human creativity, objectivization, the priority of personality and its tragic conflict with society and the world order." He observed that they would usually avoid these topics in talking with him, "lest the difference between us be intensified."

Berdyaev derived especial pleasure from meetings held at Gabriel Marcel's home—international gatherings with discussion limited to truly philosophical problems, particularly those concerning existentialism and phenomenology.

That Berdyaev could organize interconfessional meetings at 10 Boulevard Montparnasse was partly due to the fact that it was in a sense neutral territory. The American "Y" had, by the very fact of its extensive service to the Orthodox, established a reputation for interconfessionalism long before the word "ecumenical" was popular. Thus a flourishing Christian association for young men, under the name of The Lighthouse (*Mayak*), had existed for twenty years in Russia before the revolution. When the communist regime closed it down in 1918, its leaders, believing the mandate to serve Russian youth still valid, undertook work with the more than a million refugees, three quarters of them men, in all the countries of their vast diaspora. This dispersion, and the fact that no literature with a Christian basis could be produced within the Soviet Union, prompted the establishment of the YMCA Press, now the oldest and most important publisher of Russian books outside Russia. Specializing chiefly on religious-philosophical and educational literature, it has published over four hundred fifty titles in its thirty-five years, by a list of authors embracing practically every prominent Christian thinker in the Russian emigration. Its present importance as the sole source of books in Russian with a Christian background (the churches in Russia have recently been able to embark upon a limited publication program) fades beside the possibilities of distribution in a future Russia. Many of these books are of lasting interest; Berdyaev, Bulgakov, and Zenkovsky will be as pertinent later as now, and in a land where books are published in hundreds of thousands instead of the standard YMCA Press edition of three or four thousand, their influence will be greatly multiplied.

The YMCA Press printed nearly all of Berdyaev's books in their original Russian. It published *Put*, and at present issues the important journal of the St. Sergius Academy, *Orthodox Thought*. It issued the first modern Russian Orthodox literature in religious education. Probably no more significant contribution to Russian Christian culture has been made in the past fifty years. Almost from the start Berdyaev was its editor-in-chief. And he was a faithful editor. Of course there were no such things as office hours or deadlines. Berdyaev did his work at home. He personally read almost every manuscript submitted, and at stated intervals would come to the Press office for consultation and reports. His opinions on manuscripts were signally objective; as in *Put*, he admitted any serious thinker, although one occasionally noted just a trace of favoritism in his advocacy of some author suffering urgent need.

His arrival at the office was almost a ritual. He always took quite
seriously the question "how is your health?" and the reply was never
optimistic. "Not too good—you know sometimes my head aches or I
am slightly dizzy." Then the broad black hat would be placed on the
rack, the scarf—worn winter and summer—unwound from his neck.
Out of his well-worn briefcase came a black velvet beret, to be adjusted
carefully over his long hair—and after the beret, two or three manuscripts. Laying these on the desk before him, he would close the briefcase again and deposit it on a nearby bookcase before sitting down at
the desk. From one vest pocket came a small, silver spectacle case, containing the pince-nez he set astride his nose; from another, he brought
forth a stub of pencil—never more than three inches long. You could
not help noticing the graceful hands with their delicate, slender fingers—and the long nail on his little finger, a conceit of many Russian
intellectuals (one always wondered if the idea had been imported into
Russia from China, along with tea drinking). A slip of paper revealed a
series of penciled items, Nicolai Alexandrovitch's agenda for the day's
discussion. As talk progressed, these items would be checked off one by
one with a penciled X. Agenda complete, with an X across every item,
only then could other business of the meeting be considered.

Berdyaev's judgments on a given manuscript were always delivered
with evident consideration for the author's position and feeling. They
were never harsh, and an adverse verdict would often be presented with
a trace of humor. Nicolai Alexandrovitch was not a humorous man, although his sense of the humorous in many situations was strong; his
charming smile more often expressed friendliness than appreciation of
a joke. Sometimes he went out of his way to be fair. After reading the
manuscript of Zenkovsky's great *History of Russian Philosophy*, Nicolai
Alexandrovitch, despite the strained personal relationship between
them, not only accepted the work for publication but wrote the author
suggesting certain persons he might consult for prepublication revisions.

# 15

## BROKEN FRIENDSHIPS

Along with the crises in Berdyaev's relations with institutions, the years in Paris mark parallel changes in his personal relationships. Berdyaev's remark that differences in ideas "sometimes" spoiled his contact with people is an understatement. As in earlier periods, a series of broken personal ties saddened this last third of his life. In the autobiography Nicolai Alexandrovitch mourned: "I have lived in Paris more than twenty years . . . and here have been living people with whom, in the past, I was connected . . . and I have practically not met any of them." Then he listed the Merezhkovskys, Struve, Ern, Kartasheff, V. Ivanoff, Zaitseff, Muratoff. Although there was no complete break with Bulgakov, he remarked sententiously that if he and Bulgakov had met more often, the breach might have been widened. Late in 1942, Bulgakov underwent a major surgical operation. On its eve Berdyaev wrote him: "We have not seen each other often, but I always remember the road we traveled together." Soon after leaving the hospital, Bulgakov wrote Berdyaev asking to see him, and Berdyaev went to his old friend's apartment where the two spent more than an hour in conversation.

In part, these recurring ruptures were due to what seems to be a Russian trait already noted, the personalizing of opinion; if one broke with his neighbor's ideas, he broke with the neighbor as well. Mme Kuskova says Berdyaev was much easier to get along with when the two were in political agreement.[1] Part of Berdyaev's difficulty stemmed from his "bitter experience that in general people do not understand each other well." This was because "they do not listen each to what the other is saying," and in consequence "the other's personality remains an impenetrable secret." In view of what he had said about his inability to reveal himself completely—to anyone—it may be that Nicolai Alexandrovitch was here generalizing from his own experience. In reminiscing about his life just after the Vologda exile, Nicolai Alexandrovitch said "some sort of demon" seemed to possess him, driving him to break with his former friends and preventing him from making new ones.

After the break with Struve in Berlin, Struve sealed the separation with articles hostile to Berdyaev. The break with Ern occurred about the same time as that with the two Merezhkovskys. It seemed to rest largely on Ern's dislike of German idealism. One lost friendship Nicolai Alexandrovitch deeply regretted was that of Metropolitan Eulogius (see note 3, Chapter XII). No one could have been a more ardent patriot than Berdyaev. He loved Russia intensely, suffering intensely with her suffering—particularly that of the Russian Orthodox Church. If he could have nothing in common with the government of Russia, Nicolai Alexandrovitch rejoiced in his unity with the Russian Church, and when in 1927 Metropolitan Eulogius felt it necessary to break jurisdictional relations with Moscow, Berdyaev broke immediately with the Metropolitan—regardless of their long and friendly association. This one incident cost Berdyaev very dearly in the matter of personal relationships. Henceforth, Paris was full of "old friends, now no longer friends" as Hippius put it.

This decision to remain under the jurisdiction of the Moscow Patriarch caused another break in relationships. For more than three years, Berdyaev had belonged to a small study circle among whose dozen members were Dr. Ivan I. Manouchin and his wife, Fundaminsky, Fedotoff, and Mother Marie. They usually met at the Manouchin or Fundaminsky home, and discussions centered around social Christianity and the ecumenical movement. Each member in turn would present a paper, which the group would then discuss. When the question of relations with the Moscow Patriarchate arose and Berdyaev announced his personal decision, the group quietly broke up.

In 1930 the group, with a slightly different membership, began to meet again, still studying the social implications of Christianity. Out of a paper first read at one of its gatherings was born Berdyaev's book *Christianity and Class War*. Among others in this later study circle, Mother Marie, S. P. Jaba, B. P. Vycheslavtseff, G. P. Fedotoff, V. N. Ilyin, and Father Dmitri Klepinin and his wife participated. After about a year it ceased activity.

With his old friend Andre Byeli, Berdyaev never really broke relations—although these were sometimes under considerable strain. Byeli's strange figure, always in movement, constantly gesticulating ("you could almost say he danced," says Eugenie) was occasionally seen in the Berdyaev home. During the intensely controversial prewar years

Byeli was in the U.S.S.R., whither he had returned in 1923, and one wonders if his friendship with Berdyaev could have endured otherwise. So far as known, there was no correspondence between the two men after Byeli's departure from western Europe. He died in Moscow in 1934.

The German attack on Russia and the occupation of France put another heavy strain on Berdyaev's personal relationships. He hated Hitler and national socialism even more intensely than he did communism, and could scarcely hear a good word spoken for anything German. When some of his friends began having social contacts with the enemy, following the example of Frenchmen who agreed with Pétain that one had better try to ingratiate the Germans, Berdyaev's wrath overflowed. He had been estranged from the Merezhkovskys—had apparently not seen either of them for years, although they lived in Paris. Now, when he heard they had entertained a German general at tea, he condemned his former friends in no uncertain terms. As for Vycheslavtseff, the man he had defended in earlier years in Moscow when most of the university world was against him, Berdyaev felt, by some of his articles and lectures, that Vycheslavtseff had actually entered Nazi service. Vycheslavtseff wrote requesting an interview for personal explanations, but Berdyaev replied it would be better if they did not meet. When another old friend, a priest of the Orthodox Church, wrote Berdyaev explaining why he had written an article in praise of Hitler, Berdyaev refused to reply.

Berdyaev's short temper was a thorn in the flesh. It plagued him as much as it hurt many of those near him. He considered it a part of his inheritance from his ancestors, and if he ever tried to control it, the effort failed. In almost any kind of circumstance, sudden anger would cause him to lose his self-control. In his youth he could become violently angry over a card game. At a meeting in Paris, when Shestov lectured on war and others insisted upon opinions in opposition to his own, Berdyaev became increasingly agitated, thumped on the table, and shrieked in defense of his own position. Shortly after the liberation of Paris, a delegate from the Soviet Embassy called on Berdyaev with an invitation to participate in a philosophical study circle at the Embassy. Berdyaev flew into one of his finest rages. "How dare you ask me to take part in your servile study group with its slavish instructors?" he shouted as the man made for the door.

These bursts of anger could be quite unreasoned. During one of the "Wednesday evenings" at Berdyaev's home in Moscow, discussion

happened to turn to Merezhkovsky's idea of a Third Testament (the
Old Testament of the Father, the New Testament of the Son, and a
third, yet to come, the Testament of the Holy Spirit). Partly, no doubt,
because an old friend—the Catholic Father Kuzmin-Karavaeff—vigorously opposed this idea as heretical, Berdyaev hotly defended it. "How
can you refuse to accept this," he asked, "when your own Catholic Joseph de Maistre does?" "But de Maistre is on the Index," retorted
Father Karavaeff, taken aback. Berdyaev's anger suddenly blazed out.
"This is a house of freedom," he shouted. "You have outraged it by
mentioning the Index. Please do not enter it again!" A few months
later, on Lydia's suggestion, Father Karavaeff returned to the meetings
at 14 Great Vlassov Lane and was welcomed as though nothing had
happened. Ilyin points out that in excluding people from the house
Berdyaev was asserting the character of his home as a spiritual fortress.
After a break with Berdyaev, Ilyin asked for an interview. Berdyaev
agreed but fixed the meeting place in the forest of Clamart. There was
a partial reconciliation, but although the two met occasionally and
Berdyaev spoke kindly to him, Ilyin was never invited to the Berdyaev
home again.

Mme Kuskova, still a loyal marxist at eighty-three, reported an argument in her St. Petersburg home in the early days when Berdyaev was
"deserting" to the side of "idealism." She and her husband Prokopovitch thought it scandalous that Berdyaev should mix religion with politics. Tauntingly, Prokopovitch remarked: "Berdyaev doesn't believe in
God; mixing religion with politics means that you have no faith in
religion." At this Berdyaev flew into a rage, leaping from his chair with:
"I shall never enter this house again." He never did, but Mme Kuskova
reports that years later, when they were living in Prague, Berdyaev
came to see them as though nothing had happened.

Such sudden rages could have direct physical effects. Once, in the
house at Clamart, Berdyaev got into a heated argument with someone
believing that freedom existed in the U.S.S.R. Nicolai Alexandrovitch
became so emotionally upset that Lydia had to lead him from the room.
Another time, when Berdyaev was returning in the train from Paris to
Clamart, he engaged in dispute with a man he knew only slightly and
reached the house with a severe nasal hemorrhage that could not be
stopped for two days. The doctor strongly urged Berdyaev to avoid excitement, since there was evident danger the next attack might be cere-
bral instead of nasal. After that, Nicolai Alexandrovitch made efforts

to maintain his poise, and the last years of his life were not marked by such painful incidents. While his outbursts appeared to be surface phenomena of momentary duration, one wonders if, underneath, there may have been the same element he recognized in Leontieff, who broke "with friends, . . . the most clever and genial of men, when he [Leontieff] began to feel . . . too greatly dependent upon them [and] limited 'by his friends' opinions.' "[2] With Berdyaev's passionate insistence throughout life on the untouchability of his personal freedom, he seemed almost to feel that losing an argument was putting himself into bondage to his opponent.

Berdyaev always regretted these incidents and disliked the "difficult" meetings where they might occur. Returning home, he would remark how irksome it was for him to take part in them. To Lydia's question "why, then, do you give so much of your time and strength to these meetings?" he replied: "I feel it my duty to defend what I consider the truth." Berdyaev eventually learned which people were likely to upset him, and if they called (once it was a bishop at the door) would send word by Eugenie that he was unwell and unable to receive them. After an outburst of wrath he always regretted it and was not slow to say so, usually through a third person. Whether or not there was a personal reconciliation, Nicolai Alexandrovitch seemed never to hold a permanent grudge. It all boiled away in his first seizure of anger.

If Berdyaev was charming in conversation, in lecturing he was brilliant. One who saw him for the first time at a lecture in the Religious-Philosophical Academy in Paris tells of the "face so noble, the mind so clearly sincere that the tic was immediately ignored. . . . When Berdyaev spoke, it was a spiritual confession. His crystal-clear sincerity impressed everyone." And while he was a brilliant lecturer, he scintillated in debate. All his talent, all his erudition seemed to become immediately available, and unlike many who always think of the telling retort the next day, he never seemed to lack for the right argument or refutation. He remarked to Mme K: "It's unpleasant to dispute with people who are not seeking the truth but seek only to win the argument." And in debate he could be merciless in defense of what he held for truth. It was ever difficult for him to understand how others could hold to another opinion than his own—the truth, as he saw it.

Despite his very personal reactions, Berdyaev rarely in debate and almost never in his writings used the *argumentem ad hominem*—a failing of which many émigré authors were not innocent. Once when shown an article by a former pupil bitterly attacking his positions, Berdyaev read it in silence, and only later, at home, asked Eugenie not to invite the man to their house again. After Byeli had written a vicious article against Berdyaev—"The Strong Heart"—he was astonished, upon meeting Berdyaev on the street a month later, when the latter inquired about his health and why he had not recently been in the Berdyaev home. When Fedotoff published an article sharply criticizing Nicolai Alexandrovitch—"The Blinded Eagle"—Berdyaev wrote in a note to Mme Fedotoff: "I must tell you frankly that I am pained by your husband's point of view."

Loneliness was one of the characteristics of Berdyaev's way through life. He noted it with deep regret in various of his books. The English title *Solitude and Society* of his *Myself and the Objective World* was somewhat misleading, although here again, Nicolai Alexandrovitch's sense of being very much alone in the world found expression. He recognized it as partly his own fault. In youth, he had moved from his parents' home to his own apartment in search of solitude. Most of the broken relations with friends were of his own initiative, and Berdyaev attributed them partly to his own shortcomings. But a share of the blame he placed on the nature of things: ". . . a typical destiny which has fallen to the lot of many exceptional people who have passed their life misunderstood and lonely." He did not claim the solitude of a leader: "I have no need to direct other spirits." There was something of Kierkegaard's concept of the necessary solitude of a Christian before his God, although Berdyaev never expressed it in those terms. He grieved because he was never able completely to reveal himself to another: "All my life I have longed for a meeting of minds on the essential, the supreme, a conversation which would surmount distances and conventions. . . . I carried in me such a meeting, but I could not break down the wall."[3] Eugenie thinks he was less lonely after his marriage than before. This is confirmed in a phrase from one of his letters to Lydia: "When I go away alone I am uneasy, lonely, and even sad. But solitude for me has a positive value. I can concentrate, and many trenchant ideas come into my head."

Yet always his strong sense of the unreality of the world about him, of his belonging to another—real—world, set him apart from his fellow men. Sometimes he felt even God had deserted him: "I never doubted the existence of God; my torment did not lie in this. But often I have felt God's departure from the world—that he had deserted the world and man, had deserted me as well."[4] Berdyaev felt God's abandonment of human society was characteristic of the times. He spoke of it more and more frequently as the outbreak of World War II drew near. Accepting his loneliness as something salutary, he believed, like Dostoievsky, in "the redeeming and revivifying power of suffering." As he wrote of Leontieff: "Providence destined . . . his way for some higher pupose. . . . In this there is higher meaning which is a mystery to us."

Notwithstanding this long list of friends lost, some held true or were replaced. Despite his assertions "I do not have the gift of friendship. I am incapable of giving much attention to people," Berdyaev appreciated his friendships, treasuring them and seeking new ones. As noted previously, Shestov held the endurance record. Whenever the two met they argued, sometimes violently. Once, sitting around the fireplace in the evening, the debate waxed hot. Shestov sat quietly in his chair, but Nicolai Alexandrovitch raged up and down the room and around his friend's chair, firing questions at him: "You deny that? You deny consciousness! Do you think you are conscious when you are writing?" Shestov never missed a meeting at the Berdyaev home, even when the topic was something definitely Christian. Berdyaev said Shestov's religion was Old Testament rather than evangelical, but that he felt a close relationship to Luther. A great friendship vanished with Shestov's death.[5]

Berdyaev's youthful attachment to Longvinsky lasted until the latter's untimely demise in exile. One other friendship remaining unbroken to the end was that with S. L. Frank. Apparently it was not quite as intimate a relationship as with Shestov. An explanation of the difference may have been residential. Shestov made his home in Paris all the years Berdyaev did, whereas Frank lived mostly in other places. Remizoff loved Nicolai Alexandrovitch to the end but Berdyaev never recovered from his disapproval of Remizoff, who had published articles under the German occupation—and although he was formally correct, writing condolences to Remizoff when his wife died, for instance, Berdyaev never resumed the prewar ties. With Feodor Pianoff there was never a break from the earliest Berlin days to the end of Berdyaev's life, and Berdyaev leaned on Pianoff for counsel and aid in many circumstances.

Without a doubt the closest woman friend of his lifetime, aside from Lydia, was Eugenie. There were also E. Herzig in Russia and Mme de

Monbrison in France. The latter was among the new associations developing during Berdyaev's later life in Paris.

Among other associates was Fritz Lieb, Swiss professor and connoisseur of things Russian. Leaving his post at the University of Bonn because he could not endure Hitlerism, Lieb lived for several years in Clamart, partly because he sought personal contact with Berdyaev. The two men had met before, and during Lieb's stay in Clamart they saw a good deal of each other—to the great pleasure of both.

Another close friend of the Paris period was Constantin Motchulsky, talented author and critic. A score of years younger than Berdyaev, he had arrived in Paris two years before Berdyaev came. His spiritual experience there was like Berdyaev's, but telescoped into a shorter period. Somewhat of a bohemian, without the political interests that impassioned most of his fellow émigrés, his erudition was recognized by the Sorbonne and for several years he lectured on Russian literature. Somewhere at the beginning of the thirties Motchulsky came into contact with Berdyaev and then with Bulgakov. By 1933 he was lecturing in the Religious-Philosophical Academy. All the time he was writing; his great work on Dostoievsky (1937) became a "must" for students of this author. It was dedicated "with filial love" to Father Bulgakov—through whose influence he had re-entered the Orthodox Church. Berdyaev's influence on Motchulsky was also considerable, and the deep affection between them lasted until they died—only two days apart—Motchulsky on March 21, and Berdyaev on March 23, 1948.

Close friend of both Berdyaev and Motchulsky was that most unorthodox Orthodox nun, Mother Marie (Skobtsov). Poet, artist, social worker, and ex-revolutionary (she once seriously contemplated shooting Trotsky, whose secretary she had been during the first months of the Soviet regime), she was the founder and moving spirit of Orthodox Action, a social service organization expressing the faith of the Orthodox Church. No one who ever chanced to meet Mother Marie returning from a foray in the great central market, black robe soiled with the vegetables in her pushcart, hands swollen and coarse from doing menial tasks in her home for the Russian poor, will ever forget her. Her breadth of interest and scorn for convention shocked many of the more traditional-minded Orthodox. When the Germans occupied Paris, she was deported for the "crime" of having befriended Jews—and died in a concentration camp. One friend who knew them both said it was difficult to know which influenced the other more: Motchulsky's ideal of the monastic life was a quiet cell; for Mother Marie the cell was "the whole of God's world." Both were close to Berdyaev, who was interested in all the activities of Orthodox Action. When, after Metropolitan Eulogius' break with Moscow, many of the workers in Orthodox Action made the same decision to remain under the Moscow Patriarch as had Berdyaev, they were drawn even more closely together.

A significant friendship Berdyaev formed in Paris was that with Jacques Maritain. Since Meudon, where Maritain lived, was next door to Clamart, the two could meet frequently, aside from the interconfessional gatherings mentioned in the previous chapter. Other friends acquired in Paris were Jules Cain, Jacques Madole, and Professor André Philippe. Another firm friendship developed with Mme Romain-Rolland, whose interest in Berdyaev and his family continues to the present day. She is vice-president of the Berdyaev Society. Hélène Iswolsky, daughter of the last Imperial Ambassador in Paris, was another friend of the period. Her intimate picture of Nicolai Alexandrovitch in his later years, *Berdyaev As We Knew Him*, has regrettably not yet found a publisher.

Berdyaev particularly enjoyed visiting with his friends in the Clamart house after a Sunday afternoon meeting. As the guests filed out, certain chosen ones would be quietly asked to stay for supper. The gathering might include Fedotoff, Mother Marie, Motchulsky, P. Ivanoff, Fundaminsky, and occasionally Maritain and his wife. It would have the atmosphere of a party. Berdyaev relaxed and became witty and vivacious. "The 'distance' disappeared, and he would engage in discussing the most varied subjects with the verve and pleasure of a high school boy. Sometimes, at someone's witty remark, his laughter would ring through the house."

If Nicolai Alexandrovitch was at his ease in a supper company, he always felt constraint when faced with a single person. To the many requests for talks with him, largely from Russians, he never gave a refusal—no matter how busy he happened to be. But he did not like these intimate conversations. What he particularly disliked was an appeal for spiritual help or counsel. "There is something immodest about the way people will bare their souls," he told Lydia. "It makes me feel awkward." "It must be awkward to live in the world, in general," she replied. "Yes, terribly awkward," he answered smilingly. "But I am not indifferent. I sympathize with these people, and I try to help. Perhaps," he added, "I sometimes understand the man better than he does himself. But then, I am not a 'teacher of living'—my calling is something other."

Berdyaev's friends gained widely differing impressions of his personality. Mother Marie considered him a well-balanced, quiet, even gay, person. Motchulsky felt that Berdyaev was restless, tragically uneasy, dissatisfied, and a seeker after stormy weather. Many outsiders thought Berdyaev cold, supercilious, indifferent—a man in a mask; but Eugenie explains this as "his conscious method of protecting his supersensitive and refined nature from the ugliness and coarseness of life." Ni felt extraordinarily deep emotion, she says, but almost never showed it outwardly. There were moments, if not often, when he was very tender. Even at Lydia's death he did not weep, and few of those around him suspected what terrible grief he felt. Even Shestov did not understand him. In a letter to Shestov we find this phrase: "In your understanding of me there is not the slightest resemblance to me, to my interior life and my destiny." Servants always adored him whether they understood him or not, and anyone who lived in the Berdyaev home soon came to appreciate his tactfulness and tender interest in those around him.

If he suffered from misunderstanding by his friends, the failure of his critics to comprehend him was equally hard to bear. Incidentally, he found literary criticism "a type of creativity I do not greatly esteem." "Critics," not enemies—he had no enemies in the usual sense of the word, only ideological opponents. As he said of Leontieff: "He was kinder to other people than they were to him." Opposition meant attacks on his opinions, not on his character. Even his sharpest critics never accused him of insincerity or evil intent. He suffered intensely from homesickness for Russia, and from the hostility toward him of a large portion of his fellow Russians living abroad. In a letter to Shestov he wrote:

> What a strange fate is mine: the leftists consider me a rightist, and the rightists think I am a leftist; the Orthodox think me a heretic while heretics call me orthodox, and everywhere I feel that my image is distorted. Now some newspaper gossip is calling me a reactionary when my chief reaction is against the obscurantism so characteristic of the majority of the emigration.

Of Berdyaev's friends by correspondence there is a multitude. No considerable or consequent record of his side of the correspondence has been preserved, but some of the letters he received are indicative. He treated each letter seriously, trying, often at several pages' length, to help with a given problem. One man in a tuberculosis sanatorium writes that Berdyaev's letter "not only crushed my ignorant denial of . . . Christianity, but it gave peace and joy to my soul." Another letter says: "I cannot express how [this letter] has borne fruit in me, and what light it has given."

The letters reveal some of the many facets, even some of the contradictions, in Berdyaev's character. To the end of his days there was a naïveté about him that sometimes amused, sometimes alarmed his friends. This was true in matters politic. An article by a friend might lead him quite astray on some political issue. He was at first inclined to trust the Soviet newspaper articles just after the war that promised all sorts of privileges to émigrés who would accept repatriation. Writing of her husband, Hippius could have been describing Berdyaev when she says: "He had unusual confidence in others—the credulity of a child. Something of the child remained in him to the end of his life."[6] When one of his protégés was accused of plagiarism and told Berdyaev a cock-and-bull story to explain it, Berdyaev believed him implicitly.

Credulous or not, he was quick to take action if he believed his informant's freedom was threatened. While delicate in his attitudes toward individual men, he was sharp in his position with regard to ideas—"passionate, but always noble," one of his sharpest critics admitted. As for his perennial defense of freedom, he would, "in the Middle Ages, have been burned at the stake," declared Stepun. Most of his writings, books, or articles, attack some idea or its representatives. "He talks with God as though he were attacking Him in His heavenly fortress," says a friend.

In Berdyaev's character there were many contradictions—some noted by his friends, and others he said, they never knew about. He considered himself one of the Russian people of whom he wrote:

> A combination of antinomic, polar contradictions is characteristic of Russians; . . . they can equally well be called despots or anarchically freedom-loving, inclined toward nationalism . . . or the universal spirit—more than all other peoples capable of . . . cruelty and unusually humane, inclined to inflict suffering and sympathetic to the point of suffering.

Despotic or intentionally cruel Berdyaev never was, although his stern insistence on his own concept of truth and the consequent breaking off of personal relations wounded many people deeply. His friends

sometimes thought him too tolerant, particularly in contacts with
Roman Catholics; on the other hand he could be violently intolerant,
as in the case of Ern. In the last pages of his autobiography, Nicolai
Alexandrovitch explained some of the contrasting elements he observed
in himself. His innate anarchism is combined with a strong sense of
order—a habit, he explained, built up to preserve him as much as possible from the inconveniences and the effort of managing his own affairs.
He knew he was lacking in practical sense, and in order to spend as little
energy as possible on personal living arrangements, he learned to do
them by rote—with almost no thought wasted on such pursuits. It was
one of his self-recognized weaknesses that he could not stand ugliness
in any form. He disliked old clothes—it hurt him to wear a worn suit.
He disliked ill-breeding; it irked him, for instance, to see people slouch-
ing in their chairs or using bad table manners.

Although he deprecated aristocratic traits in himself, Nicolai Alexandrovitch always maintained that in some ways the aristocracy deserved
credit. "You may even recognize a certain moral superiority of the
aristocracy over the bourgeois," he wrote in *Christianity and Class War*.
"Aristocracy sincerely and openly recognized inequality, . . . but the
bourgeoisie conceals both this and its privileged position. . . . Conflict . . . in the aristocratic societies was cruel but honestly open,
while in capitalistic societies the conflict of banks and stock exchanges,
of parliamentary parties and the press, is conflict behind the scenes,
disguised. . . ." "Social class war is destroying the aristocracy. Aristocracy can stand only racial or national wars, but it cannot outlast a
war of social classes."

Berdyaev recognized another set of contradictions in his makeup.
Two psychological types were combined in him, he said, the sanguine
and the melancholy. He was quick to anger, swift in all his reactions.
And on the other hand he had known long periods of depression and
sadness with no apparent external reason—another illustration of what
Berdyaev meant when he said he was a personality living on different
levels. To critics who called him a romantic, Berdyaev replied that his
was a character of sober realism, and probably both were right. Once in
the early days in Paris, he was persuaded to attend a meeting of the
Oxford Group Movement—as it was then known. After listening to
the leader for a while, Berdyaev left quietly at the first intermission.
When a friend asked his opinion of the Movement, expecting a fairly
strong reaction, Berdyaev merely remarked: "There's not an idea in it."

# 16

## "THE LIGHT OF RUSSIA"

His personal characteristics molded Berdyaev's relations with the church. By church is meant the Russian Orthodox; although he had a strong ecumenical sense, Nicolai Alexandrovitch never considered belonging to any other. In his youth, Berdyaev's attitude toward the church had been negative. In Vologda, where there were not too many ways of occupying a young man's time, he seems never to have entered a house of worship. Even when—as "almost" Christian—he made a pilgrimage to the Zosima monastery, he had been repelled by its external manifestations of religion. The profound unrest leading to the 1905 revolution revealed the church as so closely allied with a corrupt court as to be itself not unspotted by the general moral decadence. At that time Berdyaev probably would have agreed with Hippius' devastating appraisal of the clergy and theologians (1902) dividing them into five classes, all reprehensible—while admitting that somewhere "in the depths of Russia" there must be a few men of humble sanctity. But Berdyaev would have been as unconscious of these wrestlers of the spirit as Hippius was, and his violent attack on the Holy Synod was not the only time he publicly expressed adverse criticism. One wonders if such strong aversion and censure was easier for Nicolai Alexandrovitch because he had little experienced the warm, never-absent piety of the church's life. Such contact might have softened his judgment. There was nothing soft about "Quenchers of the Spirit."

Then came the years of swift spiritual evolution; by the time the communist revolution arrived, he was avowedly a member of the Orthodox Church. He approved of the separation of church from state, and when the new government began its long-continuing effort to throttle the church, Berdyaev was as quick to defend as he had been to attack it under the Tsar. While Lydia had been shocked by what she felt were the insufficiencies of the Orthodox Church, Berdyaev came out boldly in its public defense. He even helped others into the church.

215

Kuzmin-Karavaeff tells of a conversation, shortly after the revolution, when Berdyaev inquired about his friend's approach to a Christian faith. Kuzmin-Karavaeff replied that he felt himself unready to enter the church. "My life is spiritually very poor. I feel that we should come to the church with a dowry." "No," was Berdyaev's firm opinion, "you should come into the church naked." Berdyaev used jokingly to say that Father Kuzmin-Karavaeff's conversion took place at 14 Great Vlassov Lane.

Once he had entered it, Berdyaev never wavered in his loyalty to the church—to the church as he conceived it. He saw it in two aspects, spiritual and physical, the body of Christ and the church in the world. The spiritual church is *sobornost*, the brotherhood of spirits who are consciously sons of God—the union of all those, here or in heaven, who are included in the communion of the sacraments. As a supernatural body it lives according to its own spiritual laws, unaffected by, and not to be judged by human ordinance. That part of the church which is on earth as a phenomenon of human history is humanly fallible, and Berdyaev was not blind to its faults and failures. He wrote Mme K: "Christianity in history has harmed itself, not by its aims . . . but by the means by which Christians sought to realize them." He remarked incidentally that the same was true of idealistic communism: "the first attempt to realize greater social justice in Russia is associated with tyranny and slavery." Nicolai Alexandrovitch was among the first to declare that if the church had adequately fulfilled its mission on earth, the false religion of communism could never have taken root.

But this did not destroy his faith in man—in or outside the church. "I became a Christian," he said, "not because I ceased to believe in man, in his dignity and his higher calling, in his creative freedom, but because I sought a profounder and more stable basis for this faith."[2] That it was the Orthodox Church he should enter in this search was as natural as his Russian tongue. Berdyaev under Roman Catholic discipline would be difficult to imagine, as would Berdyaev in Protestant sectarianism. Thomist he could never have become. Although he shared some of the personal qualities of Luther, he would not have been happier under the emphasis on reason in the Reformation than under the authority of the Church of Rome. But he was far from considering Orthodoxy as perfection. Historical Orthodoxy seemed to him at the time insufficiently ecumenical, too closed in upon itself, almost a sect in the world-wide church. In the Orthodox Church he valued the emphasis on spirit rather than on law, and its consequent inner freedom. He called himself a "believing—i.e. Christian—freethinker." He never pretended to be a typical member of his church. But within it he had liberty for creative thinking and fresh approaches to new situations in the world. In the one schism in the history of the Russian Orthodox Church, it was the conservative group that broke away, not the liberal. That the Old Believers were vigorously persecuted by the liberals for a century or more is beside the point.

Which brings up the matter of the church's authority and Berdyaev's thought about it. "In my religious life I do not know . . . authority," he wrote in 1927. The church in different periods of its history had too often inclined toward the realm of Caesar rather than that of spirit —where "freedom is rooted." Christianity has been guilty of the terrible falsehood of attempting to preserve freedom by liberating men from God, "when religious conscience was transferred to the church collective."[3] Like a totalitarian state, the church has at times tried to dominate man's spirit. But the spirit is of freedom. "Through . . . the immanent living out of freedom, I have come to Christ. My Christian faith is not the ordinary, inherited, family faith; it is a faith won by tormenting experience of life, from within, from freedom."[4] The spirit is freedom, but the spirit is also truth, and Berdyaev recognizes that "in its divine, mystic aspect the church is immovable, and conserves eternal truth." Thus he could write Archbishop Antony in that resounding open letter. As a believing Orthodox, Berdyaev knew the church's authority was more spiritual than normative. And the infallible spiritual authority of the church has been derived from the body of believers—not merely in the seven ecumenical councils, but throughout its history. Even the councils had no authority save as their decisions were accepted by the Orthodox people as a whole. The truths expressed in the dogmas (and no new dogma has been recognized in Orthodoxy since the seventh ecumenical council in Nicea, 787 A.D.) have been witnessed to by the outpouring of the Holy Spirit—and recognized as such by the entire body of the faithful. Yet even these truths must be sought out in each man's experience. "For the solution of these problems of the spirit, or this one problem of the relation between man and God, help cannot come from the outside. No 'elder,' even the most spiritual, can help here. . . . I myself must bring to light what God has concealed from me. God expects from me an act of freedom, of free creativeness."[5] But almost in the same paragraph he is explaining: "No single word [of this book] is to be understood as directed against the sanctity of the church." The church is the pillar and bulwark of the truth, but that is the church of the spirit rather than the man-managed institution. With the latter Berdyaev felt he had a God-given right to differ if his conscience so led him.

Of the authority of the Bible, Berdyaev was inclined to think along with the Orthodox Church. The Eastern Church does not attribute exclusive and final authority to the Bible, as does protestantism; it recognizes truth as contained in both Holy Scripture and Holy Tradition. And he did not believe all truth had been revealed once and for all, in either scripture or tradition. He felt that God is continuing His revelation—to men who respond to the call for creative effort. He knew the New Testament from cover to cover, and still, as he once said, it is extraordinary how one is always discovering new depths in it: "You may know the Gospels almost by heart, and suddenly some unexpected phrase which you have read many, many times, will open to you such profundity as you have never apprehended before, and it seems as though you were reading it for the first time." As George Seaver wisely remarks, Berdyaev was more at home with St. John than with St. Paul. Nicolai Alexandrovitch was particularly fond of the prophets. A month before his death he said he was reading them with especial concentration—to penetrate the hidden meaning in Holy Scripture. He was persuaded that, beyond the New Testament, beyond the epoch of redemption, lay a new revelation of spirit that would usher in the everlasting kingdom.

Berdyaev considered himself—and was so considered by his confessor—a loyal son of the Orthodox Church. Of Khomiakoff he wrote: "He had no religious uncertainty; . . . he was a person religiously right, calm and satisfied. In this he differs from . . . us. . . . In him there is none of the . . . torment of those who are hungering and thirsting. . . ."[6] Once satisfied, this torment of thirst for God gave him a special sense of freedom and a right to exercise it, Nicolai Alexandrovitch seemed to feel. "When a man comes to God after an experience of apostasy from God, he knows such a freedom of address to God as that man does not know who has spent his life in undisturbed traditional faith, who has obediently lived in the inherited family estate."[7] This sense of personal freedom in things of the spirit is summed up in a phrase from one of his letters to Mme K: "All my religious life is bound up with the fact that I do not accept dependence upon anyone or anything. God is my independence."

It was as simple as that. "The Christian revelation teaches us that simplicity is from God, that everything great is simple, as simple as Mont Blanc which I now see before me. Simplicity is the victory of spirituality over the lack of integrity, over confusion, division . . . indirectness," he wrote. And although he struggled to attain such simplicity, he said he was "a very uneasy person, a man of a rebellious spirit, but within me is faith and knowledge of the simplicity of the Truth."

Perhaps there was some hint of this sense of simplicity in Berdyaev's attitude toward the authority of the Orthodox Church at the time of the 1927 crisis, when the church in Russia under the leadership of its then *locum tenens*—later Patriarch—Serge emerged from the catacombs and obtained state recognition in exchange for its assurance of civic loyalty to the government. In line with the new position, Serge issued a "Declaration" that included a request to all Russian Orthodox clergy abroad to assert their loyalty to the Soviet State. The resultant situation was tragic. Almost no one on either side of the frontiers understood the situation of the other. The members of the emigration were in exile because they would have nothing to do with the bolshevik regime, and the clergy was an integral part of the emigration. Even had some wished to accede to Serge's request, they would risk personal difficulties in the country where they lived—where French or Yugoslav governments, for instance, feared and hated communism as much as did the Russian émigrés. An almost unanimous cry of protest went up, and eventually Metropolitan Eulogius left the jurisdiction of Moscow, placing himself and his exarchate under Constantinople.

Almost unanimous; there was a small group—and Berdyaev was among them—who, while signing no declaration of loyalty to the Soviet government, nevertheless so cherished their communion with the church in Russia that they could intellectually distinguish between political and spiritual affairs. Berdyaev's article "The Outcry of the Russian Church"[8] attempts to explain why he was remaining under the jurisdiction of the Moscow Patriarchate (in this, as in all matters of faith, he insisted that each man must decide for himself). How grave was the general disagreement with Berdyaev's decision is evident from the fact that some who remained his friends after the break still felt he had let his Russian patriotism overlay his religion. Berdyaev spoke on the basis of his own experience, having lived four years in Soviet Russia. The question, he said, was larger than any temporary division within the Russian Church. "We must understand the difference between the Orthodox Church in Russia and that of the emigration. The church in Russia is a church of martyrs, continuing its way of the cross to the end." Bishops in emigration did not understand what that meant—and Metropolitan Serge's declaration was really saying: "The careless words of your bishops . . . have brought us into prison, to face the firing squads."

Berdyaev had a most diplomatic phrase to characterize the compromise the Russian Church has been compelled to make under the communist regime: "The church is called to sacrifice its visible beauty and purity: it enters a world which lies in mortal sin. . . . In the name of the church, Patriarch Tichon, forgetting himself . . . agreed to speak in a language which in many calls forth moral and aesthetic revulsion." Berdyaev compares the "tremendous personal sacrifice" of Patriarch Tichon and Metropolitan Serge with that of St. Alexander Nevsky—when he submitted himself to the court of the Tatar Khan.

Émigrés or not, Russians everywhere should be loyal to their church. The emigration is a political rather than a church concept. There can be no such thing as an emigrant church. The church is above politics. The power in Berdyaev's article is all of appeal, with none of the vituperation that marked "Quenchers of the Spirit" or his defense of Fedotoff. Berdyaev understood émigré psychology well enough to recognize the problem as one of misinterpretation rather than of wrong intent.

Berdyaev's attitude of reverence for the "real" church and his scorn of many of its external phenomena carried over into his attitude toward the clergy. He seems to have had little or no contact with Orthodox priests until his St. Petersburg days, and here his one relationship—that with Archimandrite Serge—was equivocal. He admired Serge for his courage in stepping out to meet the a-religious intelligentsia, but he was displeased by the priest's unwillingness or inability to consider modern "intellectual" viewpoints. During the Moscow period he had failed in an attempt at spiritual contact with Elder Alexei, and it was only during and immediately after the revolution that he met a priest, Father Metcheff, who could offer him food for the spirit. With all his veneration for Father Metcheff, however, Berdyaev made a distinction between his spiritual and his intellectual qualities. To a friend he once remarked that Father Metcheff "had no concept of religious philosophy." In Paris, Nicolai Alexandrovitch had great respect for Metropolitan Eulogius both as hierarch and as a person. Toward the end of his life Berdyaev developed a close relationship with Father Stefan

(Svetozaroff), and their deep mutual affection was not broken by Father Stefan's return to the U.S.S.R. The two friends continued to correspond until Berdyaev's death. Father Stefan later wrote Eugenie: "I consider him a faithful member of the Orthodox Church."

Nicolai Alexandrovitch's attitude toward the sacraments of the church was typically Orthodox. Even where he found no priest with whom he could feel spiritual kinship, he accepted the communion cup as a service holy in itself, apart from the hand that held it. Despite his revolt against the milieu in which he had been nurtured, he never went to the lengths of Tolstoi, who early denounced the sacraments as a "collection of the coarsest superstitions and witchcraft." As early as 1907, before he had publicly announced his return to the church, he could write in a letter: "Philosophy is my calling, but the sacraments of the church are the very essence of life."

This complete acceptance of the sacraments grew out of Berdyaev's faith. To him the dogmas of the church were not pure rationalization, but rather something to be spiritually experienced. He said his faith did not conform to the usual teachings of Christian theology. "My faith, which saves me from atheism, is like this: God reveals himself to the world. He reveals himself in the prophets, in the Son, in the Spirit, in the spiritual experience of mankind. . . . God is truth, the world is untruth. . . . God is freedom and gives freedom."[9] What Berdyaev said of Dostoievsky in this connection is equally true of himself: "For him freedom is anthropodicy and theodicy; . . . in it one must seek both the justification of man and the justification of God. . . . God is not the Lord, but the liberator from the world's servitude. God acts through freedom. . . . He does not compel us to recognize him. . . . Even sin I feel not as disobedience but as the loss of freedom."[10]

Berdyaev's idea of the Fall was that of a misuse of freedom in the spirit world before time began rather than as an event in human history. The biblical story is a myth comprehending eternal truth. From his misused freedom, man could be redeemed only by Christ's taking upon himself God-manhood. "One can believe in God only if there is the Son, the Redeemer and Deliverer, the God of sacrifice and love." But the idea of the God-man must have its counterpart in the man-God: "The Grand Inquisitor does not believe in God, but neither does he believe in man. . . . These are two sides of the same faith. . . . Christianity demands belief in God and belief in man as well. It is a religion of God-manhood." Here Nicolai Alexandrovitch accepted the Orthodox idea of the gradual making divine and perfect of the entire cosmos

—every created thing. He offered a careful exposition of "this original comprehension of Christianity" in his *Russian Idea*. In an earlier work he expressed it thus: "The essence of evil is in the deification of the human element, separated from God. The essence of God is [in] making human nature divine, in union with God."[11] Berdyaev revolted against the idea of eternal damnation as "ugly and sadistic." He could not conceive of a God less merciful and sensitive to suffering than himself. He said he had never wanted to send anyone to hell and could not understand the psychology of those who, certain they themselves were of the elect, could take pleasure in imagining others in eternal torment. He believed, moreover, that "if one admits the existence of eternal torment, then all . . . spiritual and moral life is deprived of meaning and value, since it goes on under the sign of terror." Further, he said: ". . . the judgment of God is something quite other than that of man."[12] He often spoke of the resurrection. Orthodoxy was right, he felt, in placing supreme emphasis on Christ's rising from the dead—hence making Easter the highest festival of the Christian year. To Mme K he wrote: "For me, resurrection can be only through Christ." George Seaver points out that Berdyaev's statement of the special nature of the Trinity's third person would not be considered heresy by the Orthodox Church: "As stated by Berdyaev, however, it possesses an originality and a conviction which lifts it from the aridity of dogma into the living reality of experience."[13]

One reason Nicolai Alexandrovitch could consider himself Orthodox was that after long study he had decided Orthodoxy, in contrast to Catholicism and Protestantism, was indefinable. This suited his own temperament and gave him the freedom he insisted upon. He always denied being a theologian, although as early as 1907, when he was deep in *Khomiakoff*, he was over his ears in theological considerations —even if he called them religious-philosophical. But here there is a certain play of words, and the problems of the spirit and of man's relation to God are so much in the center of theological thinking that many would give him a place among the exponents of "the queen of sciences." Keyserling was impressed by his extensive knowledge of the church fathers, and Berdyaev's vocabulary—particularly in the earlier books—sometimes savors strongly of the theological. *Dostoievsky*, for instance, is full of much that might be called theological discussion.

But if he did not consider himself completely Orthodox, Berdyaev resented being called a heretic. There was the moment when two ultraconservative hierarchs formally proposed his excommunication. A heretic, he pointed out, is a thoroughly churchly person who expounds his personal ideas as those the church ought to hold. He, on the contrary, never claimed ecclesiastical sanction for his thoughts. He "sought the truth, and experienced as truth what was revealed to him."[14]

While he was no heretic in the Orthodox Church, some—even among his friends—thought him too tolerant of other confessions. And while he remained loyally Orthodox, his thought was constantly going out across the world to problems of the entire Christian conscience. He was inevitably ecumenical-minded. By birth and descent he belonged to both East and West. His maternal grandmother had been a Roman Catholic. His mother, brought up in that church, became Orthodox at her marriage. His wife was Roman Catholic. His sympathies were wide enough to take in the Church Universal. He could see the shortcomings in both his own and other confessions: "Freedom of the human spirit, freedom of conscience, enters into the content of Christian Truth. All this was not fully revealed by the old Christian consciousness, and least of all by Catholicism." On the other hand, he criticized Khomiakoff for talking as though the Orthodox Church were perfect— with all fault in the Church of Rome. "The mystic essence of the church in love and liberty is in Catholicism also."[15]

With Berdyaev's breadth of sympathy for the whole of the Christian Church, his approval of the ecumenical movement was natural. As for orthodoxy, he desired a fuller realization of its spiritual gifts before the world. Only thus would it attain a significance commensurate both with its old tradition and its sudden spread across the world in our day. He was well acquainted with the leaders of the ecumenical movement and rejoiced at the formation of the World Council of Churches. One of his last important lecture series was that given in October, 1946, at the Ecumenical Institute in Bossey, Switzerland. He said the Orthodox Church had suffered less in history from secularization than had others, and the triumph of the ecumenical movement must be a Christianization of the world rather than making Christianity worldly. He felt orthodoxy had much to contribute to the ecumenical movement.

A summary of Berdyaev's faith might begin with his innate sense of belonging to another world—his mystical feeling for life. To the agnostic-minded Mme K, he wrote:

> You do not sufficiently understand that I have a mystic feeling and understanding of life, and that I am a Christian. For a Chris-

tian philosopher everything in this world is a symbol of another, spiritual world. . . . From childhood there has been in me an absolute feeling of the reality of another, spiritual world, a world invisible. . . . I think in every moment of his life, man should be faced toward eternity. That negation of eternity, vulgarity, is so strong in our day! Social justice, too, must be realized for the sake of eternity.

The reality of the spiritual world, of the Spirit, was at the base of Berdyaev's faith.

Because of this he could write:

I have an absolute, unshakable faith in God. I believe in God because I do not believe in the self-sufficiency of the world or of man. The meaning of the world is God. Belief in God is the duty of nobility: in godlessness, in faith in the world, there is something vulgar. . . . The falsehood and senselessness of life of the world does not weaken, but rather strengthens my faith. The world's evil bears witness to the fact that this world is not self-sufficient.

Nobility was another phase of his belief. Christianity is the faith of an elite, he felt, of a body of free men who have placed their love of Christ before every other consideration:

My understanding of Christianity is eschatological and I set it over against historic Christianity. But my understanding of eschatology is active and creative, not passive.[16]

Here speaks the Christian philosopher. On the other hand, a clergyman who rode with Berdyaev to the cemetery after Lydia's funeral was surprised at the simplicity of Nicolai Alexandrovitch's conversation. He asked the priest's views about resurrection and the life of the soul after death, "just as," said the priest, "any ordinary workman might have inquired on the way to his wife's funeral. His faith was as simple as that of a workman."

Berdyaev's basic faith in the Orthodox Church was not always rewarded by the church's answering faith in him. But at the end of his life he was in good standing with the church as a whole. Hippius hinted, at the time, that only a freshly arrived Orthodox "like Berdyaev, for instance" could elect to continue his church relationship unbroken, when almost everyone was following Metropolitan Eulogius' move away from Moscow.

He had faith in the church for the future as well as for the present. He knew very well that the church in Russia is only tolerated by the communist regime, that its sphere of material action is severely restricted, and that its leaders have had to make what appeared from the outside to be concessions to their government. But that did not dampen his faith in the future role of the church in Russia or of the Church Universal. The church of today, presenting a disunited front against the massed demoniac powers of antireligion, stands at the end of an epoch. "We are living in the entr'acte," he said. He called on Christians to prepare for a new, creative epoch in the church's life that would "reveal, out of the depths of Christianity, power for the creation of a new, unprecedented world." But he warned against purely passive waiting for this new world to dawn, and against attempts to create new religions à la Merezhkovsky. "Go into the church," he urged, "and create a new community: we must be active as well as humble and tolerant. . . . In the religion of the Holy Spirit, the religion of liberty, everything will be revealed in a new light."

His conviction that a new epoch of Christian creativeness was coming met anything but unanimous acceptance by the authorities of the Russian Church. Acceptance would not have greatly concerned Nicolai Alexandrovitch. He spoke what he felt—regardless. Khomiakoff, writing in a foreign tongue because he could not publish in Russian, waited a hundred years before his thought found general acceptance in the church. This may be the fate of Berdyaev as well. At present, the church in Russia is marking time until some larger application of Christian principle to the whole of life becomes possible. Berdyaev understood the church's natural conservatism under such circumstances. But if the record of the Russian Church in the few months between its liberation from court domination under the Tsar and state domination under Lenin is any criterion, there can be little doubt concerning its eventual attitudes toward practical Christianity. And who of its sons has written more prophetically than Berdyaev regarding Christianity applied to daily living?

Together with his emphasis upon the practical application of Christianity to all phases of life—whether of the individual or of society—there was not a little of the mystic in Nicolai Alexandrovitch. Eugenie says he experienced even marxism "as a vague, subconscious expectation of a new world-epoch." As early as 1906, he was writing: ". . . the mystic feeling of life and personality has been the basic motive of my life." He said of himself that he was primarily a *"homo mysticus"* rather than a *"homo religiosus,"* and "for me historical revelation was always secondary as compared with spiritual revelation; . . . the inward revelation of the spirit is real." After saying all material history is only a symbol of the spiritual, Berdyaev continued: ". . . but metahistory is always breaking through into history. . . . The Gospel . . . has a significance for me which defines my destiny, not because I appropriate it from without, . . . but because I discern in it the . . . mystery of the spirit."[17] As Seaver says: "Philosophical mysticism recognizes no external authority for belief. It knows only the spirit of freedom and the freedom of the spirit." Berdyaev himself defined mysticism in his book on Leontieff: "Mysticism . . . is always the immanence of God in the human spirit. Mysticism is profoundly secret: it is always a property of the inner man."[18] In various books Berdyaev reiterated his belief that the metahistorical, the transcendental, is not only a reality but is active in the life of man. He believed this as much for himself as for society and human history. "I am firmly convinced that there is the transcendent in human life . . . and the action of the transcendental. I have felt both immersion in the lower abyss of the unconscious, and attraction to the limitless higher realms of the transcendental."[19]

This sense of the transcendental must not be confused with a feeling for the occult. During the period of the Russian renaissance when there was widespread interest in occultism, Nicolai Alexandrovitch, in line with his policy of learning what others were thinking, had many personal contacts with adepts of various "mystic" cults: the theosophists, the Rosicrucians, Hindu lore, and, as has been noted, with Steiner and the anthroposophists. He never belonged to any of these groups, although he had studied their doctrines. Some of their leaders were occasionally guests in his home. The reasons for this frequent—if only temporary—preoccupation with occultism among some of Russia's most brilliant minds offers an interesting topic for consideration. It is partly explained, one feels, in the thirst for a spiritual outlet after passions were frustrated by the fiasco of the 1905 revolution. Unlike Berdyaev, most of these fine spirits did not turn toward Christianity in their seeking. That the official church of the day had no comprehension of their problem was partly the reason why they looked to Hindu philosophy or Steinerism. Eugenie says the Russia of the period was occupied by hordes of evil spirits tempting men away from Christian truth, the most anti-Christian and powerful of which was marxism. Nicolai Alexandrovitch saw this clearly, and beginning with marxism he attacked anti-Christian forces on all fronts: in articles, in the Religious-Philosophical Society, in a thousand personal contacts and conflicts. The resultant, widely extended hostility toward his ideas and even toward his person did not disturb him. "This proves how serious the situation is. Indifference or silence would be terrible."

There was something mystic in the way not Berdyaev alone but many of his fellows in the Russian renaissance felt a premonition of coming catastrophe. It appears in Byeli and Blok, and even in Merezhkovsky. But with Berdyaev there was a difference. Whereas the others "felt," he *knew*. Right up to the start of the revolution he seems to have lived in almost hourly expectation of the outbreak of some undefined but terrible event. He once wrote to a friend: ". . . there is a great truth in revolution, but in its elements there breeds a terrible, ultimate evil. This I feel with every atom of my being." Eugenie tells how walking with her in the forest at Babaki, Nicolai Alexandrovitch would suddenly break off the conversation with: "Let's get back to the house quickly." "But what is the hurry? We haven't walked as far as the mill." "There might be news." "News of what?" "How many times have I told you," he would explain, "that we are on the verge of a terrible catastrophe?" "But on what grounds?" "Externally none whatever, but I know," and he would turn his rapid steps homeward. Through the years in Moscow those nearest him felt a constant intense expectation, an anxious uneasiness almost inexplicable in view of the peace and passivity of the post-1905 atmosphere. Most revolutionaries were dreaming of a reign of peace and freedom once the monarchy was overthrown. That no one thought the event near at hand is evident from a discussion Berdyaev reports, when representatives of various political groups at a meeting in his home placed it at twenty-five, forty, or even one hundred years away. Among his inner circle of friends, Nicolai Alexandrovitch was positive about the coming of a revolution. "It is nonsense," he asserted, "to think Russia can be saved by political programs or occult organizations. Something has broken in the depth of the soul of the Russian people, and a way of suffering lies ahead. Neither a political nor a social revolution will bring salvation, but only a religious revolution."

There was also Nicolai Alexandrovitch's sense of belonging to two worlds. "I consider erroneous the usual view which sets eternal

life over against the so-called earthly life. This is a false objectivization of eternity," he wrote Mme K. There was in Berdyaev a sense
of the continuity of life both before and after this present. He mentioned his mysterious feeling on certain occasions or in certain
circumstances, in some ancient Gothic church for example, of having
been here before in another historic period. He told Eugenie he felt
they two had met in a previous life. Many other people have felt
similar emotions, and Berdyaev did not seem to consider it of much
importance. He refused to accept the idea of "one-plane reincarnation"
—of a man's being reborn on earth. He said it contradicted the idea
of integral personality. But he believed in reincarnation on a higher
spiritual plane, as he did in an individual's previous existence: "A
man's final destiny could not be decided in this brief stay on earth
alone." He had no concern for his own possible reincarnation. That
was in the hands of God. But he did live in the clear consciousness of
a world of spirits existing about him, ever striving to influence his
thought and action. For years, in Russia, he would waken at night with
the conviction some evil being had entered his room, and with a cry of
terror he would run out into the hall. These nocturnal visitations
ceased after he left Russia. He had a special feeling about the night:
"Night always seems deeper and wider than that small strip of light,
the day. But the spiritual is also present in the night, not only the
mental; the whole of creativity is rooted in the nocturnal basis of spirit."
Sometimes, walking in the park at Babaki, he would suddenly be
seized with the feeling that another person invisibly accompanied their
footsteps. Eugenie is convinced, and apparently Berdyaev shared the
feeling, that he was protected by "good forces" (angels) from the as-
saults of "dark powers." (A small book could be written about Eugenie's clairvoyance. Once in a Moscow theater, she suddenly ex-
claimed: "Satan is in this place." Half a minute later Lenin marched
past them down the aisle.)

Another phenomenon in Berdyaev's life was his series of mystical
dreams. Many were painful and even terrifying, yet some were strangely
symbolic. In the autobiography he described one recurring dream
where, passing by a laden table with many guests but no place for
him, he felt compelled to scramble up a nearby precipice; struggling
and straining, with hands bleeding from the sharp rocks, he reached the
top and came face to face with Christ hanging on His cross. In another dream he was returning to Russia, traveling alone, and there was
no one else with him in the compartment. His train slowly approached

the frontier. With deep emotion he pressed toward the window to catch a first glimpse of Russian soil, then suddenly, conscious of another presence, turned around to find Christ standing there. Berdyaev remarked that modern psychology tries to explain such things by invoking the subconscious. But, he added, this really "explains little and decides nothing."

Like Orthodox Christians in general, and like most mystics in particular, Berdyaev was sensitive to the symbolic. There is a passage about the Cross in one of his letters:

> You speak of a magazine cover which joins the Cross with the hammer and sickle. I have seen it. Not because I have anything against the hammer and sickle do I object. On the contrary, I appreciate this symbol of industrial and agricultural labor. But you cannot join the Cross, which relates to eternity, with the hammer and sickle, [which is] related to time.

In another letter he wrote:

> It is equally true to say that the place of the Son of God is in the hearts of men and that his place is on Golgotha. In this lies the world's tragedy. The Cross is a paradox: it is born of the world's evil, and it is the world's salvation from evil.

# 17

## RELUCTANT PRECEPTOR

Life to Berdyaev was a continuous process of sharing his thoughts with others: writing, lecturing, conferences with friends. Yet he stoutly disclaimed any desire to be a teacher or found a school of thought. Nicolai Alexandrovitch refused to accept the idea of his having "disciples." Nevertheless he was constantly influencing the thought of others, intentionally striving to alter their opinions. If he truly had not wished to teach, why did he fill so much of his time with study groups —especially for young people? He rejoiced in these contacts. If that was not teaching, what was it? Perhaps Nicolai Alexandrovitch had another word for it—it does not appear in his writings.

Berdyaev once said of himself that to know the world was to wish to change it, and this surely involved changing men's minds. To what was evidently a hint from Mme K that his manner of writing was not only didactic but "imperialistic," he replied: "I do not wish to lead others [and] am not at all interested in having pupils or followers; I am quite devoid of any will to power." He showered his thoughts and books on the world almost indifferent as to how the world would receive them. In the autobiography Berdyaev describes his actions as having been both exoteric and esoteric, the latter "in only a few books and some intimate conversations."[1]

Whether or not he called it teaching, Nicolai Alexandrovitch frankly rejoiced in his influence with the younger generation. He himself felt always young in spirit. In passing, it may be noted that he was very coquettish about his age and never would tell it to anyone. He was indeed well preserved physically: at seventy-four his hearing was not impaired, and he used glasses only for reading. In this connection he wrote Mme K:

> You are right; I am very young. In my eternal age (everyone has his eternal age) I am a youth. I have no feeling of an age of maturity, of venerability, of dignity. It seems to me that I am still

that youth who used to seek for justice and the meaning of life, athirst for a knowledge of truth. The mental and spiritual bourgeois feels maturity, solidity, honorability. I hate all that.

He felt particularly at home with those of the Russian émigré youth who accepted the facts of history and looked forward rather than trying to turn the clock back. "They wanted to build a new Russia on a social basis. This was my own thought, and . . . I probably had some influence." He was sorry for the young people who "had no Moscow, no Russia" in their experience, but he had great faith in their calling. His sympathies extended particularly to the group of young Frenchmen who started the journal *Esprit*, and in this relationship he almost accepts the title of teacher. Denying he influenced the "Eurasians," a young Russian political group, he says it would be more correct to call him the teacher of the young people around *Esprit*.

In these and all his other "teaching" contacts Nicolai Alexandrovitch was ever conscious that he was unable fully to reveal himself or transmit his very innermost thoughts. It was partly due, he thinks, to his aversion to anything approaching familiarity—a sort of spiritual diffidence. Was this traceable to his unhappy months in the Cadet Corpus, one wonders? "I am always protecting my personality, maintaining a distance. . . . Having made one step toward contact, I would take two steps back. . . . Sometimes I longed to speak heart-to-heart about the most important matter, and all at once I would be caught in the pathos of distance . . . and become as conditioned as a Frenchman."[2] Finally, Berdyaev wonders whether in the last analysis it is possible for any human being to transmit to another the deepest thoughts of his soul. "Is the most pristine, and the ultimate (in thought) communicable," he asks, "or only the secondary and transitory?"[3] One of his friends once remarked that even to God most men find it difficult to bare their innermost souls, and thus what Berdyaev said about communication between men is valid for the great majority. In that respect he belonged to the majority, a position he never relished. It is doubtless one of the reasons for the refrain—recurring in his autobiography as in his letters—"no one understands me." He seemed always to have the feeling that if he could share with another his very most secret thoughts, the wall of misunderstanding would be broken down.

If he did not pretend to be a teacher, still less did he claim to be a leader. The English word itself is a deceptive one. Neither Russian nor French has a term of the exact equivalence, and the German *Führer* was forever distorted by Hitler. Not knowing English, Berdyaev's concept of leadership was confused with the *Führer-prinzip* (authoritarianism), and he was against this with all his might, calling it "opposed to the principle of personality, . . . a form of reciprocal slavery." He seems never to have understood the Anglo-Saxon idea of leadership. Certainly as a leader in the English sense of the word Berdyaev never functioned. Perhaps he never could have had he wished. In St. Petersburg his talent was recognized, but no group, however modest, ever acknowledged him as chairman or spokesman. Merezhkovsky was older and too positive for Berdyaev to have imposed his own ideas. In the movement back to the church it was Kartasheff, Boldyreff, and Bulgakov who played the leads—at a time when Berdyaev had not yet come abreast of them. In Moscow, Prince Trubetskoy enjoyed such well-established authority in the intellectual world that Berdyaev quite modestly accepted his leadership. Knowledge of his increasing fame in the world not only failed to augment his approval of himself, but on the contrary, spurred him to sharper self-criticism. These factors would not necessarily have militated against his qualifications for leadership, but another of his characteristics surely would. To be a good leader one must be a good follower when occasion demands. And following anyone else, in any sort of obedience or discipline, was for Berdyaev a spiritual impossibility.

Regardless of leadership, his books and lectures continued in an uninterrupted flow. The Paris years—after he was fifty—were the most productive of his life. The mere volume of output is surprising; the titles afford a total of nearly twenty-three hundred pages. Nicolai Alexandrovitch felt the books produced in this period were among the most significant both for himself and for the development of his thought. In his opinion they outranked earlier writings, with the exception of *The Meaning of the Creative Act* and *The Meaning of History*. He lists as most important seven of the ten finished after he came to France and before the close of the war. Those Berdyaev selects from a purely philosophical viewpoint are *Freedom and the Spirit*, (in Russian, "The Philosophy of the Free Spirit"), *The Destiny of Man*, *Solitude and Society* (in Russian, I and the World of Objects), and *Spirit and Reality*. He felt that *Slavery and Freedom* expressed some of his ideas more incisively than the rest of his writing, best revealing the sharp conflicts in a man of his spiritual type. Further, there is *The Beginning and the End* (in Russian, "Essay in Eschatological Metaphysics"), which Nicolai Alexandrovitch says best describes his metaphysics. Written during the war, it was published only in 1947. Then he cites the slim volume *The Fate of Man in the Modern World* as formulating his idea of the philosophy of modern history far better than his famous *New Middle Ages*. So simply written, yet rendering a vivid picture of man in the grip of forces threatening to overwhelm him, *The Fate of Man in the Modern World* has enjoyed remarkable popularity. It has been translated into seven languages, among them the Japanese. It is often recommended as an introduction to Berdyaev's thought. One more, *The Russian Idea,* rounds out the list of books Berdyaev considers significant. To complete the record of Berdyaev's production in Paris, the three following must be added: *Constantine Leontieff*—first published in 1926, although partly written before Berdyaev's removal to Paris—*Christianity and Class War,*—printed first in 1931—*Truth and Revelation,* and *The Origin of Russian Communism*—first appearing in 1937, in English. This last was written at a time when misguided Christian spokesmen, particularly in Britain and America, were attempting to assure the world that communism and Christianity are quite compatible. It is not polemic. Beginning with a most informative chapter on that unique phenomenon the Russian "intelligentsia," Berdyaev proceeds to explain how and why communism in Russia took a form different from anything it might have assumed in the west. It is only in a final chapter that the author confronts marxism with Christianity. And in the last paragraph, Berdyaev writes: "Man's very existence is endangered by the processes now going on in the world. Resistance to this danger is possible only by spiritually fortifying man. . . . But this can be done only by a reborn, creative Christianity, true to its prophetic spirit, facing toward the Kingdom of God."

It is interesting to review the gradual growth in influence of these and Berdyaev's other writings—from zero to world-wide esteem. He is recognized by émigré Russians as Orthodoxy's best-known representative in the west—and that practically means the world, for there is none to compare with him in influence behind the iron curtain or in other Eastern churches. There is a universality about his style like that of Mark Twain, if the comparison is permissible. One was always surprised to observe how Twain's original humor could be translated into many other tongues. Berdyaev's thought seems to have an equal appeal to thinkers of many lands and cultures. Berdyaev remarks that he is the first Russian Christian philosopher since Solovieff to be widely read abroad—and his reading public is infinitely wider than was that of Solovieff. As a matter of fact, more of his books have appeared in translation than all the works of other modern Russian thinkers, excepting the communists, put together.

The first pebble dropped into the pool of world recognition was Berdyaev's *Dostoievsky*, the first of his books to appear in translation. It was published in German in 1925, after Nicolai Alexandrovitch was already in France. Four of his books appeared in German before Hitler, and three others were published in that language in Switzerland before the war. This swift impact of one man's mind on the thinkers of a whole foreign nation is notable. It was possible, of course, because of Berdyaev's personal contacts in Germany. Keyserling helped introduce him to the Germans and then to a wider public. Although Keyserling complained in a letter to Berdyaev that the Germans were a theological rather than a religious people, Berdyaev's circle of German readers swiftly widened.

Kullmann and Anderson of the American YMCA, both resident in Berlin at that time, helped bring him into contact with German churchmen and authors, chiefly Protestant—not alone in Germany but in German-speaking Switzerland. These in turn would have spoken of Berdyaev to friends in the ecumenical movement, particularly other—French-speaking—Swiss.

Consequently, when Nicolai Alexandrovitch went to Paris he found it easy to establish contacts with Protestant leaders, and then with outstanding Roman Catholics like Maritain and Gabriel Marcel. It was Berdyaev who organized almost the first significant meetings of French Catholics and Protestants since the Massacre of St. Bartholomew. If Boegner could say once, in a meeting at St. Sergius, that the Russian Orthodox had done more for a rapprochement between French Catholics and Protestants than they had ever been able to do themselves, it was Berdyaev who took the first steps from the Orthodox side. Soon after Berdyaev's arrival in Paris his books began appearing in French. Five were printed in French before they came out in English. Accessible to groups of scholars the world around, it is difficult to say whether the French translations or their English counterparts have had wider influence.

Quantitatively, Berdyaev's works have been more widely disseminated in English than in any other language. This first came about through the Russian Student Christian Movement. Among the early outreaches of the RSCM was contact with the British Student Christian Movement. Exchange of delegates at student conferences soon brought British leaders under the spell of Berdyaev's lectures, and eventually he was invited to speak to British groups outside the SCM. Anglican interest in the Russian Orthodox Church afforded further good reason for such contacts, and soon his writings began to appear in English translation. For the wide distribution of Berdyaev books in English, credit is due first to Geoffrey Bles, whose personal interest in Berdyaev's thought led him to become a chief sponsor of these works. Sheed and Ward came next. Actually, this famous publishing house issued *Dostoievsky* in English before Bles began his extensive list of Berdyaev's works. Because many of the books published in Britain had parallel editions in the United States, the wide field of English-speaking peoples was adequately covered. Berdyaev mentions his surprise at being so popular in English.

From French and English the Berdyaev message has spread into a dozen other languages. The Scandinavian countries have made some of his books accessible to their part of Europe, and the Dutch to their own country and important sections of the Orient. Spanish and Portuguese translations have brought Berdyaev not only to their homelands but to the whole of Latin America, where, as will be seen, Nicolai Alexandrovitch has enjoyed no small influence. That it is a real, and not imagined, influence is evident from recent demands that certain passages be eliminated from a proposed Spanish edition of the autobiography. An illuminating magazine article on Catholicism in present-day Spain could be written around the passages the Spanish censor wished to delete. Of course Berdyaev's literary executors refused permission to mutilate his work. In recent years the Far East has become increasingly aware of Berdyaev's words for our time. Four Berdyaev books have been published in Japanese. The YMCA Press, which took over Berdyaev's literary estate, reports a constant demand for new permissions to translate. In the autobiography Berdyaev lists a dozen European countries where he had lectured, and mentions South America and Australia as parts of the world whence he had proof of his influence. Oddly enough he does not mention the United States. But then, Berdyaev always seemed to have a sort of blind spot for the United States, and this despite the many Americans who were his personal friends and admirers and the fact that some of the best writing about him has been done here. His rare pronouncements on capitalism in America indicated a complete misapprehension of the situation here. His apparent lack of interest was fortunately not reciprocated from the other side of the Atlantic, and interest in Berdyaev is growing. Beside books about him, numerous doctoral theses on various phases of Berdyaev's thought, in universities in the States and other parts of the world, testify further to his widening influence. How many philosophers, in their own lifetimes, have seen their works published in fifteen languages? Tolstoi may have equaled the record, but Tolstoi put his philosophy into great fiction. He was not known as a pure philosopher.

In the Russian-speaking world both at home and abroad, Berdyaev's influence cannot be said to be as extensive as elsewhere. In the emigration—that body of nearly two million Russians living in a diaspora reaching to every continent and to most of the islands of the sea—Berdyaev's fate has been that of a prophet in his own country. Several factors have helped to create this situation. As will be recalled, Nicolai Alexandrovitch disagreed with almost the whole of the emigration, upon his arrival in Berlin in 1922, on the question of armed intervention for the overthrow of the Soviet regime. His subsequent breaks with the Russian Student Christian Movement and St. Sergius again prejudiced large numbers of the cultured Russian émigrés against him. Topping it came his refusal to accept the decision of the great majority of Russian Orthodox abroad to follow Metropolitan Eulogius in his jurisdictional transition to the Ecumenical Patriarchate. Both politically and ecclesiastically he stood out against the bulk of his fellow Russians living in exile.

Philosophically he had more sympathizers among Russian thinkers. In general S. L. Frank was in agreement with him, and N. O. Lossky has not sharply disputed Berdyaev's principal theses. Vycheslavtseff never took sharp issue with Berdyaev, although Nicolai Alexandrovitch broke with him personally during the last war. In his outstanding *History of Russian Philosophy*, Zenkovsky is not very kind to Berdyaev—an attitude that may be partially influenced by Zenkovsky's intimate connection with the St. Sergius Theological Institute. Here there had been feelings of almost resentful wonder at the world's insistence upon hearing Berdyaev as a spokesman for the Orthodox Church—this despite his constant efforts to disclaim any such distinction. Among many émigré thinkers was a sense of astonishment at the fact of their compatriot's world-wide popularity. He grew up among them, no better or worse than dozens of other Russian renaissance luminaries. For most of his life he was in ideological opposition to the majority, yet his name spreads around the world while most of their works remain within Russian-language confines.

His influence has spread around the world. What kind of influence? First of all it was constructive. There was nothing of the cynic about

him. Unlike Nietzsche or the modern existentialists, he strengthened
men's faith rather than weakening it: faith in themselves, faith in the
innate nobility and creative capacities of man as an image of God, faith
in Christ and His Church. Even his ideological enemies recognize
this. He remarked, wryly, that it sometimes seemed his enemies were
more attentive to his major themes than were his frinds, and he cited
the case of a Catholic priest who, while hostile to Berdyaev's ideas,
seemed to know them better than many who accepted them. To the
rightists anyone who sees any good whatever in Marx's ideas is forth-
with branded "red." *Par contra*, the procommunists immediately
claimed such a person as their own. Some of his left-wing friends,
because they mistook his philosophical thought for political, have tried
to claim his influence in favor of Russian communism or the Soviet
regime. No one who knew the real Berdyaev, recognized by communists as one of their most effective adversaries, could ever think he
was procommunist. Particular recognition of this fact was the publication in 1953 by the Bonn government of a special edition of Berdyaev's
*Truth and Falsehood of Communism* for distribution in East Germany.

Still less could any intelligent person claim that Nicolai Alexandrovitch was favorably inclined toward the Soviet government. His attitude was perhaps never better set forth than in an article about the
sudden forced eclipse of the poetess Akhmatova and the humorist
Zoschenko, in 1946. He headed it "Of Creative Liberty and the Fabri-
cation of Souls."[4] He wrote:

> It is an elemental truth that creativeness is impossible without
> liberty. Creativeness is an act of freedom. . . . Philosophical
> thought cannot develop in Russia because only the official phi-
> losophy of dialectic materialism is permitted. . . . Even the to-
> talitarian catholicism of the Middle Ages permitted more diversity
> in thinking than does the totalitarian regime in Soviet Russia. . . .
> The basic error lies in the proposition that spirits may be manu-
> factured by means of compulsory organization.

Berdyaev's constructive influence was intensely personal. In person
and by correspondence, hundreds of men and women—not only among
the Orthodox but Protestants and Catholics as well, and others who
had not found their spiritual way—acknowledged his guidance with
gratitude. "Your writings mean more to me than I can ever tell you,
. . . you who are doing so much to bring about a saner world," writes
an American admirer. A Swiss writer says Berdyaev had a special and

helpful message for today's youth because of an "innate love of freedom that did not foam itself away in emptiness."[5] From Finland came
this note: "My younger brother, a student, was so centered on your
books in the last months before his death that you became for him, and
then for me also, a sort of spiritual father. Through your books we
came to Christianity."

The books seem often to have had the same effect of stimulating
small study-group formation as did Berdyaev's lectures. From Brazil
(1933) came news of a "circle" for the study of the present in the
light of Christianity—with Berdyaev's portrait on the wall of its meeting place. During the war a letter from a prison camp in Germany said:
"You have not only aided me to live through the long months of cap-
tivity, but you have revealed . . . the meaning of my whole life. Five
of us young French officers are studying your works." And a Belgian
reader wrote: "Your *Destiny of Man* is a revelation for me, which I
have decided to share with three of my comrades. We are studying it
together."

That his influence went beyond all confessional boundaries is clear
in letters from Roman Catholic clergymen. "Thanks to you I now
penetrate in a quite new way into the truth of man, of the world, and
of God; and everything appears . . . in a clearer light." (1945) Another priest writes (1939): "Your books express with singular force the
tenderness and thoughts which have been vibrating in me only in a
vague and despairing form. . . . I find these ideas in you, but nowhere
else." A professor of philosophy wrote: "I do not belong to any confession. It is hard for me to maintain within myself a vivid and . . .
unchangeable faith in the church invisible. . . . You have discerned
my interior solitude." And another professor wrote (1928): "Your
*New Middle Ages* struck me like a bomb. This is a real answer to the
questions which have been tormenting me, of the crisis of our culture."

While giving personal inspiration and comfort, Berdyaev's books
and letters encouraged fresh consideration, new creative thought and
action. "I am convinced," writes a fellow savant, "that Berdyaev is the
only thinker who has thought to its end 'la condition humaine,' and
that only his personalism is worthy of man. . . . Berdyaev's books are
the only ones giving renovating inspiration to the true politicians. I
think that our world will sink into ruin if men remain incapable of
appealing to those spiritual forces which Berdyaev has so wonderfully
brought to light." His friend Motchulsky is even more definite. In a
letter evidently written from the sanitarium where he spent his last

months, he writes: "Only here in forced solitude have I come fully to understand how much you have given me, how much I am spiritually allied to you. Your vital interest in my work inspired me. Without you I would not have been able to write either my *Dostoievsky* or *Blok.* The Lord has given you a great gift of sympathy." Writing of Berdyaev's *The Beginning and the End,* Jean Lacroix in the Paris *Le Monde* said· "There is no doubt that this work, so rich and satisfying, has been for many young Frenchmen the first impulse moving them toward the concept of original personal thinking." This is confirmed by the experience of many who were privileged to attend the Sunday evening groups at the house in Clamart. "He does not instruct us and makes no effort to impose his ideas on anyone, but his words have some special sort of power. They kindle in young people a creative fire. And the thought processes born in our minds are not a repetition of Nicolai Alexandrovitch's thoughts, but a sort of continuing collaboration in his creativeness." As Fielding Clarke says, ". . . everywhere there will be men and women . . . inspired to grapple with new problems, who will find new creative tasks because of what Berdyaev has revealed to them. As they read him, men think again more freshly, criticize themselves and the movements . . . they serve, and then go forward to fresh personal creation."

As these words are written, along comes a letter that would have delighted Nicolai Alexandrovitch. It is an inquiry about the Berdyaev Society. The writer says: "I am not an educated man, but found what would seem to be a mine of wonderful thought in Berdyaev, and I intend to pursue his thinking and study it intently." This would have been for Berdyaev another proof—as in Riga that day in 1926—that his message was as universal in appeal as in its content, and that it really came home to individual men and women.

Not only was Berdyaev's influence personal, it was a definitely Christian influence. It began as early as the appearance of *The Meaning of the Creative Act.* Eugenie, who was at that period emerging from the atheism typical of a majority of the intelligentsia, was aided in finding anew her Christian faith. After leaving marxism, and shaken to the core by Bulgakov's *From Marxism to Idealism,* a former intellectual—now a Catholic priest—recalls how Nicolai Alexandrovitch helped him find meaning in Christianity. The *Osservatore Romano* had good evidence for stating once that although it could not agree with Berdyaev, he had certainly brought many to the faith. No one knows how many young people, like some of the students Berdyaev knew in Berlin, returned to their church because of his influence. And for those firm in the Christian faith, of whatever confession, Berdyaev's thoughts are an inspiration. Probably no modern philosopher is more frequently quoted from pulpits around the world. As the *Osservatore Romano* said, even if one does not accept his premises, his Christian conclusions are acceptable. Through his guidance many men and women have begun to look forward toward a new world and reborn faith. Stepun remarks that the Russian revolution, like the gradual social and political revolution in the whole of Europe—or the world for that matter—is not yet ended. It can attain its fullest perfection only in the light of a reasserted and rejuvenated Christianity. This is another reason why the thought and widening influence of Nicolai Alexandrovitch will be pertinent for all thinking men, for a generation yet to be.

# 18

## THE THINKER

The huge task of a comprehensive study of Berdyaev as a thinker has not yet been attempted. Some excellent books and doctoral theses on various phases of his thought have been written, and others are known to be in preparation. Among these, the treatise (in German) by Roman Rössler is outstanding in its pursuit of Berdyaev's idea of objectivization, through fifty-five books and articles from the earliest (1900) to the latest (1948). No other work of such fundamental scholarship has appeared. The present chapter can only hint at such an over-all organization scheme, dealing principally with Nicolai Alexandrovitch's philosophic type and his methods of thinking. He was a Russian thinker, and Russian thinking differs from that of the west in its mystic overtones, its willingness to pursue a given concept to its extreme limit, its eternal search for the kingdom of righteousness. As Stepun says: "For a Russian . . . to philosophize always meant to organize life according to right and justice, . . . which gave to all philosophical discussion that . . . spiritually intense character often lacking in the thought life of western Europe."[1] From childhood, Berdyaev wrote, he remained the "Russian boy" described by Dostoievsky—tormented with "accursed questions." As early as 1909, he was outlining what might be called his own philosophical direction. He was arguing for the development of a "Russian national tradition in philosophy" and felt that it might be based on "concrete idealism, joined to a realistic attitude toward being."

Some of Berdyaev's critics have claimed he was more German than Russian, probably because of his acceptance of the neo-Kantian ideals with which his generation grew up. But he never accepted Kantianism wholly, nor any of the other philosophies that crossed his spiritual path. Each was tested, ruminated upon, and then transformed by his uniquely personal thinking into something his own and therefore, if for no other reason, Russian.

But Russian as he was to the marrow of his bones, Nicolai Alexandrovitch, like so many Russian thinkers, was at the same time universal.
He lived the whole tragedy of twentieth-century Russia in himself but
was ever conscious of its meaning for the world. Berdyaev remarks how
characteristic it is of Russia's creative spirits, something "very national
in them, [that] in seeking salvation [and] thirsting for redemption, they
suffer for the world."[2] The fact that most of his books were written after
his banishment, when he was living in the west, had little influence on
the essentially Russian nature of his ideas. Although his approaches to
the basic problems of philosophy were naturally those of the Russian he
was proud to be, he dealt with these problems in the light of their significance for all mankind.

Of course his formation was not entirely Russian. He was at one
time so deep in German philosophy that instead of sentimental verses
in the autograph book of a girl cousin, he wrote quotations from Hegel.
He has told us how his philosophic thought was a struggle for liberation, for the freedom of man's spirit. Although as a boy he classed himself outside all usual norms, and although he hated school, he loved
learning. Even the briefest acquaintance with Berdyaev's works will
convince the reader of his surprisingly ecumenical knowledge of philosophers and thinkers from Plato and the church fathers to Bergson
and Sartre. Not that he swallowed any of them whole; he was equally
generous in his criticism as in his choice of reading, and both Engels
and Thomas Aquinas and most of the thinkers in between have received his arrows of disagreement. But not in philosophy alone was
Nicolai Alexandrovitch widely read. All of a sudden, in Dostoievsky, he
launches into a comparison of the views on man held by Dante,
Shakespeare, and Dostoievsky that charms and surprises in its depth of
knowledge of all three great writers. His acquaintance with the world's
great literature and art equaled that of any other of the Russian intelligentsia of his time—which is saying much. He was one of the "new
spirits" who grew up "out of Dostoievsky, Nietzsche, Ibsen, and Kierkegaard" (although he came to appreciate Kierkegaard only later), with
the same "spiritual uneasiness and the same mental problematics, the
same conflicts and antinomies."[3]

His family tradition also played a part in Berdyaev's spiritual formation. While rebelling against his aristocratic social milieu, he grew
naturally into the acceptance of a spiritual aristocracy. The entire intelligentsia considered itself part of an elite. But it was an elite which
had crystallized into a social class. This was not what Berdyaev meant

by spiritual aristocracy. "The new intelligentsia can consist only of a selected list of *personalities* [he put it in italics] of higher . . . qualities, mental, moral, or esthetic, special knowledge . . . or prophetic gifts."[4] He never lost his conviction of the necessity, in a world that would experience spiritual progress or cultural creativeness, of a class of spiritual *noblesse.*

If there is one word to characterize Berdyaev's method in philosophy, it is intuition. The truths he defended and the theories he held came to him not by some process of ratiocination, but directly, produced in his own mind by a sort of psychological virgin birth. Considering his own philosophy, Bardyaev remarks that the "academic" philosophers seem to prefer to call him a thinker, since his philosophical processes do not conform to the usual methodical type. He admits that his philosophy never was of the professorial kind: "In me there is nothing of what is called reflection, nothing of the discursive, deductive kind of thinking, no systematic, logical, connected thought. In reality, I cannot develop or demonstrate my thought. Analysis is a . . . weak side of my thinking. I am a thinker exclusively of the intuitive-synthetic type."[5] Berdyaev says this is a Russian trait, the hostility to the formal in law, morality, philosophy. "Form introduces measure, it has a restraining effect, it sets boundaries," and this is incompatible with the Russian "leap to the final."[6]

"But the most profound intuitions are not those of academic scholars but of free thinkers. One de Maistre or Chaadaev is worth more than many professional specialists." Even in his book on Dostoievsky, he eschews both literary criticism and phychological study, wishing "intuitively to recreate Dostoievsky's world view." Despite far-ranging reading Nicolai Alexandrovitch insisted that his thoughts did not arise from books, but rather "were fed by intuitions of life." Some psychology student could have a field day exploring how Berdyaev's "intuition" was affected by his reading of different books at the various stages of his development. There is considerable truth in Stepun's remark that, like Byeli, Nicolai Alexandrovitch was of the psychological type who "had exchanged his roots for wings."

Intuition, not logic: "I have read many books on logic, but I must confess that logic never had any significance for me and never taught me anything," he writes. He feels that here again he is one with Russians in general. "This people of extraordinary spiritual gifts finds it extraordinarily difficult to discipline its spirit, more difficult than do peoples of the west."[7] His intuition, his philosophy, was born of "strug-

gle for liberation [and] conflict with the finite for the sake of infinity,"
and he "always believed in the liberating nature of philosophic knowledge." He "plunged into the concrete to discover its universal significance."[8]

His immediacy of intuition was one of the reasons why in all Berdyaev's writing there is such originality and honesty. In a passage from
the letters to Mme K, Berdyaev is explaining why he cannot be called
a politician: "I call it politics when, in conflict, men resort to falsehood,
deceit, and violence. I myself am a man of conflict . . . but I fight
with spiritual weapons and do not resort to falsehood and deceit." In
all his writing one feels that Berdyaev is rooted in his own experience—
presented with an often surprising frankness. As he said of Dostoievsky:
"He never concealed anything and hence succeeded in making amazing
discoveries." Consequently, what Berdyaev thought and wrote was
original, unrelated to and unlimited by what anyone else might think
or say on the subject. He had to be himself. He might have been describing himself when he wrote that Leontieff "had an unusually free
mind . . . bound by nothing, completely independent." And of himself he says: "I praise freedom while my epoch hates it; . . . I love
philosophical thought in a time indifferent toward it."[9]

A Belgian student of Berdyaev, A. Vermeulen, holds that Berdyaev's
thought is primarily "mythological" as contrasted with "ontological,"
but with a firm foundation in the ontological—the sense of the true
nature of being. Others have tried to show that Berdyaev's philosophy
is eclectic. Zenkovsky says "the synthetic structural power of Berdyaev
is extraordinary," but he hastens to add: "One can discern the influence of the most varied Russian thinkers on him, which does not prevent his maintaining his originality."[10] We must evidently accept Nicolai Alexandrovitch's statement that the thoughts of others produce
an immediate reaction of his own thought that he feels is original.

In some of its phases, Berdyaev's thinking while not eclectic is definitely dialectic. The last of his books he lived to see in print was *The
Existential Dialectic of the Divine and the Human.* If he is sometimes
accused of inner contradictions, his use of the dialectic is partly the
reason. Rössler calls it Berdyaev's "antinomic way of thinking" of the
inward man's ideal world and the objective world of history, saying
Berdyaev gives the phenomenon of one or the other a "double-tracked
consideration." Rightly to assess these apparent contradictions, it must
be recalled that Berdyaev's books cover nearly half a century of his
developing thought—and what a stormy development it was! A number

of his books were written under the pressure of some difficult inner crisis. As Rössler remarks, the contradictions in Berdyaev's writings may be understood by recalling "which opponent he had in mind in the given case." Shestov was not quite just in his statement that once Berdyaev moved from one stage to another he abandoned the old idea completely: "When he had to move again and leave the old man Kant behind, Berdyaev threw everything overboard, saved nothing . . . and easily slid over into metaphysics. . . . Then he cast aside metaphysics and plunged into the depths of religious revelation."[11] But that was in 1907; toward the end of his life Shestov would have recognized, as did many of Berdyaev's other friends, how something of each period, seemingly discarded entire, remained with Nicolai Alexandrovitch—all related to his central theme—and that "the evolution of Berdyaev's ideas was not at all marked by any profound inner change; . . . as a marxist he was the same fine person as now. 'The cowl does not make the monk.' " Some of his contrasting statements are more than superficial; some of them Berdyaev said were inherent in the essence of his philosophy and "cannot and should not be resolved." But, as Fielding Clarke points out, there are not a few contradictions in the Gospels, and the antitheses in some of Berdyaev's writing may be solved by reference to his central theme and to his own sound, integral personality.

Berdyaev himself recognized this: "Externally one may have the impression that my philosophical views change. But the original motive forces have remained the same."[12] The changes, he said, are "chiefly in connection with my sometimes too sharp and passionate reactions to what was dominant at the moment, but all my life I have been a defender of freedom of the spirit and of the highest dignity of man."[13] In one way there is truth in Shestov's remark about Nicolai Alexandrovitch's casting an idea completely aside. When he stood for a cause or an idea he stood foursquare; there was never anything of the middle-of-the-roader about him. Like other Russians he spoke of, he leaped directly at the final, the radical—with no "ifs" or "buts." He recognized the impracticality of such an attitude; in life in general, as in politics, "the moderates are always the ones who have influence." But in revolt against a given ideology he was merciless and extreme.

That he was sometimes hasty in his reactions has already been seen in the Fedotoff incident. Further, like many other philosophers he was also somewhat "generous"—shall we say, rather than "careless"—in the use of terminology. Like Kant or Kierkegaard, even the same word with Berdyaev may change its meaning from one period of his thinking

to another. "Idealism," "subjectivism," even "existentialism," seem
to shift their signification as Berdyaev's thought moves through the
fifty years of his writing. Then there are other words, like "objectivization" for instance, into which Nicolai Alexandrovitch puts his own
peculiar meaning. The thesis of Rössler's book is that objectivization is
the basic concept underlying all Berdyaev's philosophy. The difficulties
arising from Berdyaev's careless use of terms are augmented by his style
of writing. Berdyaev should be read as one reads the Proverbs. His
thought moves more swiftly than his pen, hence the apparent sudden
changes and lack of even progression. Take the word "existentialism"—
Berdyaev puts it down in the rush of ideas, taking no time to explain
its significance in a particular context, and the reader must ferret the
meaning out for himself. A formal scholar could make a chapter from
one of Berdyaev's paragraphs by the insertion of connecting details—
to render the thought movement smoother and less staccato.

If the progression of his thought is sometimes inconsistent, this
cannot be said of Berdyaev's purpose and basic concepts. First of all, his
philosophy was Christian. Even in the earlier phases before calling himself a Christian, Nicolai Alexandrovitch was defending essentially Christian ideas in his search for truth. The more one reads, particularly in
the autobiography, the more it becomes evident that Beryaev's life—
and hence his thought—was centered on the God-man Christ. And because he focused his beliefs on the concept of humanity becoming divine through Christ's redemptive action, Berdyaev was inevitably concerned with ethics. As he said, "the pathos of obligation has always
prevailed over the pathos of being" in his thinking. He was concerned
with how man should effect his calling of self-realization through co-
creativity with God. While he believed with Angelus Silesius—

> That God has need of me, I know:
> He could not live apart from me.
> Should e'er I cease existence here below,
> He, too, would cease to be[14] . . .

and hence that partnership is subject to man's tragic errors and insufficiencies, still he did not despair. Unlike some more single-minded
theological thinkers, Nicolai Alexandrovitch believed in the eventual
triumph of good for all mankind. There may be periods of darkness—
new middle ages. There will be tragedy and suffering, for the Cross has
a meaning for all mankind and for all time, but a new day will dawn,
probably when time shall be no more—the age when man at last at-

tains fulfillment as co-creator with God. Berdyaev included himself in the ranks of today's thinkers. "In Khomiakoff's time, creative thought had the task of overcoming Kant and Hegel; today, creative thought has the task of overcoming Neo-Kantianism and Neo-Hegelianism." In this modern effort he played a part. "The passion for ideas," he said, "is stronger in me than any other passion." In *The Russian Idea* he considered his modes of thinking as compared with others of the Russian renaissance: "I am one of the creators of the religious philosophy that developed in Russia." Then he pointed out where he "differs from others with whom he once collaborated." It all began with *The Meaning of the Creative Act*, which is consecrated to "the basic theme of my life and thought, of man and his creative calling." *The Destiny of Man*, fifteen years later, developed this theme better "but with less passion. . . . The theme of man and creativity is tied in with the theme of freedom." The "creative" theme goes deeper than man's creativity in art or science. It is "metaphysical, the theme of man's continuing the world-creative process, of man's response to God." Berdyaev said his thinking was "anthropocentric rather than cosmocentric. . . . I am a historiosopher and moralist, perhaps even a theosophist in the sense of the Christian theosophy of Franz Baader and Vl. Solovieff." Summing it up in one sentence: "Man, personality, freedom, creativeness, the eschatological-messianic resolution of the dualism of two worlds—these are my basic themes."

These words might well shape an overall outline of Berdyaev's philosophy. The anthology will make an effort to arrange in systematic order the dicta on these many problems in Berdyaev's books and articles. Here there is space only for the briefest summary. First, his thought centered on God. Not God as some abstract principle, but God as revealed in Christ. Fielding Clarke calls him "the most Christocentric of philosophers," and a recent German pronouncement says he is the most significant speaker within Christian philosophy since Kierkegaard. It was the Christ of "The Grand Inquisitor" on whom Berdyaev's thought was centered: the suffering, pitying Christ, but also the God-man who rose above all human temptations to insist on giving man his creative freedom. Fritz Lieb wrote of him: "In his whole being he was a man oriented toward 'things to come,' things which in the last analysis wait upon the true revelation of man, but also the true revelation of the reality of the Kingdom of God." In considering Berdyaev's thought one must never lose sight of this theandrism—the sense that God and man are inseparable, that each completes the other, and that in Christ, the God-man, is the gauge of man's eventual perfection.[15]

The Divine-humanity of man is another of Berdyaev's fundamental tenets: "The dissolution of personality . . . in an impersonal divinity, in an abstract divine unity, is opposed to the Christian idea of man and of Divine-humanity."[16] If he went further in the development of this idea than many church leaders of an earlier day, he did so in the conviction it was essential to Christian belief. Christ brought to man the possibility and assurance of regaining his pristine quality and again becoming divine. The whole of man's life, the whole of human history must be regarded in the light of this cardinal fact. "The mystery of Christianity is the mystery of God-manhood, the mystery of the meeting of two natures, uniting but not mingling."[17]

The two natures meet in the fact that they are both creators. *The Meaning of the Creative Act* is an exposition of man as creative, because he is himself created in God's image and likeness, and of God's expectation that man will reply to His loving call by becoming His co-creator. "God awaits from us a creative act," Berdyaev said. He considered his *Destiny of Man* which deals with the creativity theme, "probably the most important of everything I have written." His "leap into the ultimate" in predicting the third epoch of history—the epoch of the spirit and of man's full realization of his creative calling—went further than most normal Orthodox theologians are yet prepared to travel. But to Berdyaev it was a reality. It could begin any time. It might perhaps have already begun in a few choice souls, but God's purpose would not be fully worked out in and for men until the third epoch had surpassed and fulfilled the epoch of the law and the epoch of the redemption. Among Nicolai Alexandrovitch's papers was found the outline of a new work on creativeness, in which a main argument professes that man's co-creativeness with God is even more important than man's personal salvation.

In his idea of the redemption of all creation, of the eventual restoration to perfection of every creature, every bit of nature, Berdyaev is in line with the Orthodox Church. The thought has been developed from St. Paul's statement in his letter to the Romans[18] regarding the whole of creation awaiting the revelation of man's restored sonship to God. With His descent into the Jordan at baptism, Christ opened the way to becoming divine—not to man alone but to every created thing. For man and beast alike, Berdyaev said, the process of return to the pristine state of perfection is not to be devoid of suffering. Here he agreed with St. Paul about the "whole creation groaning in travail together." This suffering, this struggle, is part of the process whereby man shall learn to live in the third epoch as co-creator with God.

Struggle, Berdyaev held, is a normal part of human life and of the Christian life in particular. There is a passage in his incisive "Worthiness of Christianity and Unworthiness of Christians" where he criticized Tolstoi for thinking a realization of Christ's teaching in daily life was something easy. He even went so far as to state that regarded as regulations for daily life the Gospel precepts are unrealizable. Yet man, recognizing this impossibility, should not fold his hands and wait for a miracle. "No matter how pessimistic our feelings for the future may be, all the powers of our spirit must be directed toward realizing the Kingdom of God in the world, the . . . justice of God in life."[19] Here is where man must assert his creative capacities. The Kingdom must be taken by force: "The spirit of Anti-Christ cannot be overcome by reaction; it may be conquered only by religious creativeness."[20] Berdyaev urged that creativeness be exerted in all phases of life. Man must not be content with creativity in separate fields of culture—art for art's sake, etc.—but must strive for integrity and unity. As in the Middle Ages when all cultural effort stemmed from the church, so—although this now seems a distant ideal—the church must again become the whole of life.

It was typical of Berdyaev that he never discussed religious-philosophic ideas, even those concerning the role of the church, with churchmen. It was not in his character to talk theology with theologians, and although Bulgakov shared Berdyaev's sense of the central importance of the God-manhood idea, the two men apparently never consulted each other on the question. Berdyaev preferred philosophic mysticism, if it may so be called, to rationalistic theology. "I can enter into the meaning of Christ's words, and bend before them, only when . . . my free mystical experience . . . feels their full depth,"[21] he wrote. Despite his interest in history and his "historiosophy," Berdyaev trusted more to his present intuition for guidance than to the past. As a matter of fact, it was the future more than the present with which his spirit wrestled. "I really am not a man of yesterday, or of today, or even of tomorrow," he wrote Mme K. "I look toward a more distant future—even not the future, but eternity." Professor Spinka discerns the heart of Nicolai Alexandrovitch's philosophy when he speaks of Berdyaev's "basic, surprisingly unfaltering and constant conviction of man's supreme worth and eternal destiny."

In the autobiography, Berdyaev expressed concern lest his "creativity" motif be misunderstood. He said it is so often taken to mean creativity in the sense of creative art or literature—in other words, the banal question of whether Christianity justifies creativeness. "But I did not put the question of justification of creativeness. Creativeness needs no justification; it justifies man. . . . This is the theme of man's relationship with God and God's answer to man."[22] He explained it further in one of the Mme K letters: "The basic thought of my *Creative Act* and *Destiny of Man* is that all products of creativeness addressed to man represent a lessening of the creative fire, a lowering of levels. . . . The world could not stand a pure creative fire: it would be consumed." In Berdyaev, the concept of man's co-creativity with God grew out of the basic idea of God's love. To love, he said, is to create. And man's highest destiny is fulfilled as he, created a creator, fulfills this capacity in response to God's love.

Man may or may not strive for fulfillment. He is free to choose. God-given freedom is another of Berdyaev's basic concepts. God does not compel man to reciprocate His love. He has given man the awful gift of freedom. Already in *Problems of Idealism* Nicolai Alexandrovitch had come to this "basic conclusion." "A man . . . cannot give up his right to the image and likeness of God for any worldly values; . . . we must demand the human right to self-determination and the development of all our spiritual potentialities. And for this the . . . basic condition is . . . freedom."[23] Note how in the early, rebellious period, Berdyaev was "demanding" what he later came to see as a free, if fateful, gift from God. Stepun reviews this freedom motif in Berdyaev's experience: "Berdyaev never altered his central idea. As a marxist he stood for the liberation of the working masses. As an 'idealist' he demanded liberation of creativeness from economic forces. As a Christian, he stood out for man's freely given collaboration with God as against all attempts of authority to limit the prophetic spirit." Berdyaev called it the "mystery of freedom." His carefully developed theory of uncreated freedom—particularly in *The Destiny of Man*—is too complex to be expounded here, but it deals with freedom as something existing in what German mystics call the "*Ungrund*," the precreation chaos. In Berdyaev's view it precedes being and, once a part of man, can be used by him for or against the call of God.

Man should use his freedom creatively, Berdyaev said, both in his own life and in the life of society. He criticized Leontieff for not understanding this and likened him to "J. de Maistre and the French Catholic counter-revolutionary school. . . . Leontieff failed to understand the category of freedom . . . and the creative significance of the spirit in the life of society."[24] If man is free, he should first consider not the rights thus given him but the obligations freedom involves. In *Slavery and Freedom*, Berdyaev developed the theme. A man cannot be truly free if he enslaves others; he has become a slave to the "master idea." The ideal society will exist when no one desires to be master but where all, free men in their own right, join in common service to their Creator. And once more Berdyaev returned to the role of the church—not alone in an ideal society but in the world of today. In the little book on Khomiakoff he seemed to agree with his subject: "Khomiakoff believed unalterably that in the church is freedom . . . for a Christian, life in the church is freedom . . . the freedom of Christ." "This freedom does not reign in our country," Berdyaev wrote in 1912, "and the west is betraying it more and more." For his social ideal Berdyaev returned to the word "*sobornost*," but with severe limitations to the word's significance. Again this extensive subject cannot be compressed into a paragraph; it must be studied in the Berdyaev books themselves.

How can the ideal society be built of individual men and women? "By what means can you pass over from individual happiness to the happiness of humanity in general—a happiness for whose sake you may subordinate man to the general well-being and consider him as a means? he was asking as early as 1903, in *Problems of Idealism*.[25] Although he already harbored reservations at that time, he "continued to stand on the marxist viewpoint." But only two years later he talks about it as "this primitive gnosiology." By the time he was corresponding with Mme K, no trace of respect for marxism remained: "Marxism is one of the most immobile, hardened, dogmatic doctrines in the history of human thought. The dynamic of idiotic Russian marxism is only apparent. There is no dynamic of thought, no movement of spirit, . . . an absolutely stifling atmosphere." In another letter he explained why: "By means of tyranny you can create only tyranny; . . . violence begets violence, malice and hatred eternally give birth to the same. Freedom is not created by some forced economic organization. . . . Communism is a metaphysical mistake in consequence of which it knows personality only in the future, not the present."

No social or economic order, Berdyaev insisted, can be acceptable which does not put personality—the supreme value of the individual—first. Marx's "inhuman idea of the collective in the religion of socialism" is "fatal for mankind."[26] Mme K, whoever she was, toyed intellectually with the acceptance of communism. Berdyaev wasted no words in an attempt to disillusion her: "You are mistaken in thinking communism has found a 'real way out.' Communism is first of all a symptom of . . . the end of the old world. Russian communism has not been realized in the least; . . . it is setting up a new type of cruel bourgeois-Soviet bureaucracy." Berdyaev held that in denying man's unique spiritual value the communists have denied God—even before they became an officially godless movement. Evidences that communism denies man's individual worth is found in its substitution of collective conscience and "collective liberty"—however much these terms may outrage our common sense—for individual conscience and individual freedom.

Although he denounced communism, Berdyaev felt "ideal" socialism was acceptable as a program for the ordering of society. "But I am an enemy of socialism based on the deification of the state and of society. I am in sympathy with a socialism . . . that recognizes as the supreme value not society, not the state, the nation, or the party, but man." Despite numerous earnest but misguided attempts to reconcile communism and Christianity, what has been quoted here is sufficient indication Berdyaev recognized this as impossible.

How should the ideal society be shaped then? It must guard the supreme value of human personality and hence be God-centered. "The idea of God is the only superhuman concept that does not destroy man, does not turn him into a . . . means or an instrument."[27] The ideal society is to depend in some way upon a spiritual elite. He elaborates in considerable detail in *Christianity and Class War*, asserting that every man, manual or intellectual worker, should be recognized as a creator of values useful to society; such recognition would result in a sort of guild system having as its guiding element the spiritual aristocracy just noted.

On the whole, Nicolai Alexandrovitch was not satisfied with any existing form of state. He felt they all tended to subject higher values such as man and personality to values of a lower order. "The very last man is above 'the world' and its kingdoms—monarchist, democratic, or communist." The one true reality is the unique human personality and "the eternal conscience, as God's revelation in man. . . . This is the eternal value trampled under foot by Hitler, Stalin, and all men of power and worshipers of 'society.' " Anyone who claims the dignity of man is the central idea of communism is "jabbering nonsense—as though a chunk of material could possess dignity."

Berdyaev did not think the perfect society would be achieved in our time—perhaps not in time at all but only in eternity. "In this objectivized and alienated world, perfection cannot be realized." But he insisted upon the need for movement toward the goal now, in the present day crises of man. And this predicates spiritual revolution. "A personalist revolution is necessary, a revolution in the name of every human personality. . . . It should be a true revolution, not the masquerade that is every political revolution. . . . The falsehoods of a humanism which deforms man must be met by the positive, religious revelation about man."[28]

Another general direction in Berdyaev's thinking was toward a philosophy of history. One of his early books dealt almost exclusively with the meaning of this world's experience, a theme that kept recurring in later writings. The real world was something revealed in the depths of man's spiritual experience, a world from which he had come into this "fallen" world— To that other, real world, the "heavenly fatherland" from which he had come, he would one day return. This central fact, however, means anything but passive endurance of our "objectivized world." He is a part of it, his fate is bound up with earthly destiny, and he feels a compulsion to struggle for its salvation. Beside *The Meaning of History* (1924), two other books dealt largely with the idea: *The Fate of Man in the Modern World* (1934) and *The Destiny of Man* (1931). A main theme in this connection was the secularization of culture. Incidentally, Berdyaev pointed out the distinction between culture and civilization long before Spengler. In the Middle Ages the church was culture. It endeavored to control politics but failed ultimately to produce a social program. To this failure marxism was one of the answers. Along with secularization of culture has gone the dehumanization of man. Man has become part of a machine. Modern "progress" has failed to produce the ideal society, tending instead to disintegrate human personality. Both man and history must refer to some center. And to Berdyaev it was self-evident that the central figure of history is Christ. Only by the spiritual revolution in every man that an acceptance of the Master's teaching would mean, can the purpose of history be achieved. And thus in one sense the meaning of history lies outside history. It is "God's eternal purpose."

Despite his individualism, Berdyaev's philosophy was to a degree the product of his times. He admitted, and the student can perceive, the influence upon him of many great thinkers. On the mystic side were Jacob Boehme, Angelus Silesius, and Meister Eckhart. Representing "pure reason" were Hegel, Kant, and Schopenhauer. On the social side Plechanov, Hertzen, and Nietzsche played significant parts, while Nicolai Alexandrovitch's distinctly religious philosophy was affected by Solovieff, Khomiakoff, and Dostoievsky. And the greatest of these was Dostoievsky. For Berdyaev, as for most Russians, to philosophize meant to consider the achievement of truth and justice in human life. This explains even Berdyaev's marxist period.

Like all Russian students at a time when German philosophy set the tune, Berdyaev knew Kant and Hegel. His preference was for Kant. He considers Kant and Plato the world's greatest philosophers. Hegel, Berdyaev held, had broken away from "the inner mystery of human existence," reducing history to a nonpersonal principle. He made of man a mere instrument for the realization of nonhuman aims. Berdyaev could not entirely accept Kant either. In his earlier books, *Sub Specie Æternitatis* (1907) and *Philosophy of Freedom* (1911), he called Kant "dangerous" because he (Kant) created a rational system with no place for the eternal, substituting the dead, categorical imperative for the living Saviour. Berdyaev said no real Kantian could believe in the resurrection of Christ. In later years he altered this opinion, feeling that in Kant's very insistence upon the "real," "phenomenal" world, the philosopher had laid a foundation for Berdyaev's own type of thinking—which insists upon the primacy of the "noumenal." Schopenhauer's influence on Berdyaev's thought from the time he first read him at the age of thirteen has already been noted. Schopenhauer's "voluntarism always remained close to him."

Out of Hegel came Marx with his "scientific" answers to all the world's questions. Berdyaev's *Sources of Russian Communism* is one of his most carefully reasoned, thoroughly didactic books. It has much to teach the world about Marx's outdated pseudoscience and its baleful development under Lenin and Stalin. Nietzsche, whose preaching of the superman at one time swept the liberal intelligentsia of half of Europe, moved Nicolai Alexandrovitch together with the rest of his contemporaries. Out of his revolt against the bourgeois, partly inspired by Marx, Berdyaev felt a natural attraction for Nietzsche and, for a time at least, could overlook Nietzsche's anti-Christianity. But he soon saw that Nietzsche was essentially antihuman in his scorn for the ordinary man. Where Marx had destroyed personality in the collective, he said, Nietzsche would kill man in his achievement of the superman.

For contrast to the "realistic" theories of the Germans, Marx and Nietzsche, Berdyaev was profoundly influenced by other Germans, Boehme and Eckhart in particular. They were nearer to him than many of the church fathers. He felt more at home in their "prophetic type of mysticism" than in what the church officially recognized as such. Much of the strong mystical strain in Berdyaev's thought stems from the German mystics. He came upon them at a particularly impressionable period in his life, and often returned to them in later works. Later in his experience Berdyaev discovered Péguy, and while it could scarcely be said that the Frenchman had influenced him, Nicolai Alexandrovitch was delighted to discover some phases of Péguy so similar that the passage about Péguy in the autobiography could have been written about himself. Porret says one might call Berdyaev the Russian Péguy.

Although he knew Khomiakoff intimately enough to write a book about him, Berdyaev seems not to have been much influenced by his philosophy. Khomiakoff and Solovieff, he held, were the founders of Russian religious philosophy. Berdyaev said that with Khomiakoff's doctrine of freedom and Solovieff's doctrine of Divine-humanity something new in man had been expressed in Russian religious thinking, and Nicolai Alexandrovitch accepted both of these ideas—with some personal adjustment. Berdyaev said Khomiakoff's doctrine of "*Sobornost*" departed from the traditional: "Into it has entered European humanism transfigured in a Russian and Orthodox way." He "was a special kind of anarchist, as distinct from Solovieff, and this made him a typical Russian thinker." Khomiakoff had brilliant philosophical insights, thought Berdyaev, but failed to develop them spiritually—or in a book—writing only articles, chiefly polemics with the Roman Church.

Solovieff, "that most remarkable representative of nineteenth-century Russian religious philosophy,"[29] perpetuated Khomiakoff's religious ideas and developed them. Nicolai Alexandrovitch owed not a little of his philosophy to this remarkable Russian thinker living and writing within Berdyaev's own lifetime. Few people either read or were interested in Solovieff then, but he has gradually become recognized since his death (1900)—partly owing to younger thinkers whom he trained to carry on his ideas, among them the two Trubetskoys and Bulgakov. One of Solovieff's great passions was church unity. Berdyaev could go with him a long way, although he did not believe unity was attainable by creedal adjustment or formal negotiation. Solovieff insisted upon a prophetic role for Christianity, and here Berdyaev agreed. Nicolai Alexandrovitch could also appreciate Solovieff's attitude toward the errors of socialism. To overcome these, he said—and Berdyaev has often said it since—one must recognize what is good in socialism and strive for the realization of that good. Berdyaev sympathized with Solovieff's ideas on the oneness of all mankind, as well as of the catastrophic end of history. Berdyaev could not accept Solovieff's later period when he had turned pessimist, losing all hope of the achievement of the Kingdom in time, or even the union of the churches. Solovieff even went so far as to doubt history has meaning. Berdyaev said bluntly that Solovieff belongs to the past, yet he himself was the bearer into the future of some of Solovieff's ideas.

With Kierkegaard's thought Berdyaev became acquainted much later than the formative period when Solovieff could influence him. But he was pleased to find much of spiritual kinship with the "melancholy" Danish philosopher. With Kierkegaard, Berdyaev ranked "feeling higher than abstract reason in the . . . apprehension of existential truth." Like Kierkegaard "the foundation of his faith was in his own life; the only truth of any value for him was 'existential,' that which corresponded to his own experience."[30] In attempting to explain his concept of existentialism, Berdyaev sometimes used Kierkegaard as contrasted with Heidegger or Sartre. In a certain measure Berdyaev shared Kierkegaard's eschatological ideas. And he certainly could feel at one with the Dane in his loneliness, although he did not conceive of solitude as the only way for truly apprehending Christianity. Both men were lonely because both were near genius.

Other contemporary Russian philosophers like Lossky, Frank, and Shestov can scarcely be said to have influenced Berdyaev. He gave to each credit for creative work in philosophy. Frank had accompanied him on his painful road from marxism to Christianity, and he called Frank's *The Object of Knowing* "a very valuable contribution to Russian philosophy." Despite lifelong disputations with his friend Shestov, there were considerable areas of agreement outside the specifically Christian facets of Berdyaev's thinking. What Berdyaev said of Shestov was equally true of himself: ". . . a thinker who philosophized with his whole being, for whom philosophy was not an academic specialty but a matter of life and death."[31] Nicolai Alexandrovitch seemed to be agreeing with his friend when he wrote: "In Shestov, God is first of all unlimited possibility. . . . God is not bound by any immutable truths; . . . over against God stands the kingdom of necessity, of reason." The interaction of the two minds doubtless helped to polish some of Berdyaev's ideas.

Of all the world's thinkers, Russian or not, the man who most influenced Berdyaev's thought was Dostoievsky. Berdyaev said Dostoievsky "had a determinant significance" in his spiritual life when he was still a boy. Dostoievsky "shook my soul more than any other writer or thinker. . . . I came to Dostoievsky as to my spiritual homeland."[32] He said of Dostoievsky what he also remarked about the Gospels, that each time he reread him ever-new vistas of thought were opened. Dostoievsky helped define all the central themes of Berdyaev's thinking: man and his freedom, the problem of evil, the redeeming power of love, the individual versus society, Divine-humanity. The works of Feodor Dostoievsky were like a symphony to which Berdyaev listened all his life.

If the Dostoievsky novels were his guiding symphony, the "Legend of the Grand Inquistor" was its leitmotiv. Rössler says Berdyaev "attempts to bring the whole of human culture into relationship with the theme of the 'Legend.'" Berdyaev himself wrote that in his early youth the Legend "kindled a flame in my soul." It was the Legend that formed the central problem of his thinking and indicated what he felt was its only possible solution: "Truth makes man free, but man must freely accept the Truth. . . . Christ gives man his final freedom, but man must freely accept Christ."[33] Berdyaev called the Legend "one of the most revolutionary . . . products of the world's literature." Its theme is universal: "It gives a whole philosophy of history and contains a most profound prophecy of the fate of humanity." And summing up: "The conquest of the three temptations is the religious meaning of the future history of mankind: not to worship earthly bread, not to entrust its conscience to any earthly authority, not to unite . . . an earthly state under the power of a human Caesar."[34] Time and again in books on various topics and at different periods of his life he returned to the Legend, as inspiration, starting point, or clincher for an argument. Almost unique in modern literature is this permanent inspiration Berdyaev received from one small section of a chapter in one of a great novelist's books.

Like the boy in Hawthorne's *Great Stone Face*, Berdyaev's preoccupation with Dostoievsky seemed almost to cause a resemblance. "To understand Dostoievsky," Berdyaev said, "a special formation of spirit is essential. There should be in the knower a kinship with Dostoievsky himself, . . . something of his spirit." There were similarities in the experience of the two men. Both passed through spiritual crises. Both, from being "freethinking" revolutionaries, moved into a deep

Christian faith. Berdyaev said Dostoievsky "might be called an Orthodox socialist," and the epithet could well be applied to its author. If Dostoievsky in his Legend evinced a stroke of genius in portraying the falsehood "not alone in authoritarian Catholicism, but in authoritarian communism and fascism, in all totalitarian regimes," so did Nicolai Alexandrovitch. Both men had to struggle with a physical handicap; it will be recalled that, reprieved at the moment he faced a firing squad, Dostoievsky later developed epilepsy which was never cured. In their methods of writing the two were alike. Berdyaev said "the whole of Dostoievsky's creativeness is a whirlwind anthropology."[35] Even when he wrote Mme K: "I must admit that I do not like the person of Dostoievsky. He is even repulsive to me," there was something of Berdyaev's consciousness of his own imperfection and a dislike for the physical world that included his own person.

Berdyaev attributed the unique Russian renaissance at the beginning of this century to Dostoievsky: "Rozanoff, Merezhkovsky, the New Way, the neo-Christians, Bulgakov, the neo-idealist, L. Shestov, Byeli, V. Ivanoff . . . all are connected with Dostoievsky . . . all are trying to solve the questions he put." The influence of Dostoievsky, he said, was deeper and more powerful than even that of Tolstoi. He divided people into two groups, those naturally inclined to accept Tolstoi and those to whom Dostoievsky presents a greater appeal. And he said that while Tolstoi's influence was anticultural, Dostoievsky, who was himself a crisis in culture despite his apocalyptic tendencies, nevertheless recognized the values of history and the world's cultural inheritance. After Dostoievsky, he said, feeling for life was different than it had been before.

> We can accept the world and justify . . . its uncountable sufferings if there is a divine Reason, hidden from the "Euclid mind," if there is a Redeemer, . . . if final world harmony is to be attained in the Kingdom of God and not in the kingdom of this world. . . . The world process can be accepted if there is immortality. If there is no such thing, the world process must be refused.[36]

This, Berdyaev said, was the basic thought of Dostoievsky. He could well have been describing his own fundamental convictions.

# 19

## THE PROPHET

It has often been said that if Berdyaev was significant as a philosopher, he was more so as a prophet. The Hebrew Old Testament used three different words for the concept now translated as "prophet": one word denotes a "speaker," a second, a "speaker for" another, while the third means a "seer," one who perceives and foretells the future. Berdyaev was all of these. He spoke for his times; he spoke as he believed, for God—in the sense that he proclaimed what he had envisioned as Truth. In an unusual way he foresaw the shadow of coming events in history—and even beyond. Like the prophets of old, he spoke out of his own spiritual experience. As Eugenie says: ". . . his God-given prophetic gift may help Christians at a moment when the world is plunged into darkness."

Berdyaev was a speaker for God in his own times. Perhaps no other thinker in this century has been so convincingly able to explain to thoughtful men the ethical significance of what is happening to our world. Spengler attracted world-wide attention because he undertook to explain the events of today in the light of history, but he saw only darkness ahead. Berdyaev looked at the world in the light of God's eternal purpose, and because it was God's purpose, he saw light where Spengler saw none.

Berdyaev was among the first to sense the advent of one age ending and the dawn of another. A book might be written on the historic events occurring in Berdyaev's lifetime and his analysis of each as it came along. Long before 1914, he was saying that the mode of his parents' and grandparents' intellectual living, and of all Russia, was approaching its close. He was one of the very first who understood that the catastrophe of Russia's revolution was a catastrophe of the intelligentsia. He saw how modern industrial civilization threatened to dehumanize man, reducing God to nothingness. "The spirit of civilization is a bourgeois spirit; . . . it has been killing God." Civilization threatens to destroy itself in destroying man's soul.[1]

259

Not civilization alone is threatened with bankruptcy, Nicolai Alex-androvitch predicted, but modern culture as well. With all its mighty works in art and literature, culture has not succeeded in ennobling man. The chief reason is that culture has concerned itself only with some facets of human life; in the whole integral man culture has not been interested. The technical achievements of modern art are great, but there are neither great creators nor great art. "We are entering a period of collective, mass art; . . . the beauty of the soul is dying. . . . But there is no such thing as 'the general': only the concrete in-dividual . . . really exists." This unique individual man, his spiritual dignity and value, must be preserved at all costs. Yet with all its vast resources, culture is powerless to resolve the dilemma and save man. Only religion, only Christianity, will be able to take positive action here. Christianity can eliminate the struggle between the individual and society.

Not only did Berdyaev gaze at swift events of the present and explain what they meant in the light of eternity; he foretold in a remarkable way what subsequent historical steps to anticipate. Berdyaev foresaw that in Russia the results of the revolution would be something quite different from the triumph of freedom and humaneness many of his friends expected. This is foretold in a chapter of The Spiritual Crisis of the Intelligentsia published in 1907, ten years before the event. Here he said that when revolution came it would bring victory for the ex-tremists, hatred of freedom, and denial of God. Writing in 1945, Ste-pun could say that in the light of recent events Berdyaev's philosophy was a sort of "heavenly prologue" to the revolution. The New Middle Ages looked past these times of darkness to see the fruits of creative forces which, as in medieval times, were at work beneath the surface. In The Destiny of Man he looked ahead to man's conquest of the ethical problems plaguing him today. In The Meaning of the Creative Act he saw beyond the two epochs into which human history is divided, to a third—more perfectly human and hence more perfectly divine.

Berdyaev foretold not merely wars and revolution, and the future failures of our so-called culture; his mind leaped forward beyond the end of time. He looked forward not to an end of all human endeavor and escape from the difficulties of the present world, but to new sources of power and inspiration for living in the present. The final chapters of The Destiny of Man deal with this theme: "The Last Things"; "Death and Immortality"; "Beyond Good and Evil." Man's consummation was foretold in the perfection of Christ. In the redemption of all creation there will be "the realization of the fullness of divine-human truth, the truth of the God-man realized in life. . . . Christianity will again become the . . . final refuge for man."[2]

The last chapter of Berdyaev's *Slavery and Freedom* dealt with "active eschatology." The dawn of "Christianity in its pure form . . . will probably begin in the world only after the elementary, everyday problems of human existence are solved for all peoples and nations, after bitter human need and the economic slavery of man have been finally overcome."[3] Fielding Clarke remarks that Berdyaev gives perspectives, not programs, and in the narrow sense of program this is true. Berdyaev had seen the communist attempt to regulate every phase of human life too close at hand to wish to enunciate specific programs of reform. But in the larger sense perspective is a program. Elimination of human poverty and economic slavery, if considered in the light of each man's Christian duty as Berdyaev insisted upon doing, provides a long-range goal for creative action. His message to the world was a call for Christian action within it.

As a prophet Nicolai Alexandrovitch received a prophet's reward: he was lonely, he was misunderstood, most of his own people would have none of him. His loneliness was not due to the "sense of shame, nor timidity" which prevented his revealing himself intimately to another person. It was more because of his constant revolt. When at odds with his own, aristocratic milieu he made friends among the outcast Jews. When he revolted against marxism, he took an attitude so nearly Christian that most of his fellow "idealists" could not go along with him. Although he hated the Soviet regime, he estranged himself from most of the emigration by opposing counter revolution. And as a faithful son of the Russian Church, when the tragic decision had to be made—to remain with the preponderance of its members in the emigration or risk their ostracism and remain under Moscow's jurisdiction—he chose the lonely way. He was a prophet out of his time.

"I think of time, of my own epoch, of its evil and its problems, but I am not a well-timed thinker. I have broken completely with my epoch. . . . I sing the praise of an eschatological Christianity when my epoch recognizes only a Christianity of the everyday and traditional."[4]

And his was the fate of a "prophet in his own country." In Russia or among the million and more Rusians scattered across the world, he found few who understood or would accept his message. The émigrés considered him pro-Soviet. The Soviet government called him bourgeois and reactionary—an article in *Pravda* referred to him as the "white guard [i.e., counterrevolutionary] Berdyaev." During a month in Russia in the summer of 1957, spent in research on Berdyaev, the effect of the intellectual quarantine under which Soviet citizens have lived for forty years was clearly observable. The executive head of one of Russia's largest church districts, a man of sixty-five, had never heard of him. Neither had many other intelligent people. Librarians in Moscow, Leningrad, and Kiev knew something of this effective opponent of communism but inquired why anyone should want to write a book about him. They were visibly astonished to learn that in many parts of the free world Berdyaev is read by more people than is Lenin. Inside the Soviet Union, no one reads Berdyaev. The Lenin Library in Moscow, claiming twenty million volumes, has none of the nineteen books Berdyaev published abroad, and his prerevolution works are kept in a police-guarded "rare books" section. The public catalogue of the Leningrad Public Library (twelve million volumes) has only three cards on Berdyaev. One is a reference to *Milestones* and the other two to articles about Berdyaev. The New York Public Library catalogue has seventy-five. Almost the only published reaction to Berdyaev's thought and his person available from U.S.S.R. sources is an article about him in the Great Soviet Encyclopedia. This is so revealing that it should be quoted almost in full:

> Reactionary philosopher, idealist and mystic, white emigrant." [And Nicolai Alexandrovitch was always so proud that he had left his country under banishment, not of his own volition!] As a student . . . [he] struggled against marxism and from an idealistic Kantian position moved, after the 1905 revolution, to [the] open and senseless mysticism . . . reflected in his *Sub Specie Eternitatis* and *The New Religious Consciousness*.
>
> One of the leaders of the god-seekers, his Religious-Philosophical Society . . . became a center for counter-revolutionary ideology. . . . (He was) a contributor to *Milestones*, which Lenin called "an encyclopedia of liberal renegades". . . . Hating the Soviet system, Berdyaev emigrated in 1922. In Berlin he united [!] fugitive reactionaries and obscurantists in the so-called Religious-Philosophical Academy.

Of the two books produced in Berlin, *The Philosophy of Inequality* and *The New Middle Ages*, the Encyclopedia says they "are full of evil hatred toward socialism and the revolutionary world view." In Paris, the article continues, Berdyaev's "religious-mystic hallucinations were

suited to the taste of western Europeans, and Berdyaev became one of
the recognized leaders of the rankest form of idealist obscurantism, religious existentialism. . . . His mystic fantasies have been used to arm
the most reactionary philosophers—enemies of science, progress, and
democracy." From reading the Encyclopedia one might assume that
after his arrival in Paris Berdyaev never wrote another book. Not a
single title is mentioned, of this the most creative period in his life.

We know of one earlier attack on Berdyaev by a Soviet author. In
1935, Bucharin—leading communist theoretician of the twenties—
published a review of The Fate of Man in the Modern World, which
he had read in German translation. His review was entitled "The Philosophy of a Cultured Philistine": "The new opus of the mastodon of
'our' religious-philosophical movement deserves attention, both as a
human document and as a document of the times, viewed from the
underside." Berdyaev, says the review, is "an interesting example of
human metamorphosis, . . . having come almost the full cycle of
transformation from marxism to orthodoxy. Mr. Berdyaev was found
outside the borders of the U.S.S.R. after the October revolution [five
years after!], so that consonant with his Christian principles he could
seriously proclaim . . . the Soviet government . . . a Satanocracy,
[exercising] the power of the devil." Although the book sharply criti-
cizes capitalism, says Bucharin, "it becomes false and superficial when
Mr. Berdyaev begins casting his Parthian arrows at our movement. . . .
Mr. Beradyaev has borrowed extraordinarily much from bolshevism in
his critique of formal democracy (although not once in the entire book
does he mention Lenin!)" The review goes on to say Berdyaev has no
understanding of the common mass of people and thinks organizing
them will mean cultural decadence. "He would prefer to see the aristocracy continue its pasturing on these meadows. This is a terrible
dream," and the atheist Bucharin concludes with an old Russian phrase
—"but God is merciful."

Until recently this constituted all the Soviet public was permitted to
know about Berdyaev. But in 1955, The Communist—official organ
of the Party—published two articles for the first time recognizing the
work of Russian thinkers living abroad. Among those attacked was
Berdyaev. But again no work of his was cited. A recent number of
Science and Life has a rubric entitled "Science and Religion" in which
Berdyaev is again mentioned. The article is about Plechanov, "the
theoretician of scientific atheism," and it places Berdyaev among the
"god-seekers" (no capital letter) who called each individual, "each

unique personality," to a mystic search for a "god ideal," together with other "representatives of the bourgeois intelligentsia—philosophizing mystics like Merezhkovsky."[5] No other indication is given of the content of Berdyaev's thought. What a tremendous run on Berdyaev books there will one day be in a Russia where a free press is possible!

For Berdyaev never lost faith in Russia or the Russian people. Numerous chapters in his books are concerned with an analysis of Russian character—the much-examined "Russian soul." Berdyaev noted that Russians are a people of opposites—of strong likes and dislikes. They may always be expected to produce something unexpected. In the Russian soul, East struggles with West. The legendary Volga pirate Stenka Razin and the humble St. Seraphim are both truly Russian types. Just as in the Eastern Church its entire body of believers constitutes final authority, so for several generations Russian intellectuals thought of the common people—the *Narod*—as a sort of mystic unit, something deeper than the idea of a nation. The folk were eternal seekers for God's justice. They sought it for themselves, for Russia, and for the world. Russia was so vast even a peasant could grasp the idea of the universal, and the Russian people were always conscious of the world's as well as their own need for God.

The prophet had a poignant sense of the end of time. If the Kingdom of God is not to be realized in this world, still it will be consummated—in God's own future. Berdyaev said the Russian people "by their metaphysical nature and calling in the world, are a people of the ending."[6] The sense that Christianity has been unable to attain its "Kingdom of Righteousness on earth," he pointed out, "leads to a messianic hope, an eschatological expectation stronger in Russian than in western Christianity." The *stranniki* (wanderers), that uniquely Russian phenomenon, illustrate what is meant. "He has here no abiding city; he is striving toward the City that is to come." Berdyaev believed the Russian people were destined to create a social order more just and human than anything now existing—the better world of the future, neither communist nor capitalist.

An infusion of the apocalyptic, together with Russian—and Orthodox—religiosity, developed a type of thinking quite peculiar to the one people: dissatisfaction with the world as it is, lack of respect for the powerful, a yearning for something better and beyond—the Kingdom of God. "Russians thought . . . most important not what Russia is but what Russia brings to the world, above all brotherhood of man and freedom of the spirit."[7] From such thinking grew the Orthodox idea of Moscow the "Third Rome." The Third International is only a debased and distorted form of that idea, said Berdyaev.

He had a lively sense of living with Russian history. He felt himself a part of the historic catastrophe of the communist experiment. And while he said the bolshevik revolution was "under the sign of nihilist enlightenment, materialism, utilitarianism, and atheism," he felt the entire process was inevitable and would eventually be resolved for the healing of the nations. "When you read Soviet philosophical and literary discussions, you are impressed with horror at their colorless vulgarity." But Berdyaev insisted upon a distinction between communism and the communist government that holds Russia in its grip. He wrote Mme K in reply to one of her procommunist effusions:

> I am astonished that you are defending, not the communist idea, not the working masses, which I would fully understand, but the government. . . . There was a time when it was intellectually permissible to approve the idea of monarchy and still consider a given monarch a disaster. Now the Bolsheviks demand first of all, approval and support for their governing clique.

All this regime of oppression and terror would pass, Berdyaev believed. What are forty years in the face of history? He was certain the higher spiritual values of the Russian renaissance could not be erased; the future would see them restored as a moving force in the progress of the Russian people. In the midst of the tragic war years, when Hitlerism had inundated France and most of the rest of Europe, he wrote:

> This kingdom of very imperfect freedom will end; . . . the world is more and more enslaved by the spirit of the Grand Inquisitor. But we cannot be reconciled to the enslavement of men or of peoples. All this should not be terrifying for . . . Christians, but only for those who do not wish further to rely upon the realm of Caesar.[8]

He pointed out how it had taken more than a generation for the elementary ideas of the "liberal" Russian intelligentsia—materialism and atheism—to filter down from the leaders to the masses. And he believed that in the Russian soul these atheistic ideas would eventually be defeated by man's age-old striving for the Kingdom of Justice. In his *Cry of the Russian Church* he pictures that church's role in present and future Russian history. "The salvation of Russia will come through the Christianization of the new layers of society—by the spiritual rebirth of the workers and peasants." The church can bring this about, he said, if it remains aloof from politics. Its "separation from tsarism was a great blessing. But it is still entangled in a thousand threads binding it to historical . . . culture." The church must Christianize without engaging in political action. "The church cannot have a political ideal [and] cannot be tied to any politcal party. . . . The church will free itself from the compromises and accords it has had to accept in the past. And that will be our spiritual return to our fatherland."

# 20

## WAITING FOR THE LIGHT

As for almost every other human on this planet, the onset of World War II meant significant changes in Berdyaev's life. But unlike the majority, he was not caught unawares. His feelings about war in general had often been expressed, perhaps most clearly in *The Destiny of Man*. As a Christian he knew it was wrong to kill, but he said men may be obliged to take upon themselves the sin of causing another's death to assure the preservation of higher values and in order that, in general, killing in the world should be diminished. He was clear in his distinction between aggression, which he condemned, and defensive war, which he believed justifiable. He knew that war imposed new difficulties upon the Christian conscience. He was not deceived by nazism, characterizing it as another form of totalitarianism just as incompatible with the Christian conscience as communism. He was revolted by the nonaggression pact von Ribbentrop signed at Moscow in August, 1939. He charged Soviet Russia with betraying her allies; it was another example of dialectic falsehood, attempting to justify means by ends. He viewed the approach of the war itself in the light of the world's final destiny. One might predict two ends to the world, he said, evil catastrophes like natural disasters or wars, or the world's final transfiguration. Here he returned to his "third epoch" theme. "The Kingdom of God comes imperceptibly, with no theatrical effects. It has come in each triumph of humanity; it is coming in this world of cruelty and slavery . . . in true liberation, authentic creativeness."[1]

After almost a year of "phony war" came Germany's sudden thrust, the collapse of Belgium, and the advance on Paris. The probably German-stimulated panic swept hundreds of thousands into a tragic exodus. Half of Paris tried to get away before the Germans came. The Berdyaev family hesitated—it would be painful to leave their home at Clamart, but they dreaded seeing enemy troops occupying the city. Berdyaev consulted Hélène Iswolsky, who advised a move to Pau where

267

both she and they had influential friends. When the collapse of French resistance had ended, Pau was just outside the demarcation line of German occupation; had he gone there, Berdyaev would have been spared the sight of the enemy for another two years. But chance ruled otherwise. The family's great friend Monbrison invited them to his place at Pilat, near Arcachon. With the Germans almost at the gates of Paris, Lydia won her husband away from his decision not to run before the enemy, and they decided to leave.

The next two days brought the same hysterical tribulation that half of northern France was sharing. First came the matter of transportation from Clamart to Paris. No taxis were available, but they hired a half-winded truck into which they climbed with their luggage, including Muri in his traveling basket. Arrived at the Gare d'Austerlitz, they were caught in a sea of milling, struggling civilians all trying to get through the iron gates to the departing trains. Panic was heightened by the sound of bombs or cannon somewhere in the distance. The little group was pushed against a wall, where they remained without food or rest until nightfall. Return to Clamart was unthinkable. After hours of blundering through blacked-out streets and fruitless calls at a dozen hotels in the neighborhood, the weary trio found a small hostel that "permitted them to pass the night."

They made another attempt early the next morning. This time the crowd was not so merciless, although the press was so frightening that Berdyaev feared the two women would be crushed. They finally made the train. Eugenie tells of a characteristic Berdyaev moment in the panicky mob. Regarding the faces about him, distorted with fear and anxiety, Berdyaev had on his own face an expression of haughty disdain. To protect Muri, howling in his basket, Berdyaev held him high above his head, with the other arm doing what was possible to protect Lydia. All at once in the midst of the uproar he leaned down to Lydia and said: "I have just thought out that last chapter of my book."[2]

For three months they enjoyed the pleasant climate and restful scenery about Pilat, marred only by the presence of triumphant German troops. But in September they returned to Clamart. Anyone as outspokenly anti-Nazi as Berdyaev might well have lived in constant anxiety under the police regime of Hitler's troops. Many of his friends were imprisoned for far less cause. But although the Gestapo made several calls, questioning both Berdyaev and Lydia, they were not further disturbed. All indications point to the existence of some highly placed person in the Hitler government who parried every attempt to molest them. Once a Swiss newspaper published an item stating that Berdyaev had been imprisoned by the Nazis. Within a few days he was again visited by the Gestapo under instructions to report to Berlin if that were true. After the war, St. Sergius Institute members learned the names of two noble Germans who had been their protectors throughout the occupation of France. But Berdyaev never discovered the identity of his secret guardian angel.

Soon after his return to Paris he was offered the possibility of moving to the United States, but he refused.

Hippius wrote of life under a totalitarian regime: "A person may . . . become accustomed to such a situation if he does not die first. But then he becomes a half-person, apathetic . . . submissive."[3] Berdyaev became neither. The group of Russian friends still at liberty continued its customary Sunday afternoon meetings at Berdyaev's home. Among these was Mother Marie. One day she was discussing Berdyaev with her former husband, now a Roman Catholic priest: "What do you think of him?" she asked. "As he grows older, he is easier to talk to," said Father Kuzmin. "One can speak quietly with him, without violent argument." Mother Marie laughed: "That's exactly what he said about you."

The Sunday afternoon meetings, certainly unique in occupied Paris, rapidly became the center of Russian patriotism. Most of Berdyaev's friends among the "liberal" group attended, among them Mother Marie, Pianoff, Motchulsky, Jaba, Adamovitch, the poet Piotrovsky, Stavroff the writer with his wife, Mlle Kliatchkin, Mme Kallash the well-known journalist—and sometimes French friends like the writer Leyris or Professor Le Senne. Berdyaev sat on a hard chair (he disliked soft furniture) at the large round table, on which were laid out the latest war maps available. Eugenie describes him at these meetings: "I never saw him so lively, so easily friendly as he greeted his guests. Evidently he did not as usual feel himself alien to the situation. His heart was beating with that of Russia and he never doubted the ultimate victory." In this he was almost alone. But studying with intense interest the movements of armies across Russia, they "discussed and disputed and hoped." With those Russians who saw the Germans as liberators of Russia from the communist regime, Berdyaev broke implacably. He called them traitors. One fellow professor was thus denied access to Berdyaev until the latter learned he had broken with the Germans. Once, when the Germans sent one of "their" Russians to enlist him among pro-Hitler writers, Berdyaev put him out the door.

Berdyaev was deeply grieved when a wave of Paris arrests caught up Mother Marie, her son, Father Dimitri Klepinin, and Pianoff among others. The only thing anyone could do to help in such cases was send food parcels to the prison. Again everyone wondered why Berdyaev had escaped imprisonment. In discussing it with Eugenie, Berdyaev assured her he had no fear. He once said his highest ideal had always been that of martyrdom for the faith. This time he added a new aphorism: "The supreme hierarchic position in this world is to be hung on a cross." And when, after the war, word came back that Mother Marie and Father Klepinin had died in German concentration camps, Berdyaev felt theirs was true martyrdom.

Another real tragedy in Berdyaev's life just at the close of the war was the death of Muri, his beloved cat. The animal suffered terribly before the end, and in this Berdyaev said he lived through the suffering of all creation. In Muri he "felt himself joined with the whole of creation, awaiting deliverance. . . . The death of such a charming one of God's creatures was for me the experience of death in general." He "demanded immortality for Muri" and for himself, eternal life with his pet. "Passing Muri's grave under a tree in our garden, I have thought of immortality not abstractly, but very much in the concrete."[4]

During the difficult days preceding the close of the war, Berdyaev underwent a serious abdominal operation.[5] He remarked about it that, since he had only local narcosis, he was strongly conscious of his complete inability to move and disliked "this wall of inexorable necessity." The family, gravely concerned, was surprised at the calmness with which he prepared to leave for the hospital and his good-by as he got into the taxi. It was autumn of 1942. Both ambulances and taxis were the greatest rarities in occupied Paris. It is interesting that beside his New Testament, the only book he took with him to the hospital, and asked to have immediately after the operation, was Hertzen's *Past Events and Thoughts*—that "most brilliant of all memoirs." In the hospital the first evening he had a long conversation with his nurse, asking many questions that showed he knew almost nothing of anatomy or the nature of the next day's operation. He evidently disliked being left alone and asked that his room door be left open. Of Berdyaev's qualities as a patient, the evidence is contradictory. One nurse reportedly called him the most unbearable patient she ever had. The group of devoted ladies who in those near-starvation days kept Berdyaev supplied with dainties, insist he was a model patient. One witness pictures him after the operation walking up and down the cold corridor, on his head the huge black velvet beret he always wore (he slept in it as well), his slightly stooped figure wrapped in the inevitable scarf and a brown blanket to protect him from any possible draft. Whereas most patients in those penurious times left the hospital at the earliest possible moment because of the expense, Berdyaev seemed loath to leave and made a longer than normal stay. The husband of a Russian nurse on that floor drove one of the rare "Slota" taxis, and with his help Berdyaev got safely back to Clamart.

The last war years were shadowed by the grave illness of Lydia. A progressive paralysis of the throat caused intense suffering, and the disease was evidently incurable. In September, 1945, she died. Berdyaev wrote in his autobiography: "This was one of the most poignant and at the same time inwardly significant events of my life—the experience of her dying. I learned very much. . . . Lydia had an unusually strong faith. I have never seen such a strong faith in anyone else. . . . Hers was a lofty death, because of her intense spirituality." Berdyaev said he could not be reconciled to the idea that death is finality, emptiness. Death is not only the final evil; death is light. Only in death comes the ultimate sharpness of love. "Before she died, I told Lydia what a great spiritual support for my life she had been, and she wrote that she would continue to be. . . . With Lydia's passing," Berdyaev said, "death for me became less terrible: I discovered in it something near and dear."[6]

The close of the war brought into Russian émigré life—and that in-cluded Berdyaev—a new and painful problem. When Hitler declared war on Russia, Russians everywhere, within and without the country, had to decide whether it was an attack against the bolshevik regime or against their fatherland. The great majority in the emigration, despite their hatred for communism and the Soviet government, decided the attack was against Russia. All through the war they followed anxiously the fortunes of the Russian armies, until at the end—with Russian troops entering Berlin—their pride and satisfaction were exuberant. The first foreign mission to return to Paris was the Soviet Embassy. And very soon the Embassy was making propaganda for all émigrés to accept Soviet passports and return to Russia. Many there were who hoped and believed that a new, freer atmosphere would reign in the U.S.S.R. A much smaller number ventured to accept Soviet passports, but the question tormented all émigré minds. At first Berdyaev was also inclined to believe Stalin would give the Russian people a new freedom.

In January, 1945, while war was still raging, he had delivered a lecture in which he discussed the mission of Russia:

> What does Russia bring to the world? In a new garb, the traditional assertion of the Russian faith: peace and the brotherhood of nations. . . . Russia's purpose is pacific: only the means are military; . . . the war is being carried on for the liberation of the world. . . . After the war freedom of the spirit and of thought will be more necessary than ever. . . . After the war the world will be reconstructed; . . . one must be devoid of Christian conscience to affirm that capitalism is compatible with Christianity.

Although here Nicolai Alexandrovitch seemed to put himself completely on the side of communism, he softened his assertion somewhat by one addition:

> Only a combination of social with spiritual movement can bring the realization of the new man, who cannot automatically appear out of social changes.

Seven months later, the war in Europe ended, he was writing in the same vein:

> Insofar as Soviet Russia wants to create a new life, it must place as its cornerstone the dignity and value of living human personality, which as yet we see nowhere. This has nothing in common with the individualism characteristic of capitalist social order, which crushes human personality. . . . But we must not forget that the deepest roots of humanism, personalism, and socialism are in Christianity, pure and undistorted.

Although he never rid himself of pessimistic ideas about capitalism, Nicolai Alexandrovitch was later to change his opinions about the innocence of the Soviet government. But as late as mid-1946, he gave an interview in which he seemed to favor the émigrés' return. Although he made no approach to the Paris representatives of the U.S.S.R., they came to see him. He found some of them interesting and questioned them eagerly about life in Russia.

As word spread abroad of the actions of the Soviet government in occupied Europe, and then its attitude switch in relation to the Allies, hitherto favorable public opinion changed—placing Berdyaev in an unhappy situation. He had been living through Russia's experiences as if they were his own. Unless Berdyaev's moral suffering in this relationship is borne in mind, his later years will not be truly understood. While public reaction from the original pro-Russian feeling resulted in an equally strong hostility toward Russia and anything that seemed Russian, Berdyaev struggled to make clear the distinction between the Russian people and their government. He might accept certain positive elements in the revolution, even in the Soviet idea, but that was something separate from his belief in the mission of Russia's people. His faith in the Russian people made him an implacable enemy of the ideological dictatorship holding them in its grip. Such a distinction was hard for the rest of the world and even for the great majority of his fellow Russian émigrés to comprehend. Again he was to note in sadness: "I feel myself very much alone in the emigration."

He was already such a world figure that evidently the Soviet representatives felt every effort should be made to achieve his return to the U.S.S.R. Berdyaev and Eugenie discussed it many times. She felt that if she were younger she would return home, maintaining her Christian faith under Soviet conditions. He thought it might be possible—even advisable—for technicians, engineers, and physicians to live and work in Soviet Russia, but he failed to see how a free philosopher like himself could do any creative work in the stagnant philosophic atmosphere enforced by Russian marxism. Nevertheless, when a representative from the Soviet Embassy one day asked to see him privately, he accepted the visit. His conversation with the diplomat, as Berdyaev reported it, was interesting:

"What would I do in Moscow?" I asked him. "Write, just as you do here." "And would they publish my books?" Doubtless— of course they would dispute with you, but you would be able to publish." "Well then, when I learn that all my books written here in the emigration are distributed in Russia, sold freely in bookstores, and are on the open shelves of all libraries—then I'll return."

With this attitude, it is somewhat surprising that Berdyaev seemed interested in seeing a copy of the official registration blank for those who wanted to return to Russia. He read it through, and when he came to: "I promise to give information about any anti-Soviet activity," he threw down the sheet in disgust. A little later he was explaining his feeling to Mme K: "I have great sympathy for those returning to Russia who can work there, . . . but I am a philosopher. . . . I can exist only under conditions of absolute freedom of thought. I can neither adapt myself nor submit. I never did, during the five years I lived in Soviet Russia, and for this was banished."

His suspicions were confirmed by the suppression of Akhmatova and Zoschenko. Berdyaev wrote a full-page article about it in the Paris *Russian News*.[7] He headed it with a quotation from an earlier Russian patriot, Aksakov: "The armament of a free people is the free word." "Dictatorship over souls is disbelief in one's own people. . . . No party, no government, even in the most difficult transition period, can pretend to express the free will of the people. . . . The monolithic claim of . . . the party is a . . . false religion." After that there was less talk about Berdyaev's return to the Soviet Union.

Berdyaev never stopped writing because of the war, and once it was finished he continued his usual production. The YMCA Press was again in function, and he knew his books would be published. Two books written during the war years were issued before his death, *The Russian Idea*, and *The Beginning and the End* (in Russian, "An Essay in Eschatological Metaphysics"). The first, one of the most systematically prepared of Berdyaev's works, is an excellent outline of Russian thought of the nineteenth and beginning of the twentieth centuries. No one wishing to understand Russia should overlook it. The second has a sub-title—"Creativity and Objectivization"—as abstract as its real title. In it Berdyaev presents his very particular idea of objectivization as related to knowing and being, together with his thoughts on history and eschatology.

All the other books produced either during the war or in the three years Berdyaev lived after it have now appeared. The first was, naturally, his autobiography—of which more later. His final manuscript *The Realm of Spirit and the Realm of Caesar*, left in Berdyaev's original, uncopied script, appeared next, in 1951. In this "final message to our times" Nicolai Alexandrovitch gives his prophetic answers to many questions thoughtful people are asking today—answers many have felt but could not have stated so clearly. What are the moral limits of society's power over the individual? Can man attain spiritual power to match his technical development? What is the place of a spiritual elite in a classless society? What is the secret of the dynamic—persistent in our day—of outmoded marxism? Berdyaev's late writings put an end to all ambiguity regarding his opinion of communism—uncertainty arising from some of his earlier statements about the positive values in marxism. Here he says flatly that marxism is basically false in its philosophy and evil in its results. In some ways the book deserves to be called Berdyaev's last will and testament.

*The Divine and Human,* written during the tragic years 1944-45, was published in 1952. Its Russian title was "The Existential Dialetic of the Divine and Human," enough to frighten almost any would-be purchaser. The theme of the book can be stated in one brief quotation. "God is present in freedom and love, in truth and justice, in beauty. In the face of evil and injustice, He is present, not as a judge and chastiser, but as valuation and conscience. God is the One to whom we may go out from the world's horror, ugliness, and cruelty."

*Truth and Revelation,* although written earlier than *Spirit and Caesar,* was published in 1953. Berdyaev called it "a reconsideration of the fundamental problems of Christianty in the light of spirit and truth," the summing up of a lifelong process of thought. Berdyaev said the book was definitely more philosophy than theology, although "in the last analysis it is of the question of all questions—the question of God." He pointed out the fact that revelation to man had always come through man, hastening to add that he did not mean man need be passive—a sort of speaking tube for God's revelation. On the contrary, and here Nicolai Alexandrovitch returned to his favorite theme, man called to active co-operation with God must expand and deepen his thinking as he communes with the Spirit.

Other books were planned. The autobiography closed with these lines: "I want to write one more book about the new spirituality and mysticism. At its center will be the basic intuition of my life, of man's creative theurgic action." The outline for still another book was found among Berdyaev's papers, dealing again with the fundamental ideas expressed a generation earlier in *The Meaning of the Creative Act.*[8]

An important event in Berdyaev's life in the postwar years was the honorary degree awarded him in July, 1947, by Cambridge University. He devotes half a page to it in the autobiography: "Doctor of Divinity, *honoris causa.* This is considered a great honor. . . . It is not so much a learned degree as a recognition of service." Only two other Russians, Tchaikovsky and Turgenieff, received such degrees. He was mildly amused at the fact of this whole gorgeous medieval ceremony happening to him. "They put a red mantle and a medieval velvet cap on you." It was the only time on record when Berdyaev dressed for a part. "There is a solemn procession into a great hall full of people." He was, of course, deeply conscious of the honor shown him in England: "In no other European country have I met such sympathy, such a high appreciation of my thought." As one to receive a doctorate in theology he led the procession, and after him "at some distance walked Foreign Minister Bevin, and Field Marshal Wavell," each of whom was receiving an LL. D. Berdyaev said he watched the ceremony as though it were happening to someone else and "thought about the strangeness of his fate." So Nicolai Alexandrovitch, although he had been a professor in the University of Moscow, received his first university degree at the end of his days.

The postwar years brought further evidence of his wide fame. He was invited to be one of the speakers at the Rencontres Internationales de Genève in autumn, 1947. This very select gathering brought together outstanding intellectuals from all over Europe to discuss, that particular year, "Technical Progress and Moral Progress." After "intolerable bother with visas and such" Berdyaev reached Geneva safely. Reporting that the meetings were organized by the "bourgeois world in Switzerland, naturally very hostile to communism," he was surprised to find communism so much at the center of the group's thinking. He soon discovered he was the soundest authority on marxism present, although two of the other speakers were communists. But he knew it both from within and without, and while recognizing a certain social truth in marxism, he could devastate it completely from the philosophical viewpoint. He remarked how the very "bourgeoisity" of the Swiss organizers was so much the world against which Marx could speak with some truth, that he was hindered from speaking as strongly against marxism as he might have done in another milieu.

Berdyaev had attended another international meeting in Switzerland the previous autumn:[9] the Ecumenical Institute at Bossey, not far from Geneva—organized by the World Council of Churches. There he delivered a series of lectures on contemporary philosophy from Nietzsche to Sartre. Before returning to Paris, Berdyaev spent a few days at the home of Pastor Porret in the Neuchâtelese village of Couvet. It was only a few weeks after Lydia's death, and he loved the quiet and restfulness of the village. Even here he could not be alone. Admirers from all over the world sought him out. Porret tells of one afternoon when around the tea table with Berdyaev, himself a Russian Orthodox, were a French Protestant pastor, a Roman Catholic priest, and a Japanese secretary of the YMCA.

Aside from these two journeys abroad, the last two years of Berdyaev's life were spent in his quiet home at Clamart. Eugenie continued her role of homemaker. Berdyaev said in commenting on those years that he did not know how he could have lived without this "near and special friend" toward whom he had always had "an exceptional relation. Every day we have intellectual and spiritual conversations, sometimes disagreeing. She understands much of my thought and is near my own position." It was immensely fortunate that Eugenie was so close to Berdyaev. The present monograph owes much both to her knowledge of her great brother-in-law and to the fact that she was such an intelligent and comprehending observer.

Save for Lydia's vacant place in the family circle, life went on about as usual at the house in the rue du Moulin de Pierre. Berdyaev was deeply pained by his steady disillusionment regarding freedom in the U.S.S.R. It became evident soon after the close of the war that no change had occurred in the political tyranny ruling the Russian people. He had continued to hope the church, given a certain liberty of action, might be able to play a social as well as purely spiritual role. Before he died, however, he lost even that hope, and frequently commented on the conservative tendencies among those responsible for the church in Russia. He continued to enjoy his friends and be hurt when misunderstood. From a Scandinavian editor who had published some of his articles he received this note: "I thought I was dealing with a philosopher, and am astounded to discover that he is a Soviet patriot. If I had suspected that you could sympathize with the diabolic doctrine of bolshevism, I would never have published a word of yours." On the other hand there were dozens of letters each week from men and women all over the globe whose lives had been ennobled by contact with his thought.

The spring of 1948 seemed difficult. Berdyaev grew increasingly preoccupied with the sorry condition of the world. In a penetrating article "The Third Way," he showed the absurdity of dividing the world into two hostile camps, neither one of which could claim complete moral integrity. A third front was needed, the battle front of truth— truth to be achieved in freedom at whatever cost. Even in discussions on communism versus Christianity, he sometimes experienced difficulty in defending the latter because of errors and distortions down through its history. But he continued to write and plan as always.

The Sunday afternoon discussion group on that twenty-first of March was larger than usual, and scarcely anyone noticed a difference in Berdyaev's clarity and vivacity. One friend remarked later that Berdyaev seemed more tired than normally, and about his eyes, soft and piercing at the same time, there were new creases. A small group remained after the rest had left, to indulge in a long argument about freedom. As he went to bed, Berdyaev remarked that he was very tired. In the morning he reported he had passed a restless night troubled by cramps. The doctor called, prescribed some medicine, but said there was nothing to be alarmed about. That evening Eugenie read to him. On Tuesday he began the day's regular routine, working all morning at his desk. (He once said that if he were to picture himself in heaven, it would be seated at his writing.) At lunchtime he showed Eugenie his plans for the two new books already mentioned. She recalls bits of their conversation at the table.

"Why do you waste time in writing articles? It would be better to concentrate effort on books," she remarked.

"I cannot help writing about current events," he explained; "they take place in me and I cannot refuse to answer."

About the book on mysticism, Berdyaev remarked that the new mysticism would differ from the classic type: "Up to now, each separate mystic had his personal contact with God, and from this position he prayed for the world. The whole world will be mirrored in the mysticism of the new age. . . . The body and blood of Christ are the basis of the new world-mysticism."

After lunch Berdyaev napped as usual, then returned to his desk. When he came down for tea that afternoon he told Eugenie of his pleasure at having completed *The Realm of Spirit and the Realm of Caesar*. Shortly after he went back upstairs, he called "Genie." He was dead before she could mount the stairs, sitting at his desk. The Bible was open on one side; before him was an article by R. L. Niebuhr on "God's Order and the World's Disorder," on which he had been making notes. Porret remarks how in these latter months Nicolai Alexandrovitch had been "waiting evidently for the light." He had passed into the world of light almost instantaneously. His was now "that final, most important experience, which can be described in no autobiography."[10]

It was western Good Friday—March 26, 1948—when they buried his body in the quiet little Clamart cemetery. The moving Orthodox funeral service was held in the large salon that has now become a church. Several priests, all of them friends of Nicolai Alexandrovitch, conducted the service—among them Father Nicolas Eremin, Father Serge Schevitch, and Father Stefan Svetozaroff. Father Evgraf Kovalevsky gave a sermon on "seeking the truth." The group of mourners following the hearse was truly ecumenical; Catholics and

Protestants had joined with the Orthodox to honor their common friend. One incident at the cemetery was symbolic. At the burial, the grave was found to be too small to receive the coffin. Even in death Nicolai Alexandrovitch seemed to pass beyond the rigid frame in which this world would enclose him. That "other, altogether other world" of which he had dreamed was now for him reality.

A year later the autobiography was published. He had entitled it *Self-Knowledge: An Essay in Philosophical Autobiography.* Even his personal record must serve a philosophical purpose. The English version is entitled *Dream and Reality.* As might have been expected, it is not the usual type of personal record—but rather the story and attempted analysis of his developing thought down through the years. External facts are only of secondary importance. Berdyaev usually mentions them not in order to present the events of his life but—what really interested him—to show his own reactions to them. One reviewer complained that the book omitted so many pertinent facts: the date of his marriage for instance, and more information about Shestov and other associates who were mentioned only once or twice, with no further exposition of their relationships. Almost nothing is said of his feeling for France and the people among whom he had lived for a score of years. Reading these pages, one would never suspect that some of the world's decisive battles were being fought as they were written, or that life much of the time was clouded by privation and uncertainty. It was dedicated "to my best friend Eugenie Rapp." It was characteristic of the man that a volume of balanced, measured introspection could have been written during the turmoil of World War II. The preface was dated from Pilat, in 1940, and all 375 pages except for two brief postwar supplements were completed before 1946. As a literary work it is no more perfect than his other books; it is repetitious, unsystematic, and altogether fascinating.

In the preface Berdyaev explains that it is to be a special kind of autobiography. Then he proceeds to describe four types of such literature, concluding that his book will not be exactly like any one of them. "In its purpose this book is . . . dedicated to philosophical problematics. . . . The volume is written freely, not bound to any systematic plan; . . . it contains memoirs, but this is not the most important." The past had importance for him "only as pregnant with the future," and his story tells how he "experienced the world, the whole historic process, all the events of my time, as a part of my own microcosm, as my spiritual way." He definitely leaves out most of his relationships with people "who were of the greatest importance in my personal life and my spiritual path," and strictly biographical material is often presented "only schematically." "What interests me is not so much the characterization of a milieu, but the characterization of my reaction to it." How well he holds to this purpose is evident to any reader.

Of all Berdyaev's books none had a more extensive or more enthusiastic reception by reviewers. It was described as "the self-portrait of a great and complex personality" who "had welded together in his life and thought all the psychological and intellectual incompatibilities that have plagued and tortured man in the present age." A Swiss reviewer called him "this passionate seeker for truth . . . [who] attacks a series of problems which the school philosophers have never mentioned."[11] "One of the most original thinkers of his day, with his own views on philosophy, religion, and politics," wrote Lord David Cecil. Another writer calls it the "record of a spiritual giant."

Some comment verged on the extravagant. Reviewers called it: "The most important book of the year . . . [that] would easily tilt the scale against all the novels, essays, etc. produced in any year. . . . It is worthy of being placed alongside the *Confessions* of St. Augustine, and Rousseau. . . . One of the most important spiritual and human testimonies of our epoch. Rarely have I read a book with such perspectives of a personality and of a time."[12] "The theme of man's creative significance has seldom been presented in so far-reaching existential and religious significance and in such courageous and confessional self-presentation."[13] Some critics were less enthusiastic—finding the book "exhausting as well as exalting, and pervaded by a feeling of superiority to ordinary, stupid bourgeois persons that may be natural but is not Christian." One German reviewer sounded another note—veracity and candor: "The book is a surprisingly honest, often merciless, self-presentation." *The Oxford Magazine* said that while "Berdyaev puts the whole of himself into everything he writes, none of his . . . works is so self-revealing as this."

While Berdyaev held true to the declaration in the preface that he did not intend to "lay bare his soul," and while he did omit the most intimate facets of his life, the entire book is an amazingly frank and clear-eyed analysis of himself, his inner motives, and what he thought his life had been about. Many of his life's philosophic themes reappear: the central problem of man and his relation to God, man as co-worker with God, man as microcosm and microtheos. Berdyaev's thought on revelation as essentially bilateral, given by God, received in liberty by man, was here restated together with the philosophy of history and of what is beyond. Eternity is not merely unending time but a quality that transcends time, he said. Social, cultural, and ethical problems recur, each touched anew by some living experience of the writer, each considered *sub specie aeternitatis.*

# 21

## THE SUMMING UP

Chronologically, Berdyaev's life divides almost evenly into three quarter-centuries: the years in Kiev, the years of activity in Vologda, St. Petersburg, and Moscow, and the years abroad. Geographically his life almost boxed the compass three-quarters of the way around: Kiev in the south, the remainder of his Russian days in the north, then to the west in banishment. The final quarter of the compass, the longed-for return to his homeland, Berdyaev never accomplished. But although a third of his life—and that the most productive—was spent abroad, Nicolai Alexandrovitch never ceased to be Russian. As he wrote of Khomiakoff, Berdyaev himself was "Russian to the marrow of his bones, in his dignity and in his failures—Russian elementally and Russian consciously."[1] Although a unique genius, Nicolai Alexandrovitch was much the product of his times. In a magazine article in 1914, he was writing:

> Man is lazy and his spiritual forces slumber; great shocks, personal and national catastrophes, are needed to awaken them. . . . Why it is that in the life of some creative personalities there come periods of an inflow of creative energy [and] extraordinary creative uplift . . . remains a mystery, . . . but in history . . . periods of the increase of powers of heroic inspiration coincide with catastrophic impulses.

Although the great catastrophes of revolution, civil war, and banishment had not yet come to him, Berdyaev was speaking out of his own forty years of living in and with his fatherland. What might have been his impact on the world had he never left Russia we cannot know. The real flowering of his "extraordinary creative uplift" occurred in exile. In one of the few notes made by Lydia about her husband, this passage occurs: "Ni began to read Khomiakoff's verses to me, where Khomiakoff condemns the sins of tsarist Russia, but before he had finished he stopped—'and now it is the same, the same slavery,' he said, and bursting into tears hastily left the room. I was surprised. Ni never weeps. I saw him weep only once, when his father died." His spiritual evolution set the pattern for hundreds of his fellow countrymen and thousands of his readers. He was Russian in his love of the woods and country, in the breadth of his vision and universality of interest, in his religious life in the Orthodox Church, and in his lifelong search for Truth.

Speaking of his "inborn aristocracy," Berdyaev asserted it was a matter of the spiritual rather than social life—hence his dislike for hierarchy. He did not like to be addressed as president of a society, editor of a magazine, even as head of a family. "All hierarchic order always seemed to me to be only a masquerade," he said. He never lost his youthful passion for chivalry, "eternal by the task laid upon it";[2] the idea occurred in many of his writings. "The idea of chivalry was a forecourt of the revelation about man." Various friends have compared him to a knight of old. This was in keeping with his youthfulness—the manly mind and the childlike spirit. He said in the autobiography he never ceased to think of himself as a "youth, almost a boy"; behind his aging face in the mirror he saw himself as a young man. "This is my eternal age," he said. "I remain a dreamer; . . . there is none of the wisdom of age in me." The knightly epithet— "*sans peur et sans reproche*"—could truly be applied to him.

He was *sans peur* in all the stormy disagreements of his life. If he disagreed with the state or the established church or the majority of his Russian friends in emigration, he said so decisively and without concern for the consequences to himself. "The world" he described as "more than anything else passion and the dialectic of passion." For him contact with the world was not an amiable impact; it was protest, contradiction, and conflict. He said himself that he was always a rebel. The knight in the legend who liberated the damsel from the dragon might be considered a rebel against the monster's authority. If Berdyaev was a knight, he was a rebel knight, and his insistence on his own freedom was more than a passive refusal to accept authority or discipline; it usually meant an attack upon "whatever powers there be."

In these tilts at the dragon of authority there was nothing of the poseur—nothing done for effect. Even his bitterest opponents never doubted his sincerity. "He never had double thoughts" says Remizoff. Shining all through the autobiography is "an unfeigned sincerity . . . the pathos of candor," as one reviewer put it. It was a sincerity that applied just as well to his self-analysis as to his outward actions. There is one passage where a statement about himself, twice repeated, is followed by a psychological explanation not at all to the author's credit.

He says he is like a millionaire who can afford to be careless about his finances. There were probably two elements in this attitude: on the one hand "pride, indifference (poor), and on the other love for independence and freedom (good)." As he reread the manuscript of his autobiography, Nicolai Alexandrovitch said that he had probably often idealized himself even when he seemed to belittle his qualities. But of his basic modesty there can be no doubt. His attitude toward his writing was illustrative. It was the custom among Russian authors to ask their friends to review their newest books. Berdyaev never did that. He resisted giving one of his own works to a friend who wanted to read it: "I assure you the book is not at all interesting. I am writing a better one now." His friends recall how he passed off with joking remarks their requests to describe the ceremonies honoring him at Cambridge. And it was his friends who, after his death, discovered the facts about his famous French ancestor. Although he lived in France for a quarter of a century and knew of the Choiseul line in his inheritance, Berdyaev never troubled to look up the records.

Maritain called him "that great, lonely thinker." All pioneers have been lonely. Kierkegaard, Ibsen, and Nietzsche knew loneliness. In Berdyaev's case it was due in part to his being in such constant opposition to the world about him—and this brought him into conflict even with himself. He was lonely because he was different. It is difficult to estimate the psychological role played in his life as boy and man by that thorn in the flesh, his tic, but it certainly helped to set him apart from all his comrades. His fastidious dislike of the least hint of crudeness or ugliness was another isolating factor. While most people have had the same sensitivity to a greater or lesser degree, they have usually had to master it. Berdyaev, from childhood to the grave, was free to express his faintest whim, and that again helped separate him from others.

He suffered from causes other than loneliness. He suffered from anxiety—often intense anxiety—but only over trivial matters insofar as it concerned himself: the possible result of a slight cold, the danger of missing a train. Larger matters seem not to have troubled him. During the entire German occupation he went calmly along, knowing he was a marked man for his violent anti-Hitler writing but unconcerned as to what the Gestapo might do to him. And he suffered from homesickness. He did not say it in so many words, but it could be traced between the lines of his writings. He belonged heart and soul to Russia and longed to share her fate in body as well. His exile had been nothing of his own volition, and of this he was always proud. All the years in France, he remained terribly, poignantly homesick. A French critic was surprised that the autobiography said nothing about "his love of France." This was not strange. When it came to love of a country, Nicolai Alexandrovitch's heart had room for only one, his Russian fatherland.[3]

From his sorrows he sought refuge in his writing. It was an urge as strong as drug addiction. There was tremendous release in penning "what immediately poured itself out as a reaction to life." He said it was the only sphere of life where he could always find uplift and joy. He did not expect too much joy in his own experience, although he craved it for others. Like his other emotions, however, his joys and sorrows were kept very much within himself. He may have been suffering and lonely, but in ordinary contacts it never showed—he was kindly, gracious, a welcome member of any conversation group.

Beside writing them down, Berdyaev's greatest pleasure came from sharing his thoughts with others. The sharing process has continued to spread wherever men are thinking. His thoughts shine with originality yet put into words what many of his readers have often felt. When Berdyaev wrote Mme K: "In general I do not belong to any type," he was speaking of social classification, but the statement is valid for philosophy as well. Less than a year before his death, in a biographical summary, Berdyaev said the chief subjects of his thought deal with the philosophies of religion, history, and ethics—but above all, his thought "gives expression to the original Russian religious philosophy, tinged with eschatology."[4] This was perhaps not a complete summary, but it illustrated how Berdyaev thought in terms of general principles rather than specific programs. He said it was easier for him to write an abstract book than an article on today's problems.

"By the nature of my temperament, I clothe my tormented questionings in assertive . . . form. I put questions and problems in the form of affirmations. But in its inner course my thinking is problematic, not skeptical."[5] "Skepticism," he wrote Mme K, "is always impotence."

Professor Spinka found a peculiarly fitting epithet for Berdyaev in the title of his book *Captive of Freedom*. The unconditional supremacy of freedom was one of his central themes, grounded in the Christian conviction that freedom is the result of knowing truth. Berdyaev had defended freedom for himself and others at great cost in personal suffering and broken friendships. Criticizing some of the contradictions in his books, some have felt that here Berdyaev carried freedom to the point of irresponsibility, but he would not have agreed. He was concerned first with man's freedom as inherent in the freedom of God. This he

called one of the "basic themes of his life," not only for man in relation
to society but to the whole cosmos, "to the world's harmony." Berdyaev
thought of freedom not as some formal, abstract idea, and not only
as something man could claim as a right. For him freedom was man's
heaviest responsibility, and again he would refer us to "The Grand
Inquisitor."

If man was free, for what was he free? What was the meaning of
man's life, of the world's life, of history? Nicolai Alexandrovitch recalled that the Greeks had no concept of destiny, that only in Judeo-
Christian philosophy had one attempted to find the meaning of history,
and that even here there were two sorts of meaning. Christianity is
subject to historic treatment, but in another sense the whole of human history was Christian: "Christianity is the process of history." Berdyaev called himself a "metahistorian." Few modern writers have
shown such breadth of historic vision; fewer still have possessed such a
clear intimation of man's freedom.

Calling Berdyaev a religious philosopher is not enough; he was a
Christian philosopher. Archimandrite Cyprian called him "a believing
freethinker"[6] in the light of Berdyaev's insistence upon his own con-
ceptions of the church canons. While for the very Orthodox Berdyaev
was a difficult sheep in the fold, it must be said that he aided many
people to sense the true place and proportion of the church in their
own lives and in the world. Here, as in other phases of philosophy,
Berdyaev's thinking reached out to the universal. He was like Solovieff,
first in thinking of the mission of the church to the entire world and
then of the mission of the Russian Church to the Christian Church as
a whole. And while Berdyaev had some hard words to say about present
tendencies in the Russian Orthodox Church, living as it must under
the Soviet government, he shared Solovieff's conviction that Russian
Christianity was called to special tasks in the world's Christianity. It
could serve as a way of rapprochement between Rome and the other
confessions. His own experience in the "ecumenical" meetings at
Clamart proved the rightness of this concept.

What fascinates in Berdyaev's thought, and attracts to him the truth
seekers of so many parts of the world, is perhaps first of all his capacity
to reveal his personal standpoint for today's problems and tensions. The
thoughts he put on paper came straight out of his own living with the
same questions that Christians everywhere were facing. These thoughts
were put in words that struck deep into consciousness even if one were
"not an educated man." Not that the thoughtful seeker found ready

answers here. Berdyaev did not claim to have a solution for all the world's problems. Some of his critics say he was ambiguous. Perhaps a secret of Berdyaev's ever-widening contribution to the world's thought was his striking of new fire from human minds. To many he provided a firm basis for their thinking; others took up the questions he put so clearly and went out on their own to search for the answers.

We are led to a consideration of Berdyaev's significance for our time. He speaks to men in language they understand whether they be Catholic, Orthodox or Protestant, or seekers of other faiths. Witness that memorial meeting at the Sorbonne when a Hindu called Berdyaev his master among western thinkers. It is this universal appeal, the power to stimulate creative thought in men as far apart as Protestant Switzerland and "freethinking" Chile, that has given Berdyaev's thought such movement across our times. Exiled by a tsar, expelled by the Soviet government, at odds with most of his fellow countrymen outside Russia, never with more than a limited group of sympathizers, his influence on the entire world's religious thinking is undeniable. Professor Zenkovsky says Berdyaev was chiefly a moralist. If he uses the word in the sense of Webster's definition "a teacher of morals," it is not enough. Berdyaev never pretended to be a teacher: "I am neither a pedagogue nor a guide, but only a seeker for the truth." He disclaimed ever wanting to preach, yet his message stirred men's souls. In 1910, Nicolai Alexandrovitch was writing: "Both in the Russian intelligentsia and the Russian people a shift in will and consciousness is taking place that will lead to another feeling for life and another concept of the world."[7] Because this shift took place in him, and because he was given the words to tell it to others, the new concept of the world has crossed and recrossed the map. In a recent letter Eugenie wrote: "Our meetings continue, devoted to the works of Nicolai Alexandrovitch. Young people come to visit the room where their favorite philosopher worked. I am glad that . . . I can help, even a little, to extend the spiritual experience of Nicolai Alexandrovitch so much needed by the world." Because he had lived with the world's spiritual needs, because what he wrote came directly out of that experience, because he helped other men see their spiritual situation in the light of eternity, Berdyaev's influence will continue to expand.

Thinker and prophet and champion of freedom, how shall his epitaph be framed? In no better words, perhaps, than in what he said was the one beatitude to which he could lay claim: ". . . they who hunger and thirst after righteousness."

# Notes

Most of the sources not indicated by notes are from unpublished material such as Eugenie's manuscript and the letters to Mme K. References are to texts in English whenever such are available, and otherwise to the Russian original—indicated by (R). Because I have made my own translations in all instances, the English text referred to may not exactly coincide with that given here. Reference is made below to *Dream and Reality* wherever my translation coincides approximately with this English translation of Berdyaev's autobiography; where quotation is from the Russian original, the reference given below is "autobiography."

D. A. L.

## Preface

1. Bishop Michael in the *Journal of the Moscow Patriarchate*, No. 1 (1956).
2. Leontieff, p. 163(R).
3. Fielding Clarke, *Introduction to Berdyaev*, p. 79.
4. Philip Guedalla, "The Method of Biography," *Royal Society of Arts*, Vol. LXXXVII (London, 1939).
5. Autobiography, pp. 147-48(R).

## Chapter 1. Turning Point

1. In Russia two names are used for a given person, his Christian name and his patronymic—"ovitch" means "son of"—hence this double name indicating Nicolai as the son of Alexander Berdyaev. The double cognomen is used for any adult—be he clerk or commissar, peasant or professor. The equivalent of "Mr." is used only with a stranger, and one of the first questions put to him is "what is your name and patronymic?" Thus, calling Berdyaev Nicolai Alexandrovitch has nothing of affectation; it is the way all his friends spoke to him and thought about him. The feminine form (daughter of) is "ovna." Berdyaev's wife and her sister were Lydia and Eugenie "Yudifovna" respectively. Further explanation is necessary in this instance. "Yudif" (Judith) is a woman's name. Their father was actually named Jude, after the saint on whose day he was born; but "Judovna" sounds so much like "daughter of Judas" that the two sisters chose to call it Judif.

289

2. Berdyaev's letter to Lydia from Riga, 1927.
3. This venerable structure was destroyed during the late war.
4. Writing from Reval just after the Riga visit, Berdyaev told his wife: "I could not have imagined that I give people so much, and that they have such need of me. It appears I have had great influence in the spiritual life of many."

## Chapter 2. "Cercle de Famille"

1. An exact equivalent of this Russian rank does not exist abroad. It corresponds to the German *Geheimrat*, and approximately to our "counsellor of embassy."
2. Michaud, *Biographie Universelle*, VII, 190.
3. This was true until the reign of Peter I. He inaugurated a standing army, and reserve officers (the gentry) could be called into service as needed but were not required to bring their peasants.

## Chapter 3. *A Doll Named Prince André*

1. A *Symposium of Biographies of Men of the Cavalier Guard Regiment* (author Panchulidzev, St. Petersburg: 1901-8) gives the following data: "Alexander Michailovitch Berdyaev, a Cavalier Guard officer, son of Michail Nicolaevitch Berdyaev; born 1837, educated in the Corpus. On June 16, 1856, . . . advanced to Cornet; on October 13, 1856, for family reasons released from service as a Lieutenant. In April, 1859, married Princess Alexandra Sergeevna (born 1838), daughter of the Court Chamberlain, Prince Kudasheff. His father owned 960 souls in the province of Kiev, an entailed estate in Poland, and an estate in the province of Kaluga."
2. From one of Berdyaev's letters to Hippius, it appears this was in 1907.
3. Eugenie says that Obuchovo, the family estate near Kiev, was sold at the insistence of Berdyaev's mother.
4. M. Channing Pierce, *Soren Kierkegaard*, p. 14.
5. It was in 1936. Berdyaev wrote Lydia: "I saw Mukalov. His material situation is terrible. How to help him? This troubles me."

## Chapter 4. *The Barometer of Society*

1. P. 178.

## Chapter 5. *The Athens of the North*

1. In Russia the word "communist" was in abeyance from the 1905 revolution until Lenin, returning in 1917, brought it again into use.
2. Remizoff describes Nicolai Konstantinovitch Mukalov as "a mitchman (past mate) and an unusually noble character. No philosopher, he was courageous and kind. A big man, he was as simple as he was big, erect and well formed. He never wrote about or discussed philosophic questions."

## Chapter 6. The Unspeakable Mystery

1. Mme Kuskova reports that among others attending the first meeting were Struve, Bulgakov, herself and husband (Prokopovitch), and Petrunkevitch with his wife. There were no revolutionary extremists, and the discussion centered chiefly on what was to be done with the monarchy. About the same group attended the Schaffhausen meeting, and although the tsarist police knew all about it, no one was arrested on returning to Russia.
2. *The Meaning of the Creative Act*, pp. 180 ff.
3. *The New Religious Consciousness and Society*, p. 160(R).
4. *The Russian Idea*, p. 225(R).
5. *The New Religious Consciousness and Society*, p. 226(R).
6. *The Meaning of the Creative Act*, p. 184.
7. *Ibid.*, p. 187.
8. *Ibid.*, p. 183.
9. *Ibid.*, p. 190.
10. *Ibid.*, p. 193.
11. *Ibid.*, p. 199.
12. *Ibid.*, p. 199.
13. *Ibid.*, p. 208.
14. *Ibid.*, p. 212.
15. *The New Religious Consciousness and Society*, p. 165(R).
16. *Ibid.*, p. 222.
17. *Ibid.*, p. 215.
18. *Ibid.*, p. 209.
19. *Dream and Reality*, p. 22.
20. *Ibid.*, p. 23.
21. *The Meaning of the Creative Act*, p. 192.
22. *Ibid.*, p. 192.
23. *Ibid.*, p. 202.
24. *The Russian Idea*, p. 225(R).
25. *Dream and Reality*, p. 50.
26. *Leontieff*, p. 21(R).
27. *Ibid.*, p. 17(R).
28. *The New Religious Consciousness and Society*, p. 163(R).
29. *The Meaning of the Creative Act*, p. 194.
30. *Ibid.*, p. 197.

## Chapter 7. The Ivory Tower

1. "For the first few days joyful feelings prevailed. It seemed that the promised freedom would be immediately clothed in the form of law and realized, . . . the administration hostile to the people . . . removed, . . . the Duma . . . convoked—and that would be the end of the old regime. It seemed, also, that revolutionary activities ought to cease. . . ." S. L. Tolstoi, *Sketches of the Past* (Moscow: 2nd ed., 1956), p. 221(R).

2. *The Russian Idea,* p. 246(R).
3. This would not have been true of most of the intelligentsia of Berdyaev's own generation. They were all too liberal-minded to be easily accepted into the government apparatus.
4. *The Russian Idea,* p. 247(R).
5. Andre Byeli, *The Beginning of an Age* (quoted by Motchulsky), p. 321 (R).
6. Of V. Ivanoff, Remizoff says: "He was a sort of experimenter in cults. Besides Orthodoxy he had tried Protestantism and Roman Catholicism, plus Buddhism, anthroposophy, and the Greek mysteries. That evening was a sort of playing at blasphemy."
7. *The Russian Idea,* p. 225(R).
8. *Ibid.,* p. 225.
9. C. Motchulsky, *Andre Byeli,* p. 90(R).
10. *The Beginning of an Age* (quoted by Motchulsky), p. 75(R).
11. *Ibid.,* p. 430(R).
12. *Ibid.,* pp. 430 ff.(R).
13. Sobornost is a word that baffles all attempts at an adequate translation, not alone into English but into most western languages. A *sobor* is a council, a gathering, and the word *sobornost* has often been rendered as "conciliarity," which does not fully express the wealth of meaning of the Russian word. "Togetherness," usually togetherness in the church, is a better approximation. A French theologian, P. Congar, has recently offered a new approach that is somewhat easier in French than English. Using the word "collegiate" in its ecclesiastical sense, he produces the word "collegiality." In *Realm of Spirit and the Realm of Caesar,* Berdyaev gave his own idea of the word's meaning: "Church sobornost does not mean authority . . . rather, it is the communion in love of church people with the Holy Spirit." Then he devoted two pages to the distinction between collectivism and *sobornost,* disputing the idea that *sobornost* is mere "togetherness," and beside the element of communion in the Holy Spirit introduced the idea of "community," "which leaves judgment and conscience in the depths of man's heart, . . . something directly opposed to any authoritarian concept of the church." *The Realm of Spirit and the Realm of Caesar,* pp. 122 ff.

Chapter 8. *"Sub Specie Aeternitatis"*

1. F. A. Stepun, *Memoirs,* I, 320(R).
2. This short-lived organization must not be confused with the "Religious-Philosophical Assembly," under the aegis of Merezhkovsky.
3. Z. Hippius-Merezhkovsky, *Dmitri Merezhovsky,* p. 186(R).
4. "Liberal" is here used in the American sense. In Russia, the word does not connote the very left wing.
5. *Fakely* ("Torches"), II, 142(R).

6. *Sub Specie Aeternitatis,* p. 1(R).
7. *Ibid.,* p. 2.
8. *Ibid.,* p. 27.
9. *Ibid.,* p. 239.
10. *Ibid.,* p. 242.
11. *Ibid.,* p. 185.
12. *Ibid.,* p. 24.
13. *Ibid.,* p. 435.
14. *Ibid.,* p. 433.
15. *Ibid.,* p. 4.
16. A periodical founded in Paris. Cf. Chap. 14.
17. *Torches,* p. 145-147(R).
18. *Ibid.,* p. 146(R).
19. *Ibid.,* p. 150(R).
20. *Ibid.,* p. 153(R).
21. *Dream and Reality,* p. 156.
22. Motchulsky, *Andre Byeli,* p. 104(R).
23. *Dream and Reality,* p. 148.
24. *Ibid.,* p. 146.

Chapter 9. *"The Pillar and Bulwark of the Truth"*

1. Hippius, *Dmitri Merezhkovsky,* pp. 182-83(R).
2. Motchulsky, *Andre Byeli,* p. 162(R).
3. *Dream and Reality,* p. 190.
4. *Ibid.,* p. 189.
5. Stepun, *Memoirs,* I, 280(R).
6. *Ibid.,* p. 281(R).
7. *The Russian Idea,* p. 229(R).
8. Boris Petrovitch Vycheslavtseff (d. 1954), former *Privat-dozent* (unsalaried lecturer) at the University of Moscow, was long a collaborator with Berdyaev in the Religious-Philosophical Society and *Put.* Stepun calls him "one of the most brilliant orators of the Moscow philosophers."
9. Motchulsky, *Andre Byeli,* p. 111(R).
10. *The Russian Idea,* p. 237(R).
11. Motchulsky, *Andre Byeli,* p. 277(R).
12. Like Tolstoi, whose interest in high society and peasants was attested by his brilliant descriptions of these two social groups in contrast to generally colorless descriptions of the middle class, Berdyaev seems to have gotten on better with peasants than with the bourgeoisie.
13. *Dream and Reality,* p. 28.
14. Stepun, *Memoirs,* I, 257(R).
15. Antonov, *Russkie Svetskie Bogoslovy i ich Religiosnoe-Obschestvennoye Mirozrenie* ("Russian Lay Theologians and their Religious-Social World-Views" [St. Petersburg: 1912]) (R).

Chapter 10. A Declaration of Independence

1. Berdyaev, Bulgakov, Gershenson, Izgoeff, Kistakovsky, Struve, Frank.
2. Vyechi ("Milestones").
3. Ibid., p. 22(R).
4. V. N. Ilyin believes Joachim de Floris derived his idea from the "puri-fication" movement that developed around St. Francis.
5. The Meaning of the Creative Act, pp. 171 ff.
6. Ibid., pp. 222 ff.
7. Ibid., p. 256.
8. Russkaya Mysl (October, 1916)(R).
9. Mysl i Slovo ("Thought and Word" [Moscow: 1917]), pp. 282-98(R).
10. The Aryan Path (London: October, 1955).

Chapter 11. War, Revolution, Banishment

1. Stepun, Memoirs, I, 305(R).
2. G. Shavelsky, Memoirs, I, 164(R).
3. Ibid., I, 97(R).
4. The Destiny of Russia, pp. 7 ff.(R).
5. Ibid., p. 126(R).
6. Ibid., p. 154(R).
7. P. Miliukoff, Memoirs, II, 282(R).
8. Shavelsky, Memoirs, II, 280(R).
9. Autobiography, p. 178(R).
10. Cf., The Russian Idea.
11. A. Koestler, Darkness at Noon (New York: Modern Library), p. 267.
12. Dostoievsky, p. 12(R).
13. The Meaning of History was originally Berdyaev's course of lectures in 1919-20 Dostoievsky grew out of lectures in 1920-21. How daring these lectures were is evident from the fact that until 1955, a generation later, the Soviet government never published Dostoievsky's complete works.
14. Stepun, Memoirs, I, 191-92(R).
15. Dostoievsky, p. 83(R).
16. "Ossorgin" was a penname; his passport read "Ilyin."
17. Autobiography, p. 263(R).
18. The Spirit of Russia, pp. 39-40(R).
19. Ibid., p. 32(R).
20. Ibid., p. 9(R).
21. Ibid., p. 5(R).
22. Ibid., p. 13(R).
23. The Russian Idea, p. 254(R).
24. The New Russian Book, Nos. 9 & 10 (1922), gives the following list: B. P. Babkin, A. L. Baikov, N. A. Berdyaev, G. P. Eichenwald, S. L. Frank, I. A. Ilyin, A. A. Kizewetter, Lapshin, N. O. Lossky, Myakotin, N. A. Ossorgin, Peshechonov, V. A. Rozenberg, Pitirim Sorokin.

*Chapter 12. Berlin*

1. Zaitseff, who with his wife had been permitted to leave Soviet Russia "for reasons of health" in the spring of 1922, reports how one summer (1923) he and his wife, together with Professor and Mrs. S. L. Frank, shared a house with the Berdyaevs at the resort of Ostseebad, and how they all appreciated Nicolai Alexandrovitch's gaiety and animation.
2. The Nicolas Berdyaev Society, an international organization with headquarters at 29 rue St. Didier, Paris 16e, was founded after his death to preserve his memory and extend abroad his teachings. Its membership is open to anyone interested in the Society's purposes.
3. Metropolitan Eulogius, wise and revered leader of the Russian church, was Exarch of the Moscow Patriarchate for Russians in western Europe—a position created after the revolution and the consequent emigration. After Moscow had made what he considered political demands on his clergy (1927), he placed himself under the Ecumenical Patriarchate of Constantinople.
4. Autobiography, p. 273(R).
5. Author of the significant (and first) *History of Russian Philosophy* (1950), and Dean of St. Sergius Orthodox Theological Institute.
6. Published in English as *The End of Our Time*.
7. Zenkovsky, *Russian Thinkers and Europe* (2nd ed.), p. 271(R).

*Chapter 13. Paris in the Fall*

1. It will be recalled that this same difference caused much difficulty between Berdyaev's parents.
2. Mrs. West, Berdyaev says, was "an original and interesting person, . . . deeply religious in the Biblical-Protestant sense," interested in "the realization in life of the Christianity of the Gospels." She and Lydia were great friends, and she played a leading role in a Bible study group that met for a number of years in the Berdyaev home.
3. *Dostoievsky*, p. 90(R).
4. Lydia's recurrent dissatisfaction with their living arrangements seems to have been another cause of family difficulties. In several of Berdyaev's letters to his wife this item recurs: "I do not speak of the discomfort for me personally, . . . but every time when you . . . are in an especially difficult mood and bring up the apartment question, I feel it as a reproach—even as an accusation." (Pontigny, 1930[?]). In another letter (Nice, 1928), Nicolai Alexandrovitch says he has decided to yield to her desire and move into Paris. But how to live through the difficult period until then? "From my heart I ask, even pray you, my dear, to help me through that stage."
5. Hippius (*Dmitri Merezhkovsky*, p. 186) says: "We received a postcard from the Troitsko-Sergievsky Monastery in which Berdyaev informed us

that with his wife he had 're-entered' the Orthodox church." It was apparently in 1908.
6. Father Abrikosov was the center of a very orthodox group of Thomists having a reputation for austerity and piety.
7. Autobiography, p. 28(R).
8. Ibid., p. 34(R).
9. Eugene Porret, *Berdiaeff, Prophète des Temps Nouveaux*, pp. 123 ff.
10. Leontieff, p. 30(R).
11. Ibid., p. 249(R).
12. Autobiography, p. 195(R).
13. Somerset Maugham, *The Summing Up*, p. 16.
14. Autobiography, p. 368(R).
15. *Esprit et Liberté* (English title: *Freedom and the Spirit*).


## Chapter 14. In and Out of Organizations

1. *Dream and Reality*, p. 250.
2. Autobiography, p. 281(R).
3. Ibid., p. 350(R).
4. *Dmitri Merezhkovsky*, p. 31(R).
5. Autobiography, p. 350(R).
6. "Put," No. 49 (October-December, 1935)(R).
7. Friends of both Berdyaev and "Put" begged him not to publish this article. They warned him it would cause withdrawal of most of the magazine's regular contributors. Berdyaev was adamant. The journal never recovered from the loss of so many authors.
8. "There was a meeting in Savoie on the Swiss frontier, with the participation of Dr. Mott, at which it was decided to issue the journal 'Put.' " (Berdyaev in "Put," No. 49, p. 20.) The meeting took place at Annemasse on the French side, because it was difficult to secure Swiss visas for the Russians.
9. Autobiography, p. 276(R).
10. Pontigny, a restored and modernized medieval abbey, is a retreat house where intellectuals may live and study. For years it has been the custom during the month of August to organize three "decades," during which prominent intellectuals of France meet with their peers of other nationalities for discussions of philosophical, literary, and social-political problems.
11. Autobiography, p. 289(R).


## Chapter 15. Broken Friendships

1. "We quarreled with Struve about the amount of indemnity to be paid by Russia at the close of the war. We never had any contact afterward" (Kuskova).
2. Leontieff, p. 24(R).
3. From a hitherto unpublished chapter of the autobiography.
4. Autobiography, p. 329(R).

5. Writing Lydia, Berdyaev said: "What a fine person Shestov is—much better than I am, although he is not a Christian. But he has a slight tinge of bourgeoisity not shared by me. . . . He says that in summer, in the midst of nature, he becomes a plant. I, on the contrary, am always inwardly philosophizing." The two occasionally took their vacations together. More often, Berdyaev went to some watering place alone.
6. Dmitri Merezhkovsky, p. 64(R).


Chapter 16. *"The Light of Russia"*

1. One of the titles given to the Russian Church.
2. Autobiography, p. 191(R).
3. *The Realm of Spirit and the Realm of Caesar,* p. 109.
4. *Freedom and the Spirit,* p. x.
5. *Ibid.,* p. xviii.
6. Khomiakoff, p. 61(R).
7. *Freedom and the Spirit,* p. viii.
8. *Poslednie Novosti* (Paris), September 13, 1927(R).
9. Autobiography, p. 185(R).
10. *Ibid.,* p. 187(R).
11. *The New Religious Consciousness and Society,* last paragraph(R).
12. Autobiography, p. 322(R).
13. George Seaver, *Nicolas Berdyaev,* p. 47.
14. Autobiography, p. 199(R).
15. Khomiakoff, p. 95(R).
16. *The Russian Idea,* p. 243(R).
17. Autobiography, pp. 197-98(R).
18. Leontieff, p. 259(R).
19. Autobiography, p. 56(R).


Chapter 17. *Reluctant Preceptor*

1. Autobiography, p. 285(R).
2. *Ibid.,* p. 298(R).
3. "Put," No. 58 (January, 1939)(R).
4. *Russkie Novosti* (Paris), October 4, 1946(R).
5. *Neue Zürcher Zeitung,* February 26, 1954.


Chapter 18. *The Thinker*

1. Stepun, *Memoirs,* I, 264(R).
2. *Dostoievsky,* p. 30(R).
3. Autobiography, p. 277(R).
4. *Dukhovni Krisis Intelligentsii,* p. 3(R).
5. Autobiography, pp. 239-40(R).

6. Dostoievsky, p. 19(R).
7. Ibid., p. 22.
8. Autobiography, p. 98(R).
9. Ibid., p. 281(R).
10. Zenkovsky, Russian Thinkers and Europe, p. 263(R).
11. Torches, p. 142(R).
12. Autobiography, p. 99(R).
13. The Russian Idea, p. 243(R).
14. Berdyaev used this in the original German as the motto to head his Meaning of the Creative Act. (Translation mine, D. A. L.)
15. Cf., George Seaver's masterly chapters on man's relation to God and to Christ, pp. 27-71.
16. Autobiography, p. 195(R).
17. Ibid., p. 195(R).
18. Romans VIII, 18-25.
19. Leontieff, p. 260(R).
20. Ibid., p. 257 (R).
21. Sub Specie Aeternitatis, p. 115(R).
22. Autobiography, p. 225(R).
23. Problemy Idealizma, p. 136(R).
24. Leontieff, p. 123(R).
25. Problemy Idealizma, p. 101(R).
26. Dostoievsky, p. 99(R).
27. Ibid., p. 99
28. Leontieff, p. 261(R).
29. The Russian Idea, p. 128(R).
30. Channing Pearce, Soren Kierkegaard, pp. 29, 37.
31. "Put," No. 58(R).
32. Dostoievsky, p. 7(R).
33. Ibid., p. 69.
34. Voprosy Filosofii i Psychologii, No. 1 (1907) (R).
35. Dostoievsky, p. 45(R).
36. Ibid., p. 157.

Chapter 19. The Prophet

1. From The Meaning of History, quoted by Zenkovsky in Russian Thinkers and Europe (2nd ed.), p. 265(R).
2. The Fate of Man in the Modern World, pp. 129-30.
3. Ibid., p. 131.
4. Autobiography, pp. 280-81(R).
5. Nauka i Zhizn ("Science and Life"), No. 12 (1956) (R).
6. The Russian Idea, pp. 193 ff.(R).
7. Ibid., p. 218.
8. Autobiography, p. 306(R).

Chapter 20. *Waiting for the Light*

1. Quoted by Porret, p. 159.
2. Father Dmitri Klepinin and his wife, who were to occupy the house during the Berdyaevs' absence, moved in the next morning. They spent the following days and nights sorting Berdyaev's papers, hiding in the attic those they thought the Germans would consider incriminating.
3. *Dmitri Merezhkovsky*, p. 242(R).
4. *Autobiography*, p. 362(R).
5. In the Clinique Franklin, the surgeon was Dr. Henri Martin.
6. *Autobiography*, p. 365-6(R).
7. *Russkie Novosti*, October 24, 1946(R).
8. Its tentative title was "A Philosophy of the End."
9. October, 1946.
10. *Autobiography*, p. 370(R).
11. *Neue Zürcher Zeitung*, February 26, 1954.
12. *Stimmen der Zeit*, Vol. VIII (Munich, 1954).
13. *Rhein-Neckar Zeitung*, October 17/18, 1953.


Chapter 21. *The Summing Up*

1. *Khomiakoff*, p. 215(R).
2. *The Meaning of the Creative Act*, p. 265.
3. Some pages of the autobiography's original manuscript, critical of French intellectual life, were eliminated before printing.
4. From a biographical summary Berdyaev sent to Professor Spinka in 1947.
5. *Freedom and the Spirit*, p. xviii.
6. *Novy Zhurnal*, No. 23 (1950)(R).
7. *Dukhovni Krisis Intelligentsii*, p. 1(R).

# Bibliography

## I. Books by Berdyaev

Where no English version exists, the title is given in Russian with an English translation; *indicates a collection of previously published articles. Listing is in the order of writing or first publication; the date in the left hand column is that of first publication.

1901—*Subjektivism i Individualism v Obschestvennoi Filosofii* ("Subjectivism and Individualism in Social Philosophy," a critical essay on N. K. Michailovsky [St. Petersburg: Popov]). Pp. 267.

1903—*Problemy Idealizma* (Problems of Idealism [Moscow: Moscow Psychological Society]).

1907—*Sub Specie Aeternitatis* (St. Petersburg: Pirozhkov). Pp. 437.

1907—*Novoe Religioznoe Soznanie i Obschestvennost* ("The New Religious Consciousness and Society" [St. Petersburg: Pirozhkov]). Pp. 233.

1910—*Dukhovni Krisis Intelligentsii* ("The Spiritual Crisis of the Intelligentsia" [St. Petersburg: Obschestvennaya Polza]). Pp. 304.

1911—*Filosofia Svobody* ("The Philosophy of Freedom" [Moscow: Put]). Pp. 281.

1912—*Alexei Stepanovitch Khomiakov* ("A. S. Khomiakoff" [Moscow: Put]). Pp. 251.

1915—*Dusha Russii* ("The Spirit of Russia" [Moscow: Sytin]). Pp. 42.

1916—*The Meaning of the Creative Act* (London: V. Gollancz, 1955; New York: Harper & Brothers, 1955). Pp. 344.

1918—*Sudba Rossii* ("The Fate of Russia" [Moscow: Leman & Sacharov]). Pp. 240.

1922—*Filosofia Dostoevskago* ("The Philosophy of Dostoievsky" [St. Petersburg: Epocha]).

1923—*Dostoievsky* (London: Sheed & Ward, 1934). Pp. 218.

1923—*The Meaning of History* (London: Bles, 1936; New York: Scribners, 1936). Pp. 270.

1923—*Filosofia Neravenstva* ("The Philosophy of Inequality" [Berlin: Obelisk]). Pp. 242.

1924—*The New Middle Ages* (Russian title; published in English as *The End of Our Time* [London: Sheed & Ward, 1932]). Pp. 143.

1926—*Leontieff* (London: Bles, 1940). Pp. 270.

301

1927/28—*Freedom and the Spirit* (London: Bles; New York: Scribners, 1935). Vol. I, pp. 271; vol. II, pp. 235.
1931—*Christianity and Class War* (London: Sheed & Ward, 1933). Pp. 141.
1931—*The Destiny of Man* (London: Bles; New York: Scribners, 1935). Pp. 320.
1934—*Myself and the World of Objects* (Russian title; published in English as *Solitude and Society* [London: Bles, 1938]). Pp. 192.
1934—*The Fate of Man in the Modern World* (London: S.C.M. Press; Milwaukee: Morehouse, 1935). Pp. 84.
1937—*The Spirit and Reality* (London: Bles). Pp. 175.
1937—*The Origin of Russian Communism* (London: Bles). Pp. 240.
1939—*Slavery and Freedom* (London: Bles; New York: Scribners, 1939). Pp. 222.
1946—*The Russian Idea* (London: Bles; New York: Macmillan, 1947). Pp. 260.
1947—*An Essay in Eschatological Metaphysics* (Russian title; published in English as *The Beginning and the End* [London: Bles; New York: Harper & Brothers, 1952]). Pp. 219.
1947—*Existential Dialectic of the Divine and the Human* (Russian title; published in English as *The Divine and the Human* [London: Bles]). Pp. 248.
1949—*Self-Knowledge, An Essay in Philosophical Autobiography* (Russian title; published in English as *Dream and Reality* [London: Bles, 1950]). Pp. 375.
1949—*The Realm of Spirit and the Realm of Caesar* (London: Gollancz, 1952; New York: Harper & Brothers, 1953). Pp. 182.
1953—*Truth and Revelation* (London: Bles; New York: Harper & Brothers, 1954). Pp. 156.

## II. Books about Berdyaev

Clarke, O. F., *Introduction to Berdyaev* (London: Bles, 1950).
Porret, E., *Nicolas Berdiaeff, Prophète des Temps Nouveaux* (Neuchâtel: Delachaux et Nestlé, 1951).
Seaver, George, *Nicolas Berdyaev* (London: Jas. Clarke, 1950).
Spinka, M., *Nicolas Berdyaev: Captive of Freedom* (Philadelphia: Westminster Press, 1950).
Rössler, R., *Das Weltbild Nikolai Berdjajews* (Göttingen: Vanderhoek und Ruprecht, 1956).
The series of ten essays on Berdyaev published in Tokyo by Mr. Sadao Taguchi are almost the equivalent of a book.

## III. Other books cited

Channing-Pearce, M., *Sören Kierkegaard* (London: Jas. Clarke & Co., 1950).
Hippius, Z., *Dmitri Merezhkovsky* (Paris: YMCA Press, 1951).

Ivanoff, G., *Petersburg Winters* (New York: Chekhov Publishing House, 1952).

Izwolsky, Hélène, *Light Before Dusk* (New York and Toronto: Longmans, Green, 1942).

Miller, K., *Francuskaya Emigratsia v Rossii* ("The French Emigration in Russia" [Paris: Rodnik, 1931]).

Miliukoff, Paul, *Memoirs* (New York: Chekhov Publishing House, 1955).

Motchulsky, C., *Andre Byeli* (Paris: YMCA Press, 1955).

*Mysl i Slovo, Filosoficheski Ezhegodnik* ("Thought and Word, a Philosophical Annual" [Moscow: Leman and Sacharoff, 1917]).

Tyrkova-Williams, Ariadne, *Na Putax k Svobode* ("On the Way to Liberty" [New York: Chekhov Publishing House, 1952]).

Remizoff, A., *Kukha* (Berlin: Gazhebin, 1923).

Shavelsky, George, *Memoirs* (New York: Chekhov Publishing House, 1954). Two volumes.

Stepun, Fedor, *Memoirs* (New York: Chekhov Publishing House, 1956). Two volumes.

Zenkovsky, V. V., *Russian Thinkers and Europe* (Paris: YMCA Press, 2nd ed., 1955).

# INDEX

Abrikosov, Father, 138, 179
Academy of Arts (St. Petersburg), 10
Academy of St. Sergius, 68, 195, 201, 234, 236, 269
Akhmatova, Anna, 237, 274
Akimushka, 121
Aksakov, I. S., 274
"Alexandria," 18, 24, 26, 38
Alexeev, General, 28
Alexei, Elder, 114, 220
All-Russian Society of Writers, 152
Anderson, Paul B., 234
Andreev, Leonid, 62, 72
Angelus Silesius, 127, 246, 254
Anti-Christ, the Spirit of, 249
Antony, Archbishop, 117, 131, 138, 139, 217
Arsenieff, N. S., 166
Aussem, Otto, 58
Authors' Bookshop, 153
Avenarius, 42
Axelrod, 41
Azeff, 39

Baader, Franz, 180, 247
"Babaki," 30, 119, 120, 121, 132, 154, 176, 227, 228
Bach, J. S., 194
Bachmetieff, Sophie Nicolaevna, 12
Bakunin, Michail, 48, 49
Barth, Karl, 181
Baudelaire, Charles, 195
Beethoven, Ludwig van, 3, 194
Belaya Tserkov, 18, 22, 38
Belinsky, V. G., 101
Berdyaev, Alexander Michailovitch (father), 11, 13, 14
Berdyaev, Alexander Sergeevitch (nephew), 20
Berdyaev, Michail Nicolaevitch (grandfather), 11, 12
Berdyaev, Nicolai Michailovitch (great-grandfather), 11
Berdyaev, Lydia Judifovna (wife), see Trusheff
Berdyaev, Serge Alexandrovitch (brother), 19, 20, 21, 33, 51
Berdyaev Society, ix, 162

Bergson, Henri, 242
Bernhardt, Sarah, 137
Bevin, E., 276
Bièvres, 199
Black Heads, 2
"Black Mass," 88
Blanchot, M., 176
Bles, Geoffrey, 235
Blok, Alexander, 104, 109, 110, 140, 227
"Bloody Sunday," 81, 87
Boegner, Marc, 199, 234
Boehme, Jacob, 121, 127, 180, 187, 254, 255
Bogdanov, A., 58, 61
Bonch-Bruevitch A., 138
Bossey, Switzerland, 223, 276
Botticelli, Sandro, 133, 194
Branicky, Countess, 18, 38
Breshkovskaya, Catherine, 63
British Museum, 8
Bucharin, N. I., 263
Bulgakov, Father Serge, 65, 68, 71, 72, 83, 85, 89, 93, 97, 99, 100, 103, 104, 105, 111, 113, 114, 116, 118, 136, 138, 158, 192, 195, 196, 197, 201, 203, 210, 232, 239, 249, 255, 258
"Bund," the, 41, 71
Byeli, André, 49, 86, 87, 89, 93, 94, 95, 104, 109, 110, 112, 116, 118, 119, 127, 146, 153, 154, 204, 208, 227, 243, 258

"Cadet Corpus," the, 9, 26, 27
Cain, Jules, 211
Cambridge, 275, 284
Carlyle, Thomas, 34
Catherine II (The Great), 7, 8, 9, 11
Cecil, Lord David, 280
"Cercle de Famille," 7
Chaadaev, M., 242
Chaliapin, Boris, 137
Chartres, France, 3
Chaux-de-Fonds, Switzerland, 70
Chekhov, Anton, 72
Chelpanoff, Prof. G. I., 35
Cherepin, General, 16

Chernishevsky, N. G., 32, 144
Choiseul, Josephine-Mathilda (grandmother; m. Prince Kudasheff), 11
Choiseul-Beaupré, Marie-Gabriel, Count of (later Gouffier; great-great-grandfather), 7, 8, 9, 10
Choiseul-Gouffier, Antoine Louis Octave, Count of (great-grandfather), 7, 9, 10, 11
Christ, 16, 98, 99, 100, 105, 108, 117, 121, 139, 149, 163, 217, 221, 222, 228, 229, 237, 246, 248, 253, 254, 260
Chulkoff, George, 86, 93, 103
Chulkova, Vera, 162
Clamart, France, 170, 171, 176, 180, 188, 206, 210, 211, 267, 268, 271, 276
Clarke, Fielding, 239, 245, 247, 261
Constantinople, Turkey, 8, 9
Cyprian, Archimandrite, 286

Dante, 242
Darwin, Charles R., 44
Dehme, Frau, 160, 161
de Maistre, Joseph, 206, 243, 250
de Monbrison, Mme, 210, 268
Descartes, René, 163
Dewey, John, 181
Diaghlieff, S. P., 101, 190
Dickens, Charles, 176
Donatello, 194
Dostoievsky, Feodor, 17, 25, 48, 49, 52, 82, 88, 99, 108, 117, 167, 168, 176, 180, 187, 209, 221, 241, 242, 243, 244, 254, 257, 258
Dragomirov, Governor-General, 47
Dreling, Valentina, 62
Duma (Aug. 1905), 14, 70, 81
Duse, Eleonora, 137
Dzershinsky, Felix, 149, 152

Eckhart, Meister, 254, 255
Eichenwald, G. P., 166
Eidelman, Boris, 50
Elgin, Lord, 8
Engels, F., 107, 242
Epoch of Creativity, 135
Epoch of Law, 135
Epoch of Redemption, 135
Eremin, Father Nicolas, 278
Ern, V. F., 115, 118, 138, 203, 204, 214
Eszterhazy, Count, 9

Eugenie Rapp (sister-in-law), x, 22, 36, 43, 69, 72, 73, 111, 118, 119, 121, 122, 123, 124, 125, 126, 132, 148, 149, 151, 154, 155, 158, 159, 162, 170, 171, 172, 173, 175, 176, 178, 179, 182, 187, 188, 189, 190, 204, 207, 208, 209, 212, 221, 225, 226, 227, 228, 239, 259, 268, 269, 270, 273, 276, 277, 278, 279, 287
Eulogius, Metropolitan, 145, 163, 166, 195, 197, 204, 211, 220, 225, 236

Faulkner, William, 176
Fedotoff, G. P., 197, 199, 204, 208, 211
Fedotoff, Mrs. G. P., ix, 208
Feodor, Bishop, 114
Filosofov, D. V., 62, 89, 92, 96, 103
Florence, Italy, 11, 132, 134, 194
Florensky, Paul, 113, 117, 138
Frank, S. L., 65, 85, 99, 103, 131, 136, 158, 165, 166, 209, 236, 256
Fraternity of St. Sophia, 198
Freud, S., 74, 181
Fundaminsky, I. I., 199, 204, 211

Gershenson, M., 148
Gilson, Étienne, 200
God, 16, 91, 94, 96, 97, 101, 105, 107, 108, 126, 129, 135, 136, 163, 186, 195, 208, 209, 217, 218, 221, 222, 224, 231, 237, 246, 247, 248, 249, 252, 256, 259, 260, 263, 264, 275, 280
Godunoff, Boris, 11
Goethe, 195
Gogol, N., 180
Grand Inquisitor, 28, 88, 154, 257, 265
Greene, G., 176
Grinevitch, Mme, 128
Gudim-Levkovitch, 36
Guedalla, Philip, x

Hamsun, Knut, 137
Hauptmann, Gerhart, 71
Hawthorne, Nathaniel, 257
Hegel, George William Friedrich, 29, 242, 247, 254
Heidegger, Martin, 256
Heidelberg, Germany, 69, 70, 92
Herzig, Eugenie, 138, 209
Hertzen, A. I., 152, 254, 270

Hippius, see Merezhkovsky
Hitler, Adolf, 9, 192, 205, 232, 234, 252, 268, 271
Holy Spirit, 96, 97, 99, 217, 221, 225
Hoover, Herbert, 160
Ibsen, 49, 52, 61, 88, 137, 242, 284
Idealism, 51, 58, 61, 67, 68, 106
Ilyin, I. A., 166
Ilyin, V. N., 162, 163, 182, 204, 206
Ivan the Terrible, 53
Ivanoff, Peter, 211
Ivanoff, V., 87, 88, 118, 119, 128, 148, 203, 258
Izwolsky, Hélène, 211, 267
Jaba, S. P., 204, 269
Jashwill, Princess, 22
Joachim de Floris, 135
Judenitch, General, 151
Justin the Philosopher, 99
"K," Mme, x, 75, 78, 79, 123, 181, 186, 194, 195, 207, 216, 218, 222, 223, 228, 230, 244, 249, 250, 251, 252, 258, 265, 273, 285
Kallash, Mme M. A., 269
Kameneff, L. B., 148, 150
Kameneva, Olga, 151
Kant, Emmanuel, 29, 42, 64, 87, 245, 247
Karamzin, M. N., 25
Karsavin, L. P., 166
Kartasheff, A. V., ix, 81, 88, 99, 100, 110, 135, 141, 147, 195, 198, 203, 232
Katamenkova, Anna Ivanovna (nyanya —nurse), 20, 21
Kautsky, Karl, 50, 51
Kerensky, A. F., 70, 146
Keyserling, Count H., 164, 222
Khomiakoff, A. S., 113, 134, 188, 218, 223, 225, 247, 251, 254, 255, 282
Kierkegaard, Sören, 27, 79, 242, 245, 247, 256, 284
Kiev, 12, 14, 16, 18, 19, 20, 21, 26, 33, 35, 36, 41, 42, 43, 45, 46, 47, 48, 49, 50, 54, 58, 59, 67, 71, 72, 83, 104, 105, 117, 262, 282
Kingdom of God, 139, 233
Klepinin, Father Dmitri, 204, 270
Klepinin, Mme T. F., ix, 174
Kliatchkin, Mlle R., 269
Kniazeff, Governor General of Vologda, 54

Koestler, A., 148
Kotchubey, Prince, 16
Kovalevsky, Father Evgraf, 278
Krupskaya, Nadezhda, 85
Kudasheff, Princess Alexandra Sergeevna, 13,16
Kullmann, G. G., 234
Kulm, Battle of (1813), 11, 12
Kuskova, Mme Prokopovitch, 90, 160, 203, 206
Kuzmin-Karavaeff, 158, 206, 215, 216, 269
Laberthonnière, Father, 200
Lacroix, Jean, 239
Lambert, Marquis de, 9
Lange, F. A., 50
Latvia, 1, 2
Lenin, V. I., 33, 39, 58, 62, 104, 131, 147, 148, 157, 225, 228, 254, 262, 263
Leningrad, 158
Leonardo da Vinci, 194
Leontieff, Constantine, 7, 39, 63, 78, 79, 84, 112, 184, 185, 207, 209, 212, 226, 244, 250
Liberation Union, 41
Lieb, Fritz, 210, 247
Life's Questions, 103, 104, 105
Lipki (Kiev), 21
Lo Gatto, Prof., 168
Longvinsky, 42, 46
Lopuchin-Demidoff, Prince, 16, 36, 53
Lorenzo the Magnificent, 133
Lossky, N. O., 103, 130, 158, 236, 256
Louis VI (France), 13
Louis XVIII (France), 10
Louvre, the, 8
Lowrie, Helen, x, 176
Lubeck, Dr., 128, 153
Lubotin, 95, 119
Lunacharsky, A. V., 33, 38, 42, 44, 46, 57, 58, 59, 61, 65, 87, 104, 130, 138, 148, 157
Lundberg, A., 136, 137
Lunin, George, 162
Luther, Martin, 49, 209, 216
Madelung, E. R., 61
Madole, Jacques, 211
Maeterlinck, 49, 71, 137
Manouchin, Dr. I. I., 204

Marcel, Gabriel, 200, 234
Marie, Mother (Skobtsova), 193, 204, 210, 211, 212, 269, 270
Maritain, Jacques, 181, 199, 200, 211, 234, 284
Mark Twain, 233
Martzinkovsky, V., 192
Marx, Karl, 38, 43, 44, 48, 49, 51, 52, 144, 157, 237, 252, 254, 255, 276
Marxism, 42, 43, 44, 45, 51, 58, 59, 64, 65, 68, 83, 106, 130
Materialism, 68, 82, 83, 107, 129
Maugham, Somerset, 187, 188
Maxim the Confessor, 99
Merezhkovsky, Dmitri Sergeevitch, 72, 83, 84, 89, 90, 91, 92, 95, 100, 103, 105, 110, 111, 130, 134, 188, 194, 203, 204, 205, 206, 225, 232, 258, 264
Merezhkovsky, Zinaida (Hippius), 72, 78, 79, 89, 90, 91, 92, 93, 95, 98, 100, 101, 103, 110, 111, 141, 188, 203, 204, 205, 213, 215, 224, 269
Metcheff, Father Alexis, 155, 181, 220
Michailovsky, Nicolai, 40, 64
Michelet, Jules, 34
Miliukoff, P. N., 4, 15, 32, 39, 143
Mill, John Stuart, 29
Milutin, N. A., 16
Minsky, N. M., 72, 88, 93
Mintzlova, Anna, 127, 128
Moissy, 137
Molière, J. B. P., 137
Monod, Wilfred, 199
Morozoff, Mme M. K., 116, 138
Moscow, 33, 60, 81, 101, 105, 110, 111, 112, 113, 114, 115, 116, 117, 118, 119, 122, 125, 126, 128, 129, 137, 138, 144, 145, 146, 149, 150, 151, 153, 154, 155, 156, 159, 162, 164, 172, 178, 179, 181, 183, 185, 186, 188, 204, 215, 219, 220, 227, 231, 232, 262, 265, 282
Motchulsky, C., 210, 211, 212, 238, 269
Mott, Dr. John R., 192, 199
Mounier, Emmanuel, 200
Mozhaiskys, the, 36
Mukalov, N. K., 30, 50, 58, 62
Muratoff, N., 203
Mussorgsky, M. P., 137, 194

Nansen, F., 160
Napoleon III, 11
Nesmeloff, N. A., 127
*New City, The,* 199
*New Way, The,* 101, 102, 103
Nicolai, Baron Paul, 192
Nicolai Nicolaievitch (Grand Duke), 140
Niebuhr, R. L., 278
Nietzsche, F. W., 35, 42, 48, 49, 51, 64, 87, 180, 181, 237, 242, 254, 255, 276, 284
Novocherkassk, 12
Novoselov, M. A., 113, 114

Obuchovo, 14
Origen, 99
Orthodox Action, 210, 211
Orthodox Theological Institute of St. Sergius, see Academy of St. Sergius
*Orthodox Thought,* 201
Ossorgin, M. A., 153, 155, 156
Oxford Group Movement, 214

Paris, 1, 2, 3, 9, 18, 35, 58, 68, 83, 98, 101, 111, 115, 116, 118, 128, 143, 145, 151, 162, 168, 170, 175, 176, 188, 190, 193, 195, 197, 198, 199, 203, 206, 207, 210, 214, 233, 234, 239, 263, 267, 268, 269, 270, 271, 272, 274, 276
Parthenon marbles, 8
"Passionaria," 197
Paul I, 10, 11
Péguy, Charles, 255
Pereshneff, Claudia Michailovna, ix
Perezvony, 2
Pertsoff, 93, 103
Petchersk Monastery (Kiev), 12, 20, 21
Peter the Great, 1
Petrograd, 145, 146
Petrunkevitch, A. M., 70
Philippe, André, 211
Pianoff, F. T., 162, 164, 165, 182, 209, 269, 270
Picasso, Pablo, 117, 194
Plato, 75, 85, 242, 254
Plechanov, G. V., 41, 44, 48, 82, 254, 263
Pobiedonostseff, K. P., 103, 142
Poland, 10, 11, 14, 17
Pontigny, France, 101
Porret, Eugene, 128, 146, 184, 255, 276, 278

Potocki, Victoria, and Felix Stanislas, 10, 11
Prokopovitch, S. N., 206
Pushkin, A. S., 34, 64, 135
*Put*, 191, 198, 199, 201

Rasputin, Gregory, 141, 142
Ratchinsky, Count, 185
Ratchinsky, G. A., 115, 119, 151
Razin, Stenka, 264
Red Cross (German), 160
Red Cross (Russian), 141
Religious Philosophical Academy (Berlin & Paris), 162, 165, 168, 198, 210, 227
Religious Philosophical Assemblies (St. Petersburg), 103
Religious Philosophical Society (Moscow), 82, 100, 137
Religious Philosophical Society (St. Petersburg), 101, 141
Remizoff, Alexis, ix, 54, 55, 56, 57, 59, 61, 62, 65, 66, 83, 104, 105, 119, 283
Renaissance, 112, 132, 133, 167, 194
Ribbentrop, J. von, 267
Riga, Latvia, 1, 2, 3, 4, 5, 10
Rolland, Mme Romain, 211
Rome, Italy, 111, 134
Rössler, Roman, 241, 244, 245, 246, 257
Rousseau, J. J., 280
Rozanoff, V. V., 74, 83, 88, 100, 101, 130, 134, 136, 258
Russian Scientific Institute, 161, 168
Russo-Japanese War, 81

Sablin, V. M., 71, 72
St. Alexander Nevsky, 220
St. Francis of Assisi, 122
St. George Cross, the, 10, 12
St. Gregory of Nyssa, 127, 135
St. Isaac the Syrian, 127
St. Nicolas, Shrine of, 1, 4, 5
St. Paul, 248
St. Petersburg, 9, 16, 19, 26, 35, 40, 45, 51, 53, 56, 61, 62, 65, 69, 74, 80, 81, 83, 84, 87, 88, 93, 95, 96, 100, 101, 104, 105, 109, 110, 111, 116, 117, 131, 141, 206, 282
St. Seraphim, 122, 135, 264
St. Thérèse, 178, 179
Salvini, T., 137
Sartre, Jean Paul, 176, 242, 256, 276

Savinkoff, B., 61
Savonarola, G., 133
Schegoleff, P., 62, 65
Scheler, Max, 164
Schevitch, Father Serge, 278
Schiller, F., 137
Schlumberger, Jean, 7
Schnitzler, Arthur, 71
Schopenhauer, Arthur, 29, 34, 42, 49, 87, 254
Seaver, George, 218, 222, 226
Serge, Archimandrite, *see* Bishop Serge
Serge, Bishop, 103, 109, 196, 219, 220
Serge, Metropolitan, *see* Bishop Serge
Sezemann, V. E., 166
Shachovskoy, V., 70
Shakespeare, William, 137, 176, 242
Sheed and Ward, 235
Sheerman, V. A., 121
Shelley, P. B., 195
Shestov, Lev, 34, 48, 57, 105, 106, 108, 109, 168, 180, 205, 209, 212, 245, 256, 279
Shidlovsky, Sophie, 162
Skvortsov-Stepanov, I. I., 51
Smolensk, Russia, 11
Smolitch, I., 162
Sobor, 144, 145
Sobornost, 97, 216
Social Democrats, 39, 41, 42, 45, 46, 47, 49, 71, 83
Social Revolutionary Party, 39
Society for the Study of Eastern Europe, 160
Socrates, 163
Solovieff, Vladimir, 75, 144, 233, 247, 254, 255, 256, 286
Sologub, Feodor, 88, 93
Sorokin, Pitirim, 158
Soviet of Workers' Deputies, 81
Spengler, Oswald, 164, 253, 260
Spinka, M., 249, 285
Stalin, J. V., 9, 58, 147, 157, 252, 254, 271
Stavroff, 269
Stefan, Father (Svetozaroff), 220, 221, 278
Steiner, Rudolf, 127, 128, 226
Stepun, Feodor, 92, 101, 115, 116, 125, 150, 166, 189, 199, 213, 240, 241, 243, 250, 260

Strindberg, J. A., 137
Struve, P. B., 4, 43, 51, 62, 64, 65, 68, 69, 85, 104, 130, 161, 203, 204
Student Christian Movement (British), 175, 234
Student Christian Movement (French), 199
Student Christian Movement (Russian), 192, 195, 196, 234, 236
Stuttgart, Germany, 69
Suvorov, A. V., 10
Svatopolk-Mirsky, 81
Synod, the Holy, 103, 138, 139, 215

Taine, H. A., 34
Tauler, J., 127
Tchaikovsky, P. I., 51, 194, 275
Ternavtseff, 93
Thomas Aquinas, 242
Tichon, Patriarch, 145, 150, 198, 220
Tillich, Paul, 199
Tiutcheff, F. I., 195
Tolstoi, L. N., 16, 23, 32, 37, 38, 48, 49, 72, 82, 108, 121, 180, 181, 221, 236, 250
Trinity, the Holy, 97
Trotsky, Leon, 145, 151, 156, 210
Trubetskoy, Prince Eugene, 64, 104, 112, 115, 116, 147, 232
Trubetskoy, Prince G., 131
Trubetskoy, Prince Nicolas, 170
Trusheff, Eugenie Judifovna, see Eugenie Rapp
Trusheff, Lydia Judifovna (Berdyaev), 60, 72, 73, 79, 106, 111, 118, 119, 122, 123, 124, 132, 138, 148, 158, 170, 171, 172, 174, 175, 176, 177, 178, 179, 182, 183, 184, 185, 187, 190, 207, 208, 209, 211, 212, 224, 268, 271, 276, 277, 282
Trusheff, Mme, 119, 185
Tsar Alexander II ("Tsar Liberator"), 14, 31, 32
Tsar Alexander III, 14, 33, 38
Tsar Nicolas I, 11, 12, 14, 141, 142, 143
Tsar Nicolas II, 14, 38, 70, 140, 141, 225
Tsarina, Alexandra Feodorovna, 140
Tugan-Baranovsky, 43, 51
Turgenieff, I. S., 275

Tyrkova-Williams, Mme Ariadne, 43, 44, 85, 86, 112, 127
Union for the Liberation of the Working Class, 41
Union of Exiles, 61
Union of Liberation, 70, 71, 85, 90
Union of Russian Philosophers, 165
Uritsky, M. S., 131
Ust-Sisolsk, 55

Valery-Brussov, 62
Variags, the, 157
Verlaine, Paul, 195
Vermeulen, A., 244
Versiloff, 186
Vetrova, 45
Vichy, France, 18, 22, 23, 184
Vienna, Austria, 10
Vladimir Alexandrovitch, Grand Duke, 53, 54
Vodovozov, V. O., 46, 47
Vologda, 30, 49, 50, 52, 53, 54, 55, 56, 57, 58, 59, 60, 62, 63, 64, 65, 67, 68, 79
Voltaire, F. M., 15, 63
Vycheslavstseff, B. P., 115, 204, 205, 236

Wagner, Richard, 194
Wavell, Field Marshal A. P., 276
Wengerova, Zinaida A., 71, 72
West, Mrs. Florence, 171
Windelband, Wilhelm, 68
World Council of Churches, 223, 276
World's Student Christian Federation, 192, 199
Wrangel, Baron P. N., 4

Yakovenko, 116
YMCA, North American, 164, 165, 168, 184, 185, 199, 201, 234, 276
YMCA Press, 168, 184, 189, 201, 235, 274

Zaitseff, Boris, ix, 104, 105, 153, 203
Zemstvo, 14
Zenkovsky, V. V., 165, 192, 193, 201, 202, 236, 244, 287
Zhdanov, 61
Zhivigetov, Prof., 153
Zhukovsky, D. E., 62, 70, 103, 105
Zhukovsky, V. A., 25
Zoschenko, M. M., 237, 274
Zosima, Elder, 113